The Strutts and the Arkwrights

1758–1830

Frontispiece

JEDEDIAH STRUTT
from the portrait by Joseph Wright of Derby

The Strutts
and the Arkwrights
1758–1830

A STUDY OF THE
EARLY FACTORY SYSTEM

by

R. S. FITTON
and
A. P. WADSWORTH

MANCHESTER UNIVERSITY PRESS
AUGUSTUS M. KELLEY PUBLISHERS

© 1958
Published by the University of Manchester at
THE UNIVERSITY PRESS
316–324, Oxford Road, Manchester M13 9NR

First published 1958
Reprinted 1964, 1973

ISBN 0 7190 0019 X

U.S.A.
AUGUSTUS M. KELLEY PUBLISHERS
305 Allwood Road, Clifton, N.J. 07012

LC No. 72–375
ISBN 0–678–06758–9

Printed in Great Britain by Butler & Tanner Ltd., Frome and London

PREFACE

THIS study had its beginnings in the spring of 1950 when the English Sewing Cotton Company informed Professor Arthur Redford that a large collection of old business records lay in the West Mill of W. G. and J. Strutt, their concern at Belper, Derbyshire. Shortly afterwards I went to examine this material which, it was decided, should be transferred to the University of Manchester and Professor Redford generously allowed me to continue my study of the documents with a view to preparing a thesis on the growth of the early cotton factory system.

Investigation showed the earliest of the records to be those of Strutts and Woollat, the hosiery business founded at Derby in 1758 by Jedediah Strutt and his brother-in-law William Woollat. The remaining documents, consisting of ledgers, cash books and a variety of miscellaneous accounts, were those of the mills which Strutt, then a partner with Richard Arkwright, had established at Belper and nearby Milford in the late 1770s. Unhappily this material threw little light upon Arkwright's activities in Derbyshire or elsewhere, but some references to him were discovered in the *Derby Mercury* and in the several hundred letters comprising the Strutt Collection at the Derby Public Library. This Collection and the records of the English Sewing Cotton Company form the basis of the book.

Since the publication of *The Cotton Trade and Industrial Lancashire, 1600–1780,* Mr. A. P. Wadsworth had been continuing his researches into the early textile industry. Some of the material he had collected bore upon my own work and, in consequence, we decided to collaborate in Part One of this study. Mr. Wadsworth brought to the task not only the product of his special investigations but his unrivalled knowledge of the early cotton textile industry. It need hardly be stressed that without his contribution, much of which was completed during his last illness, this would have been a poorer book.

Together, or separately, we have many obligations to acknowledge. To the Directors of the English Sewing Cotton Company we are indebted not only for the loan of the Strutt Records but for generous financial assistance without which the book might never have been published. Our thanks are especially due to Mr. C. E. Harrison, Vice-Chairman and Managing Director, who, from the beginning, has shown a great personal interest in our researches which he has assisted in every conceivable way.

Mr. A. N. Smith and Mr. T. G. Ryde of the Belper Mills not only preserved the Strutt Records from destruction during the salvage campaigns of World War II but, with Mr. H. D. Ryde, have been unsparing in their efforts to supply answers to a large number of queries relating to local history. Mr. F. Woolley and Mr. A. Selvey, engineers at Belper and Milford respectively, have assisted in many ways and our special thanks are due to Mr. J. Entwistle, Secretary to the Directors of the Company, for his enthusiastic interest and help.

Professor A. Redford, Dr. W. H. Chaloner and Dr. W. O. Henderson of the University of Manchester have given valuable help and encouragement at all stages and Dr. J. D. Chambers, Professor H. Heaton and Professor F. E. Hyde have provided willing assistance on points touching upon their own investigations. Mr. A. H. Johnson and Professor A. W. Skempton have been most generous in allowing me to draw freely upon their paper 'William Strutt's Fire-Proof and Iron-Framed Buildings, 1792–1812', read at the Institution of Civil Engineers (Newcomen Society), in 1956. But our greatest debt is undoubtedly due to Professor T. S. Ashton who, since the discovery of the Strutt Records, has displayed an unfailing interest in the progress of our researches. His suggestions and criticisms have at all times been invaluable and he has kindly given much time and attention to the manuscript.

Mr. E. Bletcher and his staff at the Derby Public Library and the staff of the Reference Department of the Manchester Central Library have been of the greatest assistance. Warm thanks are also due to Mr. J. R. Wild, Records Clerk to the Derbyshire County Council, to Mr. E. Bor, to Mr. F. L. Wilson of Bolton, to Mr. H. Ward, Miss Janet Wadsworth and Miss Sheila Young for help in various ways and to Mr. T. L. Jones, Secretary to the University Press, for all he has done in seeing this book into print.

An earlier draft of this study was accepted in partial fulfilment of the requirements for the award of the Ph.D. degree of London University and some statistics of earnings not reprinted here have been deposited in the Library of the London School of Economics.

R. S. FITTON

April, 1958

CONTENTS

PART ONE

By R. S. Fitton and A. P. Wadsworth

PART TWO

By R. S. Fitton

APPENDICES

LIST OF FIGURES

LIST OF PLATES

LIST OF PLATES

xii

CHAPTER I

JEDEDIAH STRUTT,
WHEELWRIGHT AND FARMER

JEDEDIAH STRUTT, like Richard Arkwright, has his place on the roll of the classical inventors and industrial organizers of the eighteenth century. He was the inventor of a process which greatly expanded the hosiery industry, the making of ribbed stockings by machine instead of by hand. He became one of the backers and partners of Arkwright in his first spinning factories, and he founded a cotton-spinning firm that became the largest in the country. In character and temperament Arkwright and Strutt were contrasting figures, yet they are intimately linked. They began business in cotton-spinning together, they parted, and then, as part of the changes in the modern cotton trade, the firms they founded came together sixty-one years ago under the same ownership, though retaining their titles. The continuity of W. G. and J. Strutt and of Sir Richard Arkwright and Company is unique in textile history. The picture stretches from the first successful cotton factory of 1769 (the earlier Paul-Wyatt factories were failures) to the great combine which embraces all the fibres, natural and man-made, of the 1950s.

Here we can attempt to cover only the first third of the 189 years. The story is unbroken, the records unhappily are not. Those of the Arkwright mills hardly exist. Those of the Strutts, though more abundant, are patchy. We can, however, for Jedediah Strutt, take the study back to his youth before the middle of the eighteenth century. The records for this period are more personal than business. They are perhaps none the worse for that. They help us to get a more intimate idea of the domestic life of a textile industrialist of the eighteenth century than we have of any other. And it is possible that the broader purpose of economic and social history can be almost as well served by the study of love-letters as by ledgers. What sort of men came to the top in the great industrial expansion? Were they, as the common legend has it, thrusting, hard-headed adventurers, or might they not just as often have been sensitive, intelligent, civilized men like Josiah Wedgwood, or Matthew Boulton, or Jedediah Strutt and his sons? The first generation were mostly self-educated and self-made but, Arkwright perhaps excepted, they were hardly rough diamonds.

I. YOUTH

Jedediah Strutt, the second of the three sons of William Strutt, a small farmer and maltster, was born on July 26, 1726, at South Normanton, near Alfreton, Derbyshire.[1] It is now an ugly colliery village with an eighteenth-century core; it then lay in an attractive countryside, its only industry a little framework knitting. Jedediah's mother was Martha Statham of Shottle, near Duffield.[2] The Strutt family had long been in those parts and many of their names are recorded in the registers of Blackwell, the next parish, from the seventeenth century.

Of the father nothing is known except the tradition that he 'was a severe man, who took little interest in the welfare of his children . . .; neither educating them nor promoting their establishment in society when at the years of discretion'.[3] The eldest, Joseph (1724–94), certainly did not stay on the farm and went to London early in life. Jedediah was apprenticed away from home at 14. The third son, William (1730–1800), made less of a mark; we know nothing of him until his fortunes were bound up with Jedediah's.

The main influence in the life of the family was Dissent. Alfreton had a small Presbyterian community of which the Strutts were probably members. Joseph Strutt, when he went to London moved in Nonconformist circles. Jedediah at 14 was apprenticed to Ralph Massey, wheelwright of Findern, a village five miles south-west of Derby; his father paid a premium of £10.[4] Findern was a stronghold of Dissent, with one of the

[1] A photograph of the house, in Old Post Office Yard, was given in the *Derbyshire Times*, Nov. 8, 1930; it is now demolished.

[2] The daughter of Joseph Statham, yeoman, of Hazlewood, she was married at Duffield on Feb. 11, 1724.

[3] Britton and Brayley, *The Beauties of England and Wales*, iii (1802), 541.

[4] A photograph of the indenture is reproduced in Strutt (Hon. Fredk.), 'Jedediah Strutt' in *Memorials of Old Derbyshire*, ed. Cox (1907).

largest Nonconformist academies in the country. This was under a remarkable man, Ebenezer Latham (?1688–1754), who practised as a doctor as well as conducting the school and ministering to several congregations. His theology was liberal and he had a wide influence.[1] It cannot be assumed that Jedediah actually attended the school. His education, as he was to write later, was 'narrow and contracted', probably no more than that of a village school. But the Findern associations no doubt gave him the spur to reading and self-improvement besides personal contacts that were to prove helpful. The Woollats, with whom he lodged at Findern, were of Dr. Latham's congregation, and his master may have boarded lodgers from the school.[2]

Jedediah came out of his time at 21—in 1747—and moved to Belgrave, near Leicester, and then to Leicester. We know nothing of him in the next seven years except through his correspondence with Elizabeth Woollat, who was to become his wife. He was serious-minded, introspective, and had mechanical aptitude.[3] But he gave little promise of becoming a man of affairs.

II. COURTSHIP

Latham moved his Academy from Findern to Derby in 1745[4] and then, or before, Elizabeth Woollat went into service in his house. She was three years younger than Jedediah; they had grown up together and were much attached. Her feelings

---

[1] There is a full account of him in Dr. H. McLachlan's 'Ebenezer Latham and the Academy at Findern' in his *Essays and Addresses* (1950), 147–66. The course at Findern was for four years and the subjects taught included Logic, Mathematics, Natural Philosophy, Chronology, Anatomy, Hebrew, Theology and Hebrew Antiquities. Latham is said to have trained four hundred students, most of whom were not destined for the ministry. The fees were £16 a year for board and learning, with incidental charges for linen.

[2] Thomas Bentley, Wedgwood's friend, was a pupil at Findern during Strutt's apprenticeship there and boarded with a Mrs. Massey who, thirty years later, became Wedgwood's housekeeper (*Letters of Josiah Wedgwood*, ed. Farrer, ii (1903), 2).

[3] Felkin (*Hist. of the Machine-Wrought Hosiery and Lace Manufactures* (1867), 88), has some stories of this which may have come from Strutt's grandson, the first Lord Belper.

[4] McLachlan, op. cit., 157.

towards him were in no doubt, but Jedediah's methods of woo-
ing were exasperating. He fluttered round the candle like a
moth for seven years before he could make up his mind. Both
kept much of their early correspondence and it came down in
Jedediah's papers. Perhaps the earliest in the long series is a
light-hearted little note (without date) from Elizabeth which
may belong to her early days at Derby while Jedediah was still
an apprentice at Findern:

Elizabeth Woollat to Jedediah Strutt

A bilit so soon Jerry I fancy won't a little surprise you but I was
so a greably surpris'd when I came hom this morning to find every
thing just as I left them, the House was in a profound sylanse and
not one person got up. John I believe lay an hour after; they had
not the least suspission of my ever being out of my Room, my over
fear of being wanted at hom made me quite rude to John for I
beleive I did not speak when we parted but pray give my servis
to him and tell him yt a pleasant Gardin an open Alcove a bowl
of punch an a new sweet hart is not all Equvelant to his Good
Companny.
    I shou'd like much to know wheather your Tyranical Master
has made anny discoverry about your erly adventer last night, you
need never be at a los for to send for if you give my Brother a
Letter anny time it will Com as from him, as you say I have no
reason to suspect your sincerity. I have wrote without the least
reserve and depend upon your Goodness not to expose my Nonsense
this from your Friend and wellwisher

E: Woollat

After he left Findern he was soon writing to Elizabeth craving
sympathy in an affair of the heart. She was replying teasingly.
Unfortunately the manuscript is in tantalizing fragments; its
more coherent parts are:

Elizabeth Woollat to Jedediah Strutt

Derby March the 3: 1748

My Friend
    I rec'd your Letter of Friendsh[ip] Jany ye 16th but what shall
I say to it, surprise & p[leasure] taken place by turns ever since.
You cou'd not pay me a greater [compliment] then by ranking mee
amongst ye number of your friends, which I hope I shall allways

4

endeavour to deserve and as such sha[ll] look upon my self as a sharer in your misery. But shall I be[lieve] you to be, in jest, or are you sincear, I cant but say it a pears to [me a] little romantick, (tho theres not a Juba, a portius, a Marcus, yt [stir] ye passions in a more elagant manner.) When I compare your Letters [they] are some what inconsisttant; in ye first you say you are a vers to write-ing, in your next, that you have done all you can by Letters, [that] She is at ye distance of near forty miles, is verry young, and yet your [   ] Findern. But I will Judg favourably and immagine it to be ye effect of a m[ind] disordered, but I hope this fit of Frenzy will soone a bate, you [will] much obloige me if youl tell me who this cruel charmer [is, this] incensable fair, who lets you sigh and lan-guish, mourn and [while] away your pressious moments, which mights be rendred by her so so easy in ye injoyment of em. . . . But you desire to know where I live. I am still at Dr Lathams and I believe I allways shall be here, ye place for what I know may be enchanted for I cant get away.

But youl think I shall never have don, I will asure you I trouble you with my Letters out of interest, if not kindness: since mine to you will procure yours to me: so yt I write to you more for my own sake then yours; less to make you think I write well, then to learn from you to write better, There you see interest in my kindness, which is like ye friendship of the world rather to make a friend then to be a friend: but I am yours, as a true plain dealer &c: E: Woollat

The flow of letters ran on and Elizabeth was moved by an emotional experience to fear that their attachment had been a mistake:

Elizabeth Woollat to Jedediah Strutt

. . . Your letter came to my hand at a time when my mind was ye moste suceptable of impresstion for I was at that time a witness of a meloncholy sean of disolving nature. Mr Roe our next neibour, drew his last breath yt very day. I sat up whith him 2 nights before, just before he died, and never was I more senseably tuched in my whole life, there did I see all ye agonies yt attend a dying bed, ye cold sweat, ye dismal ruttle, ye convulsib sobs, ye deep fetch'd sighs, & all ye frightfull attendents of a speeddy disolution, youth strength & beuty (which you observe yt lady was mistress of) are no security in that war in which we are all ingag'd. Mr Roe left ye World in a peculier moveing manner, he took leave of all yt came to see him, begd their prayers, thank'd em for their kind concern for him, told em he was out of ye reech of help, took leave of his Wife & Children, gave advice to each of them, & told em how different it was to vew deth near and at a distance, and of what great importance it was to take care of their valluable and immortal souls. This puts me in mind of ye advice our late Queen upon her death bed, gave our present Duke William. She told him he would find no thort worth his care on a dying bed but how he had liv'd & if he cou'd find he had acted ye part of a man of honour & a Christian, it woud give him pleasure which he cou'd feel but not describe. When we are rightly affected with these moveing seans, what sattisfaction can the reflection of anny past pleasure, mearly innocent in them selves give to a mind made for nobler entertainments fitted for hier injoyments. Certainly none at all, we can't but look back with regret upon that time as lost, uneasiness and confusion must be ye reward, I speak from experience, tho perhaps I should not have made such a declaration, had not you first put me in mind of my own imprudence; that arbour at Findern and ye rest of ye place you mention, and twenty others which I cou'd, that Findern chichen [i.e. kitchen] and hall, yt hatefull window in my room, and every other place and circumstance which brings me to your thoughts, I look back upon as enemyes to myself & witnesses of my folly. It woud be ye greatest aleveation to my present pain cou'd I be certain you cou'd forget there was ever such a person existed as I am. Its time & that a lone I expect must compleat this. I have little news to tell you from Findern. I have been so great a traveler this summer, I have been at Birmingham, a most a greeable Journey I have had of it. My Brother sends his best, his most kind respects to you, nay I cant tell you his love better than by making youce of Dean Swift's compliment to his friend, I have, says he, but a small house and only one snug appartment, it lies on my left side, is verry warme, and you will allways be a welcom Guest to it as long as ye edifis remains in ye tenure and posestion of your humble servant. I have wrote this letter in such a hurry yt I dare say you cant reed it, and I emagin you think to your self I wish I never had, had it, and I realy am in debate with my self wheather I shoud send it or not, only ye inclos'd if it pleas you as much as it has me, will pay carridg. I am with due respect yours and &c E: Woollat

ps I beg for ye future you won't conclude your letters with those fulsom words of Lover & Admirer &c.

Joseph webster is dead, after living for some time in a very unacountable manner. Mr John Gregory, John Carver, Sarah Shipmon, little Bartle Massy is all of them in a verry bad way, & not expected to continue long.

6

Dear Betty

I was not a little surpriz'd to hear of your being at [...] for I had promise myself the pleasure of seeing you once more at [...] I have been there once I believe since you was, but felt greatly short of the pleasure propos'd since you was no longer there and only serv'd to bring to my remembrance past pleasures, which rather give me pain than any thing else, not that I was so happy as to enjoy them then, but that they are no longer to be enjoyed, for they was two sweet to last and too much in the power of fortune to continue uninterupted, for she is never constant ever wavering and perhaps equald in changeableness so much as the inconstancy of a Woman; and it is a great misfortune to Mankind, that a great part their Happiness should depend on fortune and a Womans smiles. You may think I speak a little too severely, but experience confirms me in this truth, for I can instance no one particular that has given me so much uneasiness as a too great fondness for your sex, whither I have really deserv'd ill treatment from 'em, I am not certain but of this I am convinc'd, that however I may have behav'd my self towards them I have severely suffer'd from their inconstancy, and dissimulation and if ever you have had any experience of that passion, you are not ignorant of the misery it must be to be slighted and despis'd by the object of your [...] est and most sincere Love but if you know this, it is folly [...] to resent it; and if not you will never believe it from my [...]

A Letter from Jedediah Strutt to his Wife

It was perhaps on the visit to Birmingham she speaks of that Elizabeth met the Nonconformist divine, Dr. George Benson (1699–1762), a friend of her master Dr. Latham, and then joint pastor of a Presbyterian congregation there. In 1749 he went to London as pastor of a Dissenting congregation in Poor Jewry Lane, Crutchedfriars, and Elizabeth became his servant.[1] Jedediah was late in discovering her removal; he had cooled off and apparently there had been a break in their correspondence. He resumed it on February 25, 1751:

Jedediah Strutt to Elizabeth Woollat

Dear Betty

I was not a little surpriz'd to hear of your being at London for I had promisd myself the pleasure of seeing you once more at Findern. I have been there once, I believe since you was, but fell greatly short of the pleasure proposd, since you were no longer there, and only serv'd to bring to my remembrance past pleasures, which rather give me pain than any thing else, notwithstanding I was so happy as to enjoy them then, but that they are [no] longer to be enjoy'd, for they was two sweet to last long and to much in the power of fortune to continue uninterupted, for she is never constant ever wavering and perhaps equal'd in changeableness to nothing so much as the inconstancy of a Woman: and it is a great misfortune to Mankind, that a great part of their Happiness, shou'd depend on Fortune and a Womans smiles. You May think I speak a little too seriously, but experience confirms me in this truth; for I can instance no one particular, that has given me so much uneasiness, as a too great fondness for yourself, whether I have realy deserv'd Ill treatment from 'em, I am not certain but of this I am convinc'd, that however I may have behav'd myself towards them, I have severely suffer'd from their inconstancy, and disimulation, and if ever you have had any experience of that passion, you are not ignorant of the Misery it must be, to be slighted and despisd by the object of your best wishes and most sincere Love, but if you know this, it is folly in me to repeat it, and if not you will never believe it from my words.—I am at a loss what to say, for though I have too much reason to blame your sex, yet my fondness for 'em bids me be silent on that head when at the same time I cannot vindicate my own; for men will flatter, and women disemble even their very looks dont always speak the sentiments of their hearts: tho' the pleasure reap'd by such a practice, is but a small

---

[1] For Benson see *D.N.B.* and McLachlan, op. cit., 155.

reward for the folly in committing it for it is attended with a thousand vexations which are utterly unknown to those, who are so happy as to be wiser; I have sufficiently seen this Folly myself, and hope for the future to remedy this well for it is to this end that I refrain from all private conversation with your sex and give myself up to pleasures of another kind, you know I was always fond of Books to Excess, and it is to these, that I chiefly give all my Leisure hours, as yielding perhaps the most lasting satisfaction; for good company is what I am a great stranger to, since I left Findern, and what I almost dispair of ever enjoying again, and to choose bad, and know it to be such, wou'd be an argument of great weakness and folly. I am left Belgrave, and live at Leicester, which I like much better, but am not fully satisfied, nor perhaps may never be so, for I realy don't know what I wou'd wish for next might I have it, for wishing; I am a servant and perhaps wou'd turn Master, of what or who? or wherein shou'd I be better'd? it may be worse. I am single and at liberty, and it may that may be unhappiness; but shou'd I joyn the number of Hymens followers, shou'd I be happy then? by chance it might be so, if not, it wou'd certain be the contrary. What must I do, continue as I am, restless and uneasy, or put it to the great hazard of being better or worse or for my Life. Shou'd I not study to be content. I shou'd be Exceeding glad if you wou'd write to me fro[m London] for if you cou'd not advise, you coud divert me, and besides [I should] be indulging my favorite inclination, of reading, and a [letter] from you wou'd always be a welcome guest to me, especially as it wou'd be so great a stranger.

I hear your Cousin Judith is like wise at London too, I [should] be glad to hear you are well, and like it, and that you cou'd tell me by experience, that there is greater happiness found in that great city, than in the country village, for I cant help thinking I should be much happier there than here, tho I have no reason for thinking so, but that you are there before me for honesty and innocence, Love and Constancy are oftner found in Cottages than Courts where truth seldom comes.

You'l be so good as give my Love to Cousin Judith, and accept this with the same freedom and good will that I write it, and return me an answer from under your own hand, and in so doing, you will lay, almost, the greatest obligation in your power, on your ever well wisher and admirer

J: Strutt

Leicester Februy 25: 1751

He was now nearly 25 but was still a journeyman wheel-wright. His letter was getting perilously near to becoming a proposal and there is an odd scrap in his papers addressed 'Madam' which looks as though it were copied from some improving manual of courtship; a few echoes of it crept into his letter. Silence fell again; there was a break of nearly two years before Jedediah resumed his amatory meanderings:

Jedediah Strutt to Elizabeth Woollat

Dear Betty

You will greatly wonder, after so long silence I shou'd ever trouble you with another Letter, or myself to write; But to me, it is rather matter of wonder, I have not written to you many times before this; tho' I must tell you, Letters from me are very rare things; for I can recollect but one or two instances to your sex, of now near two years. From this account of my slender correspondence, you will be ready to ask, how I thought of writing now? to this I can only answer, that if every thought for you had been a Letter, Millions perhaps wou'd not comprize the sum; tho' it may be owing to thoughtfulness alone, that gives you this trouble.

I have been sitting for some time in my window, and in some measure withdrawn from care & noise, (for all is not silence even here, nor every sound we hear agreable) till almost lost in meditating the Vanity of my own Life, and find upon the review, that except a few hours, & those chiefly spent with you, it appears, as to goodness all a blank, an Empty nothing. But there are some peculiar marks of folly (to say no worse of them) which [nothi]ng will ever erase from my memory. But the reflections in innocent [mom]ents, will always afford us pleasure, and it is in the pleasing remembrance of those happy hours, tho' few, which I have spent with you, and which yields a pleasure even now, almost equal to the enjoyment, that in a manner forces this from me. Ye Findern groves & bowers, who haunts your shades now I'm away or hears your warblers sing! Who treads your peaceful walks, or tastes your cooling springs, or counts your silent hours! O my dear Betty, can you, Can I repeat these, a thousand other happy circumstances, and not remember it was the charms of good company that rendered them so delightful, and that only that gives so much sweetness to the remembrances of them once having been and such Bitterness to think, they will no more; at least there is but slender probability of it. My own ingratitude, so long a silence, and the distance of so many Miles, and perhaps other engagements stronger than these,

9

may forbid you to indulge one thought of tenderness for me altho' when I remember your former goodness, and readyness to forgive, I am tempted to hope you will still pardon, at least vouchsafe me an answer. I make no doubt but you have heard of Bro: & I being at Findern and also the particulars of that adventure; therefore I need only tell you that the little moment I was there seemed extreamly pleasant, and when I came to leave, it was with the greatest reluctance.

But let me leave the pleasing, painful subject, and tell you as I have often done, how I am afflicted with those two constant attendants on humane Nature, viz pleasure & pain, or which may be the same thing, happiness & Misery, Joy & Sorrow, Love & hatred; for whatever is the object of true pleasure, will also be that of true happiness, Joy, & Love.

But when I wou'd speak of happiness, I find myself so perplex'd & confus'd, thro' the Error of my understanding, that what I one day look on as happiness and a blessing, the next perhaps it appears as the greatest of Misfortunes. Thus it sometimes pleases me to think I am at Newton, single, in good health, not a dying Lover, nor wounded with dispair; which must be a great blessing, that I am entering upon the world with an agreeable prospect before me and lastly I live in that pleasing hope of once more hearing from you. These, and some others I might mention all which wou'd be equally liable to objections, and are blessings, or the contrary just as we think them such, so I may say, that possibly I might have been much happier else where than here, because I have been so: and the not being in Love, may be no addition to my happiness, since the most languishing, pining Lover, perhaps never wish'd he had not Lov'd. Such a pleasing thing is Love. Besides the happiness of being belov'd may be very great; and of this [I am] utterly uncertain, because I think so, I am very liable to be deceived or [to] deceive myself. And as to business & the world they are always attended with cares & disappointments, which may often times bring more real pain than pleasure; Nay my very health may not always be a blessing, since it may sometimes lead me to vice and folly, from which sickness might have restrained me. And lastly, you, even you, who have so often, and so much contributed to my happiness, instead of indulging my wishes, or answering my expectations, may dispise & condemn both this & me. So changeable are the objects of happiness of mine at least that whatever solid foundation there may be for it yet we often place it in those things which we only think will give it us without any foundation at all. Where then shall I fix or what or whom it's true Beauty & the charms of your sex have often fix'd my attention & greatly swel'd my expectations but—Death may come! besides how can I expect that constancy in womankind which I myself never yet had.

But I am hurried away. Business & the world knock at the door and I can't think but you must be weary before you reach this part of my Letter so I will dismiss you at this time by being intirely

Yours

J: Strutt

P: S My service to Cous. Judith & if you know of a sister I anywhere have pray don't forget me to her

He was certainly a curious wheelwright. There survives an unfinished draft letter, addressed 'Dear Will', even more high-flown than the letter. It describes how he and 'a certain female who is one of the loveliest of all Womankind' sat down 'on a bank of turf under a shady sycamore', and how he 'told her I no longer lovd & that that would be the last time we should ever converse together on that subject—but I can say no more. All language fails. Here I must stop and bury in eternal Silence what coud not be uttered without Tears'. One suspects an essay in romantic fiction.

Jedediah's last letter had been written from Newton, near Blackwell;[1] he had evidently returned to his family home. About 1754 his fortunes changed. An uncle, a farmer at Blackwell, died leaving Jedediah the stock on his farm. This led him to move there and become a farmer.[2] He was soon writing to Elizabeth again, perhaps more prosaically, and on January 25, 1755, she replied:

Elizabeth Woollat to Jedediah Strutt

London Jan, 25 *1755*

The thoughts of ading anny thing to ye pleasure of a person yt is not Indifferent to me, is ye strongest motive you coud urge me to make me acknowledge yt I Recd & read your Letter with ye utmost Sattisfaction.

I cannot say I was in ye least surprisd at yt affair you mentiond as I have never been a stranger to the perpetual missunderstanding in your Family; & have been sorry for it. Methinks such Admonitions need Loud Lectures of care & prudence, that so what was at first designed to soften cares, & to be a scene of ye moste refined

---

[1] A photograph of Strutt's cottage at Newton, now demolished, is extant.
[2] Strutt, op. cit., 372.

friendship and delight, may not be changed, by an abuse of its nature, into the Greatest infelicity & burden of human life.

this surely is a state that furnishs out a large field, not only of contemplation, but the practis of every virtue; for me to say more on this head might be thought out of Charecter.

I have now the pleasure to tell your Brother Recovers very fast, has discharged his nurse & comm down into the Dineingeroome; my friend good Mrs Bettey is still constant in her attendance but begins to talk of letting go ye Dadeing string & trusting him a lone. youll please to give my service to your father & I am sure ye Dr woud have sent his had he known anny thing of my writeing, but to yt or anny thing relateing to it is an intire stranger. I cannot stay to add anny thing more then only to say this coms from your friend & Humble Servant E: Woollat[1]

The reference was to Strutt's brother, Joseph, and to Elizabeth Scott whom he was shortly to marry. She was descended from one of the ejected ministers of 1662, a Kidderminster friend of Richard Baxter, and from one of Foxe's Marian martyrs. It is not clear what Joseph's business was except that it was not in textiles. In 1770 when, with Jedediah, he took out a patent for a fire-stove, he was described as a 'glass seller' of Whitechapel.[2] He seems to have travelled the country. The two daughters of Joseph and Elizabeth Strutt married in turn Joseph Chamberlain, shoemaker of Cheapside, and the younger, Martha, was the grandmother of Joseph Chamberlain, the Colonial Secretary, and great-grandmother of a Foreign Secretary and a Prime Minister.[3]

On the back of this letter in Strutt's hand is:

Hopkns and Sternhold had great Qualms
When they Translated David's Psalms
To make the Heart full Glad
But had it been poor Davids fate
To've heard thee sing and then Translate
By Jove it wou'd have made him mad.
Let who will be Bond Slave, by Jove I'll be free.

[2] Patent No. 964 for a 'Machine for roasting, boiling and baking, consisting of a portable fire-stove, an air-jack, and a meat-screen'. Joseph's signature alone was attached to the specification. In 1774 he was of Newgate Street. When he died in 1800 he was of Rickmansworth and left '*sub* £5000' (Will at Somerset House). His widow survived him. They had two sons, John and Joseph; the former was buying goods from the Strutts in 1796–1815, when he failed.

[3] Garvin, *Life of Joseph Chamberlain*, i (1932), 5–6, 15 (quoting Sir Austen Chamberlain's *Notes on the Families of Chamberlain and Harben*, 1915). The

III. PROPOSAL AND MARRIAGE

Very soon afterwards Jedediah took his final plunge. In the light of all that had gone before his solemn letter reads oddly—and obtusely. The alliteration, the cadences, and the poetic flights almost suggest that he had had recourse to a manual of polite letter-writing, if it were not that his own literary style had been becoming steadily more turgid:

Jedediah Strutt to Elizabeth Woollat

Blackwell
Feb 3: 1755

Dear Betty

Since our first acquantance, which is now many years ago, I have often wrote to you, but never in a strain like this; nor did I think I ever shoud; for tho' we was then more intimately acquainted than since and tho' I then thought you had some degree of kindness for me, yet as my conduct and behaviour to you has been such as cou'd neither raise nor continue your regard, together with the years that has past since then, (for time often puts a period to Love as well as all other events) I did not think you coud remember me with the least pleasure or satisfaction, but rather the contrary; but when I was at London and had the opportunity of seeing you something or other told me (tho' perhaps nothing more than the last glance of your Eye when I bad you farewell) that you look'd on me with an Eye of tenderness, nay one is so apt to speak as they wish, I had liked to have said Love; and if so, that one generous instance of truth and constancy has made a greater and more lasting impression on my mind, than all the united charms of Beauty, Wit and fortune of your sex, so far as I have had opportunity of conversing were ever able to make: therefore it is upon this foundation I presume to tell you, that from a wandering, inconstant, roving swain I am become intirely yours: I am ready to be all you cou'd wish me to be, if you Lov'd me, and which is all I wish, your Husband. But suppose I shou'd have gone two far in this declaration, and my fond observation prove a mistake, how will you wish, nay rather how impossible woud it then be for you to wish even to call me by that tender name. But let me still suppose

---

elder sister, Elizabeth, married Joseph Chamberlain in 1783 and died in 1786; he married Martha (born 1762) in 1792; she died in 1824. 'Mr. Chamberlain' was buying canal shares on account of Joseph Strutt, Jedediah's son, in 1804.

13

it is not so yet what arguments can I use to induce you to leave London with all the delights it affords, or how persuade you to leave so good a master, who I know values you, and whom you both esteem and Love. Here I am at a losse and if you shoud be indifferent with regard to me, it will be impossible to say anything that will be sufficient; and indeed I am not inclin'd to flatter nor to fill your imagination with fine words only; and this is one of all the reallities I can think of, that it is not impossible but that you may be happy here, even tho' it is true, you cannot here behold the splendor and the gaiety of a great City, nor the noise and hurry of it's inhabitants, yet the London Air is not half so sweet, nor it's pleasures half so lasting and sincere. Here innocence and health more frequently reside; here the beauties of nature are ever presenting themselves, both to our senses and imaginations; here you may view the rising and the setting sun, which many in London are strangers to; here it is that you may have the morning and the evening song of many a Warbling Lark and Linnet, and as Milton expresses it, The shrill mattin song of birds on every bough. As to my self, fortune has not plac'd me among the number of the rich and great, and so not subjected me to the many temptations and follies that attend great men, some of which perhaps I shoud not have been able to withstand, and others that I would have been loth to bear; yet by the blessing of heaven I have more than enough for happiness, and by that means at this season of the year, I enjoy many leisure hours (and Oh! the blessing of leisure and retirement) some of which I spend in reading and Meditation, the rest I dedicate to Love and you.

But I shall forget myself, and learn to do a thing I never lov'd, that is, to write long Letters; and yet methinks I have a thousand things to say, but as I had rather you wish'd I had said more than less, nay if I coud have told you all my heart in one word, I shoud not now have troubled you with so many; but I have no apology to make only my sincerity and if you read with candor and with the same simplicity with which I write, you will certainly find it sincere; I hope that will recommend it to your kind reception, and obtain if possible an answer of kindness.—I saw your Brother as I passed thro Derby but did not take him the Book you desir'd me. I heard from my Brother last week, and rejoyce to hear he has been abroad. My Father often talks of the Dr. and you, and withall knows that I Love you, nay he himself loves you, and will be glad to see you here.

And now, if ever you had any kindness for me, if ever I did or said anything to give you either delight or pleasure, let it not be in vain that I now ask, nor torture me with silence and suspense;

by so doing you will lay the highest obligation on one who is in every sence of the word is your sincere Lover

J: Strutt

Elizabeth's answer left no doubt, but she still avoided a super-scription; the 'my friend' or 'Jerry' had been dropped for some time:

Elizabeth Woollat to Jedediah Strutt

London Feb: 15 1755

Yours of the 3d came safe, which I woud have answerd, before, but had not presence of mind enough for some time to lay it before my master; at length a favorable oppertunity offering it self, my Resolution got ye better of my fear; & after a short introduction gave him your Letter, which he said shewd you to be a man of sense, and he thought of honour & honesty. But as to himself he was so surpris'd Disconcerted & uneasy as I never saw him, & for some time coud say nothing more to me. At length, he became able to talk freely on yt head; bid me consult my own Happiness & not think what he suffer'd. He then offer'd to make me indepen-dent, yt so at his Death I might live where I pleas'd; not at all intending ys as a Dissuasive from accepting your Generous offer. But as a means to prevent my being Influenced by any other motive then yt alone which is essential to ye most lasting, most perfect happiness. Such, such is ye behaviour of this god-like man, may he meet all ye rewards that such Beneficence deserves in both worlds. As to myself, was I posses'd of every desireable quallification, & injoy'd ye greatest affluance, I shoud not then Hesitate a moment, but comply with what ever you coud desire; but from a conscious-ness of my own Inferiority in point of fortune, as well as every thing else, makes me extreamly fearfull you shoud find cause to repent, when its too late; if this shoud be ye case, what I must suffer, from what in me is ye least occasion of pain to you, is not for me to say, but be this as it will, you are, & ever will be Intitled to ye best wishes of your most Humble servant

E: Woollat

My servis to your Father
I wish I better deserv'd his
good opinion

But even now these two grave-minded people could not throw care to the winds. Elizabeth was prevailed on by Dr. Benson

15

to stay with him until August and she and Jedediah filled in the months with anxious discussions of the married state. (She still did not trust herself to an endearing address; that waited until after marriage.) First Elizabeth:

Elizabeth Woollat to Jedediah Strutt

London April 1th *1755*

When ever I take up my pen with a design to fix ye time for my leiving London, am allways prevented by the concern which ye Dr expresses at ye thoughts of our parting, tho hee's provided with a servant to fill up my place, his perticular dislike to strangers makes him vastly sollicitous for my staying till towards August, if you have no objection to it, I shall be Glad to oblige him.

You cannot suppose, in my present situation I injoy any great share of tranquility, ye constant fear I am in, of not answering (in every thing) your expectation renders the utmost caution necessary. I have often thought that the principal cause of unhappiness in the married state arises from the negligence of ye contracting parties, in not acquainting each other with the peculier Turn of their Dispositions, & other material Circumstances relating to the inward Temper. For, in that pleasing State of Confusion wch the Warmth of the tender affections occasions, we are apt to dwell all together upon the amiable Parts of a Character; intirely regardless of those Blemishes & Defects, wch in a greater or less Degree, are to be found in every Individual of the Human Race. No wonder then, if a person expecting to find a perfect character, & not prepared to make the necessary allowances, is miserably disappointed in his schemes of happiness.

From these considerations I am induced to give you this short view of my real temper, not doubting but your own Judgment will lead you to consider the partialities of self Love, which, perhaps may have some Influence in the following Representation. I believe, my whole Behaviour, & particularly some late Declarations, leave you no Room to dispute the sincerity of my affection. To incourage your addresses, without being conscious of a desire to answer them by a proper Regard, must have argued a Baseness of mind, of which I flatter my self, I am incapable. I have ye Honesty to acknowledge my high opinion, wch gives me the greatest satisfaction, as it is absolutely necessary in order to the Injoymt. of any Happiness in the most intimate of all Connections. Indeed, such is the natural cast of my Temper, that I must experience the greatest Pleasure or the greatest misery in that Situation. If [I a]m favored with the Common Conveniences of life, & meet with proper Returns of

16

affection from the person I love, in these circumstances no one coud be more Happy than myself; & of Consequence proportionately distressing woud be the contrary condition: I own, I am impatient of Disregard, & cannot bear the least Slight, if it comes from a person whom I am desirous to oblige. If I know any thing of myself, I am not insensible of the Benefits I receive. I think I have the Happiness to possess a grateful Disposition; but at ye same time, it becomes me ingenuously to confess, that Indignities fire my Resentment, & lead me to evidence the spirit of my sex. These I take to be the distinguishing parts of my Character—were I to say more, you might accuse me of Vanity: had I said less, you might have been ignorant of some Peculiarities in my temper, wch if unknown & unexpected, might have been the foundation of some uneasiness, & I never coud forgive my self was I to conceal whatever I thought might have ye least tendency to that; & may the same conscientious regard to what is right, that now has; always influence every part of my future conduct, that it may (*and ye Best of Blessings attend you*) is ye Ardent prayr of yours &c

E: Woollat

ps I very much wish to know how you do, shant I hear from you soon

Jedediah Strutt to Elizabeth Woollat

Blackwell Wednesday

Dear Betty

For me to have no objections to your staying till August woud be an argument of such indifference towards you which I am not willing to give for coud I be content to stay till then you might think I could always be so besides that, my interest is concern'd, & I must again tell you that I expect considerable additions to my happiness, else I would not change my circumstances; tho' the little experience I have had of the world & things sufficiently convinces me perfection is not to be found in mankind, as particularly not in Woman; therefore you might Justly accuse me of Vanity & flattering shoud I tell you I think you superior to all your sex. It may be sufficient that I think you equal to the best—I woud ask which of all your sex that was so desirous of being belov'd woud rather discover her failings to her Lover than her perfections especially if she knew him fickle and inconstant. However just that method may be in you or me at this instant. It will be to our highest wisdom for the future to act a contrary part and rather conceal than expose our folly & weakness. And here I cannot think but if Married pairs acted with the same resource in this particular

17

after Marriage as before there woud not so often be that occasion for repentance. For whatever it may be that first raises desire or kindles that desire into Love the same graceful person and winning behaviour, the same care in dress & what ever else may attract the Eye, the same temper and disposition, nay the same insinuating looks and smiles are all absolutely necessary as Oil to the Lamp which otherwise will certainly expire & die.

As to myself perhaps I may not have studied my own temper so much as you notwithstanding that I may know of many failings, others may know of many more. That I am ungrateful you can tell and I know not that I coud mention any thing worse since there is no Love for ingratitude & I can be angry too and that without reason but I can forgive—sometimes. I coud mention many follys I have been guilty of & still am which tho' they may be but trifling in themselves may sometimes be of considerable consequence. I woud not mention my Virtues nor at present is it my task only Charity and forgiveness to others is a temper I woud always wish to cultivate. I wish you could contrive something to tell me in your next that woud give more pleasure than your staying till august since that is a pain to me and how can you hurt them you Love. That artless or rather artful interrogation in the PS: to your Letter, Shall I not hear from you soon? has brought on this answer perhaps something sooner than otherwise you woud have had it. Have a Messenger waits while I write so woud only repeat your request & that I Love you and that I am your J Strutt

Elizabeth Woollat to Jedediah Strutt

London 11th May *1755*

It is with some Mortification to my vanity, so much as to suspect, you differ from me in a point I have allways held of ye utmost consequence—you certainly do not, you cannot think I ment to Justify ye practice of any known fault, no, far, very far from this I assure you, but the natural temper is not easily kept under proper Regulation at all times—therefore is it not better, to know a person before you venture upon ye Experiment, then to have your know-ledge come to late, may not this think you, be a means to prevent numberless inadvertency's yt might possiably be the ocasion of freequent, tho' undesigned uneasiness. How far I may differ in my Judgment of things from ye rest of my sex, I know not; but of this I am certain, yt it is not in my power to give you a stronger proof of my Desire for your Happiness then that late declaration &. Heaven knows how sincerely I wish it.

I shoud be glad to fix a time for my coming down yt woud be

18

more agreable to you, but to offer to leave sooner then ye time I mention'd will so distress ye Doctor yt I must beg youll excuse me & now to conclude, let me tell you theres no art I can use yt will bring me a Letter so often as I wish for it, so you must know yt your wrighting soon will give great pleasure to your most Humble servant E: Woollat

Jedediah Strutt to Elizabeth Woollat

Blackwell June 28 [*1755*]

Dear Betty,

As I have just been thinking on the uncertainty of all humane affairs I was led to this conclusion that there is scarce any thing here that will afford a lasting satisfaction for either they cannot give us that pleasure we expected or else that they soon cease to be suited. Upon looking back I can recollect a thousand things in which I once took the greatest delight and in which I now wonder how I coud be so delighted. I was once so far transported with having completed a Windmill that it was Ecstacy to see it move —And I coud have read romances with Tears both of Grief and Joy. But those are over and gone to make room for follies less innocent and more perplexing. Love has long since been my darling passion tho' it was not till lately that I had any taste for connubial pleasures but rather look'd on 'em shoud they ever be as the days of my unhappiness. But those too like the rest have had their turn and the very opposite temper of mind now takes place and is the subject of all my thoughts. Whether the joys of Wedlock will always please I am utterly uncertain but at present I know of nothing worthy the name of Love that is not intended that way And I lay not one scheme of happiness present or future with a single View only but with this additional pleasure that it may one day please another.

I have now the pleasure to see a very wilderness on the Backside of my House transformd into a most fruitful Garden but it is not formd so much for delight as usefulness, nay I know of nothing so useless in it as a littl[e] Arbour in which I have planted a shady Elm and Sycamore and that they may not yield only a barren Shade there is the Jessamine and Woodbine too to twine among the branches. This often puts me in mind of Adams Bower the Nuptial Bower and Edens Sweets the leaving which gave Eve so much reluctance. There I spend many an Hour in rambling fruitless speculations but I hope one day to spend 'em with you in the more refind pleasures of Bliss and Love. I might mention a thousand other incidents but least they shoud appear still more trifling I forbear Tho at this time I have leisure enough to say all I coud think of thro' a strain in my knee which happened a few days ago. At first I thought of nothing less than a cripple but now have for other hopes. I am not sorry that this has happend as thankful it was no worse Especially when I consider the cause—Wrestling, Leaping &c are Exercises I was ever fond of but I trust time and a few such consequences will wean me from those pursuits—

I have gone thus far without looking over your Letter or in the least considering what I was to answer and indeed I can say nothing [in] vindication of any thing I then said since I can scarce remember a word of it. I can only add that if I said any thing that lookd like too much indifference to that declaration you so frankly and generously made it was because I discovered nothing new in it. Had I been less acquainted with you, had I made less observations on your temper or conduct or had they been less just it had been greater matter of wonder to me to hear a Woman expose her failings to her Lover. But this I must suppose you ignorant of therefore that disinterested generous behaviour was not the less necessary nor woud I diminish one Jot of all the Honesty and simplicity you intended by it and am very far from thinking you would persist in any known Error. You have put a very wrong construction upon my words or at least greatly mistook my meaning. But if it be possible for me to speak what I think or convey my mind to you in any words I can conceive I woud tell you this plain truth that it is you are She with whom I intend to be happy and to whose happiness I woud contribute all in my power. Therefore whenever you shall think it a greater pleasure to come into the country than to continue in London I shall be ready to meet you not only without reluctance but with a pleasure I have not words to express. Till then I am only yours   J Strutt

tell B Scot I can never forget her

Elizabeth Woollat to Jedediah Strutt

London August 10 1755

My Derbyshire Journey begins to engross all my attention; what the event may prove, God only knows. When august was proposed for my comming I then thought of staying a month at Findern; but when I consider, how things are at present circumstanced; finde, it will be much more a greable, to spend that time with the Dr & so come directly in the Coach to Nottingham & you meet me there. I had much rather, not go to Findern till some time after-wards, if you approve of this I need nothing more to Determine me, & ye sooner you let me know, ye more you will oblige me. I have Box's also which must be there before me, how, or where, I must send them I shoud be glad to know. The Dr bids me tell you, he wishes you was at London, you shoud live with him, and he woud do all in his powr to procure Business for you; but as this cannot be, I have proposed his takeing your Brother [Joseph] into ye House to him, as Mrs Betty & he are to be married in about a month's time to which ye Dr has consented, tho upon Different terms, to what you woud have been had it, suted you to have comm. It is impossible to recount to you ye numberless instances of ye Dr kindness, & I can with truth assure you, your the only person in this World for which I woud leave this Exelent man. I have a thousand more things to say to you, which I can better tell then write. Youll please to excuse all mistakes as I have wrote this in ye utmost hurry, Mr. Strut & Mr Salte both waits in ye Chitchen for me. Yours sincearly   E: Woollat

dont forget to write soone

Jedediah Strutt to Elizabeth Woollat

Blackwell Aug 24: 1755

Dear Betty

Yours came but just in time to prevent me writing to know what coud be the reason you did not write, August being far advanced. But your Letter has put an end to a thousand thoughts many of which were but too troublesome; but now like you I am wholly taken up with seeing you here. In order so that with regard to whatever you want to send I woud wish it to be by Hall & Dawson the Mansfield Carriers rather than Clarks. You may direct em to lie till calld for Either at Nottingham or Mansfield because it will be equally easy to get them from either place. I think it might be proper to agree with 'em for the Carr: but not to pay. I fancy they Inn at the george in Smithfield but that my Bro: can tell you, & perhaps assist you in the affair.

I am infinitely oblig'd to the Dr for the kindness he expresses for me, because I am not deserving any of his favours, nor so much as known to him. If all this had happened a few years ago, London shoud have been the place of my abode, & it is with some regret that I reflect on the many advantages I shoud have enjoy'd under the Eye and influence of so good a man. He cou'd have resolvd all my doubts, answered all my objections, nay methinks I coud not have faild of being both wise & virtuous; but let it be abundantly sufficient, that he who thinks nothing too much he can do [for] the good of mankind, will not fail of his prayers & good wishes to heaven for me. I shoud have wrote sooner, but have had no opportunity till now on account of our friends from London being here till last night. You'l be so good as to let me know the day you will be at Nottingham that I may not fail to meet you. I believe it will not be possible to be married any where but here, else I had rather it had been at Nottingham, but of that I will be informd before I see you. Till that happy hour farewell from thy more than Lover

J: Strutt

ps: give my sincere thanks to the Dr for the kindness he woud have bestowd on me, had opportunity offerd for tho' I coud almost envy my Brother that happiness which might have been mine, yet since I wish him nothing that I woud not wish myself, I am contented that what coud not be mine was my Brother's Lot and Oh may I never be ungrateful!

Elizabeth Woollat to Jedediah Strutt

London Sept, 16. *1755*

I yesterday, sent by the Waggon you mentioned a Trunk, & Box, which weighed $1\frac{1}{2}$: 21: Ye Carrage 0 ·· 13 ·· 6 thay are directed for you, to lie till calld for, if you coud Conveniently send for em satturday or monday, I shoud be very glad. I come in the nottingham coach, which Inns at ye White Lyon, & shall be there on Tuesday septbr 23, where I hope to meet you, till which fair well

yours sincarly E: Woollat

I must depend on you sending for ye things,
as I shall have nothing to put on.
please to take of the matt & cord

They were married at Blackwell parish church on September 25, 1755.[1] It was a happy match although not all Elizabeth's friends thought it a good one. A cousin wrote to her a few

---

[1] The entry in the registers reads: 'Jedidiah Strutt of this Parish, a farmer and a Batchalour aged twenty six years and Elizabeth Woollat a soujourner in this Parish Spinster aged twenty six years, were married in this Church this twenty fifth day of September in the year of our Lord one thousand and seven hundred fifty and five with lisence by Me Cornelius Horn Minister. This Marriage was solemnized between us—Jedidiah Strutt—and in the

Elisabeth Woollat

presence of William Woollat
George Ranson.'
Jedediah's age was misstated.

months later to give the Nonconformist tea-table gossip at Derby:[1]

> As to what Miss Lathams said I have heard very little about it, only when they & Miss Betty Bingham & Miss Kitty was Got to Geather, they talked in a very taunting sort of a manner & wondred that you wou'd leave such a place to come & marry a wheelwright.

Elizabeth Strutt was obviously a very capable woman and perhaps supplied the drive that her introspective, self-centred husband had hitherto lacked. He was soon, with her active aid, to embark on a new career. But for the moment he was, as he described himself in the marriage register, a farmer. And in the following year he was advertising in the *Derby Mercury*:[2]

> Stolen or stray'd from Blackwell, near Alfreton in the County of Derby, betwixt the 24th and 25th of this Instant May, Two Mares, about Fourteen Hands and an Half high each, and about Six Years old; One is very dark Brown, with Brown Muzzle, a long cut Tail (if not alter'd, or ty'd up) three White Feet, a Blaze in the Face, and a Flesh Mark like this X on the near Shoulder. The other a Black, with a small Blaze, a little hollow back'd, and a Whisk Tail. Whoever will bring them, or either of them, to Jedediah Strutt, of Blackwell, aforesaid, shall receive a handsome Reward and all reasonable Charges.

This is the first public glimpse of him.

[1] Miss Dethick to Mrs. Strutt, Nov., 1755.
[2] May 28, 1756.

CHAPTER II

THE HOSIERY PATENT

JEDEDIAH STRUTT had lived all his life in the hosiery manufacturing country. Its centres were Nottingham, Leicester, and Derby, but it was spread through nearly all the villages. The stocking frame used was based on the Elizabethan invention of William Lee, the Nottinghamshire parson. Yet after over a century and a half of mechanical knitting the frame had not been adapted successfully to ribbed hosiery, which was still made by hand. It was by solving this problem that Strutt made his first industrial contribution.

I. THE DERBY RIB MACHINE

Strutt's invention of the Derby rib machine, as it came to be known, resembles the other textile inventions of the time in the way it has gathered about it much contradictory legend. We can only make guesses at the truth. The earliest form of the story, published in 1789, during Strutt's lifetime by a friend, was that a 'rude and imperfect idea' of the invention 'had been furnished by a common workman, named Roper' but it was owing to the 'labour and ingenuity' of Strutt and his brother-in-law William Woollat 'that it was ever brought to full maturity'.[1] Gravenor Henson (born 1785), a gatherer of much tradition, writing in 1831, gave it embroidery. About 1750, we are to believe, an old stockinger named Bowman, of Dale Abbey (between Derby and Nottingham), got some way towards a solution. A neighbour, Roper, of the adjacent hamlet of Locko, profiting by Bowman's partial success, tried another approach. Roper,

though an ingenious fellow, was indolent in his habits, and loved ale and company better than intense scheming, and was consequently inadequate to the task which he had to encounter; he

---

[1] Pilkington, *A View of Derbyshire* (1789), ii, 173. Pilkington was co-pastor of Friargate Chapel, Derby, of which Strutt was a trustee.

however made several specimens, which he produced with much exaltation to his pot companions at Locko, who having more wisdom advised him to display them to his master, Mr. Wm. Woollatt, or Woollett, then a hosier at Derby.[1]

Woollat consulted Strutt, who bought Roper's machine to try to improve it. According to 'a very prevailing tradition' at South Normanton, Strutt is supposed at this time to have kept pack-horses which he used to carry coals from the pits at Denby to Belper and Derby; he is reputed to have sold a pack-horse for £5 which he paid over to Roper for his machine. Then, sometimes assisted by Roper, Strutt produced what was recognized to be a highly ingenious piece of mechanism.[2] It was not an adaptation of the stocking frame itself but an attachment which was placed in front of it. A separate set of needles (barbed hooks) operated vertically among the horizontal needles of the frame, taking the loops from the latter and reversing them so as to make a rib stitch.[3]

The long low garret in the farmhouse at Blackwell, where according to tradition Strutt worked out the invention, is still pointed out.[4] All this would be about 1756, when Strutt was 30 and William Woollat possibly rather younger. If Woollat had then set up as a hosier he could not have been in a big way. In 1751 he was still at Findern and was asking his sister to find him a place in London.[5]

II. IN SEARCH OF CAPITAL

A batch of letters of 1757–8 throws light (some of it confused) on the circumstances in which the patent for the invention was launched. Strutt, with his farm at Blackwell, is seen trying to start as a putter-out of hosiery in the district and is in touch with various hosiers of Nottingham. There is talk of a

[1] Henson, *The Civil, Political and Mechanical History of the Framework-Knitters* (1831), i, 258–9.

[2] Ibid., 260. Henson suggests that 'the sum of money is most probably the only truth in the narration'.

[3] Wells, *The British Hosiery Trade* (1935), 63.

[4] Strutt, op. cit., 378–9.

[5] William Woollat to Elizabeth Woollat, April 14, 1751: 'If you can get mee into a good shop or any other beneficial place I will Endevour to Quallify my Self in Wighting and Counts.' There was estrangement from his father, who had married a second time.

lawsuit but whether it had any connection with the invention is uncertain and perhaps improbable. Mrs. Strutt has gone to London—leaving her son of nine months behind—to try to borrow money from her old master, Dr. Benson.[1] But, for reasons Professor Ashton has explained (the dearness of money),[2] she is unsuccessful. While in London she is ill. She is also canvassing for hosiery orders for her husband and brother, and has a promise from Birkett Fenn, a leading hosier of Cornhill.[3] A dealer in thread and cotton offers to supply them with material.[4] There is a nucleus of friends—through the Nonconformist connections—and relatives in London, ready to help. 'Cousin Salt' may well be the Samuel Salt (or Salte) whom William Hutton met in Birmingham in 1750 as a mercer's apprentice, who had gone to London five years later, and was to become one of the biggest warehousemen, the friend of the Strutts and Arkwrights, and of Priestley, and the encourager of Samuel Oldknow. He died in 1797 worth £100,000.[5]

Jedediah Strutt to his wife

[Blackwell, April 25, 1757]

My Dear Wife

I never wrote to you in the character of an Husband before this nor ever with greater pleasure. I did not get home till fryday. I stayd at Derby on Wednesday night and came on Thursday to Heage before it began to snow so I stayd there all night. I call'd of Nanny at Swanwick and had a good deal of talk with her husband with regard to the affair in hand. He has 2 frames of his own and will serve us when there is ocasion. He coud inform me a good deal of the proceedings betwixt Roper and Garl and that it is common to Allow 1 shilling p Dozen for putting out &ccc. I called next of Mr Malkins[6] and found them very busy papering the parlour ceiling with common blue paper. I did not think it look't well at all. Then I went to Mr Cox and ask'd him about the affair at

---

[1] To 'Elizabeth Strutt formerly faithful servant' he left £40 and to her second son, George Benson, 5 guineas. (Will at Somerset House.)

[2] Ashton, *An Economic Hist. of England. The 18th Century* (1955), 29.

[3] *Kent's London Directory*, 1754.

[4] William Seddon, threadman of Bishopsgate Street.

[5] *Life of William Hutton*, ed. Jewitt (1872), 163; Priestley, *Memoirs* (1904 ed.), 59, 62, 81; Unwin, *Samuel Oldknow and the Arkwrights* (1924), passim.

[6] Jonah Malkin (1712/13–1785) was a Dissenting minister at Alfreton from 1750–85. He and his family are frequently mentioned.

Nottingham and he wrote me a smart Letter to the gentlemen in favour of yr Bror and I intend to go over with it in a few days. I then call'd at Mr Newbolt and Mary Clark and so Home where I found all well but the New Mare had been very ill again but recoverd blessed be God & the next thing was to see thy little Billy [and] mine. He was very well and came to me with a deal of pleasure and I never was so glad to see him before. He says dad dad so prettily. He had been in some pain the day before they supposd on [account] of his teeth. I stayd some time and then up to Newton w[here] they was about agreeing the Law affair. I stayd till past n[ine] but I cannot tell you yet how it will end And now I am [writing you] this Letter. I am afraid you woud be wet and cold yesterday in the afternoon and very weary before you got to London but I hope you woud get safe. I intend to go to Mansfield on Thursday to receive your Letter that I may know how you do and the success of your Journey. I can think of nothing more to tell you at present. You may wonder how I have thought of so much when you consider I am not inclined to the talkative but I never wishd to please you so much nor ever lovd you so well as now. I woud do any thing to divert you. I am thy ever faithful loving Husband J. Strutt.

My Humbl Service to the Dr. Love to Bro: & Sister, to Dolly, to Judith, to all our friends.

Blackwell Fryday night 10 O Clock

Somebody has stole B Williamsons Old shift of the Hedge

Elizabeth Strutt to her husband

Dr. Benson's
Goodman's Fields,
London.

My Dear

I have now ye pleasure to informe you yt after a very tiresome, but safe journey I reechd London a bout 3 O Clock on Satturday, when we reechd Glen, 6 miles from Leicester I was so sick I was not able to travel further but staid behind ye waggon mor then an hour, & then walked 5 miles before I came up with it, we staid none at market harborough but went forward to Germage Inn, where we lay, we never Dined only just beat ye next day at Northampton & Lay at Lathborough, ye next Day we beat at Hockley & lay at Redfearn 4 miles Short of St Albans,[1] it has been very windy

---

[1] The waggon followed the usual Derby–London road at that time: Leicester, Market Harborough, Northampton, Lathbury, Hockliffe, Redbourn, St. Albans,

bad weather & Rained & snow'd all Day on Thursday, & I caught a very Bad Cold, I waited on Mrs Clark to her sisters in Aldersgate & then made ye Best of my way to goodmansfields where I found all friends well, ye Dr. Recd me more like a Father then a master & welcomed me a gain, & a gain, & inquir'd very Affectionately after you & our Dear little Charmer. Sister was so obligeing to follow me to ye Drs, & insisted upon my lying there wch ye Dr upon some considerations consented to, so yt I am Dispos'd on Betwixt ye 2 Houses. Cosn Salt Drank tea with me on Lords Day. I told him of our intended trade. He says he is very intimate with some of the Hosiers & will do all in his powr to serve you, on Monday I went to acquaint ye Dr. but found him so ill yt I staid with him ye whole Day & he never got out of Bed till betwixt 7 & 8 O Clock at night, to Day he is Better & gone out, I must wait for a proper oppertunity to talk him over, & hope to tell you Good news in my next, I begun ys Letter before I rec'd yours, ye post being later then Comon. I began to be in fear you had forgot me & never rec'd a letter with more true pleasure in all my Life, but can I do more then Love & thank you for it. O my Dear Jerre, what Differance is there betwixt writeing to a Husband & a Lover, I am very thankfull our Dear Billy is so well, do see him often & kiss & play with him for me, being confin'd with ye Dr Yesterday & Mr. & Mrs. Scot being to Dine with me to Day at Brothers prevents my doing anny buisness but in tend to begin in ernest in the afternoon. Mr. Seddon has begun in ye thred buisness a gain & has just been hear. He Desires his servis to you & my Brother & will be glad to serve you, on ye other side he has sent you ye lowest prises of his thred & cotton & if you trade with him will Recomend you to ye Hosiers here. Mr. Salts are come to spend ye evening with me & I have left them in ye parlour, whilst I come to tell my Dearest Jerre what pleasures it gives me to subscribe my Self thy most affectionate & ever Dutyfull wife E Strutt

Jedediah Strutt to his wife

[Blackwell, 1757]

My Dear Bett

I never waited so impatiently for a Letter nor ever receiv'd one with so much pleasure as your last. I am very sorry you was so poorly after I left you and was afraid the Wind & Snow woud beat upon you But am very glad you got safe there & that you met with so kind a reception. I am much oblige'd to the Dr for his kind inquiry

28

after me and sincerely thank him for it. I am very sorry he has been so poorly.

But to continue my journal. The Law suit being under reference I went to Nottingham on Satturday to stop Scot for coming as an evidence. I did not set out till one o Clock did business at five places and came home that Night tho' it was past 12 O Clock. Before I believe I was hinderd about 2 hours by being lost upon the forest. I found John and Betty up waiting of the cow calving. She did very well and we went to Bed about 2. I went to the gentn at Nottingham found em both at home. They had had some thoughts about it & mentiond it once or twice but as the place was distant and they had not a proper person to do the business they had dropt it a good while ago. They seem'd to listen to the proposal and shoud be glad to enlarge their trade but coud not give a positive answer but wd consider of it and let us know soon. Trade is exceeding brisk there. Boltby woud not stand to the terms of agreement he himself had propos'd. I suppose he was influenc'd by Wm Downing but my Fathers Attorny took the advantage of their proposal and has put the Tryal of till October so we let them go with all their gang to Basford and be at all the expence and lost their labour. I was at Mansfield yesterday & today have been busy in the garden. Tomorrow I am to go to Nottingham to take a Man there for getting a Bastard child. Corn still rises I believe I coud sell my worst Oats at 21s p Qr. The Duke has begun to measure the Lordship.[1] Betty does very well considering. Sally at my Fathers is got better. I have sent the cloth to the whitening there was 23 yards of it. I have just heard Boltby wants sadly to agree again they are very sick of the affair now. Father & Bro: have had no talk yet I suppose he will be at London again soon. People wonder much what you are gone to London for some say we have differ'd and you are gone away others that we are for leaving here and you are gone to see for Business because old Strutt will part with nothing and some say you are gone to fetch the Horses again that Bro: took from us for debt when they was [here]. These are the various conjectures to all which I made no reply. . . . Tell Sister Billy than[ks her for] the kind present of the Biscuits she sent him. He can mump 'em up bravely. Give my kind Love and thanks to her and Bro: Bro: Wm sends his love to them and you give my Humbl Service to the Dr to Dolly to Coz Judith & to all our Friends. I intend to write to Derby on Tuesday. It will soon be my hour for bed tho' I am not sleepy nor weary but am almost at the bottom of the paper and have said all I can think of

---

[1] The Duke of Devonshire owned half the township (Glover, *History of Derby* (1833), ii, 123).

that is materiall only that I am your ever Loving constant Husband
J Strutt

you'l excuse my many
blurs and blunders I wrote in haste.
I do not go to Nottingham today
Saturday morning 5 O Clock

Elizabeth Strutt to her husband

London 3 May 1757 6 o Clock
morning

My Dear
    I rec'd your most obligeing Letter yesterday with yt true pleasure,
which Love & Gratitude can only feel, & rejoice greatly to hear
boath you & my dear little Billy are so well, may you be ye care of a
Good & kind providence yt so we may meet each other a gain in
Health & Safety, this will be a pleasure greater then I have ever
yet known. I hope to set out on monday next, but cannot Determine
certainly ys Letter, as my Right Breast Geathers & is so painfull I
cannot wear my Stays, we poultis it by the Direction of ye Hospital
Surgions & I hope it will Break in a Day or 2. I will write a gain
on Satturday next to be at Mansfield on Monday or Tuesday
perhaps you may get somebody to call for it—ye Dr is pritty well
a gain & I have acquainted him with our scheam which, as far as
he understand it thinks it may do very well & he will do all he
can for us, & woud willingly supply us with ye money. Mr William
Cook[1] at ye same time wanted to Borrow of him one thousand
pound in order to furnish boath of us he went to ye Bank to sell
out but ye War makes ye Stocks run so very low yt he will loose a
Hundred pound if he sells out now, & thay will rise as much in
proportion if there coms a peace so yt he woud rather chuse to
Borrow for his own use then loose so much money, Ys is a great
Disopointmt to me & yet I cannot desire him to act otherwise he
says, yt he, or anny Boddy will be as much oblig'd to you for 4pr
sent, for their money, as you will be to them for it. Brother & Sister
are extreamly obliging to me & Sister has made Billy a present of a
most Beatifull new frock which I am making, Judy is making him a
Black Cap, Nancy & Kitty boath come down next week. There is
no money Left to be Dispos'd of in ye way Mr Willson mentiond
yt ye Knows of he intends to procure Mr Malkin £5 ys Summer as

---

[1] Perhaps the brother of John Cooke of Findern, brother-in-law of John
Bloodworth with whom Strutt was shortly to enter into partnership (*Derby
Mercury*, May 15, 1783).

we respect him. Sister has Bough[t] Father a handsome set of China ye Dr says its likely to be a very blooddy summer. Ye press is very hot. Tom Deathick was pressd last week but got of a gain [Remainder of Letter missing.]

Elizabeth Strutt to her husband

London May 10, 1757

My Dear

I will not add to your pain by telling you what I have suffred. I am now throe ye mercy of our Great & Good God finely recoverd & ye Surgion tould me yesterday yt he thought I might be able to travel next week without Danger, which raisd my drooping spirits greatly for I wish & long to be with you. I had my stays on a few hours yesterday & Dined & walked 3 times round ye tenters with ye Dr. He asks a great deal a bout you, & will be allways glad to see, or to serve you. Mr Fen woud have my Brother & you [be] as speedy as possible in making reddy to begin. He will imploy you in anny, or all sorts of work, Ye Dr assures me he is as safe to Deal with as a Banker, Ye Dr has given me 2 fine maps for you, I have a great Deal to say to you but as I cannot write without pain, must defer yt till I see you, which I hope will be on friday sevennight. I propose coming in yt mans waggon I came in which will be in Loughborough erly on friday where I shall be glad to meet you & perhaps we may reach Findern yt night & home on Lords Day. I am afraid you will have a great deal of trouble in procuring a Horse, tell my Dear Billy thay talk much of him at London & if he is a good Boy ye Dr says he shall be a parson & do Honour to their Cloth, I flatter myself with ye pleasure of a Letter from my Dear Jerre to morrow which will not fail to give great sattisfaction to thy faithfull Affectionate & ever Dutifull W: E. Strutt

Jedediah Strutt to his wife

[Blackwell, May 10, 1757]

My dear Love

I sent yesterday for your Letter in great hopes of hearing you woud now have been on yr way home but it did not come & this morning provd very rainy so that nobody went. I waited till noon and then sent John. I dreaded the contents as soon as I saw it was the Drs Hand. If I had known of this we woud not now have been so far asunder. I cannot tell you how to imagine the uneasiness I am in for you unless you can do it by supposing the Love equal betwixt us and I in your circumstances and you in mine. O my dear

Love those hours I spend in solititude and grief for thee are tedious hours! But I will not add to thy pain and uneasiness by telling thee of [them. It would] be more prudent if I cd say something to divert thee but [believe me when I] say I cannot be merry. Last wednesday morning I went to [? Alfre]ton on a certain occasion to Mr Horn for a Licence but after [staying] there near 2 hours & using many arguments to no purpose Cam[e] away without. As I was coming by Mr Holmes I saw him in court he calld to me askd how I did and you very kindly. The[n he asked] me to go in and drink. I told him I had just drank at Mr H—— so I told him the Errand I had been on among wh discourse he took occasion to ask me about our scheme & said Alfreton was the only place for doing business of that sort to advantage for many reasons. 1st that Mr Rope[r][1] was always drunk and neglected his business (tho' he is his Tennant) & the workmen cd not get their money, the great [expense] a week for Carrying goods and Letters, the prodigious increase of stocking makers thereabouts, that they wd be glad to work there and receive their money & so lay it out at the Market without more loss of time and that we might have room enough, that one Mr Brown a large Hosier in Nottm Some time ago wrote to him (as they had been formerly acquainted) to put out for him but he declin'd it. Then askd me again to go in and drink but I cd not stay nor did not chuse it. Then he sd he wd take a walk with me down his ground wh reaches near half way to Blackwell. I asked him to write to Brown to know if he was still in the same mind. He sd he wd but upon further consideration as he did not chuse it shd be known he had a hand in it therfore did not care to trust the Letter But if I woud go and carry it & give it to Mr Brown mysel he wd write. I thanked him [and] told him I wd. Accordingly I went on fryday. He wrote me a Letter of recomendation made me stay Tea & Ale till 8 O Clock. Next morning I set of to Nottm Saw Mr Brown but as I was not of the business cd not answer to Questions he wd have asked. He sd he sd like to employ about 10 Frames but wd come to Alfreton on fryday and will speak to Mr Holmes. I am to meet him there and have sent for yr Bro: to be there also that we may come to a resolution because I have 2 other psns at Nottm that wants to employ more hands. Those 2 that I spoke of to you before have concluded to drop it at present—I been holding My little Billy tonight. He is very fat and fresh and fair & sweet & clean & good. His Nurse desires her love to you & is truly sorry

---

[1] Perhaps the hosier about whom the following notice appeared in the *Derby Mercury* of May 23, 1766: '23 Stocking Frames also Worsted, Cotton and Thread Hose, Silk and Worsted Mitts, the property of the late Mr. John Roper to be sold by Auction at Miner's Arms in Alfreton'.

for you. I hope you will be able to write to me when you have received this. You cannot think the pleasure it will give me to hear of your recovery and that you are once more able to return. My happiness depends upon thy health and presence. Oh, how I do pity thee! Oh how I Love thee. I am afraid you sd want money. Now it happens so if you do be so good as to get what you need of Bro: Jos: and I will send it back by bro: Wm. Give my love to Bro: & Sister. My thanks & service to the Dr and Dolly for their care of you and accept your self the most sincere Love of your ever loving and Affectionate Husband

J Strutt

I have written you a deal in great haste and very poorly but youl excuse it—do write to me. Bro: Wm sends his Love to you & Bro: & Sister

Jedediah Strutt to Dr. Benson

Blackwell May 10: 1757.

Most Reverend and honored Sir

I did not receive your Letter till to night and am extreamly sorry for the Occasion of your writing and at the same time very greatly oblig'd to you for the favour. I rejoyce to hear the danger is over and have great hope that in time all will yet be well. I am fully satisfyed as to every thing that can be done for her relief. She is in the best hands in the World those of providence and you. I know she will want nothing you can do And what ever it pleases god to order I know will be for the best—But still none knows how anxious I am for the event as well as for her safe return. My Bror in Law and I are very much oblig'd to you for the pains you take to serve us. I hope to see him this week to tell him how much you interest yourself in our welfare, and happiness. I know it will give him great pleasure. I have just been with my little Billy he is very well. I sincerely thank you for your love [for him] as well as for all your other many and great favours to me [and] mine and I am with the utmost sincerity your most Oblig'd and most obedient humbl servt

Jed: Strutt

III. PATENT AND PARTNERSHIP

Early in 1758 Strutt is himself in London. He has brought with him specimens of his ribbed hose—cotton and worsted—

to show to hosiers. He finds them, not unnaturally, discouraging about the idea of a patent. Dr. Benson is more enthusiastic. He thinks it would be foolish to part with the invention for 'so trifling a gratuity as £50 a year', but is doubtful whether a patent could be upheld unless there is stronger backing behind it than Strutt and Woollat can give. An alliance is therefore sought and concluded with John Bloodworth and Thomas Stamford, substantial hosiers of Derby:

Jedediah Strutt to his wife

London 31 Jan 1758 8 O Clock

My dear love

I got safe to town on Saturday about 2 O Clock found all well and went to the Drs that evening. He receiv'd me very kindly and offer'd to go with me to Mr Fenn on Monday if we coud find him at home. On Monday Bro: and I went 4 times before we cou'd see him and then it was too late for the Dr to go there but he went with me this Morning and we saw him but Mr Fenn has no great opinion of our affair. I have this afternoon been with 3 other Hosiers. They are a good deal of the same mind but some of them think it might do very well in Cotton and Silk but none of them give any reasons of much weight. Tomorrow I intend to go to the Other end of the Town to get what information I can. They all frankly own they are the best of the kind they ever saw and very neat. Mr Fenn paid me £17 ·· 17 and gave me a Note for the rest. He Wrote last Saturday but one for 9 Doz rd hose I wish they or some of them may be here on Saturday next and the rest as soon as possible and I will endeavour to get an Order for the rest. If the man from Redford has not bro't the money nor John been for it I desire he wou'd go and fetch it if possible or I will put him to trouble. If you can do, I had rather you did not sell any Corn it rises here. Do remember to turn the Hams. Sister is not bro't to bed. The Dr was very poorly last week but is better this, he desires his kind respects to you. Mr Salt has sent the tea &cc. Your 2 or 3 lines pleased me much. I thank you for them. If you have not sent me a Letter in a bagg of Stockings I desire you woud not fail writing to me on Saturday by the post. I suppose I shall set out on Monday next but I will write to you again on Saturday and you may send for it on Monday perhaps I may send for some Stockings if they shoud come away on Monday night. I have now told you what I can think of most material only that I do not yet dispair of success but have still great hopes, that I am in perfect health both of Body and Mind and that I am your most sincerely affectionate and loving Husband J Strutt. My dear love to my dear little babes.

I have not seen the dr since I saw Mr Fenn and the other hosiers. My love to Bro: Sister desires her Love to you & your little ones

Jedediah Strutt to his wife

London 4 Feby 1758

My dear Love,

I am now at Mrs Please's. She desires her compliments to you, it is about 8 o clock. I have got the Ham and the Stocking I fancy will be very neat when dry and iron'd. I know you long to hear how I proceed which in a few words amounts only to this. The Hosiers talk so sillily and so selfishly that without you wou'd sell em fine hose at the price of coarse or ingage they shall get 2 where they get but one they give very little ear to you but thus far I learn by what they say & by the stockings I see, and the price that it woud answer all the expectations we have ever had of it if we can secure it. But this the Dr thinks we of our selves shall hardly be able to accomplish. We may readily have the patent for money enough but then he is sensible we shall have inumerable enemies that will endeavour to disturb us and afraid we shall not be able to contend with 'em (This I think is very just reasoning). Therefore he thinks that if Mr Bloodworth woud heartily engage in it and come into such measures as he and I have talk'd of his character and fortune woud bear down all opposition. To this end I woud desire my Bro: to meet me at Derby on Fryday next to come to the White Hart and stay till I can leave word where I shall find him or when he will be back because I must see him before he says anything to Mr B—I had rather before he sees him. The Dr is greatly pleasd and fully satisfyed how much it will be to our advantage if we can make the best of it. He will do everything in his power both to advise and assist us. I din'd with him yesterday. He several times wishd for you there and little Billy. I walkd with him 3 times round the tenters after dinner by which time it was near to 5 o clock when I came home and found your welcome letter. I cou'd hardly stay to read it for going to tell him the good news. I read him the most materiall articles wh pleased him much. He hoped his scheme might be bro't to bear with Mr B— He woud by no means have us either give it up nor trifle it away for so trifling a gratuity as £50 a year. I ask'd his leave to let me give my Bro: the Ham and he shou'd have the other. Sister still keeps up. I have had no opportunity of showing the Cotton Stocking but will on Monday. I intend to set out on tuesday morning on my way to Blackwell that dirty spot notwithstanding which is very dear to me on your and several other accounts. Nothing will ever make me forget or cease to Love you. I long to be happy with you again at Blackwell for I cannot be happy even here without you. Farewell my Dear Love till we meet again farewell I am thy affectionate Husband J Strutt

I have bo't 3 Silk Handkerchiefs at M[   ]s and some Cotton. I will send some sugar give my Duty to Father Brother Wm sends his Love

A partnership was formed on February 24 between Strutt and Woollat and John Bloodworth and Thomas Stamford, two of the largest hosiers of Derby. Both were trustees of the Dissenting chapel in Friargate, Derby, of which Dr. Latham had been co-minister.[1] The petition for the patent was signed at Blackwell on March 7 by Jedediah Strutt, wheelwright, and William Woollat, both of Blackwell. With the supporting affidavit it was referred by the Secretary of State to the Law Officers on March 14, returned on March 22; the bill is dated April 11, and the patent enrolled on April 19, a description of the invention to be lodged within four calendar months.[2] The following letter must be of this time:

Jedediah Strutt to his wife

Derby thursday

My Dear Love

I wou'd not willingly miss any opportunity of letting you know how we go on. We heard nothing from Mr Salt on Monday nor till today. Mr Stamford has had a Letter from him. He has paid the 60£ to the Gentn and expects it will be done in about a week. The Irish man is still here. I have been in his company once and it affords me much pleasure to find we much exceed him in point of time if not in neatness. He talks of going to Nottingham. We did nothing on Monday nor tuesday but we are now very busy in altering a frame and shall continue to be so. We have all din'd with Mr Blood[wor]th to day. His behaviour is more free and generous than ever I saw it. I have heard very little said where the frames

---

[1] Bloodworth, 'an eminent hosier', died in April, 1771; Stamford was elected alderman of Derby in 1768 and mayor in 1769 (*Derby Mercury*, April 5, 1771; May 13, 1768; Oct. 6, 1769).

[2] P.R.O., S.P. 36/139; S.O. 7/233; Ind. 6764.

36

are to be put &ccc but some thing must be determin'd soon. We are in perfect health and I have no doubt but things will (in time) turn out to our advantage. I send by Mr Malkin, the Meeting of Ministers has been today. I must conclude for fear he shou'd be gone. Mr Rawlin's has been along with us at Mr Blood[wor]ths. Give my kind love to my little babys and Duty to my father when you see him. Perhaps I may not come home till Sabbath day but hope to come then and see you. I am ever and only thine J Strutt

In September Woollat writes enthusiastically to Strutt at Blackwell about the prospects:

William Woollat to Jedediah Strutt

Derby Sept: 11 1758

Dear Bro:

This is to request you will come over as soon as you can. The Men went to Mr Stamford on Satterday to know the Higher prises we wou'd give, which we gave in Writing and they have agreed to work upon our Terms. Every thing seems to go well this Morning, they will boath get more and we shall have more Goods made by the same hands. Mr T was wth Mr Bloodworth on Satterday and spent the greater part of the Afternoon with him. He has rote to Mr Craston and I have made a Fresh Bill of Parcells of the Goods, have put Twenty p Cent Proffit on the Worst[ed] and Cotton & nearly 27 on the Silk which is thought by Mr Bloodworth a very great Proffit. He talk very freely about the affair and sais it will answer. We shall want more Frames, shou'd be glad if Jonathan wou'd Come over and Bring his frames and Prentisses but dont let any Boddy see this Letter as Mr Bloodworth and Mr Stamford wou'd not have it known what is Gain'd by the Business, youl give my Kind Love to my Dear Sister and your Little Babes

I am yr affectionate
Bro: Wm Woollat

P:S Great & Good News is just Comme. The King of Prussia has beat the Russians Kil'd and taken Fifteen Thousand 100 Pieces of Cannon their Military Chest and the Light Horse is still in Persuit of Them. Huzzay[1]

The patent specification was not, apparently, presented within the required four months and another petition ('for a

---

[1] The battle of Zorndorff, Aug. 25–6.

machine to manufacture ribbed-stockings, &c.') was signed on September 20, Strutt and Woollat being still described as of Blackwell; it was referred on November 7; the bill is dated December 7, and the grant of the patent January 10, 1759.[1]

The partnership with Bloodworth and Stamford lasted until June 19, 1762, when it was dissolved by consent. The patent was to become the sole property of Strutt and Woollat on payment of £374 14s. 10d. to Stamford and £195 4s. 4d. to Bloodworth, principal and interest in both cases. Stamford was to have 'Ten of the said Engines or Machines' and it was to be 'lawful for him at all times hereafter to use and employ the same and no more in making such Good[s] as hath been heretofore usually made thereon'. He must have been the larger supplier of capital.

Strutt had found a new backer. A connection began with Samuel Need, a wealthy Nottingham hosier, with whom Strutt was to be associated for twenty years. Need had been born in 1718, had been apprenticed as a framework knitter, and had entered the hosiery trade about 1742. He was a Dissenter who had been baptised at High Pavement Chapel but later became an Independent (Congregationalist).[2] He had a warehouse in Low Pavement, Nottingham, and lived at Arnold, outside the city.[3] Besides his support of Strutt and Woollat, Need also had

[1] S.P. 36/140; S.O. 7/234; Ind. 6764.
[2] We are indebted to the Rev. C. Gordon Bolam for information about Need's Nonconformist connections.
[3] When Need died in 1781, he left two sons and four daughters. The eldest son, John (1761–1846), a landowner and magistrate near Mansfield, for a time managed the cotton mill at Penny Foot Garden, Nottingham. Samuel (1766–1839) went into the army, served in India, and rose to be Lieut.-General. He died at Fountain Dale, near Mansfield. Hepzibah, the eldest daughter, married Edward Abney (1751–1827), a Leicestershire squire. The three younger daughters married three sons of Samuel Walker of Masborough, the ironmaster. The family were Methodists (*Memoirs of a Highland Lady*, ed. Strachey (1898), 381; *Derby Mercury*, Jan. 3, 1793). By his will Need left £5000 to each of his six children with the exception of Hepzibah whose husband had received this sum at the time of his marriage to her. In addition all Need's children were to have £125 a year for maintenance and education until they were 25. To his brother, Nathaniel, he left £50 for mourning and to his brother-in-law, Thomas Gibson, and to each of his three other executors and trustees £100. The residue was to be invested in government securities and a one-sixth share given to each child at 25 or earlier if they married with the consent of the executors and trustees. If, however, John inherited Nathaniel's estate he was not to receive more than £10,000 from that of his father (Will at Somerset House).

later a direct hosiery partnership with Strutt, but their respective spheres of operation cannot be disentangled. In September, 1762, Strutt was admitted to the freedom of Nottingham 'gratis'.[1] He had now left Blackwell and gone to live in St. Mary's Gate, Derby. His brother, William, joined him in the Derby business and the long Strutt connection with the town began.

IV. THE PATENT CONTESTED

The hosiery business grew and Strutt took the leading part in it. The London connection expanded and the firm had its agent there, Matthew Robertson. Strutt went up at least twice a year for the East India Company's silk sales. His mechanical interests did not slacken and in 1764, when the Society of Arts offered a premium of £100 for the greatest improvement in the stocking frame, Strutt entered a machine. It was passed over in favour of one submitted by Samuel Unwin of Sutton, near Mansfield. Strutt reported to his wife with chagrin:

Jedediah Strutt to his wife

London Feb 15: 1765

My Dear

I recd your Welcome Letter & am sorry to inform you I must lose the pleasure I promis'd myself in seeing you on Saturday. Since my last the frames have all been strictly examined by six chosen stocking makers, several Frame smiths & some other judicious persons & last night the Committee sat to receive their report which was in general that the Sutton frame was not nor cou'd be made of any considerable use & that mine was the prettiest & best amongst them notwithstanding which after waiting till 11 o Clock thro' the influence of two or three partial prejudiced persons we were told that none but the Sutton frame coud be admitted as candidate for the Premium. It seems very strange that a Society whose institution & whose designs can only be the public good shou'd not distribute impartial Justice to all who endeavour to promote those designs; but it is no new thing nor is there any

---

[1] *Recs. of the Borough of Nottingham*, vii (1952), 421. Daniel Lowe, another Derby hosier, was admitted at the same time. Need had been a freeman, 'burgess born', since 1739-40.

remedy for the corruption & Baseness of a great part of Mankind.
Elkington is one of the persons I mean & another that I don't
know a man of eloquence as well as impudence who hires himself
on certain occasions to gain a Majority. But it is not finally determined. I have just been with Mr Moore & he assures he did &
will do all he can in my favour & is ashamed of their proceedings
but there will be nothing done further for some weeks. I intend
setting out on Monday if I am not prevented by a summons to the
House of Commons which I am afraid of but will endeavour to
avoid it. If I escape tomorrow I shall be safe. I long to be at home.
I live here in a sort of restless uneasiness & enjoy none of that calm
pleasure and satisfaction that I find at home with you. I am in
perfect health but have had but one good sound nights sleep since
I left you. Brothers are all well & have a sort of supper tonight.
Here is Mr Mrs George & Dolly. They desire their Love to you. I am
sorry for your misfortune but I hope you was not much hurt. Tell
George his Daddy think of him & all of 'em—I am your most
Affect. Husband

Jed: Strutt

desire Bro: Woollat to put what Spun Silk hose he can in hand.
There will be a good many of them wanted. I have a few orders
but no great matters. I have bot 2 Bales of silk & some spun will
be down next week. Robertson has sold about £130 of our hose.
Hookham wants the white & Marble thread. I have been 3 times
there but have not seen him yet

Last night I wrote you the above but by some strange infatuation
it was forgot till past 12 o clock. I am very sorry because at the time
you are expecting to see me I am only writing to you but this is
not all. I went this morning to Mr Hookhams & saw him at last.
He wanted much to see me & was for sending to find me. He is a
member of the Society and ask'd me many questions about the
frames. I told him there was great partiality in the decision & if
that must be the case it would be an effectual bar to all who knew
it from giveing up their time & money whatever Premiums they
might propose. He seldom Attends but if he shoud [do so] he may
be of some service to me but he farther insisted I did not go home
till the Bill now depending in the House of Commons against the
imported [   ] French Mitts & Stockings & of foreign thrown
silk was determined. I shall be glad if I can be of any service in
this & to oblige him but am sorry [I cannot on] other accounts. I
know not which it will be but am to breakfast there on tuesday &
shall then know further about it & I will write to you again

Monday—Dudley & Unwin are still in town, Lookey set out

yesterday morning [   ] & disapointed & poor Cheatham is alternately drunk & Mad by turns and says [he] will stay here till Midsummer—it will cost him more than £20—coud you think I shoud have wrote you such a long letter—Adieu—I am ever yours

Strutt may have thought his frame 'the prettiest & best' but there was this to be said for the Society of Arts. It was persuaded that the winning frame was an improvement on the stocking frame commonly used, for work that was not very fine, and it was adjudged to be simpler, cheaper (a third of the cost of common frames), and easier to work. Next year a still cheaper frame—by John Whyman of Aston-on-Trent—was rewarded.[1] The Society gave him a premium of £100 'for Laying Open this most useful Invention for the Benefit of the Trade', but the hosiers recommended the trade to raise another £400 'rather than they should be depriv'd of the Benefit, by the obtaining a Patent for the said Invention'. It had been 'seen and examin'd by Mr. Stamford, Mr. Bloodworth, and Others in the Hosiery' who endorsed the appeal.[2]

Strutt could hardly have entered his Derby rib machine since the essence of the competition was that the machine should be generally available, and Strutt was holding closely to his patent rights. These were under challenge. He had to fight two actions, one against the hosiers of Derby[3] and one against the hosiers of Nottingham. The leader of the Nottingham infringers was Francis Jones and Strutt was already concerned about the threat in November, 1765, when he wrote to his wife:

Jedediah Strutt to his wife

London Nov 26: 1765
Wednesday 3 o Clock

Ever since I came here I have long'd for a leisure hour to write to you but none has offer'd till this that I might tell you all the little occurrences since I left you—At Loughbro I met with one Mr

---

[1] Information from the Soc. of Arts; Dossie, *Memoirs of Agriculture* (1768), i, 137, ii, 318; Wood, *Hist. of the Society of Arts* (1913), 263. Strutt did not join the Society until 1782 when he was proposed by Arkwright; he remained a member until his death.

[2] *Derby Mercury*, Aug. 9, 23, 1765.

[3] The earliest reference we have found is in Blackner, *Hist. of Nottingham* (1815), 223; his authority is supposed to have been William Strutt, Jedediah's son.

Brown of Nottm Hosier whom I once was at some pains to have made our friend but he declin'd it. This was when you was left at London. I suppose he did not know me nor did I make myself known to him. At Leicester I forgot my Baggs & had to turn again about 4 Miles. This made it a long day to Harbro. There I met with Mr Nall of Chesterfield & one Louth of Nottm. We had a good deal of Liquor & talk about patents & did not get to bed till past 12. After this I had no company nor any other occurrence worth mentioning. On Monday evening we saw Mr Seagreave & his Brother[1] & talk'd over the affair in hand, yesterday was spent in getting to speak with one Spackman a Pewterer who has a Patent for turning Oval dishes & who has had some opposition from the rest of the trade but he made 'em pay all the costs and ask his pardon so that now he is more firmly established than if they had not disturbd him. We also talked with his Attorney & are to go this evening to talk with his council if we can see him. When I got to Brothers on Monday night he was from home & had been some time but came home last night, They are all pretty well. Have not seen Dolly. I am at the Castle. Ratcliff & Lacy are here. I have Just heard young Morris is here about his patent & has had a councils opinion that there is no doubt about it. I left Brothers Letter at Mr Cooks on Monday but he was not at home. Have not seen Sally Stenson yet. There is a vast gathering at Guild Hall every day for prizes in the Lottery but the greater part are disapointed by such a Number of blanks. Tickets are dear. Here I leave off——

Thursday 2 o Clock. We went on Wednesday evening but coud not see the council till this evening at 7 when we are to go again. Tell Mr Lowe Mr Thompson is at home but I did not see him. Have seen Sally Stenson this morning, she is very well. Have bot 2 Bales of Silk today. It is very dear. I have called 3 times at Mr Cooks but cannot see him. Since I wrote the above have seen Mr Cook but he has lost all the Letters of Attorney or mislaid them.

Saturday night—Last night we spoke with the Councellor & from what he has said I am pretty well satisfyed we shall gain our point against Jones & trim somebody else.

We are to see him again on Monday. After that I hope to be with you soon. We have been out ever since morning & I am now at Mr Seagreaves. We was out last night till past 11 & probably shall not be at home sooner to night. I have mentioned sending some hose on the other side but let them be till I come. We recd Bros Letter but have not sent the hose. I have carried this in my pocket and wrote a bit & a bit when I had a few minutes to spare. I woud have

---

[1] Attorneys of Nottingham and London who were acting for Strutt.

sent it last night but Mr N persuaded me to omit it till to night thinking there might be occasion to mention some thing but I know of nothing yet. I have wrote all this for only you to read because to every one else it must appear not worth writing. I have wanted all week to hear from you but cannot & after this it will be too late—past 9 o Clock at the the Castle. The evening is very cold. From the Strand to this place is many a wh—er with cold toes. I look'd on 'em with pity but did not relieve any of them. They & the Horses seem in the same case, both hackneyed out of their lives, both are slaves to the lusts and passions of Man. This seems to be an evil not to be remidied by Law or magistrates & if it be necessary to the being of the World how is the providence of god to be justified? this may be difficult now but the time may come when even we may clearly understand it, at present it may be sufficient and for my own part I rest satisfied that he takes a proper care of all his creatures even of the abandon'd and profligates but the virtuous & good are his peculiar care & concern. I know not at present how far he will interest himself in any events relateing to myself but I am confident so far as they belong not to my own conduct they will be for the best. Here I rest. I shall use my own best endeavours to return as soon as possible & hope to meet you & the children all in health & with pleasure & in this I trust I shall not be disapointed. Have you the same hope & confidence & then you will not have much to fear

till then farewell I am yr Affect Husband

Jed: Strutt

Mr N desires his Compts. My Love to all the children. I shoud go to Broths to night

Desire Brother to look out [   ] doz Black worsted ribs & 3 or 4 Doz Marble & greys different sorts [   ] to M Robertson

The trial came on in the Court of King's Bench, before the Lord Chief Justice, Lord Camden. Samuel Need was the plaintiff and William Taylor and Francis Jones, both of Nottingham, defendants in an action touching the patent of Need, Strutt and Woollat for the sole making and vending of turned ribbed stockings and other goods. Strutt describes the preliminaries in letters to his wife. The action coincided with another of much the same kind brought by John Morris of Nottingham for infringements of his network patent of 1764.[1]

[1] See Felkin (op. cit., ch. vii) for a long account of Morris and his machine, which, like the Derby rib machine, was an attachment to the frame.

Jedediah Strutt to his wife

London 17: June 1766

My Dear

This comes to tell you we got well here last night tho' I had got a bad cold before I went from home but am very Well to day. I got very little sleep by the Way & was up last night till one o clock. We have been most of the day with Mr Seagreaves & to night with Mr Morris & Mr Bloodworth Mr Willd &c. We do not know when the Tryal will come on but it will not be this week. I have not been at my brothers. I am at the X Keys & wish you would write to me.

My love to the children   I am yrs in hast

J Strutt.

Mr Need & I have both wrote least one
of the Letters shoud Miscarry.

The Nottm people are bringing up a frame with a Machine to it & a person to work in it therefore we must have one too. So you'l pray inform Mr Woollat to take Wm Roe & Mr Webster or both to take down Weslys Little frame the Iron Work from the Wood & to get some of the Men at the building to make a Box for the Iron Work & send it if possible by the Coach on thursday in the afternoon & the woodwork too if they will take it. If not send the Woodwork on thursday & the Iron Work on Fryday but if they will not take the Iron Work all together let Mr Webster take it to pieces & put it in 2 Boxes & send part on thursday or fryday & the rest on Saturday directed to be calld for. Also send the Needle mold & Machine Mold, and some fram[e] needles, a pair of plyers, Wesleys Working needle & turning needle, Webb & cloth & a Bobin of neat Silk suitable for the frame. Also the guide & pully & everything belonging to the frame. Take care that the frame be well packd that the needles or sinkers are not damanged. If you have time shoud be glad if you would weigh up all the narrow ribd silk hose & enter them & send the price to M R & also 4 or 5 Doz 24 White Silk from 10/6 to 11/6. Mr Bwth wants left 4d Sham which [ ] with 4 [ ] worsted feet [is] the broadest rib we have. If not some of Halls or some [of] Porters broad ribs or some [other], they should be good ones. If you coud find a few of M Wrights hose they or near equal send 'em

Jedediah Strutt to his wife

London June: 21 1766

My Dear

This day I had pleasure of receiving yours & am glad to hear you are pretty well. We are now at Mr Seagreaves & have been every day that we have been here almost from morning to night. I think we have taken all the precautions possible & cannot but hope our cause is in a good way. It is first to come on on tuesday but as there are to be 2 tryals by Special Jury before ours therefore it is possible there may not be time till Wednesday. Mr Morris's comes on on Monday. Mr Need & I are subpeanied on his tryal he is very poorly & low spirited about it tho I think he has no reason. For my own part I am far from dispairing. We have a Special Jury fixed up on today. I believe we shall have Four Councill & are to meet them on Monday night. We was yesterday with Mr Dolland[1] the Mathematical Instrument maker. Our case seems to be a good deal similar to his. He has had two tryals about his & got them both. I write to you again on Monday or tuesday. Here are a vast number of evidences for All the parties. We have subpenea'd several in London. I have been down once to my Brothers but he is gone his Journey perhaps you may have seen him. Sister & the children are but poorly. I intend seeing them again to-morrow. I am not greatly elevated or cast down with this and other events but [be] assurd I am not indifferent about what I shall write to you on Tuesday or Wednesday. My Love to the Children. I am only

yours Jed: Strutt

Mr Woollatt

The back part of the frame wood work is at the Swann but nothing more. We shall be greatly disapointed if we do not receive it all by to nights coach as it must be set up on Monday. Jones has 2 frames come up. If you have not sent some silk hose please to look out all the narrow ribs you have & 5 or 6 Doz of the 24 White at different prices. M R has none to sell. He sold near 80£ worth the last fortnight. If you have any spun silk pray send them particularly 4 p of boild off spun & 2 pr white Do for Mr Hookham. We have

---

[1] Peter Dolland (1730–1820), son of John, F.R.S. (1706–61) and grandson of Jean, a Huguenot silk-weaver who settled in Spitalfields from Normandy shortly after the revocation of the Edict of Nantes. In 1750 John opened a small optical workshop for his son in Vine Street, Spitalfields, and two years later joined him at 'The Sign of the Golden Spectacles' in the Strand. The concern they founded is now styled Dolland and Aitchison (*Gentleman's Magazine*, July–Dec. 1820, 90–91).

an order from him for 5 Doz. I think Mr Seagreave has taken a good deal of pains about prepareing for the tryal. The hose for Hookham[1] shoud be 26 gage done narrow & some midling.

Mr Newham & Co.[2] wants 6 pr 4d Sham Mens full size worked with good feet 2 & 4 or 3 & 4 the man at Denbridge woud do. Send 'em if there is any dresd.

I think Pratt shoud alter his frame to 3 & 4 or 4 & 5 that he may make some of them. Mr Manning[3] wants his 2 p with worstd feet

Both Morris and Strutt won their cases but the receptions they received upon their return to the Midlands were very different. At Nottingham, when the victorious Morris returned, the *Derby Mercury* reported that

nothing but concern and Dissatisfaction were observable in the Countenance of every Manufacturer: A dumb Peal was rung on the Occasion to testify the dreadful Consequences; as it is presumed on a moderate Calculation, that no less than Four or Five Hundred Persons will be immediately turned off for want of Employment, the Mitt Manufactory being so considerable a Branch of the Hosiery Trade.

Yet at Derby

The agreeable News of the Establishment of the Patent for making Turned Ribbed Stockings, was received here . . . with a general Joy; particularly by the Workmen and others employed therein; as thereby that Branch of the Stocking Trade is secured to this Town, ONLY, for Seven Years longer, which would otherwise have been spread all over the Kingdom.[4]

The contrast is instructive, but perhaps Strutt supplied the latter paragraph.

The partners enjoyed the fruits of the patent until its expiry in 1773. Competitors were watchful of any attempt to extend it and a caveat was entered in the Privy Seal Office on May 6, 1771, 'against any Patent being passed for the making of ribbed Hose or for the renewal of any Patent that has been obtained for that purpose, till notice be given to Mr. Currie, 88 Queen's Street, Cheapside'.[5] But the patent had given Strutt a good start; he had become a man of capital.

---

[1] Of John Hookham & Co.   [2] Of Newham & Binham, Strand.
[3] William Manning, Temple Bar.   [4] *Derby Mercury*, July 4, 1766.
[5] Ind. 6766.

CHAPTER III

THE HOSIERY BUSINESS

STRUTT's hosiery business was profitable and reached a fairly large size. That at Derby was mainly in silk hose. The raw silk was bought in London and, for the most part, was prepared in the firm's Silk Mill at Derby. The thread was put out to be knitted although the firm seems to have had some frames under its own roof.[1] The chief market for its goods was London. Though the surviving records of the business relate to the years after Strutt had ventured into cotton-spinning they may be described here to show the sources of his capital and the Midland industrial background.

I. THE LONDON END

The earliest of the fragmentary records is a London Ledger, beginning in December, 1771. There is then the London agent, Matthew Robertson, in Gutter Lane, who in 1772 receives and disburses for the partners £922. The receipts—200 items in twelve months—are mostly in small amounts—below £10—cash payments from customers. His disbursements are mainly to the silk brokers through whom the raw silk was bought. In sixteen months he paid Gibson and Winter £1025 and also paid £65 for 'spun silk'. He carried stock of hosiery but a good many of the London deliveries are marked as coming from Derby, and a few from Nottingham. Most of the London customers, however, settled with the Derby firm direct. The ledger has 146 separate accounts for 1772, mostly settled by bill or note, on sales amounting to roughly £11,390. And this was a year of depression.[2]

---

[1] According to Henson (op. cit., 264) the Derby rib machines were first put in a room lit only by skylights, but this did not prevent the inquisitive from climbing on the roof to look at them.

[2] Cf. Boulton's letter to Lord Dartmouth of Nov. 10 (Dickinson, *Matthew Boulton* (1937), 83).

Credit was long and most accounts ran on for years. Balances were struck at the beginning and end of a period and the payments by bill rarely caught up. For cash or a month's bill 2 ½ per cent. discount was given but the usual credit was nearer six to twelve months. The commonest bills in 1771 were on Joseph Stenson (? of Derby) or Smith, Payne and Smith of London or were drawn to the firm's own order. Sometimes, however, the bills were made payable to the firm's silk brokers.

It was a highly detailed trade. The range of London accounts for 1772 is roughly as follows and each was made up of a large number of separate parcels:

ORDERS DEC. 1771–DEC. 1772.

	Credit No. of Accounts		Credit No of Accounts
Over £250	4	£50–£75	30
£200–£250	2	£25–£50	32
£150–£200	6	£15–£25	22
£100–£150	25	Under £15	14
£75–£100	11	Total	146

The buyers were London warehousemen and hosiers. The largest single customer in 1772 was Crafton and Colson of 9 Great St. Helens, who bought £1334 of the partners' goods, and already owed £812; their orders dropped to £416 in 1773 and £446 in 1774–5. Before the firm went bankrupt a year or two later Strutt had got nearly all his money. Indeed, the ledger suggests that the firm escaped with few bad debts. Sometimes, however, it was ready to take goods and there are quite a number of smallish per contra entries. In the main the firm stuck to dealing in its own products. In one instance, however, in March, 1772, the firm is debiting a customer (another dealer) with £11 9s. 6d. 'hose fr: Tewkesbury' and pays 12s. for '4 Doz bleaching at Tewkesbury'; this is described as 'Engine Cotton Hose'. Tewkesbury was a centre of cotton hosiery[1] and it is not inconceivable that this represents an early attempt to use Arkwright's twist for stockings.

An illustration of the more regular type of account is that of Hunt and Cunningham, St. James's Street:

[1] Cf. Wadsworth and Mann, *The Cotton Trade and Industrial Lancashire, 1600–1780* (1931), 484.

1772			£	s.	d.	1772				£	s.	d.
Jan. 6	Brot from Old					June 3	Per Bill 2 Mo.			30	0	0
		Ledger	36	3	0		,,	,,	4 Mo.	30	0	0
,, 28	To Goods		8	1	0		,,	,,	6 Mo.	40	0	0
Feb. 18	,,	,,	2	17	0		,,	,,	7 Mo.	40	2	0
,, 20	,,	,,	3	3	0							3
,, 17	,,	,,	5	14	0							
Mar. 2	,,	,,	5	11	6							
Feb. 3	,,	,,	4	4	0							
Apr. 27	,,	,,	9	14	3							
May 4	,,	,,	13	10	0							
,, 8	,,	,,	2	5	0							
,, 11	,,	,,	9	1	0							
,, 15	,,	,,	1	6	0							
,, 18	,,	,,	8	10	0							
,, 23	,,	,,	5	13	0							
,, 19	,,	,,	7	2	6							
June 1	,,	,,	17	7	0							
			140	2	3					140	2	3

The remuneration of the first agent is not shown, but in July, 1773, a salaried agent was appointed, William Harris, at £90 a year. A warehouse was rented and the rent of the agent's house paid. A porter was allowed board at 5s. a week. A successor to Harris, Joseph Mallett, acted from 1776 to 1790 when he set up for himself and was followed by Thomas Shipman. Mallett started at £50 a year and rose to £100; in 1782 he transferred to a commission basis of $1\frac{1}{4}$ per cent., raised in 1786 to 2 per cent. His sales ranged between £14,500 and £18,500 a year. The course of the London business through the agent can be roughly calculated. Since the accounting period was rather irregular, though always ending in the spring some time between the middle of February and early May, the sales are reduced to a monthly average:

Year ending Feb.–May	Av. monthly sales by agent £	Year ending Feb.–May	Av. monthly sales by agent £
1782–3	1400	1792–3	1545
1783–4	1590	1793–4	1491
1784–5	1360	1794–5	1526
1785–6	1210	1795–6	1354
1786–7	1270	1796–7	1340
1787–8	1260	1797–8	1360
1788–9	1425	1798–9	1465
1789–90	1410	1799–1800	2032
1790–1	1425	1800–1	1400
1791–2	1600	1801–2	906

In the early years most customers' payments were made direct to Derby. Mallett came to collect a much larger proportion of the London accounts and handled the bill transactions, often sending remittances through the firm's bankers, Smith Payne and Smith of London and Abel Smith and Co. of Nottingham. The firm's warehouse was in Love Lane and in 1792 Jedediah Strutt bought two houses there for £1248; the stock was insured for £2000.

As in all such London connections the agent performed many tasks for the country manufacturer. Thus Mallett was buying for Strutt wine (very occasionally), oysters, sugar, oranges, and candles. He paid Strutt's subscriptions (his annual two guineas to the Society of Arts, his £30 to the Chamber of Commerce in 1786), and obliged his friends ('Cash paid for Dr. Darwin' £2 13s. in 1792 and £1 5s. 6d. in 1793), and gave Dr. Priestley £10 10s. in 1785. The investment in lottery tickets ran one year to £46 10s. 6d. The trade purchases included recurring items of mill stores for the Strutt and Arkwright cotton mills.

II. THE DERBY SILK MILL

The London Ledgers run on to 1808; the only surviving record of the early Derby business is a cash book from the end of 1780 to the beginning of 1789. It gives a strong impression of a profitable trade, with healthy cash balances, and with Jedediah Strutt transferring large amounts to the mills he was building at Belper, Milford and Derby. But it is impossible in the absence of the partners' stock books to disentangle the various businesses—Strutt's partnership with Need, his partnership with Woollat, and that with his own sons. Clearly, however, he remains at the centre of things and is the dominant figure.

Unfortunately the precise significance escapes us of two letters from Need to Strutt in 1776 when, it would seem, a dissolution of their hosiery partnership was under discussion. Strutt may have been trying to find capital for his Belper mills then being built. The premises and machines mentioned in the letters were, it seems, in Derby. Certainly there was no break in the Strutt-Woollat business and there are references in the cash book in 1782 and 1784 to 'Need and Strutt'. Perhaps the suggested dissolution did not take place then. The 'machines' mentioned are presumably the Derby rib attachments:

Samuel Need to Strutts and Woollat

Nottingm March 28th 1776

Sir,

I Rec'd your's of the 25th Instant, but I cannot agree with you in the value of the frames, tho' many of them are out of work, these in work with Machines fixed to them are worth more, you say the Machines are not worth more than 8 or 10 a piece, pray see what you charged them when we took your stock, I think these that are out of work are charged less, & as to the goods on hand, both stuff & workmanship has been long pd for, & no Interest reckon'd upon it, & no Man can begin a business, but it will be some time before he can have a parcell of goods ready for sale. I agree with you the book Debts ought to have 3 or 4 Months Credit, for most of it, but I think the Interest that ought to be put upon the wrought goods is equivalent to the Debts, the goods in the Worsted Warehouse, I suppose Wool, Spinning &c has been all pd for, don't you think some Interest ought to be put upon them, Journey-mens Wages, Rent of the Warehouse &c are all included in that & the wrought goods. As to the premices, there may be some Engines out of Order by Ware & Tare ought to be alow'd, but I imagine there has been much more laid out in the building, the Stable, Walls &c than was added to, which I think was only £40 : 0 : 0, as to the place over the brook it was bought at your request, for you said it might be usefull sometime or other. I have reap'd no benefit from it, & if it has not pd Interest for the money it has been my loss, as to proposing me taking them, is out of the question. I am fixed in a business here, but if I was not, & was a young Man I would gladly take the whole, & think it would be of great adanvtage for any Man to come into such a business notwithstanding the great decay you mention &c. I believe it is yet far better than any other branch in the hose trade, & you know it is worth more to you than to any body else. I suppose at the time of building the Interest of the Money was lost, I don't desire to have the Goods all sold up & divide the Money, for it will be better for you to continue in the business & I would rather you would, for your advantage, if I am a loser by it, than to have things pull'd to pieces. I wish you well, & desire to have no difference, but to have things settled amicably & to your advantage, but not too much to my own disadvantage,

51

& I do think as mention'd in my last will be to your advantage. You have great advantage in the stock & frames &c. I am

Yr Humb Servt

Samll Need.

Samuel Need to Strutts and Woollat

Nottingm April 4th 1776

... As to your other letter, I agree with you that if the Machines was off the frames they would not be worth so much, but that is not the case, neither are many of them without hands, therefore the charge of the Machines putting too ought to be consider'd, nothing was ever said about the hands at the Silk Mill, which is worth something, you know Bennett asked £1000 for his, when we was about his Mill, & I am fully satisfy'd something ought to be reckon'd upon the wrought stock of hose &c & you cannot think otherwise in my opinion, for besides the Interest of above £8000 there is the Wages & Salary, Warehouse Rent, &c for the time they was making. As to the stock you had at first, if I remember, there was very few if any but unsaleable goods, & I believe some of them sold much under the value, for English had been a day or two before & bot the Saleable goods, & the Stock you now have upon your hands that are not Saleable we put under prime cost. As to the things in the Worsted Warehouse I know nothing how they was reckon'd, & I imagine the money laid out last year upon Walls, Stable &c, would amount to much more than £50 : o : o. As to your proposal of you or me taking the premises at the valuation you had put upon them is out of the question, you know I cannot occupy nor employ them, & you can, for which reason they are worth more to you than any body else. You say, you readily own if they could be occupied as they have been there would be a great advantage, for which I answer, had we continued together, they might still be occupied as before, & the keeping a large assortment of goods would always command a trade, & tire others out that make but a few articles, as it has done most that has gone into it. Upon the whole I am of the same mind as I was & think you are too much of your own side, but as I said before, I would rather have things to your advantage, that we may part amicably & friendly, so let me know in your next how you think it ought to be fix't, & if I can acquiesse in it, I will, & am

Yr Hum Servt

Samll Need.

Whatever Strutt's Nottingham connections the Strutt and Woollat partnership was based on Derby. Here it had its Silk

Mill and its warehouse. The Silk Mill employed weekly wage-earners; the wage bill ranged between £12 10s. and £15 a week in 1781 but by 1786 was between £17 and £18. The Mill was continually being extended and in 1785 another mill was built at the Morledge in Derby. This is charged to 'Building Account' in the cash book. The direct references to machinery for the Silk Mill are scanty. In 1782 Thomas Crane was paid £21 6s. for '2 Engines' (a common term for silk throwing machines) and a further £21. There are various items for bobbins, combs and wire, 'mending wheels and swifts', cogs, sinkers, files. Recurrent purchases were made of soap, charcoal, and 'ringing bagging'. The premises were insured for £1700. Other wage-earners were the menders—two at 7s. a week each, and there are regular small payments to 'trimmers'. Each December the firm gave Christmas boxes of 10s. 6d. to the 'trammers' and more to the hands at the mill—35s. 3d. in 1780 rising to 54s. 7d. in 1787. There was also, between September 27 and 29, a gift for 'expences of the candlelighting' (ranging from £3 8s. 8d. in 1781 to £5 0s. 8d. in 1788), which, as we shall see later, was a mill jollification observed also in Arkwright's cotton factory.[1]

The year 1781 appears to have been a decisive one in the history of the hosiery business. In January, Samuel Need was paid £1150, possibly an end of the partnership. He died in April and no further large payments to him or his executors are recorded. In March, Woollat received £600 and seems to have been put on about five guineas a week—possibly in semi-retirement. At the same time William Strutt, the son, was given £5 a week; he was then nearly 25. Jedediah's net drawings in 1781 were £3684. Thenceforward the accounts become more complicated and mixed up, as if they were entirely his affair.

There was a 'frame shop' in Derby and a recurring weekly item in the accounts for stocking makers' wages, an average of £145 weekly in March–April, 1802. In May–June, 1803, it ceases; the firm sold its frames to Pagets' and Byng.[2] The long

---

[1] See below, p. 99.

[2] At an average price of £12 a frame (Felkin, op. cit., 94). In 1826 Strutts wrote to Thomas Grainsdick of Lisbon: 'It is now above 20 years since we left off making hose, & we have sent your letters to Mr S. Fox Jun of this place who is our nephew & on whom you may rely with perfect confidence

connection with the hosiery trade ceased after forty years[1] and the Strutts concentrated on yarn spinning for the trade, including hosiery, and for a time at least continued their Silk Mill at Derby.

III. THE FRAMEWORK KNITTERS

As in all the domestic trades, particularly in those with valuable materials, embezzlement was the constant preoccupation of the employers. Strutts and Woollat appear with other throwsters in 1778 as founders of an association to prosecute offenders who embezzled or stole silk or silk waste from them.[2] In 1785 they paid a subscription of £1 5s. for 'prosecuting Silk Stealers'. In 1788 3 guineas to 'the Chamber of Commerce at Nottingham for procuring an Act of Parliament to prevent the destruction of frames',[3] a machine-breaking episode.

Samuel Need was the leader of the hosiers' resistance to the stockingers' attempt in 1778–9 to get Parliament to fix wages by statute. When their bill of 1779 was thrown out the crowd broke the windows of Arkwright's mill at Nottingham (perhaps because of the Need connection) and attacked and damaged Need's house at Arnold.[4] Strutts and Woollat do not appear in these trade politics. Derby was less turbulent than Nottingham (where the popular borough franchise was a factor) but there were wage movements in 1771 which suggest fairly amicable industrial relations. The framework knitters asked for higher wages because of the increased cost of living: 'If it should be judg'd you are insufficient of yourselves to comply with our Request, without the Concurrence of the neighbouring Counties, we intreat you to solicit it, and we hope it will meet with their Approbation.' The hosiers agreed about the 'enormous Price of the Necessaries of Life', pleaded foreign competition,

---

to execute any order you favr him with, & on as good terms as any house in England.'

[1] The style of the firm had been: 1762–94, Strutts and Woollat; 1795–6, Strutts and Co. (Jedediah died in 1797); 1797–1800, William Strutt and Co. (William, the elder, died in 1800); 1801–3, W. G. and J. Strutt (*Kent's London Directory*).

[2] *Harrison's Derby and Nottingham Journal*, May 21, 1778.

[3] On this see Blackner, op. cit., 434.

[4] Chambers, *Nottinghamshire in the Eighteenth Century* (1932), ch. v; *Nottingham Journal*, June 12, 1779; *Derby Mercury*, June 18, July 30, 1779.

1783

July 3 To Cash in hand 908 7

To Do of Wm Alsop on Acct of Robt Bennet 35

8 To Draft on Saml Mallet to Mr & Chr Fallon 80

To Cash of Mr Clarke wherein we paid 46 18

9 To Do of Anne Wright for our Note 40

To Draft on Bennet ... to Do 30 Jun 46 6

10 To Cash of Wm Edens Executors in full 84

To Do for a Draft on Wm Walcall 1 Mo 26 Jun 60

To Do for a Do ... Stevens Wallington & Co 130

To Do in Sale Book 2 14

J 1351 7

July 10 To Cash in hand 825 17

11 To Draft on Statham Martin & Co 1 Mo 9 July 23 9

To Do on Sam Nodd & Co 24

To Do on Hillingley Green & Son 1 Mo 11 July 30

14 To Cash of Anne Woollatt for our Note 84

To Draft on Stephens, Wallington & Co
at 1 Mo Dated July 17 20

15 To Draft on Ann Drinkwater 1 Mo 17 July 15

To Do on Chas Smith 10 10

To Do on Hancock & Wakefield Do Do 13

To Do on Peter Wise Do Do 30

To Do on Saml Hay Do Do 17 9

To Bill from R A & Co on Acct of Jed Strutt
Due 26 July 500

17 To Cash for a Bill from R A & Co on Acct of Jed
Strutt Due July 31 500

To Do on Do from Peter Ward 5 12

To Do in Sale Book 7 11

J 2106 8

July 17 To Cash in hand 1017 11

18 To Draft on Nathl Crawford 1 Mo 17 July 7 7

To Do on Benjn Holden Do Do 11

To Mr Babb's Note 5 Mo 12 July 146 7

To Josh Pettis Do 4 Mo 17 July 49 11

To Saml Wathams Draft 1 Mo 13 June 30

To Do Do 2 Mo Do 30

To Do Do 3 Mo Do 29

Carr over 1320 17

A page from Strutts

		£	s	d
43	By Draft at sight paid Wm Woollatt 29 6 0	29	6	..
4	By Cash to Tho Hare	10	10	..
7	By Do to Jno Clark	1	1	..
8	By Bill due 11 Sepr paid Do Shuttleworth	20	..	..
9	By Cash to Wm Elgar Wright to but ½ hhd wh	39	3	5
	By Profit ant Thos Stanford Bleachd wool	46	6	..
10	By Partridges Note paid in Jno Smith — ac	25	..	..
	By Cash Weekly wages to the Mill	17	9	10
	By Interest to Mrs Clarissa for an Note	10	10	..
	By Cash to Mr J Ortola for Ballance	12	11	2
	By Do to Robt Strutt	100	..	..
	By Do in Work Book	157	16	6½
	By Do in Petty Cash	2	16	6½
	By Do in hand	825	17	3½
		£ 1351	7	9½
July 11	By Cash to Winder 3 wks	1	1	..
	By Do to me Wm Roe on Acct	4	4	..
	By Do to Tho Hare	10	10	..
	By 3 Bills ant Robinson & Co	77	9	..
12	By Cash & Imprest to Ann Woollatt from N	13	4	..
	By Draft on Stephens & Wedlington ac dated July 5 Wm Woollatt due Augt 20	20	..	..
	By Cash to Wm Woollatt	50	..	..
15	By 5 Bills pd Rd & Hartshorn	75	19	..
	By Bill due 26 July ant Abel Smith & Co	500	..	..
16	By Cash to Jno Fellows Son in full	11	6	..
17	By Do Weekly wages to the Mill	17	6	6
	By Do to Robt Strutt	90	..	..
	By Do in Work Book	132	11	5½
	By Do in Petty Cash	5	7	9
	By Do in hand	1017	11	9½
		£ 2106	8	6
July 17	By Cash ant Thos Yeates	46	18	..
18	By Do to me 33.0	10	10	..
	By Bill paid me 17 Tho Ward on Acct	10	10	..
	By Cash to Tho Hare for Father	3	6	..
	Cast over	71	4	..

and were polite in their refusal of a general advance; but, 'if the present Demand for a few particular Articles, will enable us to make any Addition to their Prices, it will be done with Cheerfulness, and every opportunity of making your business more agreeable to you, shall be embraced with Pleasure'.[1]

On the actual relations between Strutts and Woollat and their framework knitters, the material is elusive. Samuel Need said in 1779 that he owned about 240 frames, most of which were of the 'common variety', and also employed many persons who themselves owned the frames in which they worked.[2] The latter would include, of course, the middlemen who owned frames as well as the stockingers with their own frames. It is doubtful how far this holds good for Strutts and Woollat. They owned some frames but in the eight years of the cash book the purchase of only four is specifically mentioned:

		£	s.	d.
1780 Aug. 19	By Cash to Josh. Moreton for 2 Frames	8	0	0
1781 Jan. 12	,, ,, ,, Wm Hill for a Coarse Frame on Acct.	6	17	0
1786 June 20	,, ,, for a 34 Gage frame & Machine & Molds No. 263	12	16	0
1787 Dec. 8	,, ,, Job Wilson in full for a Coarse Fr. & machine No. 264	2	13	0

Yet the firm assumed responsibility for some frame repairs:

1781				
June 28	Leivers for recruiting No. 13	1	14	0
July 28	repairing Cartledge's Frame	1	4	9
Aug. 20	Chris Leivers in full for recruiting a frame	1	11	0
1782				
Jan. 14	Leivers for recruiting A. Booth's frame	1	1	0
1783				
Aug. 1	Leivers ,, ,, Wm Walter's frame No 60	1	18	0
Dec. 5	,, ,, ,, Josh. Bullock's frame No. 201	1	8	0
1784				
July 9	B. Porter for cleaning & altering frames		16	6
Sep. 27	Leivers for squaring & recruiting 2 frames	2	3	0
1786				
Apr. 1	Jno Riley for recruiting Jno Brown's frame	1	8	6
May 11	Josh. Hulton for recruiting 197	4	10	0
June 8	Leaper recruiting a frame No 126	2	5	0
,, 30	Miles Bacon & Co for recruiting No 6	2	14	0
1788				
Nov. 14	Anthony Riley for Recruiting Jno Catledge's frame &c.	2	9	5

[1] *Derby Mercury*, July 12, Aug. 2 and 9, 1771.
[2] Hosiers' and Framework Knitters' examinations before Committee of House of Commons, 1780.

A dozen or so instances in nine years are not conclusive, although the numbering of the frames is suggestive. How many of the frames were in the firm's Derby workshop? It is true that, for all their mechanical intricacy, the frames stood up to hard wear. Need said that coarse frames required repairing every six or seven years and, if used by apprentices, every two or three years. They were cleaned, at a cost of 5s. or 6s., every two years or, if used by careless workers, every three months. Fine frames, he said, did not need repairing as often, and needed cleaning only every seven years.[1] But the recorded incidence of repairs in the Strutts and Woollat cash book seems low.

There is no evidence that the firm drew frame rents. They did, however, pay frame rents to a small number of owners, sometimes for a number of years:

	£	s.	d.
1780–1 John Strutt one years frame rent (for a coarse frame)	1	10	6
1781 Thomas Stenson	1	2	1
1782 Josh. Stenson 3 weeks frame rent		2	9
1784–5 John Marshall 1 years frame rent	1	5	0
1785 Miss Bailey rent of 3 frames	4	0	0
1786–7 Do. 2 ,,	2	10	0
1786 Mr Oldknow rent for 2 silk frames	1	8	6

Miss Webster drew £12 19s. 2d. in 1784 and 1785 for the rent of ten frames, and £11 12s. 6d. in 1786 and £11 18s. in 1787 for 11 frames. When the firm paid 8s. 6d. for cleaning her frames it recovered the cost from her. So also in 1783 when Mr. Oldknow paid £9 11s. for 'recruiting frames &c.' Fewer than 20 frames are here accounted for. The presumption must be that most of the frames employed by the firm were owned by the knitters or by the various types of middlemen through whom their work was put out.

Some recurring outgoings in the cash book may represent the wages of the firm's agents or middlemen. A weekly payment in the 1780s of ten guineas (with some additional payments of 5 guineas) to Jonathan Hare may be to the 'Jonathan' who was with the partners at their first setting up; it is a large amount and may represent an interest in the firm. Other recur-

---

[1] Loc. cit. The *O.E.D.* under 'recruit' quotes the *Encyc. Metrop.* (1845): 'Some hands will wear down a frame in three years; others, however, will work them twelve or even twenty years without serious repairs, or, as it is technically called, a recruit.'

ring payments, like the guinea a week to William Roe, may be standing wages to mechanics and so on. Roe and 'Mr. Webster' are mentioned in 1766, and the rent paid to Miss Webster for 10 frames in 1784 may be an inheritance.

Some work was done by outside firms—accounts for bleaching ran between £74 and £96 a year. Lamech Swift (who had the historic Old Silk Mill at Derby)[1] was paid £16 4s. in 1783 for 'throwing a Bale of Silk', £20 in 1784 for 'throwing Italian silk', and £51 in 1788 for 'throwing'. But Strutts and Woollat themselves probably did most of their own throwing.[2]

The organization of framework knitting—a complicated and difficult subject—has been well described in the books of Dr. Wells and Dr. Chambers. The Strutt papers do not help us much. The universal time-table in the hosiery manufacture was the giving out of yarn at the warehouse on Monday morning and the return of the finished stockings on the following Saturday afternoon. The weighing and the calculation of wastage took time and, as the distance to be travelled was often considerable, most of the work outside the towns was in the hands of middlemen, the 'takers-in' or 'undertakers'—the equivalent of the putters-out in the cotton districts. It was entry into the trade as such a country middleman that Jedediah Strutt was contemplating before his invention was taken up by a partnership.

Elizabeth Strutt, writing to her husband in London in February, 1774, gives a glimpse of the Saturday procedure:

Thay was very busy in the warehouse on Saturday but did very well, only was short of money, tho my son said he pd one Hundred & twenty pounds, yet one man at eight o Clock brought work to ye amount of ten pounds & went without his money.

The cash book of 1780–8 has a weekly item 'Cash in Work Book' which ranges from £80 or £90 in holiday weeks to £250 at a few peaks. This, we may assume, is the net amount of cash paid out to takers-in and individual knitters—in other words, the wages of the out-workers. There is some seasonality; the

[1] The mill had later many vicissitudes. In 1867 it was taken over by George Wrigley, and in 1897 was absorbed by the English Sewing Cotton Company.

[2] There is a frugal note of 1788 accounting for 16s. 'cash spent at Silk Throwsters Meetings three Years'.

second quarter tends to see the highest payments, and the fourth quarter the next highest. In the eight years the highest payments were in 1782 and 1783, falling (except for a slight rise in 1787) in the following years. The table shows the movement by quarters. What is most striking is the relative stability of the trade, which we saw also in the accounts of the London agent; the difference between the year of largest trade and that of least is only 20 per cent.

'Cash in Work Book'

Quarterly Totals (£)

Year	1st Qr	2nd Qr	3rd Qr	4th Qr	Annual Total
1780				1734	
1781	1632	1800	1737	1830	6999
1782	1708	1926	1999	1933	7566
1783	1970	2060	1822	1876	7728
1784	1634	1804	1781	1646	6825
1785	1673	1730	1554	1678	6635
1786	1628	1572	1526	1670	6396
1787	1678	1734	1618	1574	6594
1788	1554	1592	1491	1529	6166

If the assumption is valid that 'Cash in Work Book' is wages, it would cover a large number of workers. If 10s. to 13s. a week be taken as an average gross figure[1] the firm would be employing somewhere between 200 and 400 out-workers. The probability is that most of these lived outside Derby. Writing in 1789, Pilkington estimated that 1156 stocking frames were employed by the hosiers of Derby but that only 170 of the knitters lived in the town.[2] The silk hose branch was the best paid. Witnesses before the Commons Committee in 1779 said that a good workman on 'common altered 23 gauge silk hose' could make four pairs a week and the more skilled five; for these they got 2s. 6d. a pair and, after deductions would have about 6s. clear. The deductions—part to the hosier or his agent, part in expenses the stockinger had to defray himself, were: frame rent 1s., standing 3d.–5d., fire and candles 4d., needles 1s. 10d., sizing 1s. 3d., winding 8¼d., seaming (unspecified); 'they cannot work without a Fire to cast their Needles'.[3] The deductions

---

[1] Chambers, op. cit., 295.
[2] Op. cit., 174. Hutton said that in 1791 about 150 frames were at work in Derby and that their number had not increased over the last seventy years (*Hist. of Derby* (1791), 190–1).
[3] *C.J.*, xxxvi, 740–3.

were not clear loss for those for winding and seaming came back to other members of the family. Wives earned 4*s*. a week by seaming and children when eight years old about 1*s*. 6*d*. by winding. Putting it on the high side, Samuel Need asserted that a man, wife and two or three children could earn 20*s*. a week.[1]

[1] Hosiers' and Framework Knitters' examinations before Committee of House of Commons, 1780.

CHAPTER IV

THE PARTNERSHIP WITH RICHARD ARKWRIGHT

I. NOTTINGHAM AND CROMFORD

By 1769, when he was 43, Jedediah Strutt had become well-established and prosperous. Though not daringly ambitious, and certainly not reckless, he was not a man to neglect chances and one great chance opened up with the prospect of machine spinning. He became a backer and partner of Richard Arkwright.

In the spring of 1768 Arkwright had left Lancashire with his plans for a roller-spinning machine and, like Hargreaves with his spinning jenny about the same time, had sought his fortune in Nottingham. Nottingham was then the centre of cotton hosiery as Derby was of silk and Leicester of worsted. There was an obvious market here for cotton yarn. The Midlands were largely dependent for their supplies on Lancashire[1] where they had to compete with the other users of cotton. Nottingham, as Dr. Chambers has pointed out, had given much attention to machine spinning since the days of Lewis Paul and its mechanics had long sought after it.[2] There was also, perhaps, a less uncomfortable atmosphere for the inventor than in Lancashire, where opinion was wholly against exclusive patent rights. It would seem natural that Jedediah Strutt and Samuel Need, having profited so much from one successful patent, should be ready to exploit another in the same field.

No documents have come to light bearing on the origins of the partnership. We know much less of Arkwright than we do of Strutt; he remains one of the biographical enigmas of the eighteenth century. The authenticated facts about his life before his rise to fame are meagre; even his family could not recover many.[3] Almost all his business records seem to have perished.

[1] Wadsworth and Mann, op. cit., 269.
[2] Chambers, op. cit., 96.
[3] Seven years after his death his son, Richard, made some efforts. All he could get from one of his father's oldest associates at Preston, then a man of

Arkwright was six years younger than Strutt. He had been born at Preston on December 23, 1732, the youngest son of a large and poor family. He had been apprenticed to a barber at Kirkham, west of Preston, and had come to Bolton when out of his time. The only contemporary account of his early life was given to his son by Thomas Ridgway[1] in 1799:[2]

My first knowledge of your Father, was about the year 1750 when he came to reside in Bolton and was I think then about the Age of 18. He entred into the employment of one Edward Pollit, A peruke maker there, on whose death he remained with his widow for Sometime—He then married your Mother, and began business for himself; which he pursued with most indefatigable industry and with some success. He might now be considered in a comfortable situation; he had a decent House, a cleaner one coud not be and his friends and acquaintance always found in it a cordial reception from him. These were persons of no mean consideration in the town, but such as were in Superior Stations to himself. To these he recommended himself by his character for neatness, sobriety, industry, and good Sense. The Latter part of his time at Bolton was not so pleasant as it had been. He became necessitous in consequence of taking a public house, which did not answer his purpose and upon which he expended much money in alterations. He was obliged to leave the house and had a many interruptions caused by an inveterate asthma, which brought him very low in every sense of the word. Notwithstanding this, I believe there was only one Person to whom he owed Money, when he left the town and his credit [was] otherwise good. His customers that had employed him in his

76, was: 'Preston, 1st March, 1799. Dear Sir, I'm sorry it is not in my power to give you the whole of the information you wish. I was upwards of three years older than your Father & I do not recollect to have heard any thing particular of him only that he went apprentice to Kirkham & when he left there he went to Bolton in the year 1768. He being of the same interest as myself we knew each other & his intimacy with Mr Smalley and our own friendship—I have seen in the Register that he was baptized 31 Decr 1732 —I cant find one elderly person here that can give me any better or other information. I beg my Respectful Compliments to Your Lady who with the whole of Your family I hope will long enjoy good health—I am Dear Sirs— Your most hble Servt T. Walshman.' And even some of these facts were wrong for Arkwright had gone to Bolton from Preston before 1755; it was Nottingham he went to in 1768.

[1] Thomas Ridgway (1739–1816) who had founded, with his brother John (1733–1800), a large bleaching firm in Bolton and, in 1775, at Wallsuches, near Horwich. The firm was absorbed by the Bleachers' Association in 1900 (Sykes, *Concerning the Bleaching Industry* (1925), 81).

[2] Letter of March 25, 1799, in Strutt MSS. in Fitzwilliam Museum.

business were generally of the better sort, he might probably have done better coud he have Stooped to the vulgar, but his spirit was much superior to it, And always seemed to have something better in view. His genius for Mechanics was observed, it was perceived in his common conversation, which often turned on subjects of that kind. I well remember we had often great fun with a Clock he put up in his shop, which had all the appearance of being worked by the smoke of the chimney and we have caused a many to believe it was so; I have often seen him cut pasteboard into different shapes such as forming squares from oblongs without adding or diminishing, and a Hundred curious knackey things that one cannot find words to explain. He was always thought clever in his peruke making business and very capital in Bleeding & toothdrawing and allowed by all his acquaintance to be a very ingenious man.

He had married in his early twenties and a son, Richard, was born on December 19, 1755. His wife died and he married again in 1761.

After he gave up his public house and barber's shop he travelled about buying women's hair for wigs. It was then, in the late sixties, that he took up the idea of roller-spinning, and had his much disputed association with Thomas Highs of Leigh and John Kay, the Warrington clockmaker. Probably he took advantage of some of the discoveries of others but he certainly contributed much himself. His mechanical keenness, confidence and adventurousness have been underestimated. In January, 1768, he and Kay, as his paid assistant, were in Preston, working on the model of a machine. When their right to vote in the famous Burgoyne election of March came to be contested, the landlord from whom they rented rooms stated that they were reputed to be 'making a machine to find out the longitude'.[1]

They left Preston for Nottingham at the beginning of April. Arkwright had first sought financial help from Peter Atherton of Warrington but was more successful with John Smalley, a 'liquor merchant and painter', of Preston, who became his first partner.[2] In June, 1768, Arkwright applied from Nottingham for a patent and, twelve months later, on presentation of the

---

[1] *Palatine Note Book*, ed. Bailey, iii (1883), 263.
[2] Aikin and Enfield, *General Biography*, i (1799), 391; Baines (*History of the Cotton Manufacture in Great Britain* (1835), 150) says that Atherton was probably then of Warrington; he was afterwards of Liverpool, and also became a cotton spinner at Mold.

RICHARD ARKWRIGHT
from the portrait by Joseph Wright of Derby

specification, it was granted; Smalley signed as a witness.[1] The story goes that, on Smalley's resources giving out, Arkwright got assistance from the Wrights, the Nottingham bankers,[2] who, when progress seemed slow, turned them over to the capitalist Samuel Need who called in his partner Jedediah Strutt to pronounce on the invention.[3] But, as so often with the early textile inventions, we cannot establish the exact sequence of events with any confidence. Dugald Bannatyne's account in the *Supplement* of the *Encyclopædia Britannica* (1816 or a little earlier) is the first to mention Wright, and also the story that Need asked Arkwright 'to carry the model of the machine to Mr. Strutt of Derby' who told 'Mr. Need that he might with great safety close with Mr. Arkwright; the only thing wanting to his model, being an adaptation of some of the wheels to each other, which, for a want of skill, the inventor, with all his powers of contrivance, had not been able to accomplish'.[4] Bannatyne implies that the partnership preceded the obtaining of the patent in 1769; in this Baines followed him.[5] Some have even seen Strutt's hand in the clear specification,[6] although Arkwright's own account seems to rule this out.[7] Others put the date of the partnership in 1770 and even in 1771.[8]

The long interval between the petition for a patent and the final grant, however, supports the idea that its completion was held up for lack of money. With Arkwright's second patent

[1] Petition, June 8, 1768. The sealing of the specification was witnessed by Bigoe Henzell and John Smalley.

[2] Ichabod Wright (1700–77) had founded the bank in 1759 or 1760. He had traded in timber, iron and hemp with the Baltic (J. D. Chambers in *Nottingham Journal*, June 29, 1949).

[3] There is probably some truth in this legend; John Wright (1723–89), Ichabod's son, was named as an executor and trustee in Need's will by which he received £100. For information about the Wrights see Glover, op. cit., ii, 201; *Nottingham Journal*, Sept. 6, 1777; *Gentlemen's Magazine*, 1789, 1212; *Derby Mercury*, Dec. 23, 1789; July 22, 1790.

[4] Vol. iii, 393 (1824 ed.).

[5] Baines, op. cit., 151.

[6] Seymour-Jones, 'The Invention of Roller Drawing in Cotton Spinning', *Trans. of the Newcomen Soc.*, i (1920–1).

[7] W. D. Crofts at the trial of 1785 said that Arkwright had told him that the specification of 1769 'had been drawn from a model of the machine by a draughtsman in London' (*Trial of a Cause* (1785), 74).

[8] For 1770, Ure, *The Cotton Manufacture of Gt. Britain* (1836), i, 227; for 1771, Britton and Brayley, op. cit., 540. Smalley's name is mentioned in connection with the Nottingham mill by *Aikin and Enfield* (1799) and Guest, *Compendious Hist. of the Cotton Manufacture* (1823), 22.

there was no such delay.[1] The help of Need and Strutt would seem to have ensured the patent and have made possible the running of the Nottingham mill and the momentous decision of 1771 to develop the invention on a larger scale.

The decision to go to Cromford and apply water power to machinery still far from perfect was one of the turning points in the history of the factory system. The patent specification of 1769 had spoken only of horse power and nothing more had been attempted at Nottingham. But the possibility of water power must have been obvious. Lewis Paul's rudimentary spinning factory at Northampton over twenty years before— which in so many respects resembled Arkwright's—had been turned by water power, just as his first machines at Birmingham had been turned by horses.[2] Strutt was a silk manufacturer and familiar from his youth with Lombe's famous Derby mill, which in the sixties was being copied in other places.[3] The idea of a factory system based on water power was in the air, although we must recognize the daring of the experiment. Need and Strutt had to be prepared to risk a good deal of capital in backing Arkwright's invention and creating his factory community.

To the present-day eye it seems strange that, in a country so full of strongly flowing streams, the adventurers should have hit on so remote a place as Cromford. It had no communication by water and only poor links by road with the ports through which its raw material came and the selling points for its product. It was over fourteen miles from Derby, twenty-six from Nottingham, and nearly forty-five from Manchester. A glance at Burdett's fine county map of 1762–7 shows how different the country round Cromford appeared from what it does today. The turnpike from the North of England to Derby and London ran some miles away on the east—through Brassington—and is now a mere by-road. The direct route between

---

[1] The original Arkwright petition is not preserved but it was presented on June 8, 1768 (S.P. 44/266). A bill granting letters patent for 14 years, provided a description of the invention was lodged within four months, is dated Dec. 15, 1768 (S.O. 7/248). The patent was not granted until July 3, 1769. Fees had to be paid at every stage.

[2] Wadsworth and Mann, op. cit., ch. xxi. The use of water power for spinning had been envisaged in two other abortive spinning machines—those of Taylor (1755) and John Kay (ibid., 472–3).

[3] Cf. ibid., 305.

Cromford and Derby ran over the moorlands; the valley road, now A6, did not exist until 1820. The uplands were unenclosed moor and the roads near Cromford were unturnpiked.

The water for the Cromford mill came from a stream, reputedly never frozen, which issued from the lead mines, and joined the Derwent near Cromford Bridge.[1] The mill was built at its confluence. There was no pre-existing village of any size and, one would suppose, no labour force ready to hand except what could be gathered from the neighbouring countryside or imported. A village had to be built, the first of the cotton factory villages which were to change the Northern landscape in the next hundred years.

The first contemporary reference to Cromford we have found is in the *Derby Mercury* of December 13, 1771. The partners are advertising for clockmakers and a smith and offering employment to weavers and to women and children. The labour force is being collected. The advertisement reads:

Cotton Mill, Cromford, 10th Dec. 1771.

WANTED immediately, two Journeymen Clock-Makers, or others that understands Tooth and Pinion well: Also a Smith that can forge and file.—Likewise two Wood Turners that have been accustomed to Wheel-making, Spole-turning, &c. Weavers residing at the Mill, may have good Work. There is Employment at the above Place, for Women, Children, &c. and good Wages.

N.B. A Quantity of Box Wood is wanted: Any Persons whom the above may suit, will be treated with by Messrs. Arkwright and Co. at the Mill, or Mr. Strutt, in Derby.

Two and a half months later Arkwright writes to Strutt on the progress at Cromford; the letter gives something of the spirit of the experimental period. A few legends have come down about it, the most credible being that of Strutt using a piece of chalk to stop the 'licking'—the catching of the yarn—

---

[1] Davies (*A New Historical and Descriptive View of Derbyshire* (1811), 91) described the stream as warm, but John Farey (*General View of the Agriculture of Derbyshire* (1811), i, 487) was sceptical: 'It seems more natural to refer the circumstance [of its not freezing], as far as it is true, to the great depth and narrowness of the Valleys, preserving the temperature longer than in more open situations.'

on the front rollers of the spinning frame.[1] The letter of March 2, 1772, reads:[2]

Cromford Marh 2d. 72

Sir,

yours yisterday came to hand together with a bill from Mr. Need Value 60lb. I have sent a little cotton spun on the one spindle & find no Difficanty in Geting it from the Bobbin & Dubeld & Twistd in the maner you see it at one opration. One hand I think will do 40 or 50lb. of it in one day from the bobins it is spun upon, that is in the new whay. I am sertain of it ansuaring & one person will spin a Thousand Hanks a Day so that wee shall not want $\frac{1}{5}$ of the hands I First Expectd notwithstanding the Roaveing takeing so few. I see Greate Improvements Every day, When I rote to you last had not thorowly provd the spining; several things apening I could not acount for sinse then has proved it—I have made trial to twist it for Velverets & find what the[y] do with five operations [I] Can do with one that is duble & twist it Redey for wharping at one time, first they reel, second wind, third Duble, fourth twist, 5 wind redey to wharp, & all these done one thred at a time Except Twisting. shold Like you to try a little of this hard in a ribd fraim; i think it shold not be whet but beate. Plais to send the solft to mr. Need. One has a slacker throw then the other, naither of [them] perfect but shold like to see a stockin or part of one, pray Bring a Little with you. Mr Need spakes of wanting Thos Bell[3] & a turner but Cant see what they whant Thos. for. I spok to Coniah & dar say he will com if he was properly aployd to or they might get a man from Hibisons but there is no person at the mill that will put themselves out of their whay to be of aney Servis Except teas Mr Needs hart out with a continual want & uneasiness. As to sending aney hand from hear I cant think of doing, for where they get a Shiling cleair there shall in a few months 40, I am posative. If Mr Need thinks best Can go one or twos days pr. wheek to Nottingham & Shall Shortly Suply them with Roaveings from hear if wee cant spin 2000 Hanks a Day which I am Sertain I can in four months at the outside, and now as solfter can be spun faster than hard, stocking yarn will ansuar best & will be Dubled with very Little

---

[1] The story first appears in Felkin, op. cit., 90.

[2] Printed by Seymour-Jones, op. cit. A facsimile of the original is in the Birmingham Public Library.

[3] Thomas Bell, joiner, gave evidence in 1785 and said he had worked for Arkwright five years '17 years ago'.

Expence.—At the mill the[y] whant Cards puting on. andrew might do that as it Requiers no greate judgement, but I sopose he is a deal taken up in those Looms & the profits of wich will Scairsly pay whare house room. If he can be got to wheave by the Pees or yard & out of the mill shold sune set that plase in Better order but while he is in it is scairsly posable. Except he has his own whay no good will be don with justis or him, & what I sade to George is what I shold say again, it whas unraisenable. In a few weeks shall move for wee can do without them all. It is onley seting an other pair of cards &c, hear wee have begun of them. Shold Like to know if aney acount is come from Hallifax[1] lately; he has sent som other Cards but not the quantety I Rote for and no Letter or bill with them. Shold Rite to Mr. N. but has not time & wold when I do send to send some twe threds solft and as Even as silk. I am sertain I can [make] the first fraim, I have hands to make three frames in a fortnet. It shall be don you may depend upon it, but I whant sombody to look after the spining &c. I have rote to Kay yesterday; if he will not com can you think of sombody. A yonge man was hear this wheek sade he had spoke to you; this is his Riteing I send Inclosed. What do you think of him, he seemes a Likely person but has all to lern. I am afraide no one man will know all that I shold Expect the[y] might. Richd has hit upon a method to spin woostid with Roulers, it is quite sertain, & only altering the shape—that is Round on one side and flat on the other so that the twist gets under or betwixt them, at sertain time. It will ansuar I am sertain. Querey, will not Cotton make whipcoard as good as silk, properly Twisted. It may be don all at onst from the bobins. Pray Rite to Mr. N. what he thinks best. I Cant think of stoping this Con[c]ern hear as that at nottingm. is [not] or Ever will be aney thing in comparison to this, There is hands to be got there & if he wold have mee com over I Shall, but not take aney from hear. I askd Mr. Whard to get [me] some Let pipes to bring the [water] into the mill; they are conuini-ally fetching. It might be Brought in the Rooms. Wold it not be best to fix a Crank to one of the lying shafts to work a pump or Ingon in case of fire. Bring the belts with you. Desire ward to send those other Locks and allso Some sorts of Hangins for the sashes he & you may think best and some good Latches & Catches for the out doors and a few for the inner ons allso and a Large Knoker or a Bell to First door. I am Determind for the feuter to Let no persons in to Look at the wor[k]s except spining. The man Mr. Whard Bot. the ash Board from Calld for his money & says he will

---

[1] Halifax was then, as later, in the card-making area (cf. Crump, *Leeds Woollen Industry, 1780–1820* (1931), 8).

send the other shortly. I am tired with riteing so Long a Letter &
think you can scairsley Reed it. Excuse haist

and am yours' &c.

R Arkwright

The letter brings out how acutely aware of the possibilities
of roller-spinning Arkwright was. Though his production was
still far from perfect he was full of ideas about the use of his
yarn not only in hosiery but in the whole range of cotton
fabrics—from calicoes to fustians, and he looked forward to
worsted. (The Richard mentioned could hardly be his son,
then aged 16; it is more likely to have been Richard Priddon
who gave evidence in 1785 that he went to Arkwright in 1771,
was with him in 1775, and later was a partner in a mill with
Arkwright's son.)[1] We see too that Need was the sceptical partner who was content rather to concentrate on making a success
of the Nottingham mill than to dissipate energies at Cromford,
which must have been then more of an experimental machine-
shop than a properly equipped spinning factory. And Need
was supplying the money.

II. THE CALICO ACT

The next we hear of the partners' operations concerns their
position under the law. Early in the century, the woollen and
silk interests, in their jealousy of imported Indian cotton goods,
had secured the clapping on of a double excise duty and, for
printed calicoes, an almost absolute prohibition on sale and
manufacture. The Lancashire cotton industry had secured in
1736 a relaxation for goods of flax warp and cotton weft, a
relaxation which by custom (or subterfuge) came to cover the
great bulk of the industry's production and even, it is probable,
the growing part of it that used hand-spun cotton twist for
warps. Technically, however, from 1736, only half-cotton
material was free to be made (subject to the 3d. a yard excise).[2]

The machine-spun twist from Arkwright's patent machines
was now entering into the calico printing trade and was meeting with trouble from the excisemen. In Lancashire, where it

[1] *Trial of a Cause*, 127–8, 130.
[2] Wadsworth and Mann, op. cit., ch. vi and vii.

seems the letter of the law may have been winked at, the new printed calicoes were allowed through at the 3*d.* a yard duty; in London they were charged at 6*d.* a yard. The first hint we have of it is in an anonymous letter, which must have been inspired by the Arkwright partners, in *Prescott's Manchester Journal* of December 11, 1773. The ambiguity of the situation is illustrated by the reference to 'printed muslins' which would seem to have been explicitly permitted by the act of 1721:

To the Printer of the *Manchester Journal.*

Sir,

I shall be much obliged to any of your Ingenious Readers who will favour me with answers to the following Queries,

A. B.

1. What is the duty on Printing all cotton goods being manufactured in this kingdom?

2. Is there any law that prohibits the wear of such cotton goods, provided they are of English manufactory?

3. If there be such a law, would it not be prudent to look for redress?

4. Provided we have no such law, how must we distinguish our English printed cottons, from those printed Callicoes commonly called muslins, so much wore at this time among us?

5. Are the printed Callicoes or printed muslins prohibited? If so, what is the penalty?

6. Is it not consistent with reason, when we can manufacture goods equal to foreigners, to give employment to our own people, rather than to inrich other nations?

The partners had probably already in mind an application for redress by legislation. On February 25, 1774, their petition —from Richard Arkwright and Company of Nottingham, Spinners of Cotton, and Manufacturers of British White Stuffs —was presented to the Commons. It recited how, under the patent of 1769, cotton yarn for warps had been spun by machine, and how 'with such Warps, there are wholly made in *Great Britain*, from raw Materials, Velverets, and a Variety of other Goods, particularly a new Manufacture of White Cotton Stuffs, adapted for Printing'. A few pieces printed in Lancashire had been charged with two duties of 1½*d.* a yard, 3*d.* in all; others sold to calico printers 'in and about London' had been

F

charged as calicoes with two duties of 3*d*., 6*d*. in all. Orders had been countermanded 'to the great Prejudice of a new and promising *British* manufacture'. The petition contended that they should be charged at 3*d*. and that a 6*d*. duty would act as a prohibition. It added that doubt had arisen whether such 'White Cotton Stuffs' were not, when printed, prohibited from being used and worn in Great Britain. It went on, with some prescience:

> . . . the Petitioners assure themselves, the said Manufacture, if not crushed by so heavy a Duty as Six Pence a Yard, will rapidly increase, and find new and effectual Employment for many Thousand *British* Poor, and increase the Revenue of this Kingdom; and that it is probable that such Warp, made of Cotton which is manufactured in this Kingdom, will be introduced in the Room of the Warps before used, made of Linen Yarn (great Part of which Linen Yarn is imported ready-spun from Foreign Parts) in making *Lancashire* Cottons, in regard Cotton Goods so made wholly of Cotton will be greatly superior in Quality to the present Species of Cotton Goods made with Linen Yarn Warps, and will bleach, print, wash and wear better, and by Means thereof, find further Employment for the Poor.

They prayed that leave be given to bring in a bill legalising the white cotton stuffs, settling the duty when printed at 3*d*., and extending to them the export drawback allowed to British and Irish coarse linens.[1]

They had evidently not managed their parliamentary affairs skilfully for the petition was allowed to lie on the table; its supporters were not ready to follow it up. Strutt had come up to London to manage the case and he settled down to wait, his wife coming up to join him. On May 2 the petition was read again and referred to a committee of the House. The named members were Lord Howe the admiral, who though now member for Dartmouth, had close political connections with Nottingham,[2] and John Plumptre, one of the Nottingham members. Lord Howe reported from the committee on May 6. Jedediah Strutt had produced to it specimens of cloth, and Stephen Williams, a linen draper, had described the trouble with the

---

[1] *C.J.*, xxxiv, 496–7.
[2] Namier, *The Structure of Politics at the Accession of George III*, i (1929), 115, 117–18.

The Old Masson Mills

A drawing of the Masson Mills
(from the *Draper's Record*, September 1897, by kind permission)

London excisemen and his unsuccessful appeal to the Commissioners of Excise. Strutt, recalled, said that

the Petitioners had expended upwards of £13,000 in the said Manufacture; that if charged with the said Duty of Sixpence per Yard, it would totally hinder the Growth, and obstruct the Sale of this promising Manufacture, which, in all Probability, will become a flourishing Trade, if encouraged, and be the Means of employing many Thousands of poor People, there being already upwards of 600 Persons of all Ages employed in this Branch of Business; that Children of Seven Years old, and upwards, are employed, and they prefer Children from Ten to Twelve years old, for the preparing and spinning Cotton by the said Machine.

Leave was given to Lord Howe, Frederick Montagu (member for Higham Ferrers and a Nottinghamshire landowner), and Plumptre to bring in a bill. This had its second reading on May 17, its third on June 1, was passed by the Lords without amendment, and received the royal assent on June 14.[1]

It would seem that in the interval between the two petitions there had been negotiations with the Commissioners of Excise. In April Arkwright had presented a petition to the Treasury which was referred to the Board of Excise. He had proposed a means by which cloth could be distinguished from imported calicoes. He suggested that each piece of cloth made with cotton warp should be marked with three blue threads at both ends of the piece. The Commissioners, all nine being present, proposed to the Treasury an alternative, which would be a greater security. This was that the blue threads should be in the selvage 'running through the whole length of each piece'; a stamp at each end of the piece should have 'instead of the word Callicoe which stands for foreign Callicoes' the words 'British Manufactury'. This was embodied in the bill; the British all-cotton stuffs were to be distinguished from foreign by having three blue threads in the selvage (the first, third and fifth) and by the stamp.[2]

Arkwright himself did not figure in the Commons proceedings and he was not associated with the gift, twelve months later, of a piece of the new manufacture to Lord Howe for his

---

[1] *C.J.*, xxxiv. The Act was 14 Geo. III, c. 72.
[2] Corr. of Board of Excise with Treasury. P.R.O.

wife. This came from Need and Strutt, and the latter's draft ran:

Mr N & Mr S Compl[iment]s to Ld Howe begs his Lordships acceptance of this peice of British Calico for Lady Howe as a small acknowledgment for the great trouble we gave your Ldship last summer in obtaining the Act for the printing & wearing of them in England. We wish the *pattern* [crossed out] choice of the print may be a recommendation. The piece itself is not exquisite, has nothing extraordinary in it, but that it is British Manufacture. We have since this time 12 months made about 5000 pieces & have pleasure to inform your Lordship that when we have made the necessary allowance for the difficulties & prejudices attending all new manufactures of concern we are then so far successful. I am, my Lord, for Mr N & self yr L[ordship]s most obt most obligd & most Hmble Sert J S[1]

Eight years after the Calico Act Arkwright gave a version of this legislative episode which had some dubious points. He was putting his case for the statutory prolongation of his patent rights:[2]

By the united Effects of these important Inventions [his patents] and the Perseverance and Spirit with which the Undertaking was pursued, the most excellent Yarn or Twist was produced; notwithstanding which, the Proprietors found great Difficulty to introduce it into Public Use. A very heavy and valuable Stock, in Consequence of these Difficulties, lay upon their Hands; Inconveniences and Disadvantages of no small Consideration followed. Whatever were the Motives which induced the Rejection of it, they were thereby necessarily driven to attempt, by their own Strength and Ability, the Manufacture of the Yarn: Their first Trial was in weaving it into Stockings, which succeeded; they then endeavoured to prevail on the Manufacturers in *Lancashire* to weave it into Callicoes, but they absolutely refused. The Proprietors, therefore, themselves, made the Attempt, and succeeded; and soon established the manufacture of Callicoes which promises to be one of the first Manu-

---

[1] Written on back of a letter to Strutt from his daughter of July 2, 1775. On the same sheet is a calculation: '37 yards for 60*s*. is 1*s*. 10½*d*. p yd'— perhaps the price of the calico. In his reply of August 16 (printed by Strutt, op. cit., 380, but misdated 1785) Howe deemed the gift 'an evidence of their obliging prejudice in his favour, tho' conscious at the same time that the success of their application to Parliament was solely ascribable to the reasonableness and justice of their pretensions'.

[2] *Case of Mr. Richard Arkwright and Co.* (1782), 2.

factures in this Kingdom. Another still more formidable Difficulty arose; the Orders for Goods which they had received, being considerable, were unexpectedly countermanded, the Officers of Excise refusing to let them pass at the Usual Duty of *Three Pence per* Yard, insisting on the additional Duty of *Three Pence per* Yard, as being Callicoes, though manufactured in *England*: Besides, these Callicoes, when printed, were prohibited. By this unforeseen Obstruction, a very considerable and very valuable Stock of Callicoes accumulated. An Application to the Commissioners of Excise was attended with no Success: The Proprietors, therefore, had no Resource but to ask Relief of the Legislature; which, after much Money expended, and against a strong Opposition of the Manufacturers in *Lancashire*, they obtained.

Arkwright was then trying to make himself out to be an injured benefactor of his country, harassed by the jealousy of the Lancashire men who had filched away his patent rights. This coloured his narrative for there is little reason to believe that the partners only turned to using the yarn in hosiery and in calicoes when they had a large, unsaleable stock on their hands. The letter to Strutt of March, 1772, does not support that and a letter from Mrs. Strutt to her husband of February 14, 1774, just before the petition to the Commons, hints at a brisk demand for their woven goods:

one Waddington of Nottingm, a long with the man at yr Nottingm Cotton Mill went to Cromford & has took what Layloc Stripd was left there, then came to Derby in hopes to find ours not disposd off but there was but 2 pieces left, he said if there had been a hundred of those small patterns you took in your box he wou'd have took em all & thought him self obligd to you to let him have them, he has took a great number of white pieces from Cromford and sent to print, from what I hrd by the by betwixt your man and Waddington Arkwrigh[t] has sold the white pieces so that he wish'd you & Mr Need wou'd print no more, he told me that you might Sell them in the White as fast as Cou'd make em, we have heard nothing more either from Cromford . . .

There were then, as there had been in 1772, looms at Nottingham, Derby, and Cromford, though probably not many.[1]

[1] A letter from Need to Strutt of April 4, 1776, shows that the piece goods manufacture continued: 'I . . . have sent you 1 piece $\frac{4}{4}$ Strip'd being all I have, believe it is but 20 yds, I have wrote to Isherwood to send some, as there was above 20 pieces, at PA, I have orders for 5 or 6 pieces, I think RA

No direct evidence supports Arkwright's charge that the Lancashire manufacturers refused to use his yarn; that would have been much out of character had the price been right. Nor is there anything to show that they opposed his application to Parliament. No Lancashire members are mentioned in connection with his bill, which was a Midland affair, but equally no divisions on it are recorded. A declaratory amendment, probably of Lancashire inspiration, that the bill did not extend to 'Cotton Velvets, Velverets, or other Fustians, manufactured in *Great Britain*' was accepted;[1] this left the position of these stuffs under the Fustian Act of 1736 unimpaired. At this moment the Lancashire and Cheshire members were more concerned with pushing a bill through to prevent the export of cotton machinery. The Arkwright partners failed in their attempt to get an export bounty, which is not surprising seeing that the Lancashire manufacturers had failed four years before to get one for their checks and cottons for printing.[2]

The revenue returns for the first nine years of the operation of the new duty under the Calico Act show the enormous increase in the trade and its effect on imported calicoes:[3]

Produce of Duties on

	British Calicoes £	British and Foreign Calicoes £	Export Drawback £
1775	710	129,283	69,616
1776	1,289	125,988	52,514
1777	2,515	137,986	65,706
1778	4,824	127,688	58,436
1779	8,203	116,780	48,975
1780	14,288	124,537	35,918
1781	28,987	152,597	48,208
1782	32,939	147,645	36,978
1783	44,732	158,377	39,408

should be acquainted with this writing that is at Seagraves, Middleton was at Cromford, & said A would be here this week, but he was not come last night, J : J sent Withers 659 ps. No. 1, 2, 3, 4, £1717 : 0 : 9, there was but 26 ps No, 1, if Withers will take all we had better not apply to Leach, except he will take some that Withers throws out, there is some lies at his house, that he refused taking of those out in Octr, and we shall hear what he says of these, will Tatlow take them No 1 that now lies at London that W threw out.'

[1] *C.J.*, xxxiv, 795.

[2] Wadsworth and Mann, op. cit., 165.

[3] We are indebted to Mr. Harry Briggs for these figures which are reproduced by permission of H.M. Commissioners of Customs and Excise.

Or, in terms of yardage:

	British Calicoes Yards	Foreign Calicoes Yards
1775	56,814	2,111,439
1776	103,147	1,783,422
1777	201,253	1,947,570
1778	385,930	1,913,004
1779	656,245	1,342,744
1780	1,143,043	1,071,775
1781	2,318,972	1,194,495
1782	2,635,155	964,897
1783	3,578,590	770,922

This is the background against which the next phase of the Arkwright and Strutt enterprises can be judged.

III. EXPANSION

Mrs. Strutt had died in London on May 11, 1774, while her husband was dancing attendance on Parliament. The Calico Act was passed a month later but Strutt stayed on in London, apparently because of illness, and did not return to Derby until the late autumn. His house was left in charge of his young daughters, his hosiery business of his brother-in-law and brother, his cotton business of his partners. By September his eldest son, then aged 18, was constrained to write:

You begin to be much wanted at Home, & may also be at Cromford; I was there last Sunday but one, & heard very unfavourable accounts of Mr A's behaviour. I suppose he is going to leave you. Mrs Smalley does not seem at all happy in her new situation, & they had a bad misfortune last week for one of the Children broke a Leg.[1]

The Smalleys were then living at Cromford where, perhaps, he was a manager. Elizabeth Strutt found them 'very agreeable people'.[2] There had been an earlier hint of trouble. A draft letter by Strutt, written in London on the back of one from his wife of September 28, 1773, must have been to Smalley:

Recd yours & am sorry to find matters betwixt you & Mr Arkwright are come to such extremities (*It is directly contrary to my disposition*) & wonder he shoud persist in giving you fresh provocations.

---

[1] Sept. 14, 1774.   [2] Elizabeth to Jedediah, Sept. 5, 1774.

I said what I coud to persuade him to oblige you in any thing that was reasonable & to endeavour to live on good terms at least & my Wife has said a great deal to him. (*and what can I do more I cannot stop his mouth nor is it in my power to convince him*) nor when I come to consider the matter seriously and the circumstances I am at a loss to think about what we can do it, you must be sensible when some sort of people set themselves to be perverse it is very difficult to prevent them being so. We cannot (*stop his mouth or prevent his doing wrong*) prevent him saying Ill-natured things nor can we regulate his actions, neither do I see that it is in our power to remove him otherwise than by his own consent for he is in possession & as much right there as we. Nay further suppose we was to discharge the Man that has been the occasion of all this he may say he shall not be discharged & if they two agree what could we do to pretend to do that by compulsion that we [breaks off][1]

But there was no parting for the present. Strutt, however, was slow in recovering his health and in March, 1775, his daughter was reporting that 'he has begun to take Asses Milk and today took a ride with my Uncle before Dinner'.[2]

The next landmark was the securing of Arkwright's carding patent of 1775 in which he tried to 'sew up' the whole spinning process, older inventions than his own included. The patent was sealed on December 16, 1775, four months being allowed for the lodging of the specification. It was not witnessed and, presumably, was not fully disclosed, until April 10, 1776. W. D. Crofts, who witnessed it, gave evidence in 1785 that a few days before the due date Arkwright came to him and asked him to prepare a specification and to make it vague.[3] There is no mention of Strutt in the various stages of the patent or in any of the later trials. Yet one might have supposed that Strutt would have had better acquaintance with the mechanical facts than any one but Arkwright himself.

Great ambitions lay behind the all-embracing patent of 1775 but it is idle to speculate about Strutt's part in them. Arkwright was a domineering, self-sufficient man and the relations with his partners were not easy. He was rising rapidly in the world; the poor adventurer of the early Nottingham years had been

---

[1] Words in italic crossed out.
[2] Elizabeth Strutt from Derby to William in London, March 16, 1775.
[3] *Trial of a Cause*, 75.

put far behind; the nouveau riche had arrived. On July 2, 1775, Strutt's elder daughter, then 16, writes to him in London:[1]

Mr Arkwright came here on wednesday night & brought his daughter a very pretty letter from her Brother &—would you think it—a very elegant little watch whitch he bought for her at Manchester—on thursday morning they sett off from here to Birmingham my sister & Miss Arkwright in genteel riding dresses & provided with pen & ink & Memorandum Books that they may see which writes the best journal. They seem'd very happy & I hope they will have a deal of pleasure. They talk'd of going to France & the whole Town believes they are gone there but every body thinks they will not like it. I suppose you will see them before you receive this.

And there is a further glimpse of prosperity in a letter of July 7, 1776, from Edward Saxelbye in London to Jedediah's on, William, then 20:

I am told Mr Arkwright has set up his Carriage & parted with the greatest part of his purchase, I suppose he has made a good Bargain as he wd not have sold as he seemed very much elevated upon the strength of his own Contract with Mr Milnes; when I come into the County I shall not know Cromford, I am informed it is so much improved, I always thought it a place very capable of great additions.

This is suggestive. In 1776 William Milnes, the owner of the Cromford estate, sold it to Peter Nightingale of Lea, from whom Arkwright was to buy it in 1789.[2] Can it be that Arkwright had already bought it in 1776 but had parted with it to Nightingale, perhaps to use the money in mill building? For it was then that Cromford extensions were made and Strutt started his building at Belper. The precise relationship of the partnership to these ventures is unknown. It has been commonly assumed that it covered Nottingham, Cromford, Belper and Milford as well as Birkacre in Lancashire in 1777. It is perhaps more likely that Strutt financed Belper and Milford himself.

Belper was a village on the east bank of the Derwent, seven miles by road south of Cromford, seven miles north of Derby. There was already some domestic industry—a colony of nailers.

[1] Susannah Arkwright was then 13 and Martha Strutt 15.
[2] Glover, op. cit., ii, 358.

The first cotton mill there began work in 1778.[1] Already by that time Strutt had bought further property at New Mills or Milford, a mile and threequarters nearer Derby. Here there was a nucleus of buildings on both sides of the river which had been advertised for sale early in 1777 as:

IRON WORKS

To be sold, New Mills and Mackenay Forges in the Parish of Duffield and County of Derby, most beautifully and conveniantly situated upon each side the River Derwent; consisting of two Iron Forges; Hammersman's Forge with a Scrap Furnace, and divers Workmen's Houses, Gardens, and a spacious Yard, lying on the East Side of the River, Also a Slitting and Rowling Mill, for Iron and Copper, and a Through adjoining, with a large Building, used as a Paper or Tin Mill, a large Warehouse, an handsome Dwelling-House, with necessary Conveniences; several Workmen's Houses and other Buildings, with Gardens, Orchard, and Croft, most delightfully situated on the Side of the River, and worked by Wears made at vast Labour and Expence, and executed with great Judgment. The Situation of these Works, with the constant Power of the Water, and all their Conveniences renders them capable of being vastly improved, and altered or changed to any other Purpose or Business whatever, where a continual Supply of Water is necessary . . .[2]

The same year saw the beginning of the factory at Birkacre, near Chorley. Here Arkwright had agreed with John Chadwick of Burgh to build a spinning mill on the site of a forge on the river Yarrow. The mill, the higher and lower forges, a corn mill, a house and cottages were then leased to Arkwright on November 29, 1777, at £150 a year, with some additional land at a rent of £31—altogether 13½ acres. It is interesting that both Milford and Birkacre should be connected with iron works, a point of some utility in the making of the machinery for the mills. The Birkacre partners were Arkwright, Strutt, Need, Thomas Walshman of Preston, and John Cross.[3] It was the earliest factory on the Arkwright plan to be put up outside

---

[1] *Factories Inquiry. R. Com. Supp. Rep.* Part II, Section D1, p. 96; 1834(167) xx, 578.

[2] *Aris's Birmingham Gazette*, April 14, 1777; *Manchester Mercury*, April 29, May 6, 1777.

[3] Deeds printed in supplement to *Preston Guardian*, April 26, 1884; now in Lancashire Record Office.

Derbyshire and Nottinghamshire and it received the special attention of the rioters against machinery in 1779.

These riots, so often described,[1] were a revolt of the hand-workers of West Lancashire against machines in a time of bad trade. They were directed not only against the 'patent machines' of Arkwright but against the larger jennies also. Only the smallest domestic machines were spared; all that had been concentrated in factories—large or small—were proscribed. The rioters prosecuted at the assizes were accused of attacking ten factories, of which Birkacre was the largest. There are two lists of the machinery destroyed there, neither perhaps exact. One is in the charge at quarter sessions on April 4, 1780, when a woman was sent to prison for twelve months for taking part in the attack on Birkacre; the other the indictment of four men at the August assizes, one of whom was sent to prison for two years and another for one year. The descriptions were:

Quarter Sessions[2]		Assizes[3]
20 Spinning Frames	20 Spinning Engines	6 Carding Engines
20 Carding Engines	20 Roving Engines	20 Spinning Engines
20 Twisting Engines	20 Twisting Mills	20 Spinning Frames
20 Cotton Wheels	20 Cotton Reels	20 Spinning Wheels
		20 Twisting Mills

Birkacre had been attacked on October 4 after being under threat for several days. In the first skirmish a man was killed. The most serious apprehensions were raised throughout Lancashire; troops were called in; and Arkwright at Cromford put the place in a state of siege. A letter written from Cromford to 'a Gentleman in Manchester' on October 9, described Arkwright's preparations:

In your last you expressed some Fear of the Mob coming to Destroy the Works at Cromford, but they are well prepared to receive them should they come there. All the Gentlemen in this Neighbourhood being determined to support Mr. Arkwright, in the defence of his Works, which have been of such Utility to this Country, Fifteen hundred Stand of small Arms are already collected from Derby and the Neighbouring Towns, and a great Battery of

---

[1] Wadsworth and Mann, op. cit., ch. xxiii; Hammond, *The Skilled Labourer, 1760–1832* (1919), ch. iv; Mantoux, *The Industrial Revolution in the Eighteenth Century*, Revised Edition (1928), ch. iii.

[2] Quarter Sess. Order Book, 1780.

[3] P.L. 26. 43/3.

Cannon raised of 9 and 12 Pounders, with great plenty of Powder and Grape Shot, besides which, upwards of 500 Spears are fixt in Poles of between 2 and 3 Yards long. The Spears and Battery are always to be kept in Repair for the Defence of the Works and Protection of the Village, and 5 or 6000 Men, Miners, &c. can at any Time be assembled in less than an Hour, by Signals agreed upon, who are determined to defend to the very last Extremity, the Works, by which many Hundreds of their Wives and Children get a decent and comfortable Livelihood.[1]

But the rioters never got within fifty miles of Cromford and it was never threatened again.

The Birkacre factory was effectively destroyed and was not rebuilt as a cotton mill. The lease was surrendered on September 20, 1780, on payment of £200, the partners 'thinking it insecure to proceed in their intended Business in that place'.[2]

At Cromford, too, there were difficulties. In November, 1777, Arkwright had made inquiries of Boulton and Watt for a steam engine to raise water for the water-wheel. No order followed, but nearly three years later he took the matter up again and Watt wrote to Boulton:

Mr. Arkwright of Cromford sent for me last night, he has built a mill and the miners have lett down his water so that it cannot move. He is much more modest than he was the last time but despises your India Reels, he says he can make a thing for that purpose to answer as well for a shilling apiece—but as he does not pretend to improving the fire engine now I had little to say against him.[3]

As by this time there were two mills at Cromford, the supply of water from Cromford Sough may have proved inadequate. Boulton and Watt supplied an engine of eight horse-power.

[1] *Derby Mercury*, Oct. 22, 1779; it had appeared first in the *Manchester Mercury*, Oct. 12.

[2] The property was advertised for sale on Sept. 26, 1780 (*Manchester Mercury*); it later became a printworks.

[3] The 'India reels' were metal parts for silk winding and Boulton and his partner Rehe had a contract for their supply to the East India Company. Two months later Boulton wrote to Rehe from Cornwall: 'I hear that Mr. Arkwright came as a spy to see the reels, and that he proposes to offer something simpler and cheaper.' Nothing further is heard of this idea (Watt to Arkwright, Nov. 30, 1777; Watt to Boulton, Oct. 12, 1780; Boulton to Rehe, Dec. 4, 1780).

CHAPTER V

THE EARLY COTTON MILLS

I. THE PARTNERSHIP DISSOLVED

On April 14, 1781, Samuel Need died at his lodgings in Bread Street, Cheapside, 'advanced in Years and after a very long Illness', and 'said to have died immensely rich.'[1] With his death the cotton partnership seems to have come to an end. We do not know the financial terms of settlement. Arkwright went on with the Cromford properties, Strutt with Belper and Milford; Nottingham was working under the old name when the mill was destroyed by fire in November, 1781.[2] It was quickly rebuilt as 'Arkwright and Co.' but its subsequent history is obscure.[3]

Arkwright and Strutt went their separate ways, though linked by many ties and with joint interests in the patent rights. But there may have been personal divergences. Arkwright had now become involved, on the one hand, in big plans for the extension of his spinning interests, and, on the other, in a war against the rest of the trade. He had established a factory at Wirksworth; a large mill in Manchester was building; those at Matlock Bath and at Bakewell were probably in contemplation; he may also have begun negotiations in Scotland. Strutt may have thought Arkwright was going too fast and too far.

[1] *Derby Mercury*, April 20, 1781; *Nottingham Journal*, April 21, 1781. He was buried at Bunhill Fields with his wife's family.

[2] The fire 'raged with such Fury, that in two Hours after the spacious Building was reduced to a mere Shell: All the Machines, Wheels, Spindles, &c. employed for spinning and winding Cotton, were entirely consumed, and not a single Article contained therein, (the Books excepted) could possibly be saved, notwithstanding the Exertions of many Inhabitants, who used their utmost to preserve it and the adjacent House, from Inevitable Destruction. From what cause the Fire originated we are not able to tell' (*Derby Mercury*, Nov. 15, 1781).

[3] *Derby Mercury*, Jan. 9, 1783. The same paper (July 7, 1796), reports the death of a Mr. Hepinstall, 'master of the Cotton-mill, in Hockley, in Nottingham, (formerly in possession of the late Sir Richard Arkwright . . .)'. Blackner (op. cit., 250) states that the mill remained in the hands of the Arkwrights until 1809 and that two years later it was converted into a worsted mill.

The cotton trade was beginning its extraordinary period of expansion, more rapid than that of any other industry of the time. After the depressed year of 1779 it leapt ahead in spite of the American War. The net import of raw cotton between 1776 and 1781 had been about 6,000,000 lb. a year; in 1782–4 it was nearly double; in 1785–8 more than treble that figure. One effect of the boom in cotton twist, whether made on the water-frame or from jenny yarns, was to give a strong impetus to the building of factories, large and small. Both spinning systems rested on the use of the carding engine. Arkwright's water-frame was important but it was not the dominant form. The apologist for the displaced hand-spinners in 1780 said that the proprietors of the (Arkwright) 'patent machines' had erected them 'to the number of fifteen or twenty, in the several counties of Lancashire, Derbyshire, Yorkshire, Nottingham- shire, Denbighshire and Cheshire'.[1] This was probably not an over-estimate. But the small carding factory, which prepared cotton for home spinning on jenny or wheel, and the small jenny factories (with carding machines, the larger jennies and twisting machines) was a commoner type. It was these that were spreading rapidly over Lancashire and the adjoining counties and were defying Arkwright's carding patent rights such as they were. With their doubling and twisting machines they were formidable rivals.[2]

The best contemporary impression is that by the spinners' apologist, Ralph Mather, who in 1780 described the effect of the new factories and machines on hand labour. It is grossly overdone because the effect of the machines was greatly to in- crease the demand for labour, even if the hand-spinners were for a time hard-hit. He describes the two types of spinning:

These [Arkwright] Machines at the time of their first erection were not so detrimental to the laborious manufacturer, because one or two only of them was then built, and trade at the time every day increasing, and the Cotton exportations very large.

But since the year 1774 our exportations having very considerably abated, and the demands in the Cotton branch not being half so great, together with the rapid increase of the number of these

---

[1] *An Impartial Representation of the Case of the Poor Cotton Spinners in Lanca- shire* (1780), 2.
[2] Wadsworth and Mann, op. cit., 492–4.

Machines, which require so few hands, and those only children, with the assistance of an overlooker . . . and performing upon a moderate calculation, with the attention of a child, as much work as would, and did upon an average, employ ten grown up persons: and the other Cotton dealers, who had no share in these Patents nor in the divers erections made by the patentees, having found out Engines for Carding by water, horses or hand, which, with the labour and care of one or two persons, will perform as much work as would have employed and provided bread for eight or twelve; and also other inventions, to wit, Jennies for Spinning with one hundred or two hundred spindles, or more, going all at once, and requiring but one person to manage them: (one of which spindles was the old and usual instrument by which every poor woman obtained her bread) and likewise Doubling, Twisting, and Winding Mills, performing all these in one Machine at once, with the care of one person, and even that a child, which would have employed and found subsistence for eight or ten grown people: and these Engines (Mills or Machines) not being under the description of the Patent Machines for Carding, Roving, Spinning, &c. and therefore vesting no right in the patentees to sue the erectors for damages, has caused them to increase with such rapidity, that many are built in every town, village, and hamlet in Lancashire, and the circumscribing counties.[1]

It took some hardihood to attempt to stem this tide. In February, 1781, Arkwright opened an offensive. Three spinners who had infringed his carding patent submitted.[2] The Lancashire manufacturers organized resistance and decided to support any whom Arkwright attacked. In June he launched proceedings against nine but lost the first case that came to trial in the Court of King's Bench. It was against a small spinner at Halsall, near Ormskirk, Colonel Mordaunt.[3]

The consequence of defeat was that the trade was thrown open; the carding patent had been invalidated; the spinning patent would last only until July, 1783. If he was to retain a

[1] *Impartial Representation*, 2–3.
[2] John Middleton of Tideswell, Henry Marsland of Bullock Smithy (near Stockport), and Daniel Lees of Oldham (*Manch. Mercury*, Feb. 13, 20, 1781).
[3] Charles Lewis Mordaunt of Halsall Hall had retired from the Guards in 1765. In a letter to the Duke of Rutland in June, 1782, he wrote of 'our little work at Halsall': 'We have 600 spindles complete with all their appendages—our powers calculated to 1,300—an employment for about 160 poor children and women' (*Hist. MSS. Comm. Rutland MSS.*, iii (1894), 58).

monopolist advantage Arkwright had to fight hard. He took his defeat badly. He swore, Matthew Boulton reported, that the factory he was building in Manchester 'shall never be worked & will sooner let it for Barricks for Soldiers'; he 'swears he will take the Cotton Spinning abroad, & that he will ruin those Manchester rascals he has been the making of. It is agreed by all who know him that he is a Tyrant and more absolute than a Bashaw, & tis thought that his disappointment will kill him. If he had been a man of sense and reason he would not have lost his patent.'[1]

Arkwright now turned to other means. He had before him James Watt's success in 1775 in getting his patent of 1769 prolonged for twenty-five years by a special Act of Parliament, and Arkwright thought his claim fully as important as Watt's. The *Case* he caused to be drawn up in 1782 has to be read as special pleading. His plea about his services to mankind, the amount of money his inventions had cost him, and the wickedness of the Lancashire manufacturers was preliminary to an approach to Parliament. This was begun in a petition of February 6, 1782,[2] which asked for an act to consolidate his patents and extend the term of that of 1769 to 1789, that of the lost second patent. He was strongly opposed by the trade; as the merchants and traders of Liverpool said, he had 'realised such a Fortune as every unprejudiced Person must allow to be an ample compensation for the most happy Efforts of Genius'.[3] He failed to get parliamentary support. The Manchester Committee for the Protection and Encouragement of Trade boasted that it had frustrated his efforts.[4] Arkwright was physically threatened. He published an 'incendiary' letter he had received and offered a hundred guineas for the identification of the writer and fifty guineas to the person who posted it if he would tell who gave it to him. The letter ran:[5]

Man. 28th Nov. 1782.

Sir,

I am very sorry to hear that you still do all you can to distress the trade of Manr: after you had lost the Cause in London this town

---

[1] Boulton to Watt, Aug. 7, 1781 (Smiles, *Boulton and Watt* (1865), 302).
[2] *C.J.*, xxxviii, 687.
[3] Ibid., 882.
[4] *Manchester Mercury*, Dec. 31, 1782.   [5] Ibid.

thought you would then have been easy the remainder of your Time in the patent out. but you still keep doing all you can and not only that but you have been heard to say that you was determin'd to ruin every person that enter'd into that Business, the purport of this is to advise you that if you d'not withdraw all your prosecutions before Dec. is out I am determin'd to lay in wait for you either in this town Nottingham or wherever I most likely to find you. I will ashure shute you as your name is what it is dam you do you think the town must be ruled by such a Barber as you. Take notice if you are in town on Saturday next I will make an end of you meet you wherever I can. I am not yours, but a friend of the town of Manchester.

Arkwright was not deterred. With the prospect of the expiry in July of the 1769 patent he made another attempt. In February, 1783, he again approached Parliament and the Manchester Committee again roused its members and called for their 'timely Assistance . . . to prevent its success'.[1] A counter-petition was opened in Manchester[2] but again Arkwright was defeated.

His business expansion went on. Thus at the end of 1783 he was financing Samuel Oldknow in his newly started muslin manufacture—an outlet for yarn,[3] and in 1784 his Scottish projects were beginning. In October he was fêted at Glasgow, given a dinner, and made an honorary burgess and guild brother.[4] Six weeks later 'a Deputation of the Magistrate and Senate of the City of Perth' waited on him and presented him with the freedom of the city.[5] Manchester was justified in being uneasy. The story goes that after the Glasgow dinner David Dale took Arkwright up the Clyde valley and exhibited the utility of the Falls of Clyde; from that visit came the New Lanark mills, which began to be built in April, 1785, and were spinning in March, 1786.[6] In 1785 the Buchanans started the Deanston factory in Perthshire; and in 1786 David Dale and Claud Alexander that at Catrine in Ayrshire.[7]

[1] Ibid., Feb. 11, 1783.   [2] Ibid., Feb. 25, 1783.
[3] Unwin, op. cit., 16–17.
[4] Eyre-Todd, *Hist. of Glasgow*, iii (1934), 346.
[5] *Derby Mercury*, Nov. 18, 1784.
[6] *O.S.A.* (1795), xv, 46; Stewart, *Curiosities of Glasgow Citizenship* (1881), 51.
[7] Stewart, op. cit., 182.

II. SUCCESS AND DEFEAT

For three and a half years the trade was thrown open and there was feverish growth. A contemporary estimate was that in the period more than £150,000 was spent in erecting cotton mills.[1] But Arkwright remained unappeased, although one would assume that he was making money from the competitive advantage of his mills. He tried again for a legal remedy. Opinion at the time was that 'the very great preparations making in Scotland by Mr. Arkwright, joined by several of the most Conspicuous in the Landed and Commercial Interests of that Kingdom . . . has induced him to revive the supposed Claim'.[2] In February, 1785, he took up again his claim to the 1775 patent. The choice of defendant was significant. It was his nearest Derbyshire neighbour, Peter Nightingale of Lea, whose factory was less than two miles from Cromford, and with whom he had landed transactions. Though the case was fought out in the Court of Common Pleas, the case against Arkwright was not well marshalled; the view at the time that the action was in some sense collusive may have something in it. At any rate Arkwright won it.[3]

The cotton industry, which just then had been showing a good deal of cohesion and collective organization in its resistance to the 'fustian tax' and the Irish Resolutions,[4] turned to mobilize itself against Arkwright. It got the case reopened by a writ of *scire facias* and worked up the evidence against Arkwright.[5] In July, 1785, after a great display of hostile witnesses, Arkwright lost. He made an attempt to get the case reopened but in November was finally crushed.[6]

This is an often told story[7] on which, unfortunately, we can

---

[1] *Manchester Mercury*, Feb. 22, 1785.
[2] Ibid.
[3] Ibid., Mar. 1, 1785; *Richard Arkwright* versus *Peter Nightingale* (Court of Common Pleas, Feb. 17, 1785).
[4] Cf. Daniels, *The Early English Cotton Industry* (1920), 103–4; Witt Bowden, *Industrial Society in England towards the End of the Eighteenth Century* (1925), 178.
[5] The manufacturers employed Charles Taylor, later secretary of the Society of Arts.
[6] Espinasse, *Lancashire Worthies* (1874), 447–8.
[7] See especially Daniels, op. cit., ch. iv; Wadsworth and Mann, op. cit., ch. xxiii; and Espinasse, op. cit., ch. xiii.

offer little that is new. Arkwright's defeat was looked at in two lights. To Lancashire it seemed like deliverance from an oppressor. The trade had worked itself up into a passion. Arkwright was trying to overthrow the industry, little men and big, for his claim affected almost everybody who did carding. If he won, it was said, the trade would migrate to Ireland and Scotland, where the machines were working without restriction, and abroad. And the *Manchester Mercury* published dark hints from Glasgow about 'the great Works that are now preparing for spinning Cotton' in which Arkwright was interested.[1] There was evidently some point in his reported gibe that 'he would find a *razor* in Scotland to *shave* Manchester'.[2]

On the other side were the sympathetic views of those interested in patents of their own, like James Watt and Josiah Wedgwood. Arkwright's defeat seemed to strike at their interests. As Watt wrote to Boulton after the overthrow of 1781, 'I fear for our own'; 'I fear we shall be served with the same sauce *for the good of the public!*'[3] Watt gave evidence for Arkwright in both his trials of 1785 and after his defeat Arkwright seems to have called a meeting of patent holders which Wedgwood attended. This had a curious sequel. Watt and Arkwright got together and drew up the 'heads of a bill' for the drastic amendment of the patent law which would have got over the necessity for the public disclosure of a detailed specification.[4]

Josiah Wedgwood was of much the same view and he has left an account of a remarkable scheme that was occupying Arkwright's mind in the closing months of 1785 and early 1786. It was nothing less than that of a statutory monopoly of wool spinning. Wedgwood wrote in his Common Place Book:

The first time of meeting Mr. Arkwright was in London, on the business of the Irish propositions; and after he had lost his patent trial I attended a meeting of patent-holders at his lodgings. Upon my mentioning to Sir Joseph Banks some conversation which I had

---

[1] March 1, 1785. The company was said to consist of Arkwright, 'Mr. Dempster (Member for Dundee) and several of the most eminent Merchants'.

[2] Baines, op. cit., 193.

[3] Smiles, op. cit., 303.

[4] Roll, *An Early Experiment in Industrial Organisation* (1930), 146, 284–6, where the text is printed. The MS. is in Watt's handwriting with Arkwright's corrections and additions.

had with this remarkable man, Sir Joseph was desirous of an interview with him, and requested I would bring him to his house; but this I could not accomplish.

In the beginning of September following [1785] being at Matlock for two or three weeks, I had frequent opportunities of conversation with Mr. Arkwright and found him a very sensible intelligent man, but his views confined chiefly to mechanics. He was much disgusted with the treatment he had met with in his trial; and threatened, as they *would* have his machinery made public, to publish descriptions and copper plates of all the parts, that it might be known to foreign nations as well as our own. I strongly dissuaded him from such a step, representing how unjust it would be, that a whole nation should suffer for the imprudent conduct of a few, for his opponents were few indeed in comparison with the great body of people who would be benefited by having his admirable inventions confined to ourselves.

I afterwards found an opportunity of bringing Sir Joseph Banks & Mr. Arkwright together; when I drew up the [following] proposals. Mr. Arkwright agreed to prepare machinery for making an experiment to ascertain the practicability of spinning wool on his plan; and Sir Joseph agreed to consult his friends in the mean time relative to the obtaining of the Act of Parliament . . . alluded to.

Proposed
That Mr. Arkwright should engage to spin wool by machinery, at certain prices hereafter to be agreed upon.

To make the machinery known when it is completed, and to instruct anyone in the use of it, upon certain conditions contained in an Act of Parliament to be made upon this subject.

To accomplish the machinery, & complete the art for this purpose in ——years after the passing of the said Act.

In consideration of the above engagements on the part of Mr. Arkwright the legislature shall be petitioned to pass an Act of Parliament to secure to Mr. A. his heirs &c. the sole spinning of wool in Great Britain by machinery, for the space of —— years after passing the said Act.

A clause to be inserted in the said Act to give compensation to such persons as have at this time mills or machines employed in spinning wool, they giving up all right or claim to spin wool by machinery, otherwise than as it is provided for by the said Act.

To obviate any objection which may be made, viz. that this Act will preclude any better method of spinning wool, which may possibly be invented during the time of the said Act,

It is proposed to name a committee of mechanics to decide upon the originality and merit of such invention or inventions.

In case of death of any of the committee, the survivors to nominate others in their stead.

Mr. Arkwright engages further to spin wool 50 per cent cheaper than it is now spun, which 50 per cent will be an entire gain to the public;—and so much cheaper still, that he will himself be content with one half of the surplus profit above the 50 per cent, the other half to belong to the person whom he instructs in the business.

There will be a further advantage to the public from this invention, that one pound of wool will go as far as two pounds do now, on account of the greater fineness of the thread;—And that in virtue of this fineness, and evenness, new species of cloth will be produced, by which the wear and consumption of woollen cloths will be increased, and we shall regain the Levant, Turkey and other foreign markets which we have lost on account of the French spinning a finer species of woollen cloth than we now do.[1]

On February 21, 1786, Wedgwood wrote to Arkwright from London:

Having had the pleasure of bringing Sr. Joseph Banks and you together the last summer at Matlock upon the subject of spinning wool by machinery, Sr. Joseph told me the other day that he had taken a good deal of pains to prepare matters on his part, & would gladly proceed, but wished to know if you had taken any steps in preparing machinery &c. that he might have something certain to lay before his parliamentary friends. Being my self fully convinced that this is a subject of the first magnitude I should be happy to contribute any thing in my power towards promoting so great & usefull a work.[2]

Whether Arkwright got far with his experiments we do not know. Certainly the water-frame came to be applied to worsted spinning[3] (as he had suggested in 1772), but not to wool, which kept to hand-worked jennies until the mule came in slowly

[1] Wedgwood's Common Place Book, 325-6 (Etruria Museum).

[2] *Correspondence of Josiah Wedgwood, 1781-94*, ed. Farrer (1906), 35. Sir Joseph Banks had been President of the Royal Society since 1778; he had a house near Ashover, Derbyshire, though possibly not at this time.

[3] The first mill was at Dolphinholme, on the Wyre (1784), which had an unsuccessful start and a poor product; the second was at Addingham, near Ilkley (1787). Others did not come until the 1790s. (James, *Hist. of the Worsted Manufacture* (1857), 327-8).

twenty years later and was not widely adopted until it became self-acting.[1]

The scheme, even if the driving force were Wedgwood's, reflects Arkwright's abounding confidence in himself and also his monopolizing propensities. Of these Matthew Boulton wrote sharply a few weeks later when discussing a patent that touched him and Watt:

> Tyranny & an improper exercise of power will not do in this country . . . If he [Arkwright] had been a more civilised being & had understood mankind better he would now have enjoyed his patent. Hence let us learn wisdom by other men's ills.[2]

And it may be suspected that had Arkwright been able to apply mechanical spinning to wool he would have found in York-shire just as many obstinate individualists to oppose him as he did in Lancashire.[3]

The contemporary judgments on Arkwright were curiously mixed. Wedgwood's was more favourable than most. He was admired for his achievement, both as the architect of a great personal fortune and as one who opened up new riches for the country; he was feared for his aims. Edward Baines with his 'private source' ('by no means unfavourably disposed to Sir Richard') described how 'so unbounded was his confidence in the success of his machinery, and in the national wealth to be produced by it, that he would make light of discussions on taxation and say that *he* would pay the national debt!' And he was credited with the idea of 'buying up all the cotton in the world, in order to make an enormous profit by the mono-poly'. His 'judicious friends' thought he died none too soon.[4] His knighthood was given, like that of Jane Austen's Sir William Lucas, when he presented a loyal address. It was on George III's escape from assassination and, unusual for a man in trade, Arkwright was then High Sheriff of Derbyshire. He certainly performed the office with ostentation. His thirty javelin men were 'dressed in the richest Liveries ever seen on such an occasion'; during the assize he provided 'a plentiful

---

[1] Crump, op. cit., 24–5.
[2] March 15, 1786 (Dickinson, op. cit., 128–9).
[3] Cf. Professor Ashton's suggestive comments on the effects of Watt's and Arkwright's patents on enterprise (*The Eighteenth Century*, 107).
[4] Baines, op. cit., 196.

Table, with the choicest Wines'; and his coach with its grey horses was 'very elegant and fashionable'.[1] There was something flamboyant about him. Apart from Samuel Touchet on the Westminster stage fifteen years before, no Lancashire cotton man had yet cut such a dash. He was almost the first of his tribe.

A few years after Arkwright's death, William Nicholson, who had worked with Wedgwood and been secretary of the Chamber of Manufacturers, and was then a patent agent, made inquiries for a biography. He could not decide whether Arkwright was a 'superior genius' and a remarkable inventor or a 'cunning schemer and collector of other men's inventions, supporting them by borrowed capital and never afterwards feeling or showing any emotion of gratitude to the one or the other'.[2] Contemporaries made much of the priorities and of how much of other men's ideas Arkwright appropriated. That was natural in view of the patent trials but it belongs to the history of invention and is only incidental to his place in the history of industry. However they are looked at, the cotton factories of Arkwright and his partners and licensees in the late 70s and 80s were remarkable pieces of industrial organization which gave immense impetus to the factory system and the use of water power, and to the steam power that was pressing on rapidly behind.

The squire built his castle not far from his works. He had bought most of the land round Cromford, including the manor. He spent £3000 in clearing away a huge rock from the site of the house, roads had to be blasted, gardens laid out, trees planted, and a 'prospect' designed.[3] Yet John Byng, who looked over Willersley Castle while it was being built in 1790, and who thought he knew something of houses (and disliked manufacturers), was scathing:

> The inside is now finishing; and it is really, within, and without, an effort of inconvenient ill taste; built so high as to overlook every beauty, and to catch every wind; the approach is dangerous; the ceilings are of gew-gaw fret work; the small circular stair-case, like some in the new built houses of Marybone, is so dark and narrow, that people cannot pass each other; I ask'd a workman if there was a library? Yes, answer'd he, at the foot of the stairs. Its dimensions

---

[1] *Manch. Mercury*, March 27, 1787.   [2] Aikin and Enfield, op. cit., 390.
[3] Britton and Brayley, op. cit., 517, 521–2.

are 15 feet square; (a small counting house;) and having the perpendicular lime stone rock within 4 yards, it is too dark to read and write in without a candle! There is likewise a music room; this is upstairs, is 18 feet square, and will have a large organ in it: what a scheme! What confinement! At Clapham they can produce nothing equal to this, where ground is sold by the yard.[1]

The architect was William Thomas of London. Before it was occupied it was damaged by fire but 'most of the elegant furniture was preserved'.[2] A modern judgment on its external appearance is less severe.[3] Jedediah was less ambitious; he was not enamoured of the 'gothick'. He built his house at Milford in the main street, a neat and dignified building.

Strutt was of a different and less aggressive temperament than Arkwright which may suggest one reason why their partnership came to be dissolved. There was, however, no personal breach. The two families, Arkwright's at Cromford, Strutt's at Milford and Derby, continued on close terms and their children, who had grown up together, remained in the friendliest association.[4] The cash book of Strutts and Woollat at Derby and the London Ledger show numerous services rendered to the Arkwrights, as, for example:

1782   £   s. d.

April 18. By Cash for Carriage of a Parcel on Acct of Richd
    Arkwright & Co   2   6
May 14. By Cash to J.S. for a Bell on Acct of Richd Arkwright
    & Co. Wirksworth   6 10   0
July 31. By Cash to Thos. Moore for the entertainment of some
    boys on Acct of Richd Arkwright & Co.   5   6
Sept. 25. By Cash for a looking-Glass & case on Acct of Richd
    Arkwright Jr.   1   6   0

1783

Feb. 8. By Cash for Cheese on Acct of Richd Arkwright Jr.   4   7   3

1785

May 13. By Cash for carriage of Cyder on Acct of Richard
    Arkwright   1   7   5

On the side of another of Arkwright's partners, John Smalley, resentment smouldered. He had been his first partner at

---

[1] Byng, *The Torrington Diaries*, ed. Andrews, (1954), 252.
[2] *Derby Mercury*, Aug. 11, 1791.
[3] Pevsner, *The Buildings of Britain, Derbyshire* (1953), 105.
[4] See next chapter.

Preston and at Nottingham and was at Cromford in the early years. By 1777 they had parted company and Smalley set up a three-storeyed spinning factory at Holywell, Flintshire, where he died in 1782. Thomas Pennant in 1796 spoke of his being at Cromford 'unhappily within the baneful influence of a tyrant rival, which forced him to seek the protection of S. Wenefrede [Holywell], under which he prospered'.[1] Possibly Arkwright had settled his debt to him by a grant of spindles. The large new mills, built in 1783 and 1785 by Smalley's son, were also on the Arkwright principle and, in 1795 at any rate, were staffed by apprentice children.[2]

There is very little evidence on the all-important subject of the financial handling of the Arkwright patents. On the figures in Strutt's evidence to the Commons in 1774 and in Arkwright's *Case*, the Nottingham and Cromford period (to 1774) would account for £12,000 to £13,000; the seven following years, which included Belper, Milford and Birkacre, and the Cromford extensions, brought the total to £30,000. Against this had to be set the losses at Birkacre and Nottingham of £5,000 to £6,000.

On the royalties paid under licence to use the Arkwright machines we have only the statement of the spinners' apologist of 1780 (that the machines when sold were erected 'at the rate of 7000 l. for every 1000 spindles')[3] and an interesting letter from Thomas Walshman to Strutt in July, 1786, a year after Arkwright's loss of his patent. This refers to the Low Mill at Keighley[4], which is said to have begun working in 1780, and in which two brothers Clayton were in partnership with Walshman. (Walshman had been a Birkacre partner.) Clearly Strutt still had an interest with Arkwright in the revenues from the patent. The reference to 'overspinning' suggests that an output restriction was embodied in the licence.

---

[1] *Hist. of the Parishes of Whiteford and Holywell* (1796), 214.
[2] Dodd, *The Industrial Revolution in North Wales* (1933), 284-5.
[3] *Impartial Representation*, 2.
[4] The firm is said to have sent operatives to Cromford to be trained (Holmes, *Keighley, Past and Present* (1858), 108). The Keighley firm had an offshoot at Langcliffe, near Settle, begun in 1784, in which the partners were R. Walshman and George and William Clayton (the last married Walshman's sister). (Brayshaw and Robinson, *Hist. of the Ancient Parish of Giggleswick* (1932), 209.)

Preston 4th July 1786

Sirs,

Mr Claytons & myself have been expecting Mr Arkwright in Manchester ever since last Feby in order that we might finally settle the paymts due on account of the priveledge granted to us under the Patents. On the 25 ulto we heard of his being there and on ye 27th waited upon him—we mentioned to him our original agreement being for 4200£ and Interest which was to be paid by installments, and that those payments have been punctualy observed by us, except the last, and the reason that was not paid at the time, was we wished to see him in person & hoped some part of the payments left behind wou'd be given up, as from the loss of the Roving Patent in 1781 all the country became Spinners as soon as ever they cou'd get machinery, to the great disadvantage of those who had purchased under you, On which account we cou'd not think the Patent of the *same value* as if it had then been established &. therefore hoped some concession wou'd be made—

After talking awhile on these things, we paid Mr. Arkwright the money that was due in February last 660£ which makes the sums in all paid 4800£ which you will find is the full amount of Principal and all Interest— Now in this sum there was 600£ charged to us &. paid by us for overspinning, which we then thought exceeding hard & did not expect wou'd have been demanded as Mr Arkwright after the loss of his Patent, recommended to us, to do as much as we cou'd—that he wou'd be easy as to the payment for it—and that we might settle at ye last—

We have performed every part of our engagement in every instance & I am sorry it has not been in your powers to perform yours on which account the only request we make is yt that 600£ for overspinning be allowed us, Mr Arkwright has kindly promised to give up His part of it, if you will give up Yours &. we most cordaly hope from the equity of Your heart, that you will not have any objection—

I shall be very glad to receive your answer as soon as convenient &. am with Compts to all Your family Sir.

Your most huble Servant
T. Walshman.

Though Arkwright had a reputation for parsimony his wealth was notorious. It is unfortunate that we have not the material with which to trace in detail his investment of his capital—his acquisition of landed property, his interests in trade (of which the loans to Oldknow are an example) and his personal loans, like those to Georgiana, Duchess of Devonshire: Georgiana's gambling debts were considerable and had been contracted without her husband's knowledge. He had come to her rescue but she had not made a full disclosure to him. In 1787 she took advantage of an offer by Thomas Coutts, the banker to the royal family who, about the same time, had offered his financial support to Charles James Fox. She had also borrowed about £5000 from Arkwright, which, like the loans from Coutts, was kept a secret. Arkwright wrote to her on January 21, 1788:[1]

Not having received from your Grace as soon as I had reason, from the letter which I had the honour to receive on the 29th of last month, to expect I should, I flattered myself with the hope that everything had turned out as you wished, I am sincerely sorry to find I was mistaken. Before I can possibly have the money paid into Drummonds' hands I must beg to be informed whether the two Dfts you allude to of the Duke's acceptance are at a longer date than the one you have already sent; for if they are not payable in three months, at the latest, it will not be in my power to advance the money. I must also request your Grace will say whether I *may rely* upon the other notes being all regularly paid, as they become due respectively. From the statement annexed you will observe that some of them will fall due very soon. Mr Bennet will return on Tuesday, or Wednesday, but as he may probably be too late for the post that evening, and as I do not, for reasons I have before mentioned, wish him to call here, you will be pleased to desire your answer may be left at the Greyhound public room in Cromford; I will send for it from thence, and by that means I shall be enabled to write to London by that night's post, if I find it necessary, and it will prevent, what I have continously guarded against—suspicion.

Nothing has dropt from me to any person living that could lead to suspect what your Grace wished to remain a secret. I must beg you will at all times be assured of my best wishes.

200£	due	20 February
406·3	,,	1 March
1021	,,	25 March
1033	,,	22 June
1579	,,	25 September

---

[1] Bessborough (ed.), *Extracts from the Correspondence of Georgiana, Duchess of Devonshire* (1955), 125.

The principal was still owing in 1801 when Georgiana was in her last illness, but interest was being met and she was in hopes of early repayment. She wrote very warmly of Richard Arkwright's forbearance.[1]

Arkwright's wealth naturally created envy in the trade. The 'poor cotton spinners' in 1780[2] had already drawn a class-conscious contrast. One man

within the small space of ten years, from being a poor man not worth £5, now keeps his carriage and servants, is become a Lord of a Manor, and has purchased an estate of £20,000; while thousands of women, when they can get work, must make a long day to card, spin, and reel 5040 yards of cotton, and for this they have *four-pence or five-pence and no more.*

And the *Manchester Mercury* in 1785, attacking his monopoly, said he had 'already received by far, greater Emoluments than any Individual or any united Body of Discoverers ever did'.[3] But whatever the trade felt about him it recognised him as its leader. His name headed the trade movements, as in the fight against the East India Company in 1788, and when, in the dark days of that year the bill-holders of the ill-fated firm of Livesey, Hargreaves and Co. met to survey the wreck, Arkwright was voted to the chair.[3] (That failure, incidentally, hit him hard. Among the many houses it brought down was that of Gibson and Johnson, discount bankers, one of their London agents, with whom the Arkwrights and Strutts also dealt. In the bankruptcy proceedings Sir Richard Arkwright proved a debt against Gibson and Johnson of £32,534, his son one of £9163, and the Strutts one of £5807.)[5]

When Arkwright died, in 1792, at the age of 59, he left, as the *Gentleman's Magazine* put it, 'manufactories the income of

---

[1] Bessborough, op. cit., 244. Arkwright's notes were small in comparison with Coutts's £16,000. In 1790 the Duchess made the disclosure of her debts to her husband; he was extremely angry at his simultaneous discovery that she was pregnant by the second Earl Grey and exiled her to the Continent for twelve months.

[2] *Impartial Representation*, 5.

[3] March 1, 1785.

[4] *Manchester Mercury*, May 13, 1788.

[5] Pressnell, *Country Banking in the Industrial Revolution* (1956), 455. We are indebted to Dr. Pressnell for the debt figures from the bankruptcy papers.

which is greater than that of most German principalities. . . . His real and personal property is estimated at little short of half a million'.[1]

III. THE DERBYSHIRE COTTON MILLS

The cotton mills of the Derwent valley became one of the wonders of the Peak. The English seaside resort was then only just developing and the spas of Derbyshire were greatly favoured by tourists. The visitor to Buxton or Matlock would vary his shudders at Poole's Cavern or High Tor with headshaking or admiration over Arkwright's mills. He might exclaim with John Byng in 1790 that to the tourist[2] 'these vales have lost all their beauties; the rural cot has given place to the lofty red mill, and the grand houses of overseers; the stream perverted from its course by sluices, and aqueducts, will no longer ripple and cascade.'

Or he might rise to Erasmus Darwin's lyrical heights.[3] He might be stirred by the romantic sight of the blazing lights of the mills at night; Byng admitted it to be 'most luminously beautiful'. Benevolence might be touched by the sight of crowds of young children all saving the poor rates by earning their own living; by the chapels and Sunday schools provided for the spiritual welfare and the market and inn for the temporal support of the new community. For Cromford and Belper, like New Lanark and Mellor after them, were new communities, and in their stone and brick-built mills and cottages not uncomely. They were not precisely a new phenomenon. Ironmasters and coalowners had had to provide in some fashion for their labour in remote parts of the country; landowners had had their model villages. But the patriarchal factory village

---

[1] 1792, 770–1. He left his widow (who was to survive him by nineteen years) £500 a year; his daughter Susannah (Mrs. Hurt) £100,000 India Stock, to be divided on her death among her children; £5,000 to each of her children and to those of his son; £100 to each of his sisters and £50 to each of his nephews and nieces; £50 and £30 a year to his nephew Mr. Malyn; the remainder of his property to his son Richard, desiring him to complete in a proper manner the mansion (Willersley Castle) he had begun to build. His executors were his son, Richard, and Jedediah's eldest son, William (Will at Somerset House).

[2] Byng, op. cit., 251.

[3] The Botanic Garden (1792).

made an appeal to the sense of order and the benevolent feudalism dear to a generation that was being touched by the discipline of the evangelical revival. They were, it is easy to forget today, a deliberate creation, without assistance from the State or local authority and with no public services. The factory, the weirs and dams, the machine-shop, the houses, the roads and bridges, the inn, the truck-shop, the church and chapel, the manager's mansion—all were devised by and grew up under the owner's eye. Most of the work was done by direct labour, just as was the machine-building in the mechanics' shop. The labour had to be attracted and held. The idealized community which Robert Owen thought he had invented at New Lanark was not much different from those at Cromford and Belper that had preceded it.

The Derbyshire factories were the first model for the cotton industry. 'We all looked up to him,' said the first Sir Robert Peel of Arkwright, 'and imitated his mode of building.' Even, it would seem, in its defects. When, before the Commons Committee of 1816, Peel was reminded of his brush with the doctors in 1784 over the epidemic at his Radcliffe factory, he said: 'At that time the profits arising from the machinery of Sir Richard Arkwright were so considerable, that it frequently happened . . . that the machinery was employed the whole four-and-twenty hours' (that, of course, was on two shifts). And if the ventilation was not adequate it had been good enough for Arkwright; 'our buildings were copied from the models of his works'. Ventilation or not, the effect was beneficent; Arkwright, said Peel, was 'a man who has done more honour to the country than any man I know, not excepting our great military characters'.[1]

Night and day working was characteristic of the first thirty years of the Arkwright factory system. Medical and philanthropic opinion might be against it[2] but the hours of work for the children were actually less than they were to become under the single-shift system before its statutory regulation. Archibald Buchanan, the big Scottish spinner, who learnt his trade at Cromford in 1783, said the factory was kept going night and

---

[1] *Minutes of Evidence taken before the Select Committee of the Children employed in the Manufactories of the United Kingdom* (1816), 134, 139, 141.
[2] Cf. Hutchins and Harrison, *Hist. of Factory Legislation* (1903), 8–13, 18.

day: 'The spinning went on at night; the preparation [i.e. carding, roving, etc.] was made in the day.'[1] This suggests a shortage of labour or of power. In both series of processes children were employed. It was a twelve-hour day with (on the day shift at least) a break of an hour for dinner. William Bray, the first tourist to note the Cromford mill (he passed by in 1776 or 1777) said it employed 'about 200 persons, chiefly children', who worked 'by turns, night and day'. Another mill, 'as large as the first, is building here, new houses are rising round it, and everything wears the face of industry and cheerfulness'.[2]

It certainly was not all drabness. Indeed, Arkwright contrived a public spectacle. In September there was the annual festival of 'candlelighting' when, as in 1776, about 500 workmen and children, led by a band and a boy working in a weaver's loom, paraded from the mills round the village, where they were watched by 'an amazing Concourse of People.' Upon returning to the mills they were given buns, ale, nuts, and fruit, and the evening ended with music and dancing. The same day Arkwright and Company gave a feast to over 200 workers who, during the summer, had erected another large cotton mill, 120 feet long and seven storeys high. They were 'regaled with a large Quantity of Strong Beer, &c., yet the Day was spent with the greatest Harmony imaginable'.[3] Again, in 1778, 'according to annual Custom', the workpeople were entertained by the owners. A song, to the tune of 'Roast Beef of Old England', was rendered 'in full Chorus amongst Thousands of Spectators from Matlock Bath and the neighbouring Towns. . . . The Evening was concluded by a Ball, which Mr. Arkwright gave at his own House, to the neighbouring Ladies and Gentlemen, at which the Company was very numerous and brilliant.'[4]

The song hit off neatly, if crudely, the essence of the country factory—the all-providing 'master', the operatives ranged in order, and the regular wages:

[1] *1816 Committee*, 8.
[2] *Sketch of a Tour into Derbyshire and Yorkshire (1778)*, 119; preface dated Nov. 1777.
[3] *Derby Mercury*, Sept. 19, 1776.
[4] Ibid., Sept. 25, 1778.

Tune: Roast Beef of Old England

Ye num'rous Assembly that make up this Throng,
Spare your Mirth for a Moment, and list to my Song,
The Bounties let's sing, that our Master belong,
At the Cotton Mills now at Cromford,
The famous renown'd Cotton Mills,

Our number we count seven Hundred or more,
All cloathed and fed from his bountiful Store,
Then Envy don't flout us, nor say any's poor, &c.

Ye know we all ranged in Order have been,
Such a Sight in all Europe sure never was seen,
While Thousands did view us to complete the Scene, &c.

Likewise for to make our Procession more grand,
We were led in the Front by a Musical Band,
Who were paid from the Fund of that bountiful Hand, &c.

Ye Hungry and Naked, all hither repair,
No longer in Want don't remain in Despair,
You'll meet with Employment, and each get a Share, &c.

Ye Crafts and Mechanics, if ye will draw nigh,
No longer ye need to lack an Employ,
And each duly paid, which is a great Joy, &c.

To our noble Master, a Bumper then fill,
The matchless Inventor of this Cotton Mill,
Each toss off his Glass with a hearty Good-will,
With a Huzza for the Mills now at Cromford
All join with a jovial Huzza.

The Arkwright partners were no strangers to the arts of
industrial incentive. That entertaining physician Sylas Neville,
who visited Cromford in October, 1781, noted that Arkwright
'by his conduct appears to be a man of great understanding &
to know the way of making his people do their best. He not only
distributes pecuniary rewards, but gives distinguishing dresses
to the most deserving of both sexes, which excites great emula-
tion.[1] He also gives two Balls at the Greyhound to the workmen
& their wives & families with a weeks jubilee at the time of

---

[1] Lewis Paul at his Northampton factory had promoted rivalry by the
allurement of handkerchiefs (Wadsworth and Mann, op. cit., 437). Robert
Owen's 'silent monitor' was by comparison a horrible exhibition of
authoritarianism.

Belper North and West Mills (Reproduced from *A New Historical and Descriptive View of Derbyshire* by D. P. Davies, Belper, 1811)

each ball. This makes them industrious and sober all the rest of the year.'[1] Neville had presumably heard of the 'candle-lighting' festivities of a month before. Two years later the bonuses were lavish. Arkwright, said the *Derbv Mercury*, 'has generously given to 27 of his principal Workmen, Twenty-Seven fine Milch Cows, worth from 8*l* to 10*l* each, for the Service of their respective Families'.[2] In 1790, when Arkwright got his village a market, there was the same ingenuity. John Byng described how the landlord at the inn

has under his care a grand assortment of prizes, from Sr R. Ark-wright, to be given, at the years end, to such bakers, butchers, &c, as shall have best furnish'd the market: how this will be peaceably settled I cannot tell!! They consist of beds, presses, clocks, chairs, &c, and bespeak Sr Rd's prudence and cunning; for without ready provisions, his colony cou'd not prosper.

There was an authentic patriarchal flavour about the doggerel that was pasted on the inn door:

I

Come let us all here join in one,
And thank him for all favours done;
Let's thank him for all favours still
Which he hath done besides the mill.

2

Modistly drink liquor about,
And see whose health you can find out;
This will I chuse before the rest
Sr Richard Arkwright is the best.

3

A few more words I have to say
Success to Cromford's market day.

Byng was disturbed by the 'rustic revelry' of his inn: 'Solos, and in parts, and all kinds of chauntings, increasing with the beer, to an excess of bawling: but some of the voices I was obliged to hear, seem'd to possess much power.'[3] Of the similar inducements at that time at Belper we hear less but it too had

---

[1] Cozens-Hardy (ed.), *The Diary of Sylas Neville, 1767–1788* (1950), 279.
[2] July 24, 1783. [3] Op. cit., 252–4.

its breaks. In October, 1788, as good Whigs, if not Radicals, the Strutts celebrated the centenary of the Glorious Revolution, and at Belper 'amongst the provisions a Sheep was roasted whole; and several Barrels of Ale and other Liquors were drank, and the Day was spent with much Festivity'.[1]

Belper was ahead of Cromford in giving attention to the religious needs of the community. Strutt built a Unitarian chapel there in 1782, a solid stone building in Field Row,[2] and later one at Milford.[3]

A chapel to hold 300 had been built at Cromford in 1777. Next to it was a neat house—the partners' house—where Jedediah used to stay. The two were bought in 1784–5 by the evangelical chapel-owning Lady Glenorchy and passed out of the hands of the factory owners.[4] In any case Arkwright was an Anglican and before his death, had begun to build a church at Cromford (not completed until 1797). He bequeathed to its minister £50 a year 'for ever'.

After religion, education. In 1784 a remarkable wave of enthusiasm for Sunday schools spread over the country. It was the discovery of a cheap solvent of the twin problems of vice and ignorance. Few places in the Midlands and the North were untouched.[5] At Derby Jedediah Strutt responded in October, 1784,[6] and by February Arkwright had set up a school at Cromford; it 'already consists of two hundred children. Pleasing it is to the friends of humanity, when power like his is so happily united with the will to do good.'[7] Strutt at Belper followed in August:[8]

We hear from Belpar that Mr. Strutt has, (with a Liberality which does Honour to the human Heart) entirely at his own Expense, instituted a SUNDAY SCHOOL for the Benefit of ALL the Youth of both Sexes employed in his Cotton Mill at that Town; and provides them with all necessary Books, &c for learning to

---

[1] *Derby Mercury*, Oct. 30, 1788.
[2] Glover, op. cit., ii, 117.
[3] Ibid., ii, 326.
[4] Jones, *Life of . . . Lady Glenorchy* (1822), 477, 493.
[5] Wadsworth, 'The First Manchester Sunday Schools', *Bull. John Rylands Library*, xxxiii (1951), 302–5.
[6] *Derby Mercury*, Oct. 14, 1784. See also for local opinion on the schools the issues of Aug. 19, 1784 and Nov. 3, 1785.
[7] *Manchester Mercury*, Feb. 15, 1785.
[8] *Derby Mercury*, Aug. 25, 1785.

read and write. This School was opened on July 3, and 120 Scholars have already been admitted.—An Example worthy of Imitation by all whom Providence has blessed with Affluence. The Propriety of these Institutions, in Speculation, did not admit of a single Doubt; but since their Utility has been so amply demonstrated by Practice, it becomes the Duty of every thinking Person, in this Age of Refinement, Luxury, and Vice, to hold forth an assisting Hand, to stop the Tide of Immorality, which threatens speedily to Deluge 'The Land of Liberty'.

There was also a Sunday school at Milford.[1] The schools were, of course, the only means of education for the factory children. They worked twelve hours a day for six days a week and on the seventh had compulsory church and school. Joseph Farington described his visit to Cromford church in 1801:[2]

On each side [of the] Organ is a gallery in which about 50 Boys were seated. These children are employed in Mr. Arkwrights work in the week-days, and on Sundays attend a school where they receive education. They came to Chapel in regular order and looked healthy & well & were decently cloathed & clean. They were attended by an Old Man their School Master.—To this school girls also go for the same purpose, and alternately with the Boys go to Church the Boys on one Sunday—the girls on the next following.—Whichever are not at Chapel are at the School, to which they both go every Sunday both morning and afternoon. The whole plan appears to be such as to do Mr Arkwright great credit.

By this time the factory communities were well established. But the more one looks at the difficulties that had confronted Arkwright and Strutt in the 1770s and 1780s the greater their achievement appears. All the contemporary evidence (which Professor Redford has set out)[3] is of great reluctance to enter factories and submit to factory discipline and, in consequence, a migratory and often disreputable factory population. It was the harder problem because, though male labour was needed for supervision, for mill-building, for machine-making and upkeep, the bulk of the workers on the Arkwright spinning frames

[1] Before Samuel Slater, the founder of the American cotton industry and a Milford apprentice of Strutts, left England in 1789, a 'system of Sunday school instruction . . . had been for some time in full operation at all the mills of Messrs. Strutt and Arkwright' (White, *Memoir of Samuel Slater* (1836), 107).
[2] *The Farington Diary*, ed. Greig, i (1922), 314.
[3] Redford, *Labour Migration in England, 1800–50* (1926), 18–22.

were young children, while women and children were needed for 'picking' and beating the raw cotton to prepare it for the carding process. There were limits to the amount of adult labour that could be employed once a factory was in running order. Hence the branching out of the factory owner into the running of an estate and its subsidiary trades. The case of Samuel Oldknow has been fully described[1] but it is paralleled in the Arkwright and Strutt enterprises. Hence also the resort of owners of Arkwright's machinery to the use of pauper apprentices housed and fed by the employer.

There is no evidence that either Strutt or Arkwright took parish apprentices like Oldknow or the Gregs[2] though they may have taken individual apprentices from parish overseers. At Cromford Arkwright could draw on the families of the lead miners of the area, just as at Belper Strutt could draw on those of the nailers, a tough and rather demoralized lot of domestic workers who survived there until well on into the nineteenth century.[3] Today the English Sewing Cotton Company's mills at Belper, Milford and Matlock Bath draw their female labour in part from Derbyshire mining villages a dozen or so miles away, the workers coming in by bus. The eighteenth-century factories had a narrower range but even so workers would still come in from a radius of four or five miles.

We have seen Arkwright advertising in 1771 for clock-makers, a smith, and wood-turners—all for machine-making—and for women and children.[4] Both he and Strutt were constantly advertising for labour in the following years. Thus in 1776 Cromford was asking for 'Several Carpenters, Joiners, Labourers, &c. Also a good Forging Smith.'[5] This was for the building of the second Cromford mill.[6] In 1781 he was advertising:

Wanted at Cromford. . . Forging & Filing Smiths, Joiners and Carpenters, Framework-Knitters and Weavers, with large Families.

---

[1] Unwin, op. cit., ch. xi.
[2] Collier, 'Samuel Greg and Styal Mill' in *Mem. Manch. Lit. and Phil. Soc.*, lxxxv (1943), 139–57.
[3] Farey, op. cit., iii, 508; Wilson, 'Belper Nailers' in *Derbyshire Countryside* (1943), 21–2.
[4] See above, p. 65.   [5] *Derby Mercury*, Aug. 23, 1776.
[6] To build it Arkwright apparently dismantled an old corn mill for he advertised 'the Materials of a large Water Corn Mill, consisting of two Pair

Likewise Children of all Ages; above seven years old, may have constant Employment. Boys and young Men may have Trades taught them, which will enable them to maintain a Family in a short Time. Two or three young Men who can write a good Hand, are also wanted.

By personal Application at the Cotton-Mills Particulars may be known.[1]

There was a premium on large families. At the same time Strutt was advertising for joiners and smiths, and in 1783 for stonemasons and bricklayers at Milford.[2] In 1785 there was a more remarkable incursion which the *Derby Mercury* described:[3]

A few days since, between 40 and 50 North Britons, with Bagpipes and other Music playing, arrived at Cromford, near Matlock-Bath, from Perth, in Scotland: These industrious Fellows left that Place on account of the Scarcity of Work, were taken into the Service of Richard Arkwright, Esq; in his Cotton Mills and other extensive Works, entered into present Pay, and provided with good Quarters. They appeared highly pleased with the Reception they met with, and had a Dance in the Evening to congratulate each other on the Performance of so long a Journey.

The 'Scarcity of Work' in Perth hardly seems to be an adequate explanation of so well-organized a venture in migration. One would rather suspect that they were trainees from Deanston, Perthshire, where, in 1785, the Buchanans were setting up a cotton factory. John Buchanan had been Arkwright's first agent for the sale of his twist in Scotland; his youngest brother, Archibald, had served his apprenticeship at Cromford and then, with his brothers, built the Deanston mills.[4]

But if there was not pauper apprenticeship at Cromford and Belper there was ordinary apprenticeship and long-term hiring. The contemporary newspapers have frequent advertisements for runaways from cotton mills. In 1777 there was

committed to the House of Correction at Derby, one John Jefferies,

---

of French, one Pair of Black, and two Pair of Peak or Grey Stones, a large undershot Water Wheel, and good Shaft; also one large upright Shaft, Spur Wheel, Cog-Wheels, &c. &c.' (ibid., April 12, 1776).

[1] *Derby Mercury*, Sept. 20, 1781.
[2] Ibid., Sept. 27, 1776; May 22, 1783.
[3] Ibid., May 12, 1785.
[4] Hamilton, *The Industrial Revolution in Scotland* (1932), 127; Stewart, op. cit., 182. See also Redford, op. cit., 19.

a Gunsmith, of Cromford, for the space of one Calendar Month; and to be kept to hard Labour and corrected , he being charged by Mr. Arkwright, Cotton-Merchant, with having absented himself from his Masters Business without Leave, (being a hired Servant for a Year) and likewise been guilty of divers Misdemenors and Misbehaviour.[1]

And in 1781 Arkwright was advertising for a runaway apprentice 'by Trade a Joiner; he is a stout young Man, about 20 Years of Age, Red Hair, and has a Mole on his Face'. A reward was promised.[2] But the contracts might be with adults. In 1784 three runaways from Arkwright's Wirksworth mill were sought after: an Oldham man aged 24 and a Wirksworth man aged 27 had still over three years of their contract to serve and a Blackwell man of 28 over two years.[3] The Wirksworth mill was then new and evidently some of its labour force was recruited on long contracts; one of the runaways was an ex-soldier and another was wearing soldier's clothes. The cares of the mill manager were many; the whole success of a country factory depended on its being able to keep a labour supply.

The Derwent valley showed, perhaps, the largest concentration of mills on the Arkwright principle in the country. Pilkington in 1789 said there were then 16 in Derbyshire and his book bears the number out:

Place	No. of mills	Owner	River
Cromford	2	Arkwright	Cromford Sough (tributary)
Bakewell	1	,,	Wye (tributary)
Wirksworth	1	,,	Ecclesbourne (tributary)
Matlock	2	,, (one)	Derwent
Belper	2	Strutt	,,
Milford	1	,,	,,
Derby	2	,, (one)	,,
Darley (Derby)	1	Evans	,,
Tansley	1		(tributary)
Calver	1		Derwent
Lea	1	Nightingale	(tributary)
Wilne	1		Derwent

Pilkington may have missed one or two but not many were added later. There was Ellis Needham's Litton Mill (1782).

[1] *Derby Mercury*, Nov. 14, 1777.   [2] Ibid., Dec. 6, 1781.
[3] *Manchester Mercury*, Dec. 7, 1784.

He was extolled as an 'agricultural improver' but is remembered as a bad employer under whom Robert Blincoe, the factory apprentice, suffered. The first Cressbrook Mill, on the Wye, which looks so imposing from the St. Pancras line between Monsal Dale and Millers Dale, was started in the early 1780s, and had many changes, including a spell of Arkwright ownership; the present buildings are early nineteenth century.

Over the county border, in Nottinghamshire, there was a cluster of small early mills. (In 1794 there were said to be 29.)[1] The Pleasley mills, in which Henry Hollins, Thomas Oldknow and two others were partners, were founded in 1784–5 (with a capital of £4200.)[2] The Robinsons at Papplewick were the first in the trade to use a Boulton and Watt engine as power in 1785. And so on. Most of these had close connections with the hosiery trade, although Pleasley seems to have shared in the calico yarn boom of the late 1780s.

Many of these country mills are still to be seen; even if it has not the living continuity of Belper, Milford, Masson and Pleasley, a mill has been saved from extinction by its massive construction or its remoteness. Even Arkwright's Masson, though largely modernized, keeps in its middle portion the original six-storeyed building with its striking cupola, and some old sections, now too low in height for anything but storerooms. Cromford has become a colour works and laundry and though part of the old buildings stand, the original can be traced only with difficulty. Calver is an impressive monument; Wirksworth lies in picturesque and remote isolation; Papplewick, North Langwith, and others can still be explored. And at Styal, and, in Scotland, at Lanark and Catrine the buildings stand to link us with the first age of mill building. Like Belper and Milford they have harmonized into the landscape and have become not displeasing memorials of the early factory system. They remind one too of the extraordinary tenacity of British industry in holding on to brick and stone once a building is up.[3]

[1] Lowe, *General View of the Agriculture of the County of Nottingham* (1798), 171.
[2] Pigott, *Hollins. A Study of Industry, 1784–1949,* (1949), 35.
[3] Cf. the fine photographs of American cotton mills of the 1870s and 1880s treated as antiquities! (*Fortune,* liii, No. 4 (April 1956)).

CHAPTER VI

JEDEDIAH STRUTT AND HIS FAMILY

I. THE MAN OF SENSE

SOMETIME towards the end of his life Jedediah Strutt composed his epitaph, though it never reached lapidary inscription:

Here rests in Peace J S—— Who, without Fortune, Family or friends raisd to himself a fortune, family & Name in the World —Without having wit had a good share of plain Common Sense— Without much genius enjoyd the more Substantial blessing of a Sound understanding—With but little personal pride despisd a mean or base Action—With no Ostentation for Religious Tenets & Ceremonies he led a life of honesty & Virtue—& not knowing what woud befall him after death, he dyed resignd in full Confidence that if there be a future State of retribution it will be to reward the Virtuous & the good

This I think is my true Character

J Strutt

It was not an unapt estimate, though a little over-conscious of rectitude. But it was not unnatural that the prosperous hosier and cotton spinner, the head of communities at Derby, Belper and Milford, should never be able to forget that he was born poor and was the maker of his own fortune. The cool rationalism of liberal Dissent prevented him from giving too much credit to Providence or confessing his miserable sins. It is unfortunate that we have no contemporary estimates of Strutt beyond conventional obituary economiums. We have to judge him from his own letters and from the letters of others to him. He had a reputation for probity and he inspired confidence—Samuel Need's letters to him suggest that.[1] He was evidently an interesting but hardly an attractive man. He was withdrawn and self-centred and probably opinionated. He was a good husband and an affectionate father—according to the lights of his moral precepts; but a trying man to live with. His wife had some of the humour and the irony that he lacked; she

---

[1] See above, pp. 51–52.

was frank and not afraid to tease. He was solemn and exacting. Both were typical products of Old Dissent, untouched by the evangelicalism of the Methodist revival then active in the Midlands. There is little in their letters of the conventional religiosity of the time, although Elizabeth had been brought up in ministerial households.

Their family life was plain-living, frugal English middle-class society at its best. It was not falsely conventional; after his wife's death Strutt did not enforce a long, close period on his children's pleasures of dancing, although he took it hard himself. The essence of home life was frugality, obedience, and moral and intellectual discipline. The children were encouraged in self-reliance and industry. The emphasis was all on 'improvement'. They must make more of their opportunities, social and educational, than their parents had been able to do. The daughters must choose their friends only among those whose conversation might be 'improving'. The eldest son was encouraged to read Chesterfield's *Letters* and study to gain the confidence in polite society his father lacked. Whether because or in spite of the admonitions, the children became rather remarkable people in their own right, liberal, public-spirited, and courageous in expression of unpopular opinion.

The earlier letters to his wife have given an impression of Strutt as grave, sententious, much given to ruminating about himself, and moralizing about the world. He felt himself to be shy and awkwardly self-conscious in company, unready in conversation, more fond of pouring out thoughts on paper. They were not distinguished or original thoughts and, though he would have been horrified to have been told, they reeked of complacency. He was not ambitious of station; his Dissent and the county prejudice against people in trade limited that. But he had intense pride in his growing success and in the possession of wealth. In 1765, when not yet 39, but fully entered on his prosperity as a hosier, he could write to his wife from London:

I was this day thro' Cheapside, the Change &cc and cou'd not help imediately reflecting, that the sole cause of that vast concourse of people, of the Hurry & bustle they were in, & the eagerness that appeard in their countenances, was getting of Money, & whatever some Divines woud teach to the contrary, this is true in fact that it is the main business of the life of Man & thou knowest not how solicitous I am while life, & youth, & opportunity lasts to acquire something that you & I, shoud we live so long, may not have the two great calamities of Human Life, poverty & Old Age, come upon us together. Shoud we succeed in this & the period of our lives be lengthend out till then what think you, in that decline of our days, will afford a pleasure equal to that of being able to leave a fair patrimony to our children, & to reflect, that they are plac'd in circumstances that renders them superior to many of these difficulties we were forc'd to struggle with, this woud warm the heart however cold with age & afford real pleasure, even to a Dying parent, but think not from this that I mean to be irreligious; I the rather think that early to improve ones mind in every moral & Divine, as well as every polite & useful improvment, to the Authors of being to creatures like ourselves, who may not only help to replenish the world, but be useful in it; to provide by all honest means not only for their subsistance & our own, but for something beyond it; to spend a life of diligence, honesty, sobriety, & virtue; to have been the Author of anything great or good wherby mankind are made wiser or better; in the main, to have acted agreable to truth & ones own best reason, & in a firm belief & trust in the existence of god & his providence is truly to be religious.

The theme and the simple deism often recur. Money-getting, even if it does not have some social purpose, must be done responsibly. Ten years later, when a fortune in cotton-spinning was opening up, Jedediah could advise his son, in telling him how to prepare himself for the great world, that, though he might not become a nobleman, he might possibly be 'a Tradesman of some emminence'. (Jedediah hardly foresaw that that son's son would enter the peerage.)

The letters between Jedediah and his wife show deep affection on both sides; we may surmise that he owed much of his success to her energy and counsel. When she died he relapsed into illness and, it would seem, something like hypochondria. For many months he stayed in London, nursing his health, leaving his children to fend for themselves, while he poured forth admonition and instructions in the carriers' parcels. It is an episode hard to explain and it was followed by a similar period of illness in the following year. Yet this was only the prelude to the great burst of business activity in the founding of Belper and Milford in 1776–8.

The business always had its family character. Strutt's wife was active in it—a partner in herself; her brother, William Woollat, the co-inventor of the Derby rib machine, and Strutt's younger brother, William, were both supported by it and ran the Derby end. William, the eldest son, entered it at 14; Elizabeth, the elder daughter, was no older when she began to give a hand in the warehouse; the other sons, George Benson Strutt and Joseph Strutt, came in as they left school. The three sons were a great aid in the cotton-spinning venture, and possibly, in the early stages, Belper and Milford owed much to William, the eldest, who had reached maturity when they were started, and was to be an even greater figure as a cotton spinner than his father.

The life the family led at Derby was circumscribed. Derby was not a large town—it had perhaps 7000 or 8000 inhabitants in the 1770s—but an important communications centre. It was, Sylas Neville noted in 1781, a 'strange stragling place in a medow. Some of the streets not paved at all, others but badly paved with small pebles, & all of them narrow, except for a few, indifferent'.[1] It was a market town with silk mills, milling and brewing, a famous china works, an iron strip mill, a copper smelting works, and some hosiery manufacture. Its centre was congested because it was hemmed in between the commons and the river. But as a county town its structure was rigid; Defoe had called it 'a town of gentry rather than trade'. The county families had their town houses (like Lord Exeter's) and their exclusive assemblies. There was a gulf between them and the 'tradesmen', especially the Dissenting tradesmen, however wealthy. The Strutts found their friends in a close society—their fellow members of the Unitarian meeting at Friargate Chapel (of which Jedediah became a trustee in 1778), the Duesburys of the china works, some Nonconformist ministers and their families, and Strutt's fellow venturers in hosiery and cotton-spinning, like the Arkwrights and the Needs at Nottingham, or millers (and later cotton spinners and bankers) like the Evans. Business was always close to them. The millowner lived near his mill; the hosier near or over his warehouse. The Strutts had set up house in Derby in St. Mary's Gate, had moved to Irongate by 1763, and then to St. Peter's Street. But

[1] Op. cit., 277.

prosperous as they had become by 1774 they could still let rooms for the Derby races.

The following letters of 1773–5 are of more social than economic interest but, though there is much small beer, they are worth reproducing in sequence for their sidelights on the manner of life of a Nonconformist provincial family. They begin with Jedediah's going to London in the autumn of 1773, his return there early in 1774 to take charge of the parliamentary proceedings on the Calico Act, his wife's joining him in March, 1774, her death in May, and the conduct of the family at Derby in the long months of Jedediah's remaining in London.

The deepest impression they leave is of frugality and plain but good living. Letters pass between Derby and London in the carriers' bags of the hosiery business; a letter sent by post is a subject of apology, a relative's frank a rare gift. Jedediah is consulted about every item of expense such as clothes, and buys the family's shoes in London (was it from the Chamberlains?)— which seems hazardous. It is the self-sufficient English household, with its cow and pig and its large garden, baking its own bread, making its own cheese, brewing its own beer, making its English wines, that Cobbett was to instruct and which survives in the early editions of Mrs. Beeton.

Elizabeth Strutt to her husband

Sepbr 28 Derby *1773*

My Dear

I was glad to hear from you, & that you was well & Brothers sending by the Coach to night gives me an oppertunity not only of thanking you for writeing to me, but also of sending you 2 more shirts & 2 stocks as I wish you to go clean—if you stay longer then this week beg you will write again,—'tis our Cheese fair to Day I cou'd have wish'd you here to have bought what Cheese we might want, but I have done my best to please you, the selling price a bout six & twenty—Brother Strutt is but poorly. Billy & Bet are gone to Cromford to the Candlelighting & the rest wish to be there —Mrs Willot & Miss's send respects & will take it as a perticular favour if you will deliver the parcell to Mr Willot directed for him with your own hand, & look at his new shop & ask him a few questions concerning Business &c: that you may give a little gess how things are like to turn out, she says, to have your opinion will be some sattisfaction to her.—My love to Dolly & tell her I still Love her, but am too lazy to write at present. Be sure ask her what the fans cost mounting & pay her for them. Last friday you was hardly ever out of my thoughts the 24 of Sepber is a Day I shall ever revere[1]. . .

Elizabeth Strutt to her husband

Derby. October 11 1773.

My Dear

There is nothing that has given me more real pleasure this long time then your assuring me your well & that my last Letter was agreeable to you, there is no engagement either company or business that shall prevent my doing every thing in my power both now & at all other times that can add to your pleasure & happiness, & tho there is nothing material has hapned in your absence that obliges me to write now, yet I canot omit writeing a line or too, to tell you how much we wish to see you, which we hope will not be long. First the children are all very well & very good & send their Duty, Bet is in the Warehouse & works hard. After repeated mes-sages by word of mouth from Mr Milnes we have this day had a letter which I here inclose that Mr Need & you may consult togeather what is to be done with it: I have wrote my self to Day to Mr Milnes in the best terms I cou'd to beg he will wave his resentment till he hears what you both say when you return, he is quite impatient of disregard & will no longer be trifled with.—I wish you was got well throe your other cross affair—there is also great complaints of Brother Woollats conduct in the Warehouse & Billy is uneasy & thinks the money is not took proper account on, Brother Strutts is a silant Disapprobation so we have no great harmony amongst us, but trust there will be more when you come. How does the face of one we love stifle every contending passion, & smiles & sunshine immediately appear.—I am chiefly concerned a bout you least you shoud want shirts and other things as your stay has been so much longer then expected, I am sorry Brothers coud not take you in, I fear your quarters are not the most agreable, be sure you take care of your self, as you vallue her which has the [Hon]our & Happiness to subscribe herself your truly Affectionate Wife E: Strutt Mr Lowe sends respects to you. He will be in [? London] in less then a fortnight.

---

[1] Their wedding anniversary was actually Sept. 25.

113

Elizabeth Strutt to her husband

Derby Feb 14: 1774

Well my Dear, & so the cork came out of the Bottle & you was thereby depriv'd of your Dram, 'its no matter, you will allways have your own way, but I will not Chide, as your so ingenuous to acknowledge your fault, & my superior judgment *in small matters,* so for the future I shall expect you will submit a little—

I rejoiced to hear you got so well & so early to London, & wrote to me so soon, 'tho you said not one word when, or where, you met Mr Need, nor how you was convey'd to London nor one word of Brother Willm &c, its true these are but trifling, but to me interesting particulars, & I shall expect you to indulge me a little when you have nothing else to do,—I hope before now you have got a fresh Bottle of the tincture which I injoyn you not to forget nor neglect, & then I will promise you I will endeavour to be boath easy & cheerfull, the nights is the worst, as thay are but indifferant in general.—we shall put into the bag tonight an odd shoe, Mr Morris has sent, & says you will find one of those you took is less then the rest & he will be oblig'd to you to send it down directly, as the owner wants it, I long to know your suckcess with regard to the affair your gone about.[1]

. . . —the children are all very good & diligent & beg their Duty to you,—be sure let no engagement what ever ma[ke] you neglect your health, let that be your first, & principal care, as you have any regard for a family that most ardently & most tenderly Loves you, —I shall send you to night in the bag 2 shirts & a pair of clean flanel linings & a few lines Dr White has wrote to you, you will find them pin'd to one of your Shirts don't forget to look for it,— so you lye at my Brothers, well, I hope a kind providence will ever attend you, the fear of fire at one House & the torment of Bugs at the other, wou'd quite divide me—give my love to Dolly, & Miss Willot when you see them we wish much to hear Sister's opinion of her Daughter Martha, Bet talks of wrighting to you with a franch quotation, english'd on ye other side which you must keep out of sight, & try Jack or Bet to read you the french by this means you will be a Judge of their proficiency in that Language.

8 o clock I have this moment put your things into the bag youll observe there is 2 shirts with what you have with you, makes eight, one cravat now makes three, & eight stocks you took with you & 4 pocket handkerchiefs—dont forget to send the shoe down the first oppertunity yours is in the bag—I hope you will not be angry at my sending you a post letter, as the greatest pleasure I

---

[1] The omitted passage is quoted above, p. 57.

have is in writing to you & hearing from you, & of you, thay have had a few lines from you to Day in the ware-house. I am glad, truly glad to hear you hold well. I am your truly

Affectionate wife

E: Strutt

I beg to be remembred to all Brothers family do you lye in your Cotton Sheets & upon the mattriss we made, did you get your Box Satturday or Sunday

Elizabeth Strutt to her father

[Derby, February, 1774]

My dear Father

Permit me to testify to you how sensible I am of your goodness: be persuaded that I shall endeavour to make myself more & more worthy of it by my conduct. I assure you that I employ all the diligence & application imaginable to perfect myself in french. May it please God to preserve you, & grant you the accomplishment of all your wishes. I am, with the most profound respect, & the most tender affection

My Dear Father,

Your most dutiful Daughter

Eliza: Strutt.

Martha Strutt to her father

[Derby, February, 1774]

My Dear father

Tho my sister has wrote to you first I would wish not to be thought an inch behind her in affection & Gratitude to you & will take as much pains as I can to perfect myself in my French. My Sister has rec'd a french Letter from Miss Need but it is very Imperfect & is now writing to her again. My Uncle is just returned from Cromford, all goes on well there only my Grandfather Complains of his very bad neighbours but you know he was never easy long together. Here has been a sale of Horses by way of Auction at Simpsons. There was some very pretty ones. How I do wish for a Horse, I would do anny thing for a Horse may I not hope

I am my Dear Father your

Affectionate Daughter

Martha Strutt

Ma chere Mere se porte beaucoup mieux, nous vous souhaitton

parfaite Santé & un prompt retour presentez nos respects á mes Cousines.

My Mother is much better we wish you perfect health & a Safe return present our love to my Cousins.

Elizabeth Strutt to her husband

Derby Feb: 23 1774

My Dear

I am very glad to hear you hold rather better, & I wou'd not have been so long before I had told you so, and also have thanked you for your short Letter; but did not chuse to write in the companys as that goes to the warehouse & is liable to be opend by others besides yr self—if there be no probability of your being at Home before, I will write next week in the bag, but what will you say, if I shou'd surprise you by a visit in a week or too; as I am most exceedingly press'd by a Gentleman of our acquaintance to take a place in his carriage, & not to mention a word of it to you, till you see me. But I cou'd by no means promise him to do that.—Mr Low has just call'd in upon us, he is just returnd from his journey to Manchester Leeds, Norton &c. He will be in London very soon, youll say these are but trifles to write about,—but as we go on in the old round, you know my way of Life does nor furnish much matter for conversation, or entertainment to you,—it may perhaps give you some pleasure to hear we are all very well, I have not been better this long time then I have been, for this week past, patty says 'tis because you are better, indeed you are generally the subject of conversation amongst us, & the end of every thought wakeing & sleeping,—if we have any thing my family thinks good to eat, one cries my Father wou'd like this, another says I wish he had a bit, Joe says let us send him some poor Daddy,—& then a gain if any thing is propos'd to be don, the answer is, but will it be a greable to my Father, what will he say to it, we had better let it a lone, & ask him when he coms Home, which we hope will not be long first, for as health, chearfulness, & Good-humour &c, are but enjoyed in part without you, think of us, & hasten to compleat it —there is one thing is a check upon our innocent amusements, & that is, that silant Gloom, which you know at times used to hang a bout my Brother Strutt, it never was more visable then since his return from London, & I think till yesterday I never saw him smile, the children took pains to devirt him with an account of futball play on shroves—tuesday, such a match you never saw, poor peeters got the Day at last, after 5 hours hard strugle, but nothing will please him, betwixt you & I, he has met with some dissopointment at London, I h[e]ard him say Mr. Duesberry had been at great expence in fitting up a grand warehouse at London, but was provided with a person to take care of it—I shall tire you with this long letter but before I conclude I must tell you 'tis at the joynt request of the House, you are desir'd to try Cosns Jackc & Betsys, a billitys at the french Letter on the other side—but a bove all let me know, how you do & if you take any tincture now, my Daughters was to visit Miss Stamfords yesterday, but I have never been out of the House since you left it, accept on Sunday to Meeting I am your Most faithfull & Affectionate Wife

E: Strutt.

Our Loves to Brothers family

Elizabeth Strutt to her husband

Derby March 9 [1774]

My Dear

Your most kind & Obliging Letter I sincearly thank you for, but am very sorry to find your business is likely to detain you so long from home, & indeed that very circumstance makes me very wavering with regard to my takeing a Journey to London, for I long to see you, & to see you there, & well, wou'd to me be a pleasur superior to every thing in the Whole metropolis beside—Mr Lowe will be in town a bout the 27 or 28 of this month & has had a letter from his Father informing him mother is so much better that Miss now has some hopes of coming with him, if that shoud be the case Mr Low presses me hard not to let slip the oppertunity, & he will take all ye care in his power to make it a greable, & Mrs. Willot wou'd by all means have me come, Dr White says he shou'd have hopes the journey wou'd be of servis, if I take care & not hurry a bout too much when I am there,—you say nothing in your last, how your health is now, I am affraid of the expence of my journey, we are all well as usual. Patty observed you took no notice of her Letter & with tears said she thought you partial to her sister. Mr Baker calld here on Sunday night but brought neither a letter nor the shoe, 'tis a dissoopointment to Mr Morris let me hear from you soon which will oblige your Affectionate Wife E: Strutt

My comts to all that enquire of me.

Note on back in another handwriting

Have ordered a good deal of thread from Gardom but have received but little yet. Wm. Shepherd at Hucknall has left. They get so much better thd from Sutton—Have wrote several times to Nottingm but cannot learn what sort of White thread there is.

Suppose there is none ready yet. We never get any that the men like so well as Gardoms. Have sent a parcel of the 24 Narrow Ribs to see how they are Approvd of. Butterworth says he cannot work them at the 3d Advance

Elizabeth Strutt to her children

[London,? March, 1774]

. . . Sukey Need coming to see me, so we only [made] a turn round St Pauls & so home a gain, indeed I am not much dispos'd to walk for I have got so bad a cold I know not what to do with my self, it lies very much in my Head, & cold shiverings, in other respects I do very well, your Cosns are all very obliging to me, & very readdy to wait upon me, & I think Cosn Betsy greatly improved, & very Notable, she wash's all the small clothes & Irons them, & at their Great wash, She hangs out & folds all the linnin & Irons all her own, & her sisters clothes. Sister thinks Patty not in the least improvd, but she dares not give her self any Airs, before her Mamma, for I can assure you thay are all kept at a propper distance & are made [to] do the most servile work when ocasion requirs, thay have a large House, kept exactly neat & but one servant, the rooms are all scourd every week & the counting House & Chitchen & stairs every Day. You may tell Miss all this—your Father is better toDay, but has been but poorly, he is gone to Lord Hows & wont return till late, I am going to Drink tea with Mrs Willot this after-noon, I was there monday morning for an hour or so. My kind Love to Mrs Willot & Miss & Mrs Rosel & tell them I am quite charm'd with Mr. Willot's sittuation 'tis in my opinion, by far the most pleasant I ever saw in London, & as to the family, there is harmony, Economy, & industry appears to me, to run throe the whole of it & thay will not hear a word of Miss leaving till the latterend of the summer & then Mrs. Willot will come down with her & bring the little popit with her, I did not see it, 'twas a sleep, I wonder how she will part with it as there is no more to be expected at present—I have just now recd my Dear Girls Letter & thank her for it, I am much obligd to patty for her concern a bout me, I allmost repent not bringing her up with me, but some future time perhaps you may boath come—I have no objection to your waiting upon Miss Moresby as I fancy thay are ingenious sober Girls, I like Miss Kitty very well. She has quite a taste for painting & is comn to London for instructions, she much wishd she had known patty before she had left Derby, as their tastes woud have been simmelar, she was very sick upon the Rode but we got a bit of broild Bacon for her & after that she was quite well, she promisd to call upon me but I have not yet seen her—I much want my White Cloke as the weather is fine, you may inquire if any boddy is coming up, you can send it by, or if Brother wou'd be so good if they send any thing by the Coach as to carefully put it in, be sure don't neglect the very first oppertunity & dont let it be crushd or rubd, My sister & cosns all beg their Love to all of you, we all include your Uncle & tell him I have talk much a bout him & he shall hear from me soon, tell joe & George I expect to hear of their being very good, to each other, I think of you all every Day & hope to meet you shortly in Health & safety. I think I shall surprise you all with what I shall bring down with me, for I shant forget one of you. Your Father joyns with me in Love to you all

I am your most Affectionate Mother

E: Strutt

Elizabeth Strutt to her children

[London,? April, 1774]

My Dear children

I am much obligd by all the pritty letters you send me, I every Day think of you, & wish to be with you, but don't know when that will be as your Fathers business goes so slowly, we rec'd the Gingerbread & Butter boath safe & sound each excellent in their kind. I have been most of the Day to Day buying hats & Ribband for you boath, now for your shoes, thay say Green will be prittyest, but I know not what we shall fix on, as my son Willm has wrote to me a bout nothing & made a pritty good Letter of it, he may depend upon his Buckles &c—I was yesterday at the Romish cheppel & was entertaind, have been at Coxs Museum, & intend seeing a play if I hold but well enough, but I dont hurry my self as you immagin for your Father Complements me with a Coach every where. My Love to both my Brothers, & tell my Joe he has had a present made him to Day, 'tis now in my pocket. I am my Dear Children your most effectionate Mother E: Strutt

Elizabeth Strutt to her children

London Aprill 4 [1774]

My Dear Children

You know I have no inclination for writeing, which makes me allways include boath my D[aughter]s in one letter, as it wou'd be needless to say the same thing twise over, in the first place let me tell you I rec'd all your Letters safe and was much pleasd with them, there was no room at all for Betsy to remark your letter, or

laugh at it, & pattys second letter was quite a master pies, your Father said it was a very pritty letter, Betsy worked very hard indeed to finish my ruffle so soon, it came safe & I have made them, the gingerbread was very good & we wish you to make us a pound or two more just such & send it the first oppertunity you have, you may on friday take six pounds of Butter & send it us in the Roles, you might put the Butter & gingerbread in a basket togeather & sew a cloth fast over it & send by the carrier on munday, directed for your Father in Woodstreat—the chese & Miss Willot's pettecoats came safe. She was here when thay just come in. We had been at the jews synogogue to hear the famous [ ] sing for there was nothing else we coud understand, their whole devotion appears nothing but a confused clamour. However we was so much entertaind that your Father went a gain this morning—on friday we went to Westminster Abby & walk'd in the park &c till I was quite weary & was forc'd to take a coach home, you will give my love to Mrs. Willot & to Mrs. Rosel & to misses & tell Miss Peggy I am much obligd to her for her kind Letter & I will write to her soon— George was very good & Joe was very good to write me such pretty letters, thay must also be good to their sisters & do every thing thay bid them & thay may depend upon a reward,—No, 'tis impossiable you shoud think what I shall bring, I am even surprisd my self at what your Father has bought for us all, but I wont tell you till I see it, this I can assure you it is not a Carriage,—I am sorry to hear there is any more disturbance about the school sweeping but to put an end to it you have now our orders to send the money directly, get down what it is thay demand & pay it—our Loves to your uncle & Aunt Woolat, & tell your Aunt I have not yet bought any Wosteds, but thay are to be had at many shops in Newgate street & Cheapside—our Loves also to your uncle Strutt & tell him I have been punctual in delivering his message & it is now in debate & he will hear more of it by, & by,—Miss Morsby & I have been a little unlucky, She has been to see me twice & I have been to see her once, & never cou'd find each other at home—tell Billy as he forgets me I will try if I cant forget him—the messenger waits so I am obligd [to] Conclude my self your very Affectionate Mother
E: Strutt

My Cold is Better but I am but indifferant. Your Father is purely. I [wish] my Dear Girls will write to me often.

William Strutt to his mother

Derby April 10th. 1774

Hond. Mother

I have at last sat down to write a few Lines to you as you desir'd, Irksome as it is to me thro' my Inability to write about nothing, for I know of nothing to tell you except that we are all very well & should be glad to see you at Home as soon as convenient, but suppose there is no prospect of that at present. Am afraid you will be Tir'd of staying long in such a Hurrying place. We all go on very well & your absence which at first (as you expected) render'd it lonely & dull is now become more agreeable & pleasant than one would have Imagined. A Gentleman has just called here with a Parcel & a Letter Inclos'd for Mr. Wm. Strutt who is just set off for Arnold. Mr. Wright would have brot. it, but the Coach was just going out & he had not time to call for it, are glad to hear by him that you are pretty well. My Uncle Woollatt is got much Better but not quite well. Brothers & Sisters are all very anxious to know what it is you have Bot. for them & join with me in Duty to my Father & you, Love to Uncle & Aunt, Cousins &c &c. Joe says he will write to you soon. I think of nothing more now therefore conclude myself your ever dutifull Son

Wm. Strutt

Elizabeth Strutt to her children

London Aprill 20 1774.

My Dear Children

the Day you receive this, it will be just a month since I left you, & your Fathers affairs nearly in the same sittuation, very little forwarder by what I can learn—I want very much to be at Home, but at the same time shall be very uneasy to leive your Father behind me, surely a week or too more will produce some alteration in their affairs—it gives us pleasure to hear you go on so well & spend your time agreably, be sure be Loving, kind, & obliging to each other, let there be no contention amongst you, but which shall behave best, you will allways find if you act upon that principal it will carry with it its own reward, your now comn to years of Discretion & are capable of Distingwishing what is most Amiable in Minds & Manner & I doubt not, your care to a dobt what appears to you to be so.

tell Alice I wish she wou'd collect all the feathers She can find & pick em, clean & rub them throe a sive then put them into a wide roomy bag & hang them up in the stove till I come, because

I shall have ocasion for them at Cromford directly, I hope to find the Garden put into a little order & things made to look a little decent, we must depend upon your uncle for his care about these things,—I wish he wou'd be so kind to tell Dr. White we can't get him a Kitchen like ours for less than too guineas and a half. Ours cost that, if thay chuse one let us know, your Father desires you will take six pd more Butter on friday (that is the day you receive this) & put it into a clean cloth in a Basket without a pot, & the Basket put into the bag of stockings, there is a round B: in the safe woud hold it. We have not rec'd the silver cup you said woud come by the Coach. I hold better, your Father is purely. I have such a pen I cannot write more then that we give Love to all of you & are your most Affectionate Mother & Father J & E: Strutt. Let us hear how you all do soon. Tell Joe & George we are pleasd to hear thay are good. Your Aunt & cosns send love to all of you.

On the back in Jedediah's handwriting:

I have enquired at other places & coud have a Kitchin very near for 46 or 47/- if Dr White chuses but not for less of that shape & size. Mine cost me 50/-. I have inquird of Mr Dolland about the gloves & he sells them for the same that Mr Adams does of the same size. Shall be glad if he has any commands for us

Elizabeth Strutt to her children

London Aprill 27. *1774.*

My Dear Children

We are very sorry, that an unforeseen train of consequences, in your Father[s] affairs prevents our return to Derby, & to our own Dear fire-side so soon as we cou'd wish. I fear it will be a month still before all that is absolutely necessary will be finished. I have not your Fathers patience, that 'tis quite uncertain wheather mine will hold out, but as we hold tolerable well, will be one means of making our absence more a greable to us, & the confidence we have, of your not only behaving well to each other, but the Good Economy you will now have an oppertunity of shewing how much your Mistriss's of a steddy, regular uniform behaveour, with a Genteel frugallity, a long with that principle of morallity wch I have often observd with pleasure in all your Conduct, will make you, not only Dear to us, but Amiable in the Eyes of God & Man, & as a confirmation of our most tender & indulgent regards, the trifles we have sent you by Mr. Lowe[1] will testify.—Your Good

---

[1] In 1769 Thomas Lowe opened a shop at the Corn Market, Derby (*Derby Mercury*, Dec. 22, 1769).

Fathers present to you is, 2 pares of Stone Buckles for his Daughters, a pare of Silver for his son Willm. and a pare of knee Buckles, and there is also a glass plaything to exercise his philosophy to find out the use of it—I have sent each of my Girls a hat, & a few ribbands for their Caps but I wou'd wish you to buy White for the hats thay look neatest, & put on in any forme you like best & a large beau on the left side & long ends. Send me a bit of my strip'd gown I will try to match it for pattys coat. Yr things will all now want puting in to order for the summer, & George & Joe must want their Clothes Made. I wou'd have you see if Mr Lowe the mercer has ever a good Cloth light Blew that he cou'd recomend to me, I wou'd have them both the same with white Buttons. Tell Mr Breary I hope I may rely upon his Honour to make them as neat & as with as little stuff as if I was at Home to give the orders myself. I would have them made frock fashion with a small start up Collor like Joe's Brown ones & don soon, I woud have both full suits. Your Brother William must chuse for himself as to the Colour, he might as well have them of Bobby if thay have what he likes otherways of Bob Grayson,[1] he may have them as soon as he pleases, & to sattisfy his scrupelous Consiance you may assure him from me, I dont mention these things with out first procureing the approbation of his Good Father—Well the next thing to be don is that Wine in the Celler to be Bottled, be sure take great care that the bottles are clean & dry & well cork'd, dont let it be wasted by any means—how is your bear now, perhaps when the wine is bottled Alice might make a few Gallons of treacle Bear & put upon the Raisins, I think it wou'd be very good, and any Bottoms of the Casks thats dead &c. let them be bottled & drank when ripe. Give our respects to Alice & tell her we shall be obligd, by her best care of every thing in our absence—how does the cow do, has she not calved yet.

We beg our Respects to Mrs. Willots family & will be obligd to Mrs. Willot if she will buy for me 5 or 6 pecks of Cowslippeep's where she buys her own. You will pay her for them, & lay a clean Cloth upon the floor & spread the peep's upon it & let them ly till I come—I have sent Mrs. Dolphins silk. Shall be glad if she likes it, you will carry it to her your self Betsy, and give our Complements to her & Miss,—& Miss White & Miss Bing[ha]m & every boddy that inquires after us. We expect a long letter & doubt not but your gratitude will lead you to oblige us. I ask Miss peggy Willots pardon I have not wrote to her of all this time but

---

[1] Robert Grayson, a Derby linen draper (*Derby Mercury*, March 10, 1758).

do intend it. We are your Sincearly Affectionate Father & Mother
J & E: Strutt

I am sorry to informe you the Box will not be at Derby till Satturday sevennight & long to know how you all do. The figs are for Joe

Elizabeth Strutt to her mother

Derby May 2d 1774

My dearest Mother

We were yesterday morning reading your letter with that secret pleasure which the mind always feels on being assured that the object of its sincere regard & veneration is in health & safety; we flattered ourselves with the pleasing thought, that you was then employed as we were in enjoying the fragrance of May morning.— But how suddenly are our fondest hopes damped with the melancholy news that this dull morning brings! We are now mourning your absence & wishing your return. Pray write as soon as you receive this, for we shall be impatient till we hear better accounts.

We are very much obliged to my good Father & you for the things you have sent us, & hope we shall endeavour more & more to merit them by our conduct. Joe will want a new hat before he can wear his new cloaths, pray must we buy him one. Patty will paint the ribband she intends to put round her hat.—We are all mercenary enough to join in requesting that Miss Willotts may have no more proofs of your regard. It is vexatious to put ones self to expence to please people, & scarcely to receive thanks for one's kind intentions. Miss M. Willott has informed me that her sister & the child will come to Derby this week; she says she intends to take her little neice a walking every day; I told her she would then be deprived of the pleasure of walking with Her acquaintance; she replied: 'no indeed I shan't, for I shall make nothing of taking *you* along with me, & making you carry the child.' She will find herself mistaken: I have been her sisters maid, but I will never be hers.

The bacon has been hung up some time: every body that sees it says it is spoil'd; but we have eat some of it & it tastes very good; we never failed turning it once a day & I generally went into the cellar with alice to see that she rubbed it well. The Butcher sent the hams at the time you fixed, but has not yet called to be paid, & I did not think it right to send the money by the man who brought them. I cannot say they look well now that they are hung up, but they have been taken all possible care of.—I will endeavour to execute all the orders given in your last letter, & don't doubt but with Patty's advice & Alice's assistance everything will be done to your satisfaction. I have nothing more to say but that we are all very well & join in duty & love wherever due, *pray* write soon.

I am your affectionate & dutiful daughter

Eliza: Strutt.

Martha Strutt to her mother

Derby, May the 3 [1774]

My Dear Mother

I hope by this time you are much better than when my Sister wrote. I wish I was with you & then I should not be so uneasy but I hope we shall soon meet again. We have not yet seen Mr Lowe only at the Meeting. We shall be very agreeably surprized with our things on Saturday. I am sure I did not expect such nice Buckles. I hope you have rec'd the Butter safe & good. Mr Lowe brought his Lady to Derby last night but not Mr Dan'l Lowe. I have sent a pattern of the Silk. I wish you may match it, must have it made up this summer. We all continue well & send Duty to father & Mother Uncle & aunt love to Cousins

from your affectionate & Dutiful

Daughter Martha Strutt

I hope my Cousin
patty will nurse you
as she did at Derby

Elizabeth Strutt to her mother

Derby May ye 5 1774

My Dearest Mother

You could not be more surprised at not receiving the butter, than I was when I read my Cousin's letter; & am very sorry to hear that you think pleasure of any kind could make us forget you, or any of your orders. After your unbounded generosity to us, we must be utterly destitute of gratitude, and filial affection, to neglect even the most trivial of your requests. I can assure you the greatest pleasure I have had since you went, has been the hearing that you was tolerably well: you know that much visiting is my aversion, & that I am soon weary of any thing of the kind; how then can pleasure have made us forget ourselves? My uncle & brother said the butter could not possibly be sent in the bag; we therefore put it carefully into the basket, & sent it at the time you ordered: Mr Stenson[1] delivered it into the man's hands him self & saw it entered

---

[1] Probably John Stenson, hosier of Derby, whose death, aged 67, is reported in the *Derby Mercury*, March 10, 1780. In 1811, three Stensons—John, James Smith and Thomas—were trustees of the Friargate Chapel.

along with the bag. What must we do? *I* would buy the same quantity to-morrow, & send it on monday; but patty thinks that would be foolish indeed, as it is probable you may have it before you receive this.

We have bottled all the wine: I hope I may say well. I have also been to Mr Lowes about my young brothers cloaths; neither he, nor Mr Earl have any light blue, but Mr Grayson has a good cloth at six & sixpence a yard almost as light as my Fathers. Mr Lowe was married last monday to Miss Snelson of Hanbury. I called upon Mrs Willet this morning, she is pretty well, but says she had rather not go out anywhere as her stay is so short. I like my shoes vastly, they fit very well, & I am most obliged to you for them. We are very sorry to hear you have been so poorly, but hope you will soon get better. We are all very well & join in duty & love.

I am your most affectionate & dutiful daughter

Eliz. Strutt

Martha Strutt to her mother

Friday May the 6th [1774]

My Dearest Mother

As Mr Grayson is going to set off I have not time to say more than that we have just rec'd the Box. Never was I more surprized in my life but I will not say more at present than that you may expect some Letters by Mrs Willott. I think the Child is very ordinary. Mr Sisters Letter is sealed up or else I might have said this in hers. We are all well & join in Duty to Dear father yourself & remain

your affectionate Daughter

Martha Strutt

I hope you
have rec'd the Butter

Jedediah Strutt to his children

London May 7: 1774

My Dear Children

It is with the utmost concern I am oblig'd to tell you that your Mamma is very Ill of a Fever. This is the 10th day since she began & since which she has been growing worse & indeed I have been under the most painful apprehensions that you woud never see her more. Mr Willatt has attended her & a Phisician (Dr Pitcarn) & to day I have some hopes she is something better but am still very doubtful of the event. You will guess what I feel by what yourselves will feel on this occasion. Her Love to you & me was without

126

bounds & it will be impossible ever to forget it but I cannot dwell on the Subject—you may be assurd that nothing that my best affections can dictate shall be wanting to restore her to myself & you. I cannot say more. Farewell. Bettsys & pattys Letters are rec'd I am

yr most afft Father

J. Strutt

I will write you again
in a day or two

William Strutt to his mother

Derby May 8th 1774

Hond. Mother

It is the deepest sense of Gratitude that obliges me to write to thank you & my Father for all the favours I have received from you but especially for what you have now sent, tho' I want Words to express my sense of the Obligation you have conferr'd upon me, let my Actions & Conduct witness the sincerity of my resolutions to please you & to conform to every thing that is Virtuous & Praiseworthy. The Buckles are very neat and exactly what I could have wished, as for the Glass you have sent I am at a Loss to know the Use of it for I have not had time to examine it yet—Joe & George send their Duty and Thanks and are equally pleased with their Presents. They are very good & say they will Endeavour more & more to deserve the good things you have sent them, we last Night received a Parcel from my Father but to our great disappointment not one Word about you. We are all very anxious about your Health & beg you will write soon & let us know how you do, [we] are very glad to hear my Father holds so well, hope it will not be long before you both come home. I shall not have occasion for any cloathes till then. Since I wrote the above my Sister tell me Mrs Willott has received a letter from her Husband acquainting her that you are still worse which makes us very uneasy, but what increases our distress, is, she seems shy of telling them & says it is by your desire, hope you will write to acquaint us with particulars, that Heaven may preserve your Life to the latest desirable period is the constant Prayer of your Dutiful Son

Wm. Strutt.

Martha Strutt to her father

[Derby, May 8, 1774]

Hon'd Father

It is with pleasure known to few I take up my Pen to thank you

127

in the greatfulest manner I am capable for all your unbounded generosity to us. Your goodness has reached far beyond what we could ask or think: but may it tend to make us good, Virtuous, & happy. May your life be spared to cultivate our growing minds. Train us like yourself to all that's good & amiable in the eyes of God & man. May we be blessings instead of curses & our best endeavours be to please you in every thing. Tell my Dear Mother not to think we are too much taken up to neglect executing all her orders for our study is to make everything agreeable against your return, which I hope now will not be long. Don't you wish to retire from busy bustling London to your own arm Chair & homely fireside, where after the bussiness of the Day you can nod a bit undisturb'd. When we rec'd the Box which was Friday we took it up Stairs, opened it, found every wrote on so carefully, took all the things out one by one, still, & still more surprized! but I am at a loss to express myself & to thank you & my good Mother enough so I will leave you to think & Conclude myself

your Affectionate & Dutiful Daughter

Martha Strutt

We did not show joe & George the things till Sunday for we thought that overjoy would make them not mind their Books. George is surprized with his Buckles for he thought you had forgot him. They likewise desire to join in *grateful* thanks.

Martha Strutt to her mother

[Derby, May 8, 1774]

My Dearest Mother

As Mrs Willott sets out for London to day my sister & I have wrote to my father by her to thank him for all his unexpected goodness. The things are what we could all have wished. If we had been there ourselves we could not have been pleased so well. The Buckles & shoes are quite handsome. In short every thing is beautiful. Hearing of your being so poorly has made me very uneasy especially to think of your being angry at us but I will flatter myself it was oweing to your illness for I hope when you once get home you will find every thing done to your satisfaction. We have bottled the wine & I think it is [not] as sweet as it was at first but it is very clear & good. There is twenty one quarts & 8 pints. Alice has made some Treacle beer & turned it upon the Raisins.

I have just run down to look at the sweetest horse I ever saw in my life. It is to be sold for 11 pounds or less but I cannot expect it now my father has bought us so many fine things & my Uncle says he will never meddle about it for he shall never ride it. I hope we shall have a letter soon to know how you do. I wish you would come home & go to Matlock. I believe Billy will write to his father but fear you know [what] was always his troublesome companion. Joe says he thinks he has almost forgot his mammy's face she has been so long away. We are all very well & that your health may be restored & a safe return to your family & friends is the constant prayer of your affectionate & Dutiful Daughter Martha Strutt

I suppose you will see Miss Malkin soon in London & she proposes to return thro' Derby. Polly Henson woud be glad to know if you have heard of a place for her. We took the Silk to Mrs Dolphins she thinks it extremely well done. She is but poorly. Poor Mac gives her duty to you, she thinks it a long time before you come, she has had a bad fall down stairs & is very poorly. Her old husband is worse again & brought her a shilling. Joe thanks you for his nice figgs.

These last letters from her children probably did not reach Elizabeth Strutt before her death on May 11. She was buried in the Dissenting burial ground at Bunhill Fields on May 15 and the bill for the funeral was as follows:

Mr. Strutt   Dr.

For the Funerall of Mrs. Strutt

	£	s.	d.
1774			
May			
15th			
To a Strong Elm Coffin with a Double Lid & Coverd with fine Black Cloth, Close Drove with the Best Brass Cased nails & Double Pannelld, a Double Borderd Metall Plate with Inscription, 3 Pair of the largest Patent Handles with wrought Gripes & Embellishd with a Glory & an Urn & 8 Dozen of Ornamentall Drops all neatly Guilt the Inside Lined & Ruffled with Superfine Crape	6	6	
To a Suit of Superfine Crape consisting of a Shroud Sheet Cap & Pillow	2	2	
To 2 Men in with the Coffin & putting in the Body		3	
To Screws Pitch & fixing in the false Lid & making up the Body		2	
To the Use of the Best Velvett Pall		10	
To 15 Plumes of the Best Black Ostrich Feathers for the Hearse & 4 Horses	1	16	
To a rich Armozine Scarf for the Minister	1	14	
To 3 Silk Hatbands	1	4	
To 6 Pair of Mens Plain Kid Gloves		13	
To 3 New Crape Hatbands		10	6
To 4 Pr of womens Plain Kid		11	11
To the Use of 3 Cloaks the Mourners		3	
To the Use of 4 Hoods & Scarfes		6	
To a Hearse with 4 Horses to Bunhill fields Burying Ground	1	2	

To 2 Coaches with Pairs to Do	1	2
Paid for fetching Company	1	
Paid for Carying the Minister to Lowlayton	6	
To 2 Porters with Staves Coverd with silk Scarves & Cloaks	10	
To 2 Hatbands & 2 Pr of Gloves for Do	7	
To 3 Cloaks 3 Hatbands 3 Pr of Gloves the Coachmen	13	6
To 6 Men in Black to Bear the Body & attend as Hearse Pages with Caps & Truncheons	1 1	
To Silk favours & 6 Pr of Gloves for Do	12	
To a Hatband & a Pr of Gloves for the Men that attended the Funerall	3	6
Paid for Turnpikes	1	1
Paid for Beer for Men	2	
Gave the Grave Digger	1	
Attendance at Funerall	3	6
A Man fetching Company	1	1
	£22 4	9

Recd May 18th 1774 the Contents of the above
p Robt Grayson

II. FATHER AND CHILDREN

The children did not come up to London for the funeral—time was too short. But a little later Jedediah was sending his reflections to them and continued to instruct them at long range. It is well to remember their ages. Jedediah was then 47, his eldest son William was just short of 18, Elizabeth was 15 and 7 months, Martha 14, George 13, and Joseph not yet 9.

William Strutt to his father

Derby May 14th 1774.

My Dear Father

We yesterday received your kind but dreadfull Letter. You will easily guess the Transports of Grief we were in upon first reading it; had we not in some measure been prepared for it the day before by my Uncles Letter it would have been almost insupportable but even then I was not without some hopes that I should have seen my Dear Mother once again, but I never must, therefore shall endeavour patiently to submit to the will of God, who knows what is better for us than ourselves.

Oh; if I had known when she left Derby that that would be the last time I should ever see her, what a Tender parting would there have been but Mr. Moresby's Family being here early in the Morning we had scarce time or Opportunity to bid her Farewell: now, all the little neglects & Omissions of our Duty towards her crowds into our Minds; I had promised myself the satisfaction of seeing her again & of rendering to her all the little offices in my Power, but I am disappointed. I live in hopes the time will come when we shall all meet together in the Blessed Regions of Bliss & Immortality, never more to part—Oh: what did she say of me. Had I thought she would never more have seen me she should not have wanted my Letters, but Future events are very wisely hid by Providence. To have seen her in her Illness & last Agonies would have greatly increased our Affliction. We sincerely pity you & doubt not but Reason will, in Time get the better of Grief, since we are satisfied it is for the best.

You may depend upon it we shall do every thing in our power to render the remainder of your Life as easy & happy as may be by strictly adhering to the rules of Virtue & Religion since we are certain that will meet your Approbation. I can at least Answer for myself—

On Tuesday we Received a very pretty Note from Mrs White who is ever ready to do any thing in her Power for us; & Miss White has this Day brot us two Sermons very suitable to the present Melancholy Occasion. She & Miss Bingham have been here twice since we received the Fatal news & are very obliging. Miss Peggy Willott is now here advising with my Sisters abt their Mourning. She is very much affected as well as all my Dear Mothers Friends at Derby.

Mr Breary will get our Cloaths done as soon as Possible according to your orders. We stopt George's & Joe's Blue ones being cut off when we heard my Mother was so dangerously ill. We were much obliged to you for your kind Letter & hope you will not fail to write to us soon & often to comfort & support us under this Affliction but hope it will not be long now before we shall see you here. It might have been your Lot to have Died first & then her Tender Heart would soon have broke with Grief. We have reason to be thankful she has been spared to us so long, & that we are blessed with so Kind, so Tender, & so Indulgent, a Father who I am fully persuaded will do every thing in his Power to make up the Loss we have sustained; may God Bless you & support you under this severe Trial & may you live many Years to taste the pleasures of Filial Duty & Affection. My Brothers & Sisters send their Duty to you &c and are pretty well & my Uncle Strutt & Uncle & Aunt Woollatt send their kind Love to you. I wish to see you as soon as Possible & Remain your ever Dutifull Son

Wm. Strutt

Jedediah Strutt to his children (draft)

[London, May, 1774]

I recd both your pretty Letters & am pleasd to think you will bear the Loss of your dear Mother in a becoming Manner. Indeed it seems natural to submit to Necessity & to be resignd to those Ills we meet with in Life for which we can find no remidy. Death is Inevitable—& if in the present case he had been put off a little now yet it woud not be long before he woud call again. Nay it will not be long at longest before he will call on every one of us & when he calls we must obey. To Die is so frequent & the Instances so Numerous that one wd think the very habit woud render it familiar under all Circumstances—but it is not so & I have tryed the Common Arguments on those Occasions such as that it was the Will of god that the Dead if they have no enjoyment they are at least free from every pain & every grief. But it is possible they still exist, or that they will exist again in some other better World than this That we may again live with them there in unmix'd and everlasting happiness. Oh happy day how often shall I wish for that day for however these things may be or whether they will be at all or how or in what manner we cannot tell but this we know that it will not be long before we also shall add to the number of the dead, shall be as they are & know all that they know. One might call this reasoning but alas how weak, how short, how unsatisfactory. I try by reflecting on my own case & circumstances in how many Instances they might have been so much worse. I might have been in want & Indigent circumstances. I might have been sick or infirm or unable a thousand ways to take care of my family & affairs, or you my dear children might have been afflicted with Ill health or decrepit or Insane or you might have died also or it might have been all these together & how coud I have prevented any of them. I sometimes compare my own case to that of others in the like circumstances & recollect numberless Instances of Affliction & distress so complicated so big with Woe that they woud Esteem mine a blessing. But these & a thousand other arguments when I woud apply as reasons or remedies to the relief of my own distracted mind all appear empty as air, they are in vain, they are as nothing.—The first transports of grief Indeed are now in some measure abated for it is not in the Nature of extreams to last long. It is become less evident but more constant. I am best diverted when I am obligd to be engag'd about business but most happy when alone. Company does not please me but it is time only that can restore me (if any thing can) to that happiness & tranquillity I enjoyd but a few weeks ago. I know not whether I do well or Ill in writeing to you in such a way as this but it is because I Love the subject & I have nobody will understand me so well as you. At present I feel so bewilder'd, so lost, so wanting some how or other, so but half my self that I can scarce believe things to be in the manner they are. I doubt not every repetition of this kind will affect you but it will wear off especially in mind[s], young as yours are. Other objects will make other impressions but you I trust will never forget your dear Mother who loved you so well. I hope you will always retain much of her goodness of temper, disposition & affection, that you will imitate the example she has set you of virtue & goodness, of Benevolence & kindness (for they are most amiable virtues), that you will study the same sentiments of Sobriety, Temperance, Diligence, Frugality, Industry & Occonomy that you observd in her. Your own recollection will bring to your minds so many things that were to be found in her so worth your attention & imitation that I need not here enumerate them.—Nor is it needful I shoud tell you what in her you shoud not imitate fof she had no vices. She had indeed some failings & infirmities (who are without some) but shoud one attempt to draw her character they would sink into the shade & be lost among so many excellencies. I Loved her with all her failings & the more the longer I lived with her. Indeed she is gone & never knew *how* well I loved her.

I should have wrote to you sooner but either I have been ingaged about nessessary business or I have been immersd in thinking or so confused as scarcely to be able to think at all or I have not been in the Humour to write. I was in hopes I shoud have had a Letter from one of you but have not but I beg you will write to me soon. You should not wait for my writing. I want you to tell me how you do & how you go on & how you manage affairs and all the little things you can think of, they will all please me from you.

Martha Strutt to her father

[Derby, May, 1774]

My Dear father

We rec'd your very affectionate & pretty Letter with great plea-sure & am glad to hear you are tolerably well & I am sure your Letters will always give us as much pleasure as ours can give you. You need not question doing well in writeing to us on this present Melancholy subject for it gives us pleasure & it will be impossible we should ever forget my Dear Mother whose affection for us all could not be greater than it was. It is not her loss, tis only ours. She woud have liked to have stayed with us a few more years but it pleased God she should not therefore we must submit or in his Anger he may send some other greater affliction upon us. We do not yet know how happy she is but if we are good there will be no doubt but that,

> When the great, the awful Trump shall blow,
> We shall again behold her face to face;
> Shall smile at all our troubles here below,
> & gain in heaven with her a Glorious place.

if she does still exist how happy must she be. Let us then only prepare to meet her, for it will not be long before we must all meet. All her friends are very much greived for she had many good friends & I hope those who loved her will love us. But we must love one another & be friends amongst ourselves, to you we must impart all our Greifs. But you desir'd we would tell you all we could think on. The Cow has calved above a week ago a Bull Calf & my Uncle sold it for Seven & sixpence. We have great plenty of Milk, we hardly know what to do with it now we have never a pig. Should we make any Cheeses but they was not good before. There is some pieces of Muslin come for Miss Sally Whites Negligee. Mr Lowe has had a large family. Mr & Mrs Lowe of Nottingm & Master & the maid Mr & Mrs Hardman & Miss & the Maid we all drank tea there yesterday. I have had a ride this morning upon the blind mare & Billy upon David. The Garden is very nice, there is a vast many Gooseberrys & Currants & Apples & every thing & we want you at home very much to see and taste of all of them. Billy sends his Duty to you & he has got a good deal of Money for you & will collect all he can. Captain Boothby had paid all. My Uncle & Aunt Woollatt sends their kind love to you & all your friends desire to be rememberd to you & Mrs Willott will be obliged to you to give that parcel to Miss Willot. We are all very well & join in Duty to you from your ever affectionate Daughter

Martha Strutt

Martha Strutt to her father

Derby May 18 1774

My Dear Father

The inclosed my sister wrote last night but the parcel did not go so I thought I would write a line to tell you we rec'd your pretty Letter and are much obliged to you for it & you desired we would tell you all we could. All our friends are very good. Mrs White has wrote us two very pretty Letters & lent us two sermons very good ones for the Occasion. Miss White & Miss Bingham have directed us about our Clothes. My grandfather came here on sunday & is just returned. He has a suit of Clothes & joe & George one each which I think will not serve them for sundays & every day long. We are all pretty well & I hope you will take care of yourself for our sakes & as we cannot call my Dear Mother from the Grave we must follow her good example & as long as it pleases God to spare you to us we must endeavour to render life tolerable without that best of women. But the Parcel waits so I must conclude myself your very affectionate & Dutiful Daughter

Martha Strutt

I hope you will excuse this poor short Scroll but I thought you would like it better than none. We saw the cotton mill mentioned in the paper. I hope you will not be long before you come home. We do wish to see you. Miss Dolly Milnes[1] was to be married to day to Mr Gell of Hopton.

I think if my Dear Mother knew she would very much approve of every thing you have done. I will write to you again soon I hope you will.

Elizabeth Strutt to her father

[Derby, ? May, 1774]

My Dear Father

We received your very affectionate & instructive letter along with the books & drawings, I cannot tell you how much I am obliged to you for them. You may be assured that my endeavors shall never be wanting to make my mind & manners agreeable to you, but I have so many things to learn, all of which will require so much vigilance, & care, & attention, that I am much affraid I shall never be the agreeable person you describe, but the satisfaction that will arise from such a behaviour together with the thoughts of makeing myself aimiable in the eyes of God & you will be sufficient to banish from my mind every meaner thought & pursuit & encourage me to exert all my powers to arrive at so much excellence. Never was advice given in so pleasing a manner nor ever received with so much transport. I will think of it over & over & I *will* put it in practice.—Miss Malkin went from here to Chesterfield about ten o'clock on friday morning; & her sister came here last night along with Mr Astley, who came to preach at Derby to day, & Mr Wilding went to Chesterfield: she will return tomorrow. As my Brs George & joe had but one suit of cloaths each & have wore them every day they begin to look shabby for sundays & will not last them all summer. I was thinking that if George's green and joes brown ones could be dyed they would do to wear every day & save buying them another suit.

---

[1] One of the daughters of William Milnes of Cromford she was married to Philip Gell (*Derby Mercury*, May 20, 1774).

I wish you was here to advise us—The Cow gives a deal of milk & the butter is very good. We sell all the old milk; for the cheeses that were made of it last year you know were far from being good—Miss Bingham & Miss White are very kind. The latter has given me a pretty hymn to Providence.—we are glad to hear that your business is almost done. Pray come as soon as ever you can. We all join in duty to you & my Uncle & aunt. I am your affectionate & dutiful daughter

Eliza: Strutt

My sister desires to thank you for the drawings & will write soon Sunday night.

William Strutt to his father

Derby June 28 1774

Hond Father

I was in Hopes that by this time we should have had no occasion to converse in Writing, but from what you say we are not yet to expect you, sure it will not be long now before you will come home, we have got the Garden in very good order now & plenty of every thing in it. Patty takes great care of the Pigg and they both manage very well in the House. Betsey thinks she had better not send her Shoes. She likes them much & they will not be too little they will do to wear some future time, but Patty has sent hers & would be glad to have some Black ones as soon as Possible, when does Miss Willott come home. Mrs Willott is preparing her house over the Bridge to go to it very soon. You will find some alterations in Derby since you left it, but it will renew your Grief to see again those places where you have so often conversed with the dear Object we Mourn, she allways enlivened the company & Conversation—never was there a more Tender Mother or a more affectionate Wife, how exceedingly anxious did she use to be for the Health & preservation of us all, but she is gone, I hope, to reap the rewards of all her cares & Labours in another & a better World than this & we must submit to the all wise disposal of a Just & Good Providence for these are not Ills else would they never fall on Heavens first Favourites and the best of Men—this brings to my Mind those lines of Mr. Addison which She has very often repeated to me.

> The Ways of Heaven are dark & intricate
> Puzzled in mazes & perple'd with Error
> Our Understanding traces em in vain.
> Lost & bewildred in the fruitless search;
> Nor sees with how much art the windings run
> Nor where the regular confusion ends.

It is a pleasure to hear & read of great & good Men bearing up under all the weight of Misfortunes with Equanimity & Firmness of Mind & rising superior to all their sufferings, Glory in the Triumph. We are much obliged to you for all the kind & very affectionate Letters you have sent, some of which I never did, nor I think I ever shall read but in Tears. It is grand Consolation to us to think we are still blessed with so Tender and so good a Parent & hope I shall ever use my utmost Endeavours to merit his regard. We are all very well, to hear you was so would give us the greatest pleasure but particularly your ever Dutiful Son

Wm. Strutt

PS. Patty would be glad if you would chuse her shoes rather larger as these sent are too little.

Elizabeth Strutt to her father

[Derby, June, 1774]

My Dear Father

I am affraid you will think it long before you hear from some of us. We should have wrote sooner but had not till now any opportunity of sending a letter except by the post. I have but just now seen your last letter. My sister would have wrote today but says she is not in the humour for it but will write in a day or two. We have got joes cloaths dyed but Georges are already too little & they will run up with dying so my Uncle thinks they had better be laid by for joe till he is big enough for them & let George have another suit of black but he can do without them till you come. My brother & sister went to Cromford last Sunday & did not return till Wednesday noon. Mr Arkwright has lent Patty his horse till she has got one of her own & yesterday she took a ride on it single & I went behind my Uncle but it provd quite too strong for her & we were forced to have the saddle & pillion changed upon the road—it is now gone back again. We have washed this week but Alice makes the cloaths her own way now & they are not so good a colour as they used to be. She is to go to smally [Smalley] wakes next monday & stay till tuesday night.—I suppose my uncle has told you that we have got a pretty pig, we will be sure to take care of it.—We have very good milk & gather 6 pounds of good butter a week & it has not that disagreeable taste it used to have—I went to Dr Whites last thursday & had a very agreeable afternoon. Mrs White lent me the Life of Queen Caroline, & will lend me any other book that they have. I believe I have told you every thing I can think of. We are all very

137

well. I wish you had said so in your Letter. We all desire our duty to you. I am your affectionate & dutiful daughter

Eliza Strutt

I like the books you sent me vastly.

(*On back*)

I have hardly had time to tell you these particulars for did not know that the parcell would go so soon & Mr Gardiner was here which made it so long before I could write that it had like to have been too late. My Br will write to you on sunday.

Elizabeth Strutt to her father

Derby july 9 1774.

My Dear Father

I esteem it as a favour that you will take the trouble to tell me of any thing you think inelegant in my letters; but it was the haste I was in, & my unwillingness to omit writing to you when I had so good an opportunity, that induced me to send you my unconnected thoughts just as they arose in my mind: your telling me of my faults is a proof that you love me, & I will do all in my power to improve, but I am much afraid you will be tired before you have taught me to speak & write elegantly.—I have sent you the receipt for the powders & am very sorry to hear that you are so indifferent as to have occasion for them, I beg of you for our sakes to be careful of yourself, the least intimation of your declining health is sufficient to alarm us. I wonder when we shall have the pleasure of seeing you here again, I never wished so much to see you as I do now; you have been gone at least 5 months, is not that a long time? but however 'The joys of meeting pay the pangs of absence' & I am now in pleasing expectation of those joys, & when will they arrive?

When I wrote last to you I did not know that there was any thing very inelegant in saying I liked the books *vastly*, but when I came to think of it I thought it did not sound well; will it be better if I say that, I am much pleased with them, I have found (as you told me I should) many passages that have entertain'd me, some that have renewed my grief, but that wants no renewal, for tho' my thoughts are often diverted by company, amusements, family affairs, yet when I am alone they will return to you & to my dear Mother. I know not how it is, but there is something so pleasing in my grief that I love to indulge it.—As to the management of the house we do every thing that we can recollect she used to do. Alice grows careless, & we must grow more & more careful; I must endeavour to acquire that steadiness & diligence which will conduct me easily through all

138

the difficulties of this life. But I am of strange unsteady temper, 'This moment resolute, next unresolved.' Perhaps you my dear Father could point out some way for me to get the better of it. I know not what I should do without so experienced a guide. I often read your pretty advice with great pleasure.—Alice has just been in to tell us that she intends to leave her place the 8th of next month, sure you will be at home before then, we shall not like to have another while you are away. I think she might have staid till you came home, but perhaps we may get one as good as she & we must learn every thing we can of her before she goes, with regard to cooking & cleaning that we may be able to direct another, otherwise we shall appear very silly in the eyes of the world if she should be ill natured enough to expose us.—

I have not done any thing in the warehouse lately & indeed we have too much work to do to admit of my being there long together, however I will be very diligent & improve in my french as much as I can & when I have time I will assist Molly. We are all very well & desire our duty & love to you & to my uncle's family. I am my dear Father

your affectionate & dutiful daughter
E: Strutt

The receipt[1]

Pulv: Ipecacuana gr 3
Spec: Aromatice gr 2
Pulv: Rhei gr 8 p Pulv:

Martha Strutt to her father

[Derby, ? July, 1774]

My Dear Father

I now take up my pen with an intention to write you a long Letter, & tell you all I can think of. Last thursday we was surprized with a visitor from London, which we did not expect, it was sally Beardmore My Dear Mothers old favorite servant, she staid till this afternoon, friday, & then went to Headge where she intends staying a month with her sister, & calling on us again as she returns to London. We were very civil to her & did all in our power to oblige her, she is very thin, she says she called on you just before she set out but did not see you for you was gone to Gravsend. When she came nobody knew her, it was not likely we should for it is now 13 years since she left Derby. She says Mrs Dolly talks of sending us some Gold & Silver fish which she keeps in a glass of water but she does

---

[1] Jedediah, it would seem, was suffering from a stomach complaint.

not know how to send them. May be you could bring them. We are much obliged to you for your goodness in complying with anything that will make us happy. I likewise thank you for the pretty drawings you sent me, but I fear they will be too hard for me & I have never a pencil. If you think they are any better at London than Derby please to bring me one. Last night Monday night my uncle treated us to Mr Steven's Lecture upon heads. He perform'd in the New Theatre. There was a deal of Company & I was never better entertained. He shewed us the Picture of a Lady. On one side she was painted in very good humour & on the other in a very bad one & there was such a contrast that I think I shall endeavour to be always good humoured. I have the pleasure to tell you that George & joe have never been beat but once since whitsuntide, they are very good & send their Duty. We manage pretty well & take care of all the things. We are busy makeing & mending all the Boys shirts & when we have done them my sister will help Molly. I dont know what is the matter with Molly but she has begun to take Snuff & does very little work. I will not say any more about a Horse as you think it will be better not to have one. My uncle has bought himself a new saddle & Bridle new Stirrups & spurs. I dont know what he intends to do with them. I should like to go one other quarter to the dancing if you think proper. Mr Simpson has a many scholars.[1] Mr Frud does not teach any more at Derby. Miss Bingham has asked us to go there this afternoon which obliges us to break off. You will be surprized at the Date of this Letter but since I begun to write it I have wrote a bit now & then as things have hapened till there was an opportunity of sending it. We are very sorry to hear you are but indifferent & you dont say anything of coming home. You cant think how we want to see you. I hope Mr Harris's is not an infectious sore throat. Pray take care of your self. I think there has been more deaths this spring than ever was known. We still learn French & we will go forward as best we can; Bessy Laluriel went to Burton on Sunday. She has taken to learn french & we are to write to one another. You say you would have us acquainted only with those which we can learn something from. There is Miss Whites & Miss Bingham, Miss Willots & Miss Evanses are as good a set of acquaintances as we can have. There is Miss Balguys & Miss Duesbury want us to go & see them but we had rather not go for I am sure we can learn nothing there. Mrs Willett is coming to live at her own house where my uncle Woollatt lived. She has lett her other house & shop all together. They are building a smart new house where Whittingtons lived. We

---

[1] Mr. Simpson's dancing school was held at the Old Assembly Room, Derby (*Derby Mercury*, April 16, 1778).

are all very well & the Cow & the Pig but the mare is lame of both her fore feet & my Uncle thinks she never will be well again. I should be obliged to you to send my shoes as soon as you can for I have none to wear on sunday. We all join in duty to you & my Uncle & Aunt & love to Cousins from your affectionate & Dutiful Daughter

Martha Strutt

My Uncle & Aunt Woollat desire their love to you. We hope to hear from you soon. Betsy will write soon

Martha Strutt to her father

Derby july 27th 1774

My Dear Father

I receiv'd your pretty Letter with great pleasure & thank you for it. My Sister told you in her last Letter that Alice was going to leave us I suppose to be married. We enquired of Mrs White & everybody we could think of for one & have at last heard of one, she has just been here & we think she will do if you approve of the wages she expects which is at least 4 pounds. She has lived at several places in Derby, Dr Butters and Mr Coopers the Excise Officer & is now with Mrs Chatterton in the Iron Gate who is a very clever woman & we must have one that knows how to do most things as we are not clever enough ourselves at present to teach one, but must learn what we can of them. The young woman is willing to come for a month or a quarter of a year upon trial but we shall not say any thing to her till we hear from you as Alice says she will stay till you come which I hope will not be long. Mrs White thinks she has used us very ill in accepting the mourning if she did not intend to stay as servants usually stay the year they wear the mourning. Wednesday fortnight my uncle, Sister & I took a ride to Cromford. I rode Single of my Uncle Woollatts horse. On thursday we dined, drank tea, & supped at the bath & stayed till twelve o clock. My sister danced but we did not know the Gentleman. There was a deal of Company but none that we knew except Mr & Mrs Thompson of Nottingm & Mr & Mrs Johnson of Glasgow. On friday my Uncle dined at the New bath[1] with Mr Thompson but he would not come to Derby. On sunday my Brother went to Cromford & came back on tuesday morning. He met with young Mr Salt & Mr Arkwright & they all went to Bonsall

---

[1] 'At Matlock are two baths, the old and the new [wrote William Bray in 1777]. The company dine together in a large room at two, and sup at eight, after which there is music for those who choose dancing, or cards for those who prefer them. The charge for dinner is one shilling, and the same for supper; every one drinks what he likes.' (Bray, op. cit., 125–6). Another description of the Baths is given by Cozens-Hardy, op. cit., 278.

wakes & Mr Salt came to Derby. Sally Beardmore came to Derby last wednesday to take a place in the coach for tomorrow & when she gets to London she will call on you with a Letter from some of us. You desir'd I would send you word when danceing begun. The second quarter begins next Monday & I suppose you mean for me to go then & I will endeavour to learn all you desire me. Mrs Willott has come to her own house & they like it very well. When you write please say if you would have Alice brew for all the Burton drink is gone sour & there will be none fit for you to drink when you come home. Master bobby Malkin has given me a very pretty bird, a proud Taylor.[1] It whistles very well, & my uncle has bought a cage for it, cost 5 shillings. I have not time to write more as the parcel is going so must conclude. We are all very well and join in Duty to yourself, Uncle & Aunt and love to Cousins from your ever affectionate & Dutiful Daughter Martha Strutt.

pray write as soon as you can.

Elizabeth Strutt to her father

Derby August 10th 1774.

My Dear Father

I am very much concerned to hear of your indifferent state of health; you have my best wishes & my constant fervent prayers for the restoration of it. Your business has detained you so much longer in London than I expected, & you have so often said you thought you should come soon that now you are so poorly I sometimes think you will never come. I wish I could see you. I received your letter dated the 25 of july & desire to return my sincere thanks for it, for I am really pleased with it & am obliged to you or any one else that will tell me of my faults, they are innumerable, & will never be expelled without great attention, & I am often inattentive.

That bashfullness you tell me of is indeed very embarrassing to myself, & must make me appear silly to others; but I think it will soon wear of if I accustom myself always to speak & act as I should do if I was in company. As to my speech I must say that I never observed any lisp in it, & if there is excuse me if I say I think it is natural, & what I cannot remedy; however I can observe how others speak, if that will be of any use to me & I will do it with attention. I always thought there was something disagreeable in my reading but did not know till now what it was; now I do know I shall certainly endeavour to rectify it. I confess that I have suffer'd myself to spend too much time in bed, but your advice & the desire I have of pleasing you, have so far animated me that I now rise about 5

---

[1] Proud tailor, dialect name for a goldfinch.

o'clock. I am thoroughly convinced that youth is the season for improvement & that if I live I shall have reason to regret the loss of every mispent minute; & tho' I know this how many minutes & hours do I mispend. I think my sister already much improved in her dancing, she has something of that graceful agility, & that air of ease, which I have often admired in good dancers, but which I now despair of ever attaining.

Since my sister mentioned a servant to you in her last letter who we thought would do, I have enquired her character of Mrs Butter, & we all think she will by no means suit us, so we are yet unprovided. I beleive alice will stay with us till you come but I dont know. I wish so much to see you, that if you could fix a time for coming down how impatiently should I reckon the days & hours till I saw you. That my dear Mother will not meet you here when you come is very certain; but your dutiful & affectionate Children will meet you, they will load you with their caresses & endearments, they will endeavour to mitigate your grief, & when you are not well they will treat you with that excess of tenderness which your departed Consort would have poured over you, in every thought, word & action they will strive for your approbation; I in particular will do this, being with much gratitude, your affectionate & dutiful daughter Eliza: Strutt

Dr. White of Nott[ingha]m called here on monday & desired his respects to you. We are all very well & send our duty to you. Pray write a line the first opportunity; I think you would if you knew how anxious I am for your better health. When you are better, I shall be obliged to you if you will continue your admonitions.

Martha Strutt to her father

Derby Augt 17: 1774

My Dear Father

As I have an opportunity of writeing to you & was not willing to omit it tho' you do owe me a Letter for to one of yours there ought to go three or four of mine to make up for the Inelegancies of them but I hope I shall improve though I flatter myself poor as they are that they give you some pleasure. Billy will be very glad to hear from you for he thought you had almost forgot [him. He] went yesterday to Tutbury Bull running &c & [came back] last night. George has been very poorly but he is got better & gone to school. This week is danceing week so I have not time to write so much as I would. I hope I shall improve by going. We are learning the Cotillons. Mr Simpson has about fifty Scholars. I need not tell you how glad I shall be to see you for we all join in the affectionate Letter my sister wrote to you. Our races are in about 3 weeks & if you are not come home by

143

then please to send us word whether you would have us lett the Lodgeings. We are all very well & the Boys are good. Today is joe's birth day & he is to have a plumb pudding but I must go to the Danceing & must conclude this short Letter but I will write you a longer another time. Our Duty to Uncle & Aunt & love to Cousins & am with ardent wishes for your health & safety your affectionate

& Dutiful Daughter
Martha Strutt

My Uncle & Aunt Woollat send their love to you

Jedediah Strutt to his son William

London, August 17 1774

My Dear Billy

Some time ago I happened to see some of the Letters wrote by the late Earl of Chesterfield to his son which pleasd me so well that I determined to buy the Book & on perusing it find so full of good sense, good language, & Just observations that I am charm'd with it—

The late Lord Chesterfield was a Nobleman of the first Rank, had all the advantages of a learned & polite Education Joind to a ready witt & good understanding. He had seen & conversd, & been Employd in most of the Courts of Europe: Indeed he had spent a Life of many years in the most polishd & refind company that were any where to be met with to all which advantages he added the most diligent, the most careful & most Justest observations—The son to whom he wrote these letters I suppose was his only son, & the letters show how much he loved him but not being born in Wedlock he coud not inherit his Fathers Estate & Honors; therefore it was that the Father endeavourd first to qualify him for the highest posts of honor & advantage in the State & then intended to use all his influence which was a great deal to bring him in to these posts, in order by his Learning & good sense, by his great knowledge of Men & things, by his acquaintance with the Language, Government, & Manners of Foreign Courts as well as those of his own, by a Masterly Manly Eloquence in Speaking & Writeing, & lastly by the most consumate politeness, Address & graceful behaviour to enable him to make his way & his Fortune in the great World. It is to such a son so circumstanc'd, & to such a Father so qualified that the world owes these Letters.

It is very true that the Rules & Precepts contain in these Letters are appliciable only to those of the same Rank & circumstances (and perhaps there are some passages to loose or too Immorral to be

Applied to any circumstances whatever). But there are many others deserve to be well attended to by all who have the least desire to be amiable in themselves or agreable to others, who woud in the least adorn the Rank & Station they are in the world whatever it is—I need not tell you that you are not to be a Nobleman nor prime minister, but you may possibly be a Tradesman of some emminence & as such you will necessarily have connections with Mankind & the World, and that will make it absolutely necessary to know them both; & you may be assured if you add to the little learning & improvement you have hitherto had, the Manners, the Air, the genteel address, & polite behaviour of a gentleman, you will abundantly find your acct in it in all & every transaction of your future life—when you come to do business in the World. It is impossible for you now to think how necessary it is to have these accomplishments as well as those of a more solid or more important Nature—You may believe me in this for I now feel the want of them by dear experience. If I woud I cannot describe to you the awkward figure one makes, the confusion & the imbarrassment one is thrown into on certain occasions from the want of not knowing *how* to behave, & the Want of assurance to put what one does know into practice—I look on it now as a real misfortune that in the beginning of my Life I had not sense nor judgment enough of my own nor any friend that was able or kind enough to point out to me the necessity of any easy agreeable or polite behaviour. Indeed so foolish was I, that I looked on dancing & dress, the knowing how to sit or stand or move gracefully & properly as trifles not worth the least expence of time or money, & much below the notice of a wise man—I observe in you a good deal of the same temper & dispositions with regard to these things that I myself had when I was your age; but if you will believe me as the best friend you have in the World, they are wrong notions, & must be eradicated & chang'd for those of a different nature if ever you mean to shine in any character in Life whatsoever. Indeed it is almost as necessary to learn a genteel behaviour, & polite manner as it is to learn to speak, or read, or write. Nay there are not many virtues that require to be inculcated, cultivated, improv'd, attended to, & practis'd than these little arts of address & behaviour which you now think & I once tho't so trifling, & so unnecessary. —It is from the necessity there is of learning these things & of youth being the only time in which they can be learnt, from my own inability to teach them you, having never learnt them myself, that I here make you a present of these letters as containing the best reasons as well as the best instructions for obtaining those necessary accomplishments that I have any where yet seen, & I injoyn, & intreat you to read them with love and Attention & endeavour to put in practice what you find necessary to be practisd so far as is agreable & consistent with your rank & circumstances. By diligently & Attentively doing this you may in a little time acquire more real knowledge of the world of Mankind, & be better qualified for the various [require]ments of business & amusement than it is possible you coud without such an help, & without such Attentions. I have just lookd over all the volumes & as I went along have marked with my pencil a great number of these passages I thot worth remarking, but shall here take no further notice of them; your own Judgement I have no doubt will lead you to take proper notice of all those that appear more immediately to concern yourself, & leave the others to whom they may concern.—

I am the more urgent with you about this affair of your manners as I am sure you stand in great need of improvement in that respect. You are naturally very modest, & consequently very bashful; there is a Backwardness in going into company, & shyness when in it that prevents you saying or doing those things, or not in a proper manner that you are very well qualified to say or do if alone, or only with some intimate acquaintance. These things if they belong at all are rather the overflowing of [your] duty, are what may be called being too modest; they are not true modesty & there should be attention & care taken to remove them. I think it may be truly said, that if a man of great modesty indulges himself in seeing but [not participating in] company, he will never have assurance enough when forced into it to behave with that ease, freedom & gracefulness, that is the very life & soul of pleasing. There will always hang about him that foolish, sheepish, Bashfulness that will ever make him appear ridiculous however well he may be [qualified in] other respects. I speak this from experience & very feeling [for I] always had the same feeling without the proper means for rem[edying it until] too late. But you are young & yet to what you already know [if you] add ease & attention & every other proper means of improvement [that is] in your power, you will certainly improve, & you will as certainly find it will well [repay] all the pains & trouble you may bear: but there must be a diligent attention & observation—

Lord Chesterfield will tell you, that the company of Women will best teach you the manners & the graces & give the highest polish to politeness & good Breeding, & you may believe him; but then, it must not be with the Low, the vulgar, the Ignorant or the abandond; but with the Genteel, the Gay, & the sensible part of the Sex. With some of them I am sure some time may be spent very profitably, very innocently, & very agreeably. But you will say all this will be attended with a great deal of expence of money, of Dress, of time & a great deal of trouble. Now with regard to the expence, the company I woud wish you to go into will never run you to any great lengths & I think you are too sober & have too much sense to run into idle, debouch'd, extravagant company, there is nothing to be learnt there, so let not the expence hinder you from going into such company *if possible* that is something older, & something superior to your own; you will there most likely see & hear something you had not seen & heard before, & come away the wiser & the better. And when ever you want, that you think necessary in your Dress to make you appear, at least not below the company you frequent, have it, & I will most willingly pay for it, & I will only ask in return, that you make a wise & a proper use of it; you will have the advantage & I shall have the pleasure.

The trouble you will be at will help to keep both your mind & your body in a proper habit of disposition & the same I reckon will [not] be lost if you make a proper division & disposition of your time to your business, your improvement, your pleasures, & add the [   ] use thereof to each, you will have time enough for all. What is [   ] redeeming as time, is like gaining some that had been lost, & improving it is like makeing it more than it is: It is like makeing of time.—Now all I mean by all this is, that I think you abundantly deficient in the great points of assurance, address, & politeness & if ever you will learn them it must be now while you are young. I therefore intreat you will not now neglect things, read over the Letters I have sent you on the subject again & again: they will abundantly inform & assist you, attend to them, practice them.—I woud have you also endeavour not only to retain what you have already got of the Latin & French Languages, but to improve in them, particularly your French, which you may do a great deal by a little practice, & by endeavouring to converse with your Sisters in it, & that woud improve them also at the same time. You cannot now tell what pleasure it may give you & what advantage it may be if you come to live any time in the world. What you have learnt of Algebra will do you no harm, but I think you will tire of it for it is a dry study, & not adapted either to a man of business or pleasure. To understand common plain Geometry wd be of much more use to you in life & I wd wish you to learn about as much of Musick as I have learnt, which to be sure is but very little, & may soon be learnt, but by knowing so much of the first principles & foundations, you will always have more pleasure from hearing it than you can possibly have without some such knowledge.

[You] say you are very far from being perfect in danceing but I would ha[ve you en]deavour to make your self more so, either by going to school [or by] entering company & assembly where you can improve your s[elf]. Tho' these Letters are more immediately applied to the use of yo[ung noblemen] & gentlemen, yet there are so many things contained in them [that are of] general use that they may be read with advantage by people of [both] sexes, especially the young, that I woud have your Sisters read them as well as you, & George too: but they must read them with attention, & then they will find many things well worth their observation.—I have at different times wrote you this long Letter & sometimes think of many more things that I have to say but not now. I shall be glad if you will write to me, & tell me any thing you have to say, & your opinion of the books. I am not very free in conversation but I love to write to you. I think I am better in my health this week & hope in time I shall be very well again. I apprehend no danger but am not so well as I could wish, I desire my love to your Sisters & Brothers & am your most affect. Father

J. Strutt

Elizabeth Strutt to her father

[Derby, Sept. 5, 1774]

My Dear Father

I am obliged to you for your last favour, & should certainly have returned you thanks for it sooner, if I had had time, which till now I assure you I have not. You have wrote me a longer letter than I expected but not longer than I wish'd. I am glad to hear in your letter this morn: that you have had an agreeable journey, & that it has been of service to you; & I am sorry that you was disappointed on your return in not finding a Letter from Derby. We have received the letters from Miss Needs but how we were surprised & mortify'd from what you said in my sisters L[ette]r. We expected two elegant Epistles from them giving an account of their travels ever since they left Nottingham & also something sympathetic & friendly; but instead of that, we had the mortification to find these the contents of both letters:—that they just wrote a few lines (though it was with difficulty that they could spare the time) to apologize for their long silence; to let us know where they are; that it is a pretty house, & to give us a list of the names of the Nobility now at Brighthelmstone. What answer can one send to such stuff inelegantly expressed? I never was more at a loss for a subject.

I was at Cromford last Wednesday but one along with my Uncle, & we return'd on Thursday. Mr Smalleys family is there. They seem to be very agreeable people & I could spend a week with them with great pleasure. I have not seen any of Mr Milnes's since last summer. I had a letter from Miss Dolly during my dear Mother's illness whilst my mind was rack'd with a thousand hopes & fears. I could

148

not answer it then—in a few days after she was married—& I have never answered it—I suppose it would be very improper to renew the correspondence now, having deferr'd wishing her happiness so long —if you think it would not, & can tell me how to address her in her elevated station it would be very agreeable to me, for there is something improving in her letters. I have a peice of news to tell you. Last Thursday but one Alice said to my Sister I shall go (for she never says may I) to Smally next Sunday, I shall like to go before dinner, & shall come back on Monday. Accordingly on Sunday she left of her mourning, drest herself very fine, & set of in the midst of very heavy rain which was likely to continue—a few minutes after she was gone the bells began to ring—we enquired into the cause & found it was for Alice's wedding—I was much surprised but not angry; but my Brother & Sister were very angry, said she had used us very ill, & declared she should never come again—but when they had considered that the Races were so near, that they were not provided with a servant, & did not know when we might, & that it would not be long before you came home, they agreed for her to stay till then, which she is willing to do. Most People think she uses us very ill in leaving, the year she wears her mourning; but she thinks there is nothing amiss, either in leaving at this time, or being married without letting us know, & says that if it was all undone she would do just the same again. I asked her if you had given her a note & she said you had not, & that besides her wages there are two new Gowns owing her. When her wages were raised which is 4 years since my Mother promised her a new gown every year that she took no veils [vails], & she has only had two of them: She will look upon the crape one as a third, unless we choose to take that for another servant & then she will expect two—she has had one of our Cotton but she is willing to stay till you come home & then you can settle these things to your own satisfaction.[1] We have at last heard of a woman that is likely to suit us. She has a good Character, & I shall send to her as soon as I have an opportunity, she lives at West Hallam. For so young a House keeper this is a very difficult affair & I am sorry it happens so soon because it makes me appear to great disadvantage. Having never been used to Cooking or any thing of the kind I am not capable of instructing a servant, & those that do understand their business are very hard to be found; but Mrs Willott & Misses have given me their advice & assistance in a very friendly way. If when you come home you should not find such good

---

[1] The movement for the abolition of servants' tips (vails) had been spreading south. Evidently Mrs. Strutt had substituted gowns for the irritating imposition on visitors. Cf. Hecht, *The Domestic Servant Class in Eighteenth-Century England* (1956), 158–68.

Economy nor have things so nicely cook'd as they have been, I hope you will be so kind as to excuse it at present, & when I have had more practice (for nothing but practice will do it) I don't fear but I shall be capable of managing the house to your satisfaction. We have not had a single person to enquire for lodgings, & I believe there will not be so much company at the Races as was expected. My Brother sends his duty to you & thanks you for the books. He is highly delighted with them. He went to Cromford yesterday otherwise he intended writing to you. He will write next sunday for he has no time but on those days. He returned to day & was to have brought Miss Smalley along with him but she was taken ill last night & could not possibly come.

I apply very closely to my french & don't doubt but with care, attention, & practice, I shall be able to translate any french book that falls my way; but as to converseing in that language, the pronunciation is so very difficult, that I am afraid I shall never do it with elegance & fluency. I see that the word expell'd was very improperly used in my last letter, & I am obliged to you for taking notice of it: remedied would have been much better. I have not time to write to Miss Need this afternoon, but I will write as soon as the races are over & send it to you to read.

I am my Dear Father your affectionate & dutiful Daughter
Eliza Strutt

pray give my Duty to my Uncle & Aunt & love to Cousins, I am glad to hear they are well.

William Strutt to his father

Derby Sepr 14th 1774

Hond. Father

I hope this will be the last Letter I shall have occasion to write, before we see you again; I little thought you would have staid so long, for it is now more than seven Months since you left Derby[1]. . .

. . . I received your kind, Instructive, & very long Letter, with great pleasure, and the Sunday after the Books which you were so good to send me, for which I return you my most sincere thanks. I had just seen one of the Volumes before, and was highly entertain'd with it, I wish much to have them myself, but never tho't I should. Indeed you could not have obliged me more. I am now perfectly convinced of the Utility of Learning & practising a Polite, easy, graceful Manner & Behaviour, and these Books will I am sure be a very great help towards giving me in some degree all those little arts

---

[1] The omitted passage is quoted above p. 75.

of address and behaviour which makes a Man at first sight (without many other Qualifications) so much admired & esteemed, and which I am conscious I stand in very great need of. I am particularly pleased with those passages on the employment of Time, the remarks are very Just: for I think that Man must be very unhappy who knows not how to employ every Minute of his Time some way or other to advantage; also the stress Lord Chesterfield lays on Diligence, Application, & Attention to whatever one undertakes; and I admire in every Page, & every Line, the purity, ease, and Elegance of his Diction, the Justness of what he advances, but above all, the pleasing agreeable manner in which he communicates all his Instructions and which indeed in that respect I have great need to make notice of & to improve; for, whenever I would express my Thoughts either in Writing, or in speaking, I am puzzled, and at a loss to do it in that easy Elegant manner I could wish. In short the more I read these Letters the more I am instructed & delighted by them. I have read the first Volume and begun the second, and you may be assured that I shall read them all with care & attention and endeavour to put in practise every thing that I think applicable to myself. I am very glad you marked those passages which you tho't worth remarking, I cannot agree with Lord Chesterfield in thinking that Time totally lost, or worse, which is employed in Mussic, provided it be done at a proper time & place. I shall certainly endeavour to Improve all I can in the French Language, both by reading & speaking it; as for Latin, I must confess I do not at present know what use it would be of to one in my station, but perhaps you could inform me, it is difficult, & must take up a great deal of Time, otherwise I should like to understand it. Algebra, & other Branches of the Mathematics, I only endeavour'd to learn enough of, to qualify me to read, & understand those Books which (in my opinion) treat on some subjects worth knowing—we are all very well & hope it will not be long before we see you, I am your most dutifull son

Wm. Strutt.

Elizabeth Strutt to her father

Derby Sepr 14 1774.

My Dear Father

I ought to make a number of apologies for my carelessness but as they cannot mend the matter now they will be as well left out—the moment I had seal'd my last letter to you I recollected that I had put no date to it and was most heartily vex'd with myself. It was wrote on Monday the 5 of septemr. Mr Br. has just brought me your letter & I am sorry that I have finished mine to Miss Need for I have said just the reverse of what you tell me to say & I have taken so much pains in the writing that I am loth to do it over again. I have said nothing about myself. However I think I will send it as I have an opportunity & then you will see it & if you think it a very improper one and not fit to send please keep it & I will write another. I am exceedingly rejoiced to hear you will be at home so soon & I hope nothing will happen to occasion your staying longer than next week. Miss Malkin & Miss Smalley from Alfreton came here last thursday and would have gone back that afternoon but we prevailed on them to stay till the next day & my brother & young Arkwright who was here two days treated us to the Play each night. Mr John Willot[1] was married at Leeds last saturday fortnight & his two sisters from Derby are to set off thither tomorrow to make a stay of about two months. My sister would have wrote to Miss Sukey Need today but it is dancing week & she makes the common excuse—want of time. I have not yet been to see her dance but intend going to night as they dance by candle light for the first time. We took notice that you did not begin Pattys letter in the usual manner but all thought it was done without design. And now my Dear Father the greatest pleasure I have, or can have is in the thoughts of seeing you, & that I shall see you in so short a time. I am your most affectionate & most dutiful Daughter

Eliza: Strutt

Haste has ocasioned my making so many mistakes in writing this letter so ill: but we are ironing today, & I really have not had time to take as much pains with it as I would otherwise have done.

III. THE DERBY HOUSEHOLD

Early in 1775 William Strutt spent some months at the London warehouse and in the summer Jedediah was there with his daughter Martha for several months, but in ill-health. While he was away the second son, George, was sent to school at Chesterfield, a school kept by Thomas Astley, the Unitarian minister there.[2] The letters show a pretty interplay of sisterly jealousy between Elizabeth and Martha.

[1] A linen draper of Leeds he was married at Clitheroe to a Miss Robinson of Chatburn. (*Derby Mercury*, Aug. 26, 1774).

[2] Thomas Astley (1738–1817) was at Chesterfield from 1773. For an account of him see McLachlan, *The Unitarian Movement in the Religious Life of England* (1934), 100, 119.

Jedediah Strutt to his son William in London

Derby Ap 10 1775

Dear Son

We recd yours this Day & shall send what we can of the things you mention—I wish you woud get your Uncle or your Cousin John to go with you to Dr Williams with my Comp[limen]ts & shoud be obligd to him to send a Bill of Cotton I left with him & I think he was so kind to say he woud tell me how he did it—I desire my Love to your Uncle & Aunt & to all the Children & if your Aunt can get us a few pounds, more such Tea as the last or such like if it be 2, 3, 4 or 6 will not signify & also if she can meet with a few pounds of Chocolate that she thinks good & a few pounds of Tea of a better sort if she has opportunity & you must pay her for them all & for every thing else that you have & I will repay you—I wish you to send her every thing that you have opportunity to & know & if your Uncle or Cousin go with you any where do not let them be at any expence about you—I want a glass syphon such alike one that your Coz Jn has to empty his fish globe with. You may get one at the Weather glass makers in Holborn & also a small funnel to fill it with —I am a great deal better than I have been and intend going to Cromford this afternoon. Your Sisters & Brothers are very well but think you very deficient in not telling them all you see and hear. However they expect great things from you when you come home. If your Uncle can spare Coz Jno to come down with you we shoud all [be] very glad to see him & flatter our selves for a few Weeks it woud be very agreable to him but however We expect to see your Aunt this summer & somebody along with her. I am yrs

J Strutt

Elizabeth Strutt to her brother William in London

Derby April 18 1775

Dear Brother

If the letter which Mr Evans brought last night was design'd for me I am much obliged to you. I hope you will excuse my writing sooner as you know my dislike to that employment. Miss Malkin sets out for London to night which is a good opportunity of sending to you. I therefore under the supposition that you have wrote me two letters could not omit answering them. You cannot think how often we talk of you & how much we wish to see you. We hope you will be much improved & that the mauvaise honte will have entirely left you. We have been to see Miss Duesbury two or three times lately & she says there is a Miss Cooper that wants to come down & has nobody to come with that she knows. [She] will be glad to come with you provided it is agreeable to you & don't think the care of her too much trouble—surely you will not. Miss Duesbury seems to me to add to her great beauty much good nature & I cannot see that pride the people here talk so much of. My Father has got cold & has been but poorly this day or two but he is rather better to day.—You dont say how you like London or whether it answered your expectations, or exceeded them, or what—but I thought you would be entertain'd at a Play or with the singing you was likely to hear. We are obliged to my aunt for the tea & shall be glad to have some more when she can get it. I desire my duty & love to all that family. My sister would have wrote this afternoon but she is going to see Miss Fox. We are all very well & I am your affectionate sister

E: Strutt.

it is rude to leave Miss Malkin alone & that I might not do it long I have wrote this so fast you will scarce be able to read it. Com-[plimen]ts to Miss Willott.

Elizabeth Strutt to her father

Derby july 2d 1775

My Dear & Honor'd Father

I received your letter yesterday & was glad to hear you got so well to London. I do not wonder at your being exceedingly tir'd for such journeys are very fatigueing to people in perfect health. I am glad to hear my Uncle's family are well (I wish you could have said you were so) but as to my Brother's writing to them I dare say he never will for I never remember to have seen more than one letter of his & that was to you & so as the saying is if they are angry they must be pleased again. Mr. Astley has sent word that he does not know what Books George will want but he must take all he has so he has put them all together in a Box to be sent next friday & I shall work very hard to get his shirts & other things done to send along with them. Bro: Wm. & George set off this morning about 11 o'clock. They will stay at Cromford all night & go to Chesterfield tomorrow. George says he will be very good & Joe has been very good today. They both send their duty to you & joe desires you will bring his Cousin joe down with you if he gets better.[1]

. . . Miss Bingham call'd here on friday. She says there is no knowing when you will come down for Mr. Lowe said he should stay but a month & is not return'd yet. Dr. White has been in town a day or two, & is got pretty well. He went to Nottm yesterday. I have made you a night shirt & shall send it tomorrow in the bag along with the

---

[1] The omitted passage is quoted above, p. 77.

shirt that you left to have a button hole made in the wrist band. When you receive that you will have 7 shirts, 6 stocks & three pocket handkercheifs. I did not go to the meeting this morning because it rain'd so I have wrote my Sister a french letter & shall send it with her flannell petticoat & a letter to Miss Willott which she forgot to take. It is almost dark so I wish you a very good night,

> I am with the greatest affection
> your dutiful Daughter
> E: Strutt

I shall be exceeding
glad to hear from you
as often as ever you can write.

Teusday

My Aunt Woollatt desires to be remembered to you & will be obliged to you to buy her a handsome silver Cream Jug such a one as you would buy for yourself.

William Strutt to his father

Derby, July 5th 1775.

Dear Father

We Received your last Letter with great pleasure, as it Brot an account of your continuing pretty well which hope will be the case while you continue in London, I suppose before this Patty has arrived there with Mr. & Miss Arkwright from their short Tour, please to tell her we expect to have a long Letter with all the particulars of her journey, the most entertaining part of which she will easily collect from the Journal she was to keep and, also how the City of London answers her expectations, I went with George on Sunday to Cromford, and from thence to Chesterfield on Monday. He seem'd much pleased with the situation of the House & School but could not help shedding Tears when I left him—Mr. Astley says besides the Books he now has he will be wanting in a little Time, Caesars Commentaries, Virgil, Turners lattin Excersises, Chambaud's French Fables—French Rudiments & a French Dictionary, some of these French Books we have here but as they are wanted at home suppose he must have others. My Uncle has gone to Cromford to Day. Please to call upon Peter Vallotton, there is a deal of Money Due, Give my love to my Uncle's family, I should have written to them before now to thank them for all their Kindness, but I will write to Cousin Jno soon. We are all very well but the family is small. We are lost without you. I am your Dutifull Son

> Wm. Strutt

There are 2 or 3 Letters in the Bagg

Martha Strutt to her brother William at Derby

[London, July, 1775]

My Dear Brother

As our stay in London will be much longer than we expected I have defer'd writing (as I always do) in hopes of having a better opportunity & more inclination, but your unexpected favour rouzes me & I am ashamed when I think how rude as well as unkind it is to be so negligent but I hope you will not impute it to indifference but for want of courage & resolution which I always want in writing. I believe I do not want Matter for I have seen a great deal but I do as you did save it up till when I got home. I am very glad to hear Pegg has learnt to canter. I often wish I had her here or that I could come to Derby & take a ride with you for a few hours & come back to London again for I dont wish to come & stay with you at presant & I beleive my Papa will stay the sale of Silk over & if we can prevail upon my Aunt shall bring her along with us. I wish I could leave behind me those awkwardnesses you tell me of, I believe one is walking which you have often told me of & there is no doubt but that by attention & care a genteel Carriage & Polite behaviour might be attained, but you know I want attention.

Last Sunday we took a ride to Hampstead & drank Tea with Mrs Roper, it is a very pleasant place situated on a hill about four miles from London. On Monday I went to see Miss Willot & staid with her till wednesday. I was tir'd of mantua making, she wondered Miss Bessy did not write to her. I have been at Sadlers Wells & was amazed to see the rope dancing & walking the Ladder about which you told me of. I have not yet seen the King & queen but shall see them soon as I am told they go to Footes every wednesday. Our journey into France is postponed till some future opportunity or else if we had gone I saw the insurance office for lives when we set out from Derby I intended going. Please to tell Mr Stenson that I have call'd on Mrs Major & they were all very well. I shall call again. Give my love to joe & tell him that his cousin joe is so good a boy & learns his Book so well that he cannot leave school to come to Derby at presant but will come when he is a big Boy. Did you know my Papa has had a letter from George, he does not say how he likes school. I shall write to him very soon. I think I did not tell you we had been at Bedlam but I shall never desire to go again for I never expected to get out alive, the men that are at liberty follow you about & look so wild tis quite terrifying. I am to go to Mr Witherses & to Mr Johnsons with my Papa some day to Greenwich to Gravesend &c. &c.

Please to give my Compts. to Miss Almond & if I can spare time from all my pleasures I will write to her, also to Miss Robinson & to my Cousin Dolly. I am glad to hear she likes school. My Papa is got pretty well & has begun to Bathe. My Aunt & Cousins join with me in Love to you all. I will write to sister soon & now I think I have wrote you a very long Letter. However I [have] told you all I could think on, so if this will force another Letter from you, you will oblige your very affectionate Sister

M. Strutt

Elizabeth Strutt to her father

Derby july 24 1775

My Dear Father

Mrs Dolly got here about 9 o'clock on saturday night and was very much fatigued with her journey, my uncle & I went with her yesterday to Findern, it is needless to say how surprised & glad her friends were to see her—her aged Parents hung with fondness o'er her, & mindled tears of joy—she is an agreeable sensible woman; & I Love her because I am sure my Mamma loved her much. I believe she will come & stay a week here before she returns to London. Findern is a strange desolate place now—I used to think it very fine & have spent many a happy day there, but I think I am happier now—everybody is surprised when they consider what we are, & what we have been. I often think of it—& I never think of it but my heart & eyes overflow with joy & gratitude. I can never thank you enough, nor ever repay the vast, vast debt I owe you. Mrs Dolly told me you was getting better, & I am very glad to see it confirm'd in your letter this morning: I hear too by her that Patty is very well, that she is a very fine Girl, has a very pleasing manner, & is admired by every body; & I hear it with pleasure. Pray give my love to her & tell her, I should be very glad if she would overcome some pleasure to write to me a little oftner, I shall be very glad to see her & you at Home again, but she is so well pleased with London now that she does not want to come it seems.

I shall send the Loom Quilting you mentioned to night & pray tell Cousin Betsy that I think of her & will write to her soon—I have long been in great wants of a white petticoat myself, & should be very glad if you would give me leave to have one now, because the summer will be over soon—I have wrote to Brother George twice since he went to school & have desired him to write to me, but he has not.

I believe the hay was got pretty well but they have drank all the Beer & we are brewing again to day. I forgot to tell you in my last that Mrs Gell was brought to Bed of a Son & Heir about a fortnight ago & that Peggy (my Uncles Mare) was gone to school to learn to hold her head properly—I desire my Duty & Love at my Uncle's & am my Dear Father your very affectionate & dutiful daughter

Eliz: Strutt

My Uncle Woollatt desires his best respects. Phillip Wakefield bought us a little Pig last Friday & gave 19s for it.

My Bror has desird me to mention his having another suit of Grey Cloaths. I believe we shall wear second mourning all the summer & as his Coat will be much too shabby (he being obliged to wear it every day) We all think there will be no extravagance in his having a coat & waistcoat of light grey narrow Cloth because he may wear a light one out of mourning & it will be very useful when he travels. He desires his Duty & love & would write to Patty but he has *nothing* to say.—Mr Lowe called here yesterday & desired his respect to you. I cannot help telling you that he took up Lord Chesterfields Letters and cried 'Hum—a strange Hotch-podge I believe.' Farewell once more my Dear Father! I have told you a many trivial things but Women talk of nothing else.

George Strutt to his father

July 27 Chesterfield 1775

Dear Pappa

I Received yours a few days since & was greatly rejoiced to hear from you. I like school full as well as I expected, & will improve as much as ever I can, both in manners, & learning: for Mr Astley takes a great deal of pains. I received a letter from home last saturday, they were all very well. Did Brother wright to you about some books which I were to have because you was saying you could get them at London. If he has not I should be glad the next time you wright you would mention it to him; because Mr Astley gave him an account of what sorts I must have; for I shall want them as soon as possible. I have begun of making themes, & like it very well, & I hope shall continue so, & intend to have a good many against I come home, which I expect to do at christmas: but Mr Astley gives no holidays, but leaves it to their friends. But they all go & for that reason it will be very disagreeable to stay by myself. But you will tell me when you come hither which I hope will be soon & bring cousin Joe with you to Derby. I often think of your kind letter which you sent me but you never told me how you did, for I made shift to read it. Mr Astley wishes I might learn to wright & I do to because if I do not it will be too late, for I should chuse to wright better than what I do. Miss Malkin whent to Derby last week, & is not come back yet, but

158

intends coming in a few days. I saw miss Nanny last week, she was very well. I shall wright home soon, because I never have since I came; & Sister thinks me long, for I promised her would wright home very often but I have had nothing to say. I am very glad Sister likes London, but Sister told me you will stay a month longer, but I hope you will not exceed that. I expected Miss Arkwright would have stayed till you came; for you might have come togeather. You will give my love to Sister, Uncle, Aunt & Cousins, & all that inquire after me.

I am your most dutifull
& affectionate Son.
George Strutt.

Elizabeth Strutt to her father

(first page missing)

Now I have a favour to beg of you which I hope you will not refuse—it is that you will buy for Miss Bessy Willott a pretty fashionable pair of silver or plated Buckles—my Mamma often used to make them presents of little things & they have given us their advice & done us all the good offices in their power ever since her Death without any return & I think we should not forget them. I mentioned Buckles because I heard Miss Bessy wishing she had a pair. I am much pleased that you gave me leave to have a Petticoat & thank you for it. We are all very well & desire our Love to all. Goodnight may your sleep be sound & unbroken for without that there can be no perfect Health. I am most affectionately your Dutiful Daughter

Eliz: Strutt.

Monday

I waited impatiently for this mornings account of your Health & am sorry to find it such a bad one. I hope you will consult Dominiceti & every body else that you think can be of service to you. I am very anxious for you to come home not only that I may see you but because you would be better here than at London. I beg you will not stay a day longer than you can help. I am often very dull having nobody to talk to but I shall not grow melancholy. I read the determination of the American Congress yesterday & am sorry to see what distress they are brought to. How sensibly they write with what courage & coolness! What havock & bloodshed can a few ambitious men create amongst whole nations! Fare you well my dear Father & may the God of Heaven preserve you!

Elizabeth Strutt to her father

Derby August 20 1775

I can assure you my Dear Father I have not wanted inclination to tell you how much I was rejoiced to hear of your being so well for some days: to what do you impute it to & is it likely to continue? I have wished to hear from you, & know all particulars—indeed I should have wrote to you before now but I have had a bad cold, & I have been very busy lately, & several other things have happened to prevent me. John Strutt Esqr called here last week with one of his Son's in his way to Matlock & was so obliging as to write two Franks one of which I now send you; he did not stay many minutes but would not go through the Town without calling upon us. Pray tell Patty I wish her much pleasure but I am sorry she said she did not want to come Home: for now was I in her place & she in mine, I should think how much she had to do, & wish to be at Home merely to assist her: besides, I could wish that Home was more agreeable to her, & every one of the Family than any other place.

We have drank tea this afternoon at Mr Lowe's along with Mrs Tate of Chesterfield. She has been at Derby a fortnight & brought me a long letter from George, he writes very prettily, & she says they all think him an attentive, diligent, good Boy, & indeed we hear frequent & good a counts of him from other people—he has sent for a Prayer Book that he made use of at home & says he is not happy without it, he also wants some Books that Br. was to send to you for but he is gone to Cromford & I know nothing about them. I have been twice to drink tea with Mrs Dolly at Findern & she is to come here tomorrow & stay a week or a fortnight & my Uncle talks of taking her to Matlock for a day or two because she was never there.

Jedediah Strutt to his daughter Elizabeth

(draft on back of her letter of July 24, 1775)

You have wrote me two Letters since I came here. I thank you for them both. I have read them over & over—many times because they gave me pleasure & I am led by them & other instances of your affection to think that it is neither from Motives of Interest nor Duty that you behave to me with such tenderness and respect. I flatter my self it is because you Love me. I know not how it is unless it be *that you have no Mother* that I cannot see you nor think of you but with a pleasure & concern that I know not how to express. When I see in any of you signs of a good temper and good disposition, When in any of your words or actions you discover marks of ingenuity of a turn for improvement of good sense & of a good understanding & that

160

you improve in these as you increase in years what pleasure does it not give me and if, as it will sometimes happen that you fall in error and do wrong, yet how ready do I feel myself to forgive, to excuse, to attribute it to your youth, to inadvertency or inattention because I think it does not proceed from a bad heart or a vicious disposition of mind in any of you & because I am sure it is because [of] tl..t I Love you. This being so as I am certain it is you may most firmly rely on my cheerfully & willingly doing every thing in my power that will contribute to your interest, your happiness, your improvement, and even your pleasures & amusements—& you on your part if you love the truth & be honest, if you are wise & good & virtuous, if you will be grateful & love me as your best friend you will then abundantly repay all I have ever done, all I ever can do for you. I am very sorry to hear you have not been well & hope you are got better. I woud now & always have you be very careful of your health for after peace of mind & a good conscience it is the best blessing you can have in this world. I am better to day than I have been for some days past.

Elizabeth Strutt to her father

Derby August 30 1775.

My Dear Father

I received your very affectionate Letter last Saturday, & Pattys on Monday, I am very glad if there was any thing in mine that gave you pleasure, but I was in so much haste when I wrote them, that I cannot now recollect any thing I have said; but let the sincerity of whatever expressions of affection I made use of reccomend them to you. All your Letters; your Readiness to do every thing in your power to oblige, & give us pleasure; in short every thing you do or say, are so many fresh instances of your Love and affection for us; & I hope we shall never prove ungrateful: be assured then that in return I do, & always shall love you as my best Friend, & that being fully satisfied I have neither a bad Heart, nor a vicious Disposition, I will be diligent, temperate, & virtuous; I will love the Truth, & be grateful to you, & love you, with all the tenderness & affection, that your goodness can inspire me with: I cannot say that I will be wise, but will endeavour to improve, & learn & know all that I can. May we none of us disapoint your fondest hopes! Mrs Tate went to Chesterfield to day, & I wrote to George by her & sent your Love to him, she drank tea here last Monday. I wonder whether you are better than when you wrote last, or whether you are gone to Chelsea. I wonder too what your quack medicine was that did you so much good. I think London does not agree with you & that you would be

better if you could come home. I often think of you, & as often
heartily wish you was in perfect health, for there is very little
enjoyment without it. Wearisomeness, want of sleep, loss of appetite,
indigestion, how tiresome are they! I experienced them but for a
week, and how did I enjoy the reverse of them, that is, Health, when
it returned; every thing felt & look'd & tasted better because I was
so, I met with a very pretty Stanza of Mr Gray's in the last Months
Review

> See the Wretch that long has tost
> On the thorney Bed of pain,
> At length repair his vigour lost
> And breathe, and walk again:
>
> The meanest floweret of the vale,
> The simplest note that swells the gale,
> The common Sun, the Air, the Skies,
> To him are opening Paradise.

Health is a great blessing & worth taking pains to preserve; but like
many other things its value is best known by its loss. May you bear
its loss no longer! Mr Arkwright brought his Sister to Derby last
Teusday but one to go to School at Mr Latuffieres, & the thursday
following, Mrs Dolly being here, my Uncle & I went along with her
to Matlock, we had a very agreeable journey & came back on
saturday morning. Mrs Dolly was obliged to go to Findern the same
evening but I beleive she will come for a day or two before she goes
to London. Mrs Need & Misses went through Derby yesterday in
their way to Matlock, Misses call'd here but Mrs Need was so poorly
that we were obliged to call on her at the George; they are to be at
our House at Cromford for they are quite full at both the Baths, &
a deal of the Company lodge at other places. Pray give my love to
Patty and thank her for the Letter, I have sent the Handkerchiefs
she mentioned & will write soon. It was very hard you should go to
Mr Withers's to Dinner & have none when you came there. Miss
Needs desired their Com[plimen]ts to Patty & Miss Sukey will write
to her soon. I am much obliged to you for buying the riding Hat; I
long to see it. I have asked Molly about staying another year & she
says she intends staying till you come home but she thinks her place
is not profitable enough, she has had two old petticoats (one I gave
her today) & a bed gown but I suppose she thinks she deserves a new
gown for she has bought herself a new gown lately to wear every day,
& she tells me the neibours say I have not forgot all my Mamma's
rules, for they see I have given her a new gown; there is great notice

of, & many remarks made on every thing I do, it requires much more thought and care than I am Mistress of, to act with propriety in my situation—Molly will stay till you come & if you can agree about wages, she will stay another year. There are some things to be objected to in Molly, but it may be very difficult to get a better, & very easy to get a worse, therefore I could wish her to stay again, for changing is very troublesome. You cannot think how glad I shall be to see you at home again. I desire my love to all my uncles Family —I wish it may please God to bless you with better Health—I am your most Loving & affectionate Daughter

Eliza: Strutt.

We are all well & send love to you.

IV. LAST YEARS

The records of the last twenty years of Jedediah's life are scanty. He went to live near his cotton mills and built his mansion, Milford House. The Derby house was kept on and, apparently, the eldest son and the two daughters lived there until their marriages. Jedediah remarried about 1781 or 1782; his wife was Anne, widow of George Daniels of Belper, yeoman. One wonders whether she was his housekeeper. The marriage was not well received by the family and Strutt seems rather to have withdrawn into himself. He died 'after a lingering illness' on May 7, 1797, aged 70. In 1795 he had bought Exeter House, Full Street, Derby, an historic mansion where the Young Pretender had stayed, and he died there. He was buried in a vault under the Unitarian Chapel at Belper; the tablet bore the simple inscription:

JEDEDIAH STRUTT

THE FOUNDER OF THIS CHAPEL

DIED A.D. 1797, AGED 70 YEARS

To the careers of Jedediah's sons we shall return in the next chapter. George had married in 1783 and William and Joseph within a week of each other ten years later. The two daughters married late but well. The younger, Martha (Patty of the letters), married in 1791 Samuel Fox of Osmaston, but died in 1793. An entry in the cash book of 1786 of 6 guineas to Samuel Eyre 'for learning Mr Fox to work in frame &c' possibly refers to his initiation into the hosiery business. The

163

Foxes were an old Derby family. Martha had had earlier interests. In 1787 young Arkwright had written chaffingly to his friend Samuel Oldknow: 'There is certainly something going on between Miss S. and you, and of a very serious nature too' and a few months later had hinted 'They say Mr. Macmurdo and Miss Strutt are on good terms.' But Oldknow remained a bachelor; Martha's brother, William, told the news of the marriage to his friend:

> I suppose you have heard that my sister is at last married to Mr. Fox. It was time to make an end of it & the attachment had lasted too long and was too strong to be broken. They are now at Brighton & we are left a forlorn herd of Bachelors. What will become of us the Lord knows, Adieu.[1]

The elder daughter, Elizabeth, was the more striking character of the two sisters. She married in 1785 William Evans of Darley Abbey, on the outskirts of Derby, who was of a family of millers, cotton spinners, paper manufacturers, copper smelters, and bankers. They had long been close friends of the Strutts and William Strutt married an Evans. A disagreement between Elizabeth and her father just after her marriage provoked one of the most self-revealing of all his letters. As he grew older his capacity for brooding evidently did not diminish:

Jedediah Strutt to his daughter Elizabeth Evans

New Mills March 23: 1786

My dear Bettsey

If it were possible you could consider & see, how slender once my former fortunes were, & how narrow & contracted my education, & the habits of the former part of my life have been, & join these to my natural disposition to frugality, Oeconomy & industry you cou'd not wonder at my surprise on seeing such an enormous bill of cost for what in my opinion tends only to make you appear ridiculous—

I had *thought* upon the subject & concluded that if I gave you 10 or 15 Guineas for a new suit or so as you had already so good a stock of cloaths it would be very well. And if you chuse to make miss W—a present of something to the amount 2 or 3 guineas I shoud have no objection & these are still my sentiments—What you have

---

[1] Unwin, op. cit., 240.

laid out for Mrs S—I also mean to pay you for—But your Acct &, my opinion on this matter are so very different, that when they are compard, it cannot but appear, either, that you have been exceedingly profuse & extravagant, or that I am exceedingly penurious & caucteaus, even to meaness—Which ever way it may be I cannot now change my sentiments. Experience & observation of Mankind & the world has long since convinc'd me that to be industrious, temperate & frugal are wise Maxims & worthy to be retaind, & observd even by the rich & the Affluent—that a fantastick Vanity, a tho'tless profusion, Wilful or careless extravagance may sometimes gratify a silly pride or please a sensual & foolish apetite for the moment; but will never be the source of true pleasure or solid happiness.

Your reference to my leaving Derby being the cause of many of your inadvertances brings to mind one of the most blamable parts of my own conduct during my whole life—If it was to do again I coud not believe it possible that with such a temper & disposition as I am possessd of I shoud suffer other persons to squander away the money I had taken so much pains to acquire, in so profuse & so extravagant a manner, directly opposite to my own Judgement & inclination, without my leave or consent & in many cases without my knowledge of the matter—It is true I first hinted—then disapproved—was Angry—kept away—but avoided quarrelling because that woud give me more uneasiness than the loss of the money —the consequence is, that from having but little pride & no ostintation of my own, not being fond of finery & dress, not thrusting myself into what is calld Genteel Company, not frequenting Assembles, Ball, Concerts plays & shews, not going every summer at no little expence to see & be seen as the fashion is to some or other of the polite Watering places—From not using these great means of popularity & from that most humiliating circumstance to the pride & honor of my family, my late Marriage, tho' evidently concerted so as not in the least to lesson their fortunes or hinder their enjoyment: I am but little known & but little regarded. Few people imagine that the house at Derby belongs to me, that I have my concern in the business there, or that you are my children. When I am there strangers view me as a stranger also, & acquaintances seem not to be acquainted, nay in looking sometimes at some persons, I think their Eyes wished they did not see me: some of these I coud pity for the Weakness, & others I despise for their haughtiness.

Since I recd your Letter I have tho't over these things at different times, more than I had ever done before, and coud just now say a great deal of the subject; but will only observe further that I think with regard to business, building, furniture, Dress, expences &c I have not been properly consulted. And tho' you have all treated me personally with all the affection & regard I coud wish, yet in respect to my Marriage when it is duly considered I have been treated very disrespectfully & in a Manner I did not desire on that account. It woud have been easy for me to have enforcd a very different behaviour in my own family (& for other people I care not a pin) but I know it woud be all constraind, & constraint in all things lessons the pleasure. I have willingly given time & opportunity. I have asked but civility, because civility to my Wife would have been respect to me but how hard to obtain even that. Contempt & dislike in ones own family, soon begets a dislike in others. I desire not to be misunderstood to mean all this to you only, I mean it generally, but not equally, for I have observd a good deal of difference—I will only add that my wish & desire has ever been & will ever be, that you be wise, & virtuous, & happy. If you have any of you been less so than I expected, perhaps, I expected too much, & it was necessary I shoud be disapointed. If in your husband you have found a real friend, a kind & faithful monitor, you have found a great treasure & long may you live to enjoy that & all your other blessings is the sincere wish & prayer of your affectionate Father & constant friend

J. Strutt

Elizabeth bore six children before her husband died in 1796; in 1797 she married his half-brother, Walter Evans of Darley Hall, and died in 1836. By him she had a son, born in 1800. Elizabeth had inherited her father's florid style and was even more a child of her age. In October, 1793, she writes to her brother Joseph in ecstasy over Godwin's *Enquiry Concerning Political Justice* (which had been published in February in two volumes at three guineas):

Elizabeth Evans to her brother Joseph

Darley, Oct. 24, 1793

Mrs Drewry tells me you are impatient to see Godwin's Enquiry. —I am impatient that you should, & therefore send you the first volume which you may be getting on with, while I finish the second —& oh my dear Joseph read attentively, meditate, discuss, disseminate these precious opinions, these divine truths, with all the zeal which their importance demands. They have penetrated my heart, may they raise yours above prejudice, enable you to despise riches, & finally dispose you to use all your efforts to ameliorate the condition of mankind. The grand desideratum in Politics is the diffusion of knowledge & morals amongst the poor.—This the manufacturer has it in his power considerably to promote & is culpable in the neglect of it.

The time may be long in coming, but I indulge myself with the delightful hope that it will come, when the tyrants & the slaves of the earth will be converted into one great alliance of friendship & of brotherhood. You may have the pleasure of accelerating that blissful period—and would to God that you would set about it.

I am ever your truly affectionate sister

E. Evans.

This letter of the daughter, wife and sister of eminent cotton spinners reminds us that Robert Owen, then a struggling mill manager in Manchester, was not quite the pioneer in applied social doctrine that he thought he was.

Elizabeth was still more gushing in her letter to her bachelor uncle, William Strutt, in 1798, the year after her father's death. Of William, who died two years later, we know hardly anything outside the family letters:

Elizabeth Evans to her uncle William Strutt

Darley 6th Decr 1798.

Mr dear Uncle

If I had had the misfortune to lose you in your late dangerous illness; or if you had not recovered your faculties I should have been inconsolable for not having performed what I have long meditated: which is, to make you a formal declaration of those sentiments of affection & gratitude which are indelibly engraven on my heart.— For tho' there are cases in which I am convinced 'gratitude would be a *vice*;' that is, that it would be unjust: yet in the relation I stand to you, my dearest Uncle, I hold it to be an indispensable duty, a positive & indubitable virtue.

From my youth upwards, even to the present time, you have been my kind and dis-interested benefactor—& this from the purest motives—from respect for my mother's memory—and from the benevolence of a heart which has always found its chief gratifications in the enjoyments of others. You have so conducted yourself through life in the relation in which you have stood towards me, as to leave upon my mind but one full, pure impression of gratitude; unmingled with any of that bitterness or alloy which often arises between the best friends, from various little coldnesses, omissions, or neglects, none of which have I ever experienced from you. On the contrary,

167

I look back upon my past life, & recollect, with a pensive & most indescribable pleasure, that in all the events which have attended me through it, my *Uncle* has been my never-failing friend!

My mother died, & my father did not return to us for more than nine months. Who was then my watchful guardian? Who beheld with tender pleasure the fortitude & resolution inspired by my father's letters, which animated my endeavour to supply the place of that excellent mother?—My Uncle. Who taught me to ride on horseback—accompanied me in my rides; & showed me all of my native country & neibourhood that his convenience would permit:—endeavoured to inform my understanding & promoted all my innocent recreations? My Uncle. Who visited me with most frequency & cordiality when I left my paternal home & was married?—My Uncle. Who attended me in my indisposition at Bath during 4 or 5 weeks? My Uncle. Who came to me again at Bath, after my husband's death, & made that long & necessary absence from my children tolerable to me? My Uncle. And lastly, who gave his open countenance & support to my second marriage & left his home to assist me to obtain it? My Uncle. And I will venture to say he will never repent it, & that I shall always consider it as the consummation of his good deeds towards me.

You have probably now done all for me that you can ever do in this world: and all the return I can make you, is the testimony of an honest heart; & these tears of gratitude which fall while I acknowledge these important benefits. I thank thee also God of Nature! for enabling me to shed them at forty years of age, with the same sensibility as I should have done at twenty.

I have made these acknowledgements with the more pleasure as I cannot now be suspected either of flattery or of interest. I have nothing more to expect—I want nothing. I shall have your picture & I shall prize it as the resemblance of him, who has ever been my zealous, dis-interested, & faithful friend.

So farewell my dearest & honoured Uncle! May God bless you! and grant that the remainder of your life may be tolerably comfortable, & your death easy.

Eliz: Evans,

CHAPTER VII

THE SECOND GENERATION

UPON Jedediah's death in 1797 his businesses passed to his three sons all of whom, since leaving school, had taken an ever-increasing part in the management of their father's concerns.

Though, as we have seen, they did not remain long in hosiery, their cotton business, now styled W. G. and J. Strutt, continued its growth. Under them it became the largest in the country, celebrated not only for its size and for the excellence of its buildings and equipment but for its efforts to ensure the well-being of its workers. It was a model, spoken of in praise by such severe critics of the factory system as Owen, Faucher and Gaskell.[1]

There was, it seems, a broad division of function between the Strutt brothers. George, resident at Bridge Hill House, Belper, saw to the management of the mills there and at Milford and to the estates.[2] From Strutts' headquarters in Derby, William and Joseph looked to the technical and the commercial sides respectively. All were diligent in business. In 1800 when Joseph lay seriously ill in London, William, busy making arrangements for their friend Dr. Darwin to go there to attend him if need be, wrote that should he himself go up to London it would be the first time that he and his brother had both been away from Derby since the day Joseph had left school. And Strutts' Letter Book for 1824 to 1827 contains but a few pages written in a hand other than Joseph's.

---

[1] Owen, *The Life of Robert Owen* (1857), 211; Faucher, *Manchester in 1844* (1844), 94, 96; Gaskell, *Artisans and Machinery* (1836), 90, 294. For a more recent appreciation see Hammond, J. L. and B., *The Town Labourer, 1760–1832* (1917), 42, 49.

[2] We know little of the early years of the Strutts' estate except that Samuel Slater's father, William, a timber merchant, negotiated the purchase of a piece of land containing a water privilege for Jedediah some time before 1782. During the next thirty or forty years, however, the estate was extended greatly and by 1820 covered an area of 1,450 acres, stretching along both banks of the Derwent between Belper and Milford (White, op. cit., 31; Strutt MSS.).

Jedediah's sons were all men of distinction. Eminently successful in business, they had little personal ambition. Never putting money-making first they were always warm-hearted and open-handed. Their interests were diverse and their capabilities in many fields manifest. Of great personal charm, of progressive outlook and of profoundly humane thought and emotion they gave of their talents freely and lavishly in the service of Derby and of the county where, as Deputy Lieutenants and Justices of the Peace, they shared the power of the squirearchy and also its responsibilities.[1] It is to them that we now turn.

I. WILLIAM STRUTT, F.R.S.

William Strutt inherited his father's mechanical abilities. An architect of taste and distinction he became, as we shall see, the builder of the first multi-storied fire-resistant buildings and it was largely owing to his ingenuity that the Strutts' mills were the best equipped of their day.[2]

He was, as the President of the Royal Society said of him in 1831,

the author of those great improvements in the construction of stoves, and in the economical generation and distribution of heat, which have of late years been so extensively and so usefully introduced in the warming and ventilation of hospitals and public buildings. He possessed a very great knowledge of mechanics, and employed himself through the whole course of a very active life in the furtherance of objects of public utility.[3]

Although it was Strutt's mechanical genius that secured his election as Fellow of the Royal Society in June, 1817, when he was 60, he maintained throughout life an unflagging interest in many of the branches of pure science. His reading was wide —it included the works of Newton, Euler, Blair, Priestley, Lan-

---

[1] Cox, *Three Centuries of Derbyshire Annals*, i (1890), 48, 178. Joseph, an alderman of the borough of Derby, was elected first mayor under the Municipal Corporations Act, 1835, and served a second term in that office (*The Illustrated London News*, Feb. 3, 1844, 67).

[2] See next chapter.

[3] *Abstracts of the Papers Printed in the Philosophical Transactions of the Royal Society of London from 1830 to 1837*, iii (1860), 84.

den and Vince—and many of his friends—like Darwin, Edge-worth and the Benthams—were of the same bent.

About the time of his election to the Royal Society he was engaged upon problems connected with centrifugal force and in a letter of November 17, 1817, to his son Edward, then a student at Manchester College, York,[1] he wrote of the progress of his work in this field:

I have shown my paper on spinning tops to Mathematicians & Philosophers [he said] & am surprized to find that they are *all* ignorant of the subject. But I find an Englishman (Mr Landen) a profound Mathematician has written at length on the question. He says that Euler & other foreign mathematicians who have treated it are wrong. I have therefore only to prove that he is wrong (which I shall find very easy or so says Mr Sylvester)[2] to give more importance to the paper which however must be rewritten. What however excites more interest in the paper is a description of a Bullit which will have all the effect of a rifle though shot from a common Barrel. It seems of great importance & the subject must be further investigated. Do ask Mr Turner[3] whether he can give any information as to the theory of Spinning Tops. I hope in a few years you will be worthy of being commended for the R.S.[4]

Strutt, ever anxious that his son, soon to go up to Trinity College, Cambridge,[5] should make fullest use of opportunities that he himself had never enjoyed, wrote to him of the new

---

[1] Edward had been at Manchester College since September, 1817. His cousins John and Joseph Douglas entered there in 1810 and 1811 respectively (Kenrick, *A Biographical Memoir of the late Rev. Charles Wellbeloved* (1860), 250-6). Joseph Strutt was President of Manchester College from 1817 to 1826 and his brother George from 1837 to 1840 (Davis, *A History of Manchester College* (1932), 207).

[2] Charles Sylvester, a friend of the Strutts and author of *The Philosophy of Domestic Economy* (1819). The work was dedicated to William Strutt.

[3] William Turner, tutor at Manchester College. He was the grandson of William Turner of Wakefield, a student of Latham at Findern and a friend of Joseph Priestley and Paul Cardale, the Radical Dissenter of Evesham (McLachlan, *The Unitarian Movement in the Religious Life of England*, 80, 247). 'I am glad Mr Turner approves of the doctrines of Malthus,' Strutt wrote to his son on June 2, 1819, 'I suppose his opponents, if the subject were in any way connected with what they call the benevolence of the Diety would controvert the elements of Euclid.'

[4] Edward was elected F.R.S. in 1860.

[5] Strutt graduated B.A. in 1823 and M.A. in 1826. After going down he settled in London to study law, being admitted to Lincoln's Inn in 1823 and to the Inner Temple two years later. He was never called to the Bar.

horizons that were soon to open before him. He told him of his methodology and, in terms reminiscent of Jedediah, went on to stress the importance of acquiring a liberal education and of cultivating the social graces. These were the constantly recurring themes of his letters:

Derby April 8 1818

My dear Edward,

It gave me very great pleasure to hear from Mr Well[belove]d that your conduct merits the approbation of the Tutor himself and also that the examination passed off so well & you past at least. The pleasure which this must give you must be worth a good deal, independently of the proper legitimate object, *real knowledge*. You are now I hope so well grounded in most of these requirements which appear dry and crabbed to young people, that you have nothing before you but the pleasure which must result from a successful pursuit of it. With respect to languages you will begin to relish and appreciate their beauties & with respect to Science how I delight to have ones curiosity perpetually gratified by being able to comprehend all that others have thought & done & discovered by patient persevering reflection & experiment & then being in possession of & familiar with an immense number of facts, bound together by theories, you will be placed in a situation in your turn, to combine & recombine & to try the result of your penetration by asking natur questions; then you will undoubtedly stand in the ranks of those by whose powers of mind we have been so much elevated in the scale of being. And it is highly probable your success will be in direct ratio of the intensity & time with which the other qualities are applied, for it should be a maxim that no efforts are wholly lost. There is no magic in all this. Newton you know said all that he did was only by patient thinking. We *must* reason from what we know & inventing is only looking at all sides of a thing & putting it in different points of view & by long habit & a great store of ideas this becomes almost mechanical. There are to be sure degrees of sagacity, but anyone who will persevere can not but sooner or later blunder upon something valuable.

What I saw of the tutor at midsummer gave me exactly the impression you now express. There is nothing however in which a tutor is of less use to them who are determined to know than in Mathematics but before another Year we shall know more. What you say respecting the debating Society is very gratifying. I care not how you have spoken provided you have overcome the dislike of speaking; practice & a grasp thoroughly of the subject will do all the rest, and so far as importance is desirable will in your situation give you more than anything else can do. . . .

I do not like your Uncle Joseph's plan of taking a long journey in foreign countries especially with Women. So many things may occur which may be painful or even fatal at such a distance from home. There is a great difference between that and travelling in England.

You will probably visit these Countries but travelling in a country without a good knowledge of the language may almost as well be let alone. Remember that by going on with French you are only consulting your greatest good (I mean *pleasure*). Upon the whole as you say nothing about it I do not know whether you have any aversion to it. Was it but a lesson or two in a week it would be very useful.

With respect to dancing Country dances will soon form but a small part of a Ball, formerly there was nothing to do & everybody bobbed as they could but now Quadrilles &c. are all the fashion in which to dance ill is to be laughed at. To see D. Gor & S. Evans dance country dances shows such a mean education, it is almost like going to a Ball with a coat cut at the elbows, besides to dance well is the first step towards a Woman's heart. The very exercise will be a relief from your other occupations.

Farewell my Dr Boy affectionately Yrs
Wm. Strutt.

II. FAMILIES AND FRIENDS

The Strutts' position in the cotton world, their support of religious and political freedom, their efforts to better the lot of the labouring classes and, not least, William's scientific attainments, earned for them the regard of some of the ablest of their contemporaries.

In the years during which he embraced Republicanism and Unitarianism and, with Southey, toyed with the idea of creating a Pantisocracy on the banks of the Susquehanna, Samuel Taylor Coleridge was a frequent visitor to Derby. Here he stayed with Jedediah's daughter, Elizabeth, the widow of William Evans of Darley Abbey. He was there in January, 1796,[1] when Jedediah gave him a letter of introduction to John

[1] Letter to Rev. John Edwards, Unitarian minister of the New Meeting at Birmingham, in *Collected Letters of Samuel Taylor Coleridge*, ed. Griggs, i (1956), 179.

Fellows, silk merchant of Nottingham and a prominent member of the High Pavement Chapel where Need was baptized.

Coleridge found Derby 'full of curiosities, the cotton, the silk mills, Wright, the painter, and Dr. Darwin, the everything, except the Christian!'[1] On February 6, 1797, while at Stowey, near Bridgwater in Somerset, he wrote enthusiastically to John Thelwall[2] who, imprisoned in the Tower in May, 1794, had been tried for treason and acquitted later that year. His lecture at the Baptist Chapel in Derby was to be the scene of a serious riot instigated by a Tory mob:[3]

You are going to Derby! I shall be with you in Spirit.—Derby is no Common place; but where you will find *citizens* enough to fill your lecture room puzzles me.—Dr Darwin will no doubt excite your respectful curiosity. On the whole, I think, he is the first *literary* character in Europe,[4] and the most original-minded Man. Mrs Crompton is an Angel; & Dr Crompton[5] a truly honest & benevolent man, possessing good sense & a large portion of *humour*. I never think of him without respect, & tenderness; never (for thank heaven! I abominate Godwinism) without gratitude. William Strutt is a man of stern aspect, but strong, very strong, abilities: Joseph Strutt every way amiable. He deserves his *Wife*—which is saying a great deal—for she is a sweet-minded Woman, and one that you would be apt to recollect whenever you met or used the words lovely, handsome, beautiful &c—'While smiling Loves the shaft display, And lift the playful torch elate.'—Perhaps, you may

---

[1] Letter to Josiah Wade, Jan. 27, 1797 (ibid., i, 177).

[2] Ibid., i, 305–6.

[3] The mob, drawn together by drum and horn, broke the chapel windows, wounded many people with stones and bricks and did much damage. Thelwall, however, walked through their midst pistol in hand, threatening to shoot the first person who molested him, and thus escaped any injury (*Annual Register*, March 24, 1797).

[4] Maria Edgeworth, a friend of Darwin and of the Strutts, did not share Coleridge's opinion. She wrote to her aunt, Mrs. Ruxton, from Liverpool on April 6, 1813: 'At dinner Darwin's poetry was mentioned, and Mr. Roscoe [of Allerton Hall, near Liverpool] neither ran him down nor cried him up. He said exactly the truth, that he was misled by a false theory of poetry—that everything should be picture—and that therefore he has not taken the means to touch his feelings; and Mr. Roscoe made what seemed to me a new and just observation, that writers of secondary powers, when they are to represent either objects of nature or feelings of the human mind, always begin by a simile: they tell you what it is like, not what it is' (*The Life and Letters of Maria Edgeworth*, ed. Hare, i (1894), 195–6).

[5] Dr. Peter Crompton of Derby. A friend of the Strutts he later lived at Eton House, near Liverpool.

be so fortunate as to meet with a Mrs Evans whose seat is at Darley, about a mile from Derby. Blessings descend on her! Emotions crowd on me at the sight of her name—We spent five weeks at her house —a sunny spot in our Life!

In February, 1802, Coleridge met Joseph Strutt in Davy's Lecture Room in London and was, he wrote to his wife in Keswick,[1] 'pressed . . . with great earnestness to pass thro' Derby . . . and stay a few days at his house among my old friends'. Whether Coleridge ever took advantage of Strutt's invitation we do not know. In 1806 he abandoned Unitarianism and with it, it seems, his Nonconformist associations in Derby.

William Strutt's 20-year friendship with Erasmus Darwin, in whom Coleridge had displayed such lively interest, began in 1781 soon after his arrival in Derby from Radbourne.[2] Three years later the pair were amongst the ten who, meeting at Darwin's house in Full Street, founded the Derby Philosophical Society.[3] Darwin, the first President, continued in office until his death in 1802; he was succeeded by Strutt who also held the position for the remainder of his life.[4]

The Strutts, one suspects, owed many of their connections to Darwin. It was he who, in 1793, introduced William to the eccentric and celebrated R. L. Edgeworth,[5] a member of the Lunar Society, a group of radical and scientific outlook founded by Darwin during his residence at Lichfield. Amongst those who frequented its meetings were Matthew Boulton James Watt, William Small, Samuel Galton, Joseph Priestley, James Keir and Josiah Wedgwood.

Lifelong friendships between the Edgeworths and the Strutts and their families ensued. Whenever Edgeworth came to England he called upon William and presented to him many of the score of children of his four marriages. The year 1810

---

[1] Griggs, op. cit., ii, 789.

[2] *A Memoir of William Strutt*, 13. This typescript, believed to have been written in the late 1890s by or on behalf of the Hon. Frederick Strutt, is in the Derby Public Library.

[3] Glover, op. cit., ii, 458. He errs in stating that the Society was founded in 1783. In 1858 the Society was amalgamated with the Derby Town and County Museum (*Derby Mercury*, Sept. 22, 1858).

[4] *A Memoir of William Strutt*, 14.

[5] *Memoirs of Richard Lovell Edgeworth, Esq. Begun by Himself and Concluded by His Daughter Maria Edgeworth*, 3rd edn. (1856), 334.

saw the turn of Sneyd, 'not the mechanic of the family but
. . . [one] not ignorant of such subjects', 1811 that of William,
'bred an engineer', and at the same time Strutt was given 16
years' notice of the introduction of the then one-year-old
Francis Beaufort, (father of Francis Ysidro the economist),
'intended for the navy and [who] . . . must therefore be mayed
a good mechanic'.

On March 15, 1813, Edgeworth advised Strutt of his proposed visit to England. 'We have some thoughts of taking
Liverpool & Manchester in our way,' he wrote, 'pray tell me
what litary & Scientific people there are in these places whom
we ought to see. We propose to pass one *whole* day with you.'

Edgeworth had, however, seriously miscalculated his time-
table. On April 25 his eldest daughter, Maria, was to write to
her sister Honora:[1]

We have been now five days at Mr. Strutt's. We have been treated
with so much hospitality and kindness by him, and he showed
such a high esteem, and I may say affection for my father, that
even if he had not the superior understanding he possesses, it
would be impossible for me not to like him. From the moment we
entered his house he gave up his whole time to us, his servants, his
carriage; everything and everybody in his family were devoted to
us, and all was done with such simplicity of generosity, that we
felt at ease even while we were loaded with favours. This house is
indeed, as Sneyd and William described it, a palace;[2] and it is plain
that the convenience of the inhabitants has everywhere been
consulted: the ostentation of wealth nowhere appears.

Seven hours of one day Mr. Strutt and his nephew Jedediah
gave up to showing us the cotton mills, and another whole morning
he gave up to showing us the infirmary: he built it—a noble building; hot air from below conveyed by a *cockle* all over the house.
The whole institution a most noble and touching sight; such a
GREAT thing, planned and carried into successful execution in so
few years by one man!

We dined at Mr. Joseph Strutt's and were in the evening at Mr.

---

[1] Hare, op. cit., i, 195–6.

[2] Strutt had lived at St. Helen's House (now Derby School) since 1800
(*A Memoir of William Strutt*, 50). Built by the Gisbornes, Hutton wrote of it
in 1791: 'a house that would honour the first orders of nobility, but in a
situation which does not merit a dwelling of £500. Wherever we find so
expensive a work, we may fairly conclude the proprietor was either very
rich, or did not dread poverty' (op. cit., 30).

George Strutt's; and I will name some of the people we met, for Sneyd and William will like to know whom we saw:—Dr. Forrester; Mr French; Miss French, who has good taste, as she proved by her various compliments to Sneyd; Miss Broadhurst, not my heiress, though she says that, after the publication of the *Absentee*, people used to turn their heads when she was announced, and ask if that was Miss Edgeworth's Miss Broadhurst! She met Sneyd in Dublin; has been lately at Kilkenny, and admired Mr. Rothe's acting of Othello. We saw a good deal of Mr. Sylvester, who is, I think, a man of surprising abilities, of a calm and fearless mind: an original and interesting character. Edward Strutt is indeed all that Sneyd and William described—a boy of great abilities, affectionate, and with a frank countenance and manner which win at once. One of our greatest pleasures has been the hearing everybody, from Edward upwards, speak of Sneyd and William with such affection, and with such knowledge of their characters.

The families' correspondence covered not only matters of personal interest but also a whole range of scientific and engineering problems. Thus shortly after William Edgeworth's visit to Derby in 1811 he was sending Strutt information he had obtained for him from Dr. John Brinkley, Bishop of Cloyne and first Astronomer Royal for Ireland. At the same time his father was writing about the niceties of centrifugal force, his plan for a spire 'of iron ribs covered with slates' for 'our little church' at Edgeworthstown and of suggested improvements to Strutt's washing machine. He also disclosed the abandonment of his scheme to build under the Menai Straits an iron tunnel fourteen feet in diameter, a project he had first outlined to Strutt some six months earlier:

I have declined [he wrote] not for any doubt of being able to execute it in the manner & for the money proposed; but because a bridge has been proposed by Mr Telford at the estimate of £150,000; and because I think a bridge at that price preferable to a tunnel at £100,000—the original estimate for a bridge was 270,000. To such an enormous expence I should prefer a Tunnel.

The Strutts assisted the Edgeworths in the revision of their manuscripts. 'William tells me that Mr Ewart[1] and Mr Holland mentioned some errors (God knows there are many) in Practical

___

[1] Peter Ewart (1767–1842), cotton spinner of Manchester. He was a friend of the Strutts.

education,'[1] R. L. Edgeworth wrote to William Strutt in June, 1811:

> When any strike you or your friends pray invite some of your young people to note them down that I may correct them. In the 3d edition we have altered some things which were too *strong* about servants—I had thought it was not necessary always to say that we meant bad servants.

And on February 26, 1824, William Edgeworth told Strutt:

> I am very glad you were pleased with the alterations that Maria made in her work in consequence of the very patent & accurate perusal you made of it.[2]

Shortly before William's death in December, 1830, Maria wrote to his daughter, Frances, from North Audley Street:

> If at any moment you could give him pleasure by mentioning to him my unceasing and affectionate regard pray do me the justice to do so. I learned from my dear father fully to estimate Mr Strutts generous character and talents always directed to the most useful and benevolent purpose. And all I have ever seen or known of him myself has confirmed my fathers judgement. Besides I am grateful to him for the friendship he has ever shown me & many of my family—my dear brother William in particular who really loved him as if he had been his own son.

Edward Strutt was to remain on the friendliest of terms with Maria until her death in 1849.

The Strutts' intimacy with Thomas Moore began soon after his settling at Mayfield Cottage, near Ashbourne, in 1813. What was perhaps his first stay with them is described in his letter of October 23, 1813, to Mr. Power:[3]

> Bessy and I [he wrote] have been on a visit to Derby for a week . . . We were on a visit at Mr. Joseph Strutt's, who sent his carriage and four *for* us and back again *with* us. There are three brothers of them, and they are supposed to have a million of money pretty equally divided between them.[4] They have fine families of daughters,

---

[1] R. L. and Maria Edgeworth, *Practical Education* (1798).

[2] The reference is to *Harry and Lucy*, 4 vols., 1825.

[3] *Memoirs, Journal and Correspondence of Thomas Moore*, ed. Russell, i (1853), 365–6.

[4] This was, perhaps, not an overestimate. Apart from generous bequests to his servants Joseph Strutt left the whole of his £160,000 real and personal estate to his sole surviving child, Isabella. William left £1,000 to each of his

and are fond of literature, music and all those elegancies which their riches enable them so amply to indulge themselves with. Bessy came back full of presents, rings, fans &c &c. My singing produced some little sensation at Derby, and every one to whom I told your intention of publishing my songs collectively seemed delighted.

Of a visit in 1814 Moore wrote to Miss Dalby:[1]

I suppose you have heard that we have been to Derby; and a very pleasant visit we had of it. I like the Strutts exceedingly; and it was not the least part of my gratification to find a very pretty natural girl of sixteen reading the sixth book of Virgil, and not at all spoiled by it. This is Joseph Strutt's eldest girl, a very nice dancer as well as a classic, and a poetess into the bargain. Indeed, they have quite a nest of young poets in that family; they meet every Sunday night, and each brings a poem upon some subject; and I never was much more surprised than in looking over their collection. I do not think I wrote half so well when I was their age. Then they have fine piano-fortes, magnificent organs, splendid houses, most excellent white soup, and are, to crown all, right true Jacobins after my own heart; so that I passed my time very agreeably amongst them, and Bessy came away loaded with presents of rings, fans, and bronze candlesticks.

The next we hear of Moore is on January 31, 1828, when he was chairman at a dinner held at the King's Head Inn, Derby, by the Subscribers and other Friends of the Lancasterian System of Education of which he was President. His diary records the events of the day:[2]

Breakfasted in my bed-room [at Joseph Strutt's], and took a few hours to think over what I should say in my speeches to the Lancastrians. . . . The company at the dinner larger than ever they have had at any public dinner in Derby before; at least so they told me. About a hundred sat down, all good Whigs, I took for granted; good materials for Whigs, certainly, being chiefly dissenters,

---

three daughters 'as a token of my regard having already provided for them by a family settlement'. The residue and the 1200-acre estate at Kingston-on-Soar, Nottingham, he left to his son Edward and his heirs (Wills at Somerset House). The Kingston estate, formerly owned by the Babingtons, had been bought from the Duke of Leeds in 1796 with Barbara Evans' £20,000 fortune at the time of her marriage to William Strutt (Burke, *Vicissitudes of Families*, Third Series (1863), 231; *A Memoir of William Strutt*, 34).

[1] Russell, op. cit., ii, 31.   [2] Ibid., v, 256.

unitarians, Nottingham editors, &c. &c. Three long tables, and my chair at the top of the centre one placed with the back close to a large fire: should have melted away, had I remained in it, but abdicated, and joined Strutt at the head of one of the other tables, leaving my chair like Banquo's during dinner. All went off famously: made them about ten or twelve speeches, and was cheered most heartily throughout. My brother orators *not* such as it was difficult to eclipse; one of the 'gentlemen of the press' talked of the duty of 'heditors lifting up their woices'. A party of amateurs sung glees occasionally between the speeches, and one of their performances being 'The last Rose of Summer', the mayor, who sat on my right hand, confided to me in a whisper his regret that they should choose such *dull* things for such an occasion: told him I heartily agreed with him. Retired from the chair between ten and eleven, and adjourned (tired as I was, and covered not only with applauses but with fish-sauce) to a party at William Strutt's, where I found duets on the harp and pianoforte going on; and, in spite of my dozen and one speeches, was obliged to muster up voice enough for the same number of songs. Slept at Joseph Strutt's.

Among the toasts proposed by Moore was one to Henry Brougham[1] who, in a letter in *The Times* of February 9, 1825. had advocated the foundation of a great University in London, The same year he had introduced into the House of Commons a measure, which was abandoned on technical grounds, for the purpose of providing university education at an incorporated College in London for all those unable to proceed to Oxford or to Cambridge.

Proposing 'Success to the University of London' Edward Strutt 'observed that the establishement of this institution must be particularly gratifying to the friends of the Lancastrian system of education. . . [and] that he trusted the London University would not only extend the means of instruction to a greater number of persons, but that it would also enlarge the limits within which a university education had been hitherto confined. How far this institution would be successful remained to be seen; but considering, as he did, that it could do no harm, and that it might do great good, he could not but think that the public were deeply interested in its welfare, and that they owed a debt of gratitude to those

---

[1] Henry Brougham (1778–1868), M.P., F.R.S., 1803; cr. Baron Brougham and Vaux. He was a Member of the first Council of the University of London.

philanthropic and enlightened persons who had exerted themselves in its support.'[1]

Edward Strutt was to take an active interest in the new university. He became Vice-President of University College, 1862–71 and President 1871–9.

Of other of the Strutts' connections only tantalizing fragments of correspondence remain.

William's association with Josiah Wedgwood perhaps came about through Darwin or through R. L. Edgeworth. Or perhaps it arose from the Strutts' membership of the General Chamber of Manufacturers, a body founded by Wedgwood in 1785 in which industrialists united to defend their common interests from the threat of taxation and competition from abroad.[2]

About William Strutt and the Benthams we can say a little more. It seems likely that Edgeworth supplied the link some time in 1793, the year he met Strutt. Certainly Jeremy was writing to Strutt in July, 1794, when engineering problems were under discussion.

An eleven-year gap in our information is broken on July 20, 1805, when Samuel Bentham, on the eve of his departure on a government mission to Russia, wrote to Strutt as follows:[3]

I am exceedingly sorry to find that it will not be possible for me to make my intended tour to Derby previously to my leaving England. . . . I was in great hopes of being able to spend a day or two with you first not only because I know no one whatever with whom I converse with so much satisfaction; but I also particularly wished to consult you on the drying of wood artificially . . . as it is I must send someone else to extract what they can out of you on these subjects and in the meantime I would beg you to let me know how soon in your opinion fir or oak plank 4, 6 or 10 inches thick may be dried fit for use without cracking or splitting more than if dried gradual as usual. If you have any business in the country I am going to or wish for any information from it be assured that it will give very great pleasure to be anywise useful to you while I am there.

Samuel did not return from St. Petersburg until the autumn of 1807 and we have, unfortunately, no other reference to him.

[1] *Derby Mercury*, Feb. 6, 1828.   [2] *A Memoir of William Strutt*, 21.
[3] Letter in Strutt MSS. at the Fitzwilliam Museum. Bentham was at this time inspector-general of Navy works.

In August, 1823, Jeremy asked Edward Strutt, then on the Continent, to visit him in London upon his return to England. Advising his son of this William observed:

Mr Bentham the son of Sr Saml has been here, and also has visited Scotland; after his return to London he wrote to me to say his Uncle (Jeremy Bentham) desire to request that on your return (which he concluded wd. be through London) you would call upon him. I returned him for answer that I was sure you wd. do that. I feel highly honourd by the invitation and an honour I think, it is, for I believe he is very select in his acquaintance, & I have no doubt that in Lincoln Inn it will be a feather in your cap to be invited by him. I enclose a letter of introduction which I think you had better deliver personally & not otherwise. When you call perhaps you had better send in your card or you may not be admitted. Mr Abercromby[1] I understand also means to invite you. He you know is a first rate man both as to his talents & connections—this will of course lead to attentions from the Duke of Devonshire. These things are coming in some degree to your own merits, and some how or other derived from Cambridge I suppose. I think I remember observing to you that the Eye of the public would be upon you at a certain time, that time is arrived, and you are beginning to be thought of for a publik Station, of which more when we meet— but say nothing abt it.

In later life Edward became an intimate associate of Jeremy Bentham and also of such distinguished contemporaries as Macaulay, John Romilly, McCulloch, John and Charles Austen, George Grote and Charles Buller.

One of the Strutts' most fascinating connections went back no doubt to the publication of Robert Owen's *New View of Society* in 1813–14 for in his autobiography Owen tells us that:[2]

of men of great practical knowledge who were [then] much interested in my views and practical measures were Mr. William Strutt, . . . and his brother Joseph, two men whose talents in various ways and whose truly benevolent dispositions have seldom been equalled.

Our next glimpse of Owen is in 1818 when, stopping at a 'superior hotel' midway along the Swiss shore of the Lake of

---

[1] The Hon. James Abercrombie (1776–1858); M.P.; P.C., 1827; Speaker of the House of Commons, 1835–9; cr. Baron Dunfermline, 1839. He was a Member of the first Council of the University of London.

[2] Owen, op. cit., 211.

Geneva, he met 'my old and respected friend Mr. Joseph Strutt . . . with his two daughters'. The parties thereupon agreed to prolong their stay for another day and, to celebrate their unexpected meeting, they asked the hotel proprietor if he could supply 'a bottle of genuine old hock grown upon Prince Metternich's estate'. 'The bottle was brought,' Owen concludes, 'and certainly, in the estimation of Mr. Strutt and myself, it was the most delicious wine we had ever drunk. Its price was ten francs.'[1]

In April, 1819, Owen, 'looking uncommonly well', called upon the Strutts in Derby. He had earlier been to see Edward at Manchester College. 'Mr Owen spent Sunday evening here and we were well pleased to hear of his visit to York especially as he gave a *tolerably* good account of your Lordship,' wrote Anne Strutt to her brother on April 18; and five days later her sister Elizabeth quipped, 'perhaps his countenance brought a glow from your fine face. At any rate I had more pleasure in looking at him from thinking how short a time it was since he had been "sunning himself in your eyes".'

On July 20, 1821, the eve of the Coronation of George IV, Edward, then in London, met Owen who, he wrote to his father, was 'enthusiastic as ever and says he shall soon raise £60,000 to build a parallelogram'.[2]

Strutt's family, one suspects, regarded Owen as something of a bore and an oddity. Certainly the letters of Elizabeth and Anne convey more than a hint of this and the impression is strengthened by the following letter of May 28, 1830, from Edward to his sister, Frances. He had, he said, dined at Dorset Square:

The party was somewhat dull, as the conversation turned chiefly on subjects connected with Mr Owen's plans. Mr O. was inclined to be prosing as usual, but Mr Rough far outdid him in the quantity, the dulness, & the absurdity of his discourse.

---

[1] Ibid., 173. William had considered his brother's Continental tour ill-advised (see above, 173).

[2] For Owen's scheme to build Villages of Co-operation to help relieve unemployment see Cole, *The Life of Robert Owen*, 2nd edn. (1903), ch. x. Edward, 'having spent the evening which was a very fine one at Covent Garden and Vauxhall', viewed the Corporation procession from 'a very excellent front seat on the north side of the Abbey quite close to the platform for two guineas'. He was, he wrote, 'at my place by 3 o'clock'.

Owen had in all probability been disclosing his plans for establishing producers' co-operatives and for a system of labour currency.[1] Having returned from America in 1829 after losing £40,000 or four-fifths of his fortune in his New Harmony experiment he was now entering on some of the busiest, and immediately the most influential, years of his life.

Edward was to hear more of these ventures. Owen wrote to him on September 4 from 43 Bedford Square:[2]

> Great events may be looked for before the end of the year. The value of the supposed *miser* of the modern political Economist will be put to the test before that period.

Our last information about Owen is that contained in the following extract from his letter of December 23, 1830, to Edward Strutt:[3]

> I fear [he wrote] we must not indulge the hope of again seeing your father restored to health—that society must lose the services of one of the most valuable men that the last century has produced.

III. PUBLIC LIFE

The Strutts played a distinguished part in the public life of Derby, labouring incessantly to better the amenities of the town and the welfare of its inhabitants. They had power and they used it wisely and in the public interest.

If the tasks they set themselves called for hard work, unusual ability and an unflagging attention to detail they were at least not hampered for lack of room in which to operate. The public and social services of their day were conspicuous only by their absence. Not until 1833, when it made a grant of £20,000 to the Societies founded by Lancaster and Bell, did the state begin to recognize that the education of the masses was a national responsibility; another thirteen years were to elapse before it made any provision for the training of teachers. In 1842 only one Lancashire town, Preston, was able to boast of a public park and another, Liverpool, of public baths. The Health of Towns Commission reported in 1844 that of the fifty large towns of England there was scarcely one in which the drainage

---

[1] See Cole, op. cit., ch. xv.   [2] *A Memoir of William Strutt*, 91.
[3] Ibid., 92.

was good and only six in which the water supply could be so described. In 1850 the House of Commons was told that great towns like Leeds and Sheffield were without public libraries of any kind.[1]

Before the coming of state aid the provision of these and other services was left to private enterprise and to such measures as were approved by private Act of Parliament. The Strutts did their best for Derby and in 1833 Glover wrote what was in fact a remarkable testimony as to their achievements:[2]

The town of Derby [he said] is rapidly becoming distinguished among the provincial capitals of the kingdom for improvements, which blend the two characteristics of perfection—elegance and utility. The streets, particularly the main thoroughfares, are gradually being divested of obstructions, and with the approaches to the borough in every direction, have undergone the process which gives smoothness and safety to the carriage ways. In public buildings, Derby probably surpasses every county town of similar extent. We cannot look around us without discovering proofs that the Improvement Bill obtained some seven years ago, has been acted upon with energy, taste and judgement, and the commissioners merit the thanks of the community for the spirit, intelligence and prudence with which they have employed the parliamentary powers entrusted to them.

This was, indeed, a remarkable transformation since Sylas Neville's visit half a century earlier.[3]

William Strutt began early. In 1788, when he was 32, he took an active part in obtaining an Act of Parliament authorizing the construction of a new bridge over the Derwent at St. Mary's and the widening of its approaches.[4] Four years later he was instrumental in securing a further Act providing for the paving and lighting of the town, the costs of which were to be defrayed by the levy of a small rate and by the sale

---

[1] For further information about the provision of public services see J. L. Hammond in *A Century of Municipal Progress, 1835–1935*, ed. Laski, Jennings and Robson (1935), ch. ii.

[2] Glover, op. cit., ii, 467.

[3] See above, p. 111.

[4] 'Memoir of William Strutt, Esq., F.R.S.' in *Derby Mercury*, Jan. 12, 1831. The article is unsigned but Baines (op. cit., 205) attributes it to Edward Strutt. Work on the new bridge began in 1788 and was completed in 1793. The cost, including the purchase of property at the approaches, came to £2875 (*A Memoir of William Strutt*, 18).

of Nun's Green Common.[1] So beneficial was this latter Act that in 1825 Strutt was elected chairman of a commission which successfully sought Parliament's consent to borrow £20,000 at 4 per cent. in order to improve still further the amenities of the town.[2]

William designed many of Derby's bridges and did much to establish and to support institutions like the Friendly Societies, the Savings Bank and the Gas Company.[3] The Derby Infirmary, built at a cost of £17,870 and opened in 1810, was considered by many to be his masterpiece. He was responsible for its design and displayed in it the whole range of his architectural and mechanical genius. It became a showpiece visited by medical authorities from all parts of the country and from the Continent. Towards its construction the Strutts each contributed £300.[4]

The provision of educational institutions for the benefit of ordinary people was always a concern near to the hearts of the Strutts. Joseph was largely responsible for founding the Sunday school connected with the Friargate Chapel. To its children he gave prizes for meritorious conduct and entertained them in the grounds of his house.[5] In 1812 he took the initiative in establishing a Lancasterian School at Derby, providing it with money, books and paintings. He or William never failed to preside at its annual meeting.[6] In 1824 Joseph made enquiries of James Shuttleworth, the Strutts' agent in Manchester, about the rules of the Mechanics' Institutions there, at Glasgow and at Edinburgh, and the following year, ably assisted by Edward Strutt, he founded an Institution at Derby. To it he gave 20 guineas, an annual subscription of 2 guineas and 500 books 'in almost every branch of science, history, travels and amusement' carefully selected from amongst the volumes in his own library.[7]

---

[1] *Derby Mercury*, Jan. 12, 1831. [2] Ibid.; Glover, op. cit., ii, 466.
[3] *Derby Mercury*, Jan. 12, 1831.
[4] Ibid.; Sylvester, op. cit. Glover, op. cit., ii, 531. Arkwright gave £1,000 towards the cost of construction of the Infirmary (*Derby Mercury*, Jan. 31, 1805).
[5] *The Illustrated London News*, Feb. 3, 1844, 67; Noah Jones, *Life and Death; A Discourse on Occasion of the Lamented Death of Joseph Strutt, Esq.* (1844).
[6] *A Memoir of William Strutt*, 55.
[7] *Derby Mercury*, March 23, 30, 1825. The Strutts later founded a Mechanics' Institution at Belper. In 1846 its library of 1,000 volumes was housed in

The Strutts held that education should not end with the three R's or with the spread of scientific knowledge amongst intelligent artisans. They believed that the labouring classes (not to mention those more fortunately placed) must learn to appreciate and to respect such amenities, public and private, as were available for them to enjoy.

As contributions towards the achievement of these ends Joseph opened his residence, St. Peter's House, with its large and valuable collections of paintings and statuary to all who sought permission to view it[1] and in 1840, in the closing years of his life, he gave to the citizens of Derby an Arboretum or park. Planned by J. C. Loudon, the distinguished landscape gardener, the Arboretum was almost 11 acres in extent. It had 1,000 trees, several thousand evergreens, more than 6,000 feet of gravel walks and two lodges with rooms for the use of the public. Its cost amounted to £10,000.[2]

Handing over the Arboretum to the committee appointed for its management Strutt said that there had of late been a great expansion in the trade and population of Derby and that, while the provision of amenities had not been neglected, nothing had so far been done to supply 'a scarcely less urgent want of the inhabitants of a large and increasing town—the opportunity of enjoying with their families, exercise and recreation in the fresh air, in public walks and grounds devoted for that purpose'.[3]

After giving details of the size, layout and management of the Arboretum Strutt concluded in a strain that provided a fair summary of his social outlook:[4]

I have [he said] purposely omitted any endowment to keep the Arboretum in order as I know by experience that I shall best provide for its future preservation by entrusting it to those who

---

their Long Row schoolroom. Members paid 1s. a quarter and had singing and other classes. Jedediah Strutt was treasurer (Bagshaw, *History, Gazetteer and Directory of Derbyshire* (1846), 290).

[1] *Derby Mercury*, Jan. 17, 1844; *The Illustrated London News*, Feb. 3, 1844, 67. For the contents of Strutt's collections see *A Catalogue of Paintings, Drawings, Marbles, Bronzes, &c. &c. in the collection of Joseph Strutt* (1827 and 1835), (Catalogues in the Derby Public Library).

[2] *Derby Mercury*, Sep. 16, 1840; *Christian Reformer*, N.S., Vol. 1, No. II (Feb. 1845), 75; Burke, op. cit., 223; Pevsner, op. cit., 119.

[3] *Derby Mercury*, Sep. 23, 1840. [4] Ibid.

will enjoy and profit by it, and who will take an interest in its permanence.

It has often been made a reproach to our country, that in England collections of Works of Art, and Exhibitions for Instruction or Amusement, cannot, without danger of injury, be thrown open to the public. If any ground for such a reproach still remains I am convinced that it can be removed only by greater liberality in admitting the people to such establishments—by thus teaching them that they are themselves the parties most deeply interested in their preservation—and that it must be the interest of the public to protect that which is needed for the public advantage. If we wish to obtain the affection and regard of others, we must manifest kindness and regard towards them; if we seek to wean them from debasing pursuits and brutalizing pleasures, we can only hope to do so by opening to them new sources of rational enjoyment. It is under this conviction that I dedicate these Gardens to the Public; and I will only add, that as the Sun has shone brightly on me through life, it would be ungrateful in me not to employ a portion of the fortune which I possess, in promoting the welfare of those amongst whom I live, and by whose industry I have been aided in its acquisition.

Admission to the Arboretum was free on Sundays, except during service time, and on one other day of each week. At other times a small charge was made to provide for the cost of upkeep. The Arboretum was much frequented by the people of Derby while excursion parties came by the newly built railways in order to spend the day there and to take tea in its grounds. On such occasions the charge for admission was usually reduced by one-half.[1]

IV. SOCIAL AND POLITICAL CHANGE

William Strutt, his son has recorded, 'was a warm friend of toleration, and a sincere enquirer after truth; and as such, he was a zealous advocate of the right of free enquiry, and ree discussion on all subjects, moral, political and religious'.[2]

This was true of the entire Strutt family. As Whigs they supported the campaigns for Free Trade and for the First Reform Act, a movement in which Edward, since 1830 one of the

[1] *Christian Reformer*, N.S., Feb. 1845, 75; *Derby Mercury*, July 7, 1841.
[2] *Derby Mercury*, Jan. 12, 1831.

Liberal Members of Parliament for the borough of Derby, played his part.[1] They rejoiced at the abolition of the Slave Trade, at the repeal of the Test Act and at the passing of the Roman Catholic Relief Bill.[2] With an equal, if misplaced, consistency they sent George Henry Strutt to London in April, 1818, to oppose Peel's Factory Bill. 'Mr O[wen] will not like this but interference is bad in principle,' William wrote to his son.

In the Derbyshire Treason Trials of 1817 Joseph Strutt made great efforts on behalf of the accused whom he felt to be the victims of a plot. His son, Joseph Douglas, one of the thousands who witnessed the executions of Brandreth, Ludlam and Turner before the County Gaol, echoed the sentiments of the whole family when he wrote to Edward on November 7:[3]

Your sisters no doubt told you all about the Special Commission & by what you hear from them & read in the paper I think you will have learnt the most prominent parts of this business so dreadful to contemplate & so harassing to the feelings of those who have a spark of feeling remaining in their breasts. . . . People are flocking into Derby to witness this dreadful sight—the horse guards are parading our streets; I am glad you are spared the feeling which these things could excite in your bosom. The time for the execution is drawing near & I am going to be a witness of it tho' my heart is ready to burst at the very idea. Good God are these things to be suffered much longer in our once free and happy land.

Like their fellow Unitarians the Strutts were amongst the most stalwart supporters of political freedom both at home and abroad. They avowed sympathy with the Americans during the War of Independence and were roused to enthusiasm at news of the outbreak of the French Revolution.[4] Later, deeply

---

[1] Edward Strutt represented the borough of Derby, 1830–47, Arundel, 1851–2 and Nottingham, 1852–6. In 1856 he was created Baron Belper of Belper. From 1846–8 he was Chief Commissioner of Railways and from 1852–4, Chancellor of the Duchy of Lancaster. He never took an active part in the family business.

[2] Strutt MSS.; *Derby Mercury*, Jan. 12, 1831; *The Illustrated London News*, 1844, 67; Noah Jones, op. cit.

[3] For the full text see *V.C.H. Derby*, ii, 153–4. The original letter is at the Public Library, Derby. An account of the proceedings at the Trials is given in the *Derby Mercury*, Oct. 2 to Nov. 13, 1817, and an estimate of their significance in J. L. and B. Hammond, *The Skilled Labourer*, ch. xii.

[4] Strutt MSS.; *Derby Mercury*, Jan. 12, 1831.

moved by its excesses, they were, on the eve of Britain's entry into the conflict, amongst the conveners of a meeting held to confirm 'our Determination to support and defend our excellent Constitution, consisting of King, Lords and Commons';[1] and in 1803 Joseph became Lieutenant-Colonel and George, Captain in the newly formed Belper Volunteers, one of the many regiments raised throughout the country to meet the threatened French invasion.[2] Nevertheless they continued to work for peace and in August, 1812, William was chairman 'at a numerous and respectable Meeting of the Friends of Peace, assembled from the counties of Derby, Leicester and Nottingham, held at Loughborough' which resolved unanimously that 'the two Houses of Parliament . . . take such measures as their wisdom may deem effectual to restore to our country the blessings of a just and permanent Peace'.[3]

After the Treaty of Vienna the Strutts sided with those liberalizing movements that sought the overthrow of autocratic monarchs and the removal of reactionary governments.

Joseph Douglas Strutt, a witness of the Austrian suppression of the risings at Naples and Messina in 1821,[4] wrote home in horror about what he had seen and in 1823 the Strutts did their best to organize assistance for the Spaniards in their unsuccessful resistance to the French troops, authorized at the Congress of Verona to restore the absolutism of the tyrant Ferdinand VII

Your Uncle Josh & I have been endeavouring to promote a subscription at Derby for the Spaniards but have made nothing of it [William told his son on August 10]. We have subscribed £100 each but I believe the Town and County together will not raise another £100. It is much the same through the Kingdom, the consequences of success or failure of the Spaniards seems too remote for the stupid public to be raised to exertion. I suppose they cannot see that probably the liberty or slavery of Europe may depend on the event— there is however I think but little to fear.

---

[1] *Derby Mercury*, Jan. 3, 1793.
[2] *A Memoir of William Strutt*, 37. For an account of the Belper Volunteers see *V.C.H. Derby*, ii, 149.
[3] *Leicester Journal*, Sept. 4, 1812.
[4] Leaving England in June, 1820, Strutt visited France, Switzerland, Italy and Greece before being 'seized with a malignant fever' while on a voyage from Smyrna to Constantinople where he died on Aug. 26, 1821. He had intended to go on to Egypt (Strutt MSS.; MS. 4173, Derby Public Library).

Milford Warehouse to-day

News of changes in the political climate at home or overseas always held a prominent place amongst the Strutts' interests. In his last illness William was cheered by the success of the July Revolution which placed Louis Philippe on the throne and sealed the fate of the ancient monarchy of France.[1] And in December, Edward, then in London, was quick to pass on to his sister Frances information about the revolutions in the Swiss cantons and in Poland.

Yet, unlike discontented reformers and revolutionaries who sought salvation in a complete break with the past the Strutts did not expect results overnight or suffer the illusion that humanity could be reformed solely by Act of Parliament:

I observe [William wrote to his son on June 2, 1819,] that all permanent alteration of public opinion are made slowly & by degrees but the red hot democrats seem to desire revolution more than gradual reform. Even if their abstract principles are perfectly correct they would gain more, & proceed faster, by aiming at less.

[1] *Derby Mercury*, Jan. 12, 1831.

The Milford Mills

CHAPTER VIII

THE MILLS

I. THE SIZE OF THE FIRM

THE cotton trade has always shown an extremely wide range in the size of its firms and the number of people they employ. This goes back, as we have seen, to the earliest days of the factory system. In the 1770s and 1780s there were, at the one end, the Arkwright and Strutt mills, multi-storeyed buildings with 300 or 400 workers apiece; each mill had its own water-wheel and the group was added to by building similar mills close by. The progenitor had been Lombe's Derby silk mill. At the other end of the scale were the little workshops with a carding engine, a few spinning jennies or twisting frames, driven by hand or horse or rudimentary water power. As mule spinning came in, and as steam became auxiliary to, and then superseded, water as power, the same variations in scale persisted. In 1786 'a stranger approaching the town [Manchester] only saw one high chimney, which was of Mr. Arkwright's mill';[1] but there were scores of small workshops, like those with which Robert Owen and McConnel and Kennedy began.[2]

The evidence on Peel's factory legislation between 1816 and 1819[3] gives a striking impression of this variety. From the Strutts with their factory villages, almost towns, and their 1500 workpeople, we move downwards to the host of small men with their factories of less than a score of workers, clustered on country streams (Keighley had '20 to 30 mills on one little

---

[1] *1816 Comm.*, 317.

[2] The number of cotton and woollen mills registered in Lancashire in Jan. 1803, under Peel's act was 148, of which 85 were in the Salford Hundred; 65, employing 8475 people, were in Manchester. Only factories with over 20 workpeople and over 3 apprentices were registered (*Manchester Mercury*, Jan. 11, Feb. 15, 1803). This would give a Manchester average of 130 and still exclude the smaller concerns.

[3] The Commons Committee of 1816 and the Lords Committees of 1818 and 1819.

brook'),[1] or converted cottages in villages and towns (as at Oldham, where 'many are made from cottages, a steam-engine attached to them, and the rooms laid together').[2] It was among these small factories that the worst scandals of insanitation and overworking were found. James Watkins of Bolton, an independent-minded magistrate, said that of the mills he visited those with an average of 15 persons employed were 'the worst of all' and that similar to them were 'some large Mills, whose respective Stories are let off to different Occupiers'.[3] This room- or floor-letting system was especially common in Manchester and Stockport. (The Lower Carr mill at Stockport had 27 'masters' in it, employing in all 250 people.)[4] The large employer did most of the speaking before the parliamentary committees but he was hardly the characteristic figure of the trade. There were actually very few 'cotton lords'. The statistical evidence presented was most deficient on the small factories. The large firms were active in their own defence and went to some pains to present a case; they were, as for a generation afterwards, very critical of their small uncouth competitors. The Strutts stressed the contrast to the Factories Inquiry Commission of 1834.[5]

Judged by the numbers employed, it would seem that the two largest cotton undertakings in the country in 1816 were Robert Owen's New Lanark mills and the Strutts at Belper and Milford. Owen said he employed '1600 or 1700';[6] the Strutts employed 1494 in 1815 and 1613 in 1818.[7] If we add the Strutts' Derby mills they would easily come first. The two firms were essentially factory colonies. Both had been begun in the early Arkwright years; both were made up of mill units;

[1] *1816 Comm.*, 117.

[2] Ibid., 197.

[3] *1819 Comm.*, 280–1.

[4] *1819 Comm.*, 442. Clapham in his note 'Some Factory Statistics of 1815–16' (*Econ. Jour.*, 1915, 477) does not take this important system into account.

[5] *Supp. Rep.* Part II, Section D1, pp. 96–7; 1834 (167) xx, 578–9.

[6] Possibly an overstatement, as Owen's evidence was not very satisfactory. He said that 2297 people were 'supported by the New Lanark manufactory and establishment', of whom 266 were from 5 to 9 years. This would leave only 300 or 400 to cover the under-fives, the aged, and the wives who did not work in the factory (*1816 Comm.*, 20, 113).

[7] *1816 Comm.*, 217; *1818 Comm.*, 216. They had in addition 383 workmen and labourers and 122 bleachers.

both depended on river water-power (the Clyde and the Derwent); both had remained faithful to water-spinning. When Owen and his philanthropic partners bought New Lanark in 1813 it had four mills, three of them of seven storeys, one of six; a long narrow store-room; a machine shop; a brass and iron foundry; and a building, then unused, designed to house a school, lecture room, and church.[1] The Strutts' buildings, as we shall see, were of much the same scale.

There were a few other large country colonies of the same type but smaller. Buchanan's Catrine, in Ayrshire (another Arkwright foundation) had 875 workers in 1816.[2] Monteith and Bogle at Blantyre, Lanarkshire, had two spinning (water and mule) mills, a power-weaving mill, and a dyeworks, with altogether 750 operatives.[3] Deanston, Perthshire, had, however, contracted:

> The Cotton Works . . . were erected in the Years 1784 and 1785, and were filled with Hand Jennies and Water Spinning Frames, till the Introduction of Mule Spinning, and employed 600 to 800 Workers. Owing to the Improvements in Machinery, fewer Workers were found necessary, and about the Year 1800 not above 500 Workers remained.

The works were closed in 1805-6; they had only 377 employees in 1818.[4] Henry Houldsworth had 635 at Glasgow—at Anderston (steam) and at Woodside (water).[5] In North Wales there was the Holywell Twist Company (now owned by William Douglas), which went back to the earliest years, with 840 in 1818, and his mills at Pendleton, near Manchester, with 531.[6]

Arkwright at Cromford had 727 in 1816. His empire had never been so compact as the Strutts'. He had had, he said, 'about 1800 or 1900 in mills which were my own, and in mills with which I was connected'.[7] This was at an earlier period and most of the concerns were now on their own feet, like the Manchester factory of J. and R. Simpson, or held on mortgage, like Oldknow's mill at Mellor.[8] There were a few other largish

[1] Podmore, *Robert Owen, a Biography* (1906), i, 98.
[2] *1816 Comm.*, 240. [3] Loc. cit.
[4] *1819 Comm.*, App. 104. [5] *1816 Comm.*, 240.
[6] *1819 Comm.*, App. 45. [7] *1816 Comm.*, 277, 281.
[8] Oldknow had 418 in 1797, including 100 apprentices; in 1812 he had 380 including 35 apprentices (Unwin, op. cit., 195, 203).

country mills of the factory colony type, but all probably of smaller size.[1]

The other great firms of the trade were of a different kind. They were the big town factories, steam driven, and containing mules. Although the urban factories were numerous little more than half-a-dozen employed more than 600 people each. They were:

Manchester	*1816*	*1818*
Adam and George Murray	1215	
McConnel and Kennedy	1020	1125
Philips and Lee	937	
Thos. Houldsworth	622	736
Ancoats Twist Co.	376	612
Thomas Marriott	649	
Preston		
Horrockses	704	
Blackburn and (1818) Manchester		
Birley and Hornby	549	1028

Altogether these large firms accounted for only about 14,000 of the 60,000 operatives covered by the various figures given to the parliamentary committees. Both among the town and country mills the small firm was predominant. The figures given to the 1816 Committee will suggest the ranges:

No. of Workers	*Man-chester and Salford*	*Scotland**	*Preston and District*	*Bury and District*	*Notting-hamshire*	*Oldham*	*Lanc-ashire*
1–99	10	6	9	1	3	2	4
100–199	14	17	7	2	1	4	5
200–299	7	10	1	3	4	1	1
300–399	8	2			1		
400–499	3	2		1	1		
500–599	2	1					
600–699	2	1					
700–799		1	1†				
800–899		1					
900–999	1						
1000–1099	1						
1100–1199							
1200–1299	1						
	49	41	18	7	10	7	10

* Excluding New Lanark's 1600–1700 workpeople.
† Horrockses' six mills.

[1] There are, for instance, no figures for Sir Robert Peel's mills at Tamworth. The factory colony of the Gregs at Styal had 252 workers in 1816. John Bott and Co. at Tutbury, had 190 (*1816 Comm.*, 374).

The returns gathered by the Manchester millowners in 1818 are fairly full for England but are weak for Scotland:[1]

Area	No. of Mills	No. of Workers
Lancashire		
Manchester, Salford, Eccles	80	19,923
Ashton-u-Lyne and district	34	4470
Oldham	19	1643
Bolton	19	3262
Preston	15	1898
Chorley, Blackburn	9	1219
Bury	7	1111
Rochdale	7	796
Wigan	8	616
Warrington	5	648
Cheshire		
Stockport and district	30	4823
Macclesfield, Wilmslow, Congleton	10	1461
Derbyshire	7	4073*
Nottinghamshire and Staffordshire	10	1314
Cumberland (with Backbarrow, N. Lancs)	7	847
Yorkshire	30	2029
North Wales	2	1176
Scotland	38	6014†
	337	57,323

* Including Strutts.
† Not including New Lanark. The 1816 figures in the previous table were said to include all but New Lanark and totalled 41 firms and 10,000 workers.

II. THE STRUTT MILLS

Strutts were always a rather specialized firm of spinners, concerned mainly with hosiery yarns, while the other big firms, such as Arkwright and Owen, spun for the cotton piece-goods markets and for yarn export, or specialized in fine counts like McConnel and Kennedy and Houldsworth. Strutts' roots were in the Midlands, although they did a good business in Manchester through their agent there. At Derby, however, they did for a time enter the general trade. Writing in 1789, Pilkington said: 'Mr. William Strutt the younger is endeavouring to transplant the manufacture of calicoes into the town and its neighbourhood. He employs 112 looms, 40 of which are within

[1] *1819 Comm.*, App. 110.

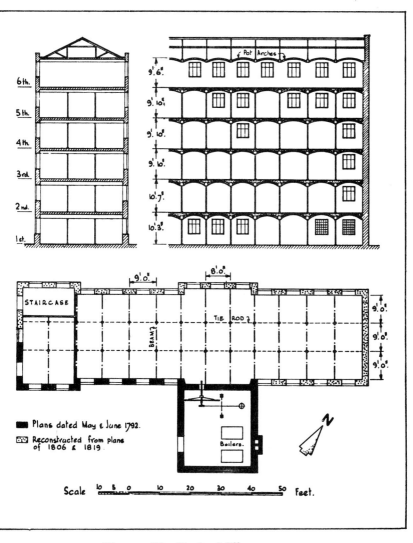

Fig. 1.—The Derby Mill, 1792–93

(Reconstructed from drawings of May 28, 1792, and Portfolio 84 in the Boulton and
Watt Collection at the Birmingham Public Library and from E. W. Brayley's map
of Derby in 1806 and Chatterton and Swanwick's map of 1819)

the town.'[1] He also embarked on mule spinning at Derby and
built the Calico Mill,[2] later referred to as the Derby Mill.[3]
His son credited him with being among the earliest pioneers of
the self-acting mule—before 1790; 'but we believe that the inferior workmanship of that day prevented the success of an
invention which all the skill and improvement in the construction of machinery in the present day [1831] has barely accomplished'.[4] In January, 1795, £255 was spent on 'mules, &c.'[5]
The Strutts had, however, given up their mules some years
before 1816.[6] These developments were part of the cotton boom
that followed the depression of 1788 and lasted until the crisis
of 1793. The Strutts must then have invested heavily out of
their accumulated profits.

The 1780s saw a great stirring of interest in the use of cast-
iron in building and constructional work, and William Strutt
was much alive to it. In March, 1789, Samuel Oldknow, then
planning his Mellor mill, was proposing to put up a stone
bridge over the Goyt and sent the plans to Strutt. He replied
(on March 1) suggesting that before there was a final decision
Oldknow should consult 'some learned mathematician'. He
went on:

a man has got a patent for making Iron Bridges cheaper than of
stone and has prepared a plan for one over the Schulkill in America,
—but I suppose you will not wait. Indeed, if we are to wait for the
perfection of every proposed improvement, this age is so improving,
we should all sit still and do almost nothing.[7]

---

[1] Pilkington, op. cit., ii, 176.
[2] Calicoes were being sent to London, on account of the spinning firm, to
be sold by Thomas Shipman, the agent of the hosiery firm, from 1800. He
received a commission of 3d. a piece. The amounts were:

Period	No. of pieces
April, 1800	2036
May, 1801	3220
Aug., 1801	4040
Feb., 1802	5343

[3] See below, pages 200–205.
[4] *Derby Mercury*, Jan. 12, 1831.
[5] Belper Ledger.
[6] G. B. Strutt's evidence, *1816 Comm.*, 307.
[7] Unwin, op. cit., 222. For its development see Gloag and Bridgwater,
History of Cast Iron in Architecture (1948).

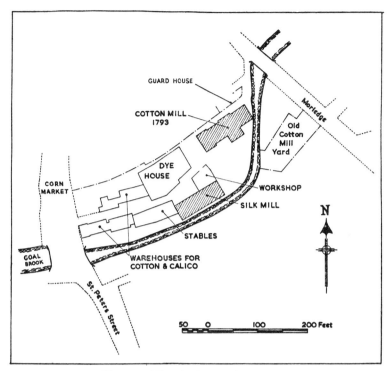

Fig. 2.—The Derby Mills in 1820

(Drawn from *Particulars of* [the Strutts'] *Derbyshire Estates According to the Surveys of 1819 and 1820*)

The man was Thomas Paine, who had patented his iron bridge in 1788 and was in 1788–90 in England, concerned with the Walkers, the Masborough ironmasters, in casting and testing a sample rib.[1] Strutt was a customer[2] and friend of the Walkers, three of whom had married daughters of Jedediah's old partner Samuel Need.[3] It is not likely that he met Paine—their

---

[1] Moncure Conway, *Life of Thomas Paine* (1892), i, 253–67.

[2] In 1788 Strutts were buying 'Barrs of Iron' from Joseph Sykes, Son and Co. of Hull, a large importer of Swedish iron, in 1788–9 cast steel and 'Barr Steel' from John Walker and Co. of Sheffield and in 1790 from the sister concern Walker, Booth and Crawshaw of Masborough, near Rotherham. In November, 1794, Ebenezer Smith and Co. of Griffen Foundry, Chesterfield, offered to supply 'Pillars for the [West] Mill with their appendages @ £11. 10. 0. p Ton'. The foundry was the second largest in Derbyshire (Farey, op. cit., i, 396).

[3] See below, page 327.

political sentiments were much the same—and that Paine visited Derby or Belper.[1]

Strutt's mind turned to another practical application of cast-iron and he became the builder of the first multi-storey fire-resistant buildings. The problem of building fire-resistant cotton mills was a pressing one to factory masters. The early timber-framed structures were most vulnerable. Rooms were imperfectly ventilated; methods of dust extraction were primitive; oil from the machines dripped on to the wooden floors; the machinery contained much wood; the lighting was by oil lamps and candles; and fire-fighting was inefficient. Few firms escaped loss at one time or another; Arkwright's Nottingham mill had been destroyed in 1781, one at Cressbrook on the Wye near Tideswell, was burnt down in 1785 and the Evans at Darley Abbey lost one in 1788.[2]

Perhaps the final stimulus towards a solution of the problem came in 1791 with the destruction of the Albion Mills in London, the most advanced industrial building of the day.[3] Certainly the following year Strutt began to erect at Derby the first successful fire-resistant mill:

He was the first person [his son wrote of him in 1831] who attempted the construction of fire-proof buildings on a large scale in this country, and with the most perfect success. The great improvements made of late years in the formation of Castings in iron, have given great facilities to this mode of construction, which is now very extensively in use.[4]

The Derby Mill, 1792–3, and a four-storey warehouse Strutt built at Milford at the same time were not only the first multi-storey fire-resistant buildings, they were the starting point of an entirely new form of structure, the iron-framed building from which the modern steel-framed structures have evolved.[5]

[1] Paine wrote on June 17, 1789: 'I have been to see the Cotton Mills,—the Potteries—the Steel Furnaces—Tin plate manufacture—White lead manufacture' (Moncure Conway, op. cit., i, 265).

[2] *Derby Mercury*, Nov. 15, 1781; Nov. 24, 1785; Dec. 3, 1788.

[3] *Annual Register*, March 3, 1791. In 1802 Simon Goodrich (1773–1847), who served under Samuel Bentham at the Admiralty, submitted a design, explicitly based upon Strutt's mills, for 'Rebuilding the Albion Mills Fire-Proof'. The Mills were, however, not rebuilt.

[4] *Derby Mercury*, Jan. 12, 1831.

[5] This is the conclusion reached by H. R. Johnson and A. W. Skempton in their paper 'William Strutt's Fire-Proof and Iron-Framed Buildings,

The Old Mill, Milford (3rd storey)

Milford Warehouse (3rd storey)

Hollow-pot roof, Milford

The Bleaching Mill, Milford (ground floor

The Derby Mill, wrote Britton and Brayley on Strutt's information,[1]

is remarkable for its floors being constructed on brick arches, and paved with brick, by which means it is rendered absolutely indestructible by fire. This building is six stories high, 115 feet long and 30 feet wide; it was erected in the year 1793, and was the first *fireproof* mill that was ever built.

The use of hollow earthenware pots and tiles was coming into favour at this time.[2] The latter were used in the construction of the Théâtre du Palais-Royal in Paris in 1789–90 and in planning his Derby Mill Strutt explored the French method. On October 29 1792, John Walker wrote to him from Ashbourne on enquiries he had made in Paris:

I am afraid I shall have more difficulty in getting you the drawings than I was aware of. As soon as I received your letter I wrote to an English architect in Paris for them. But three days before I left London a Frenchman who had made his escape informed me that the massacres of the 2nd September had driven him to England, as they did all ye English, and notwithstanding my enquiries I cannot learn where he is. . . . Previous to your letter I had ordered one of each sort of the hollow bricks, of which the Arches are composed, to be sent to me, and I expect soon to hear of their being arrived in London. . . . Unluckily I only saw the building the evening before I left Paris, at a time when I was unwell, so that I have not so perfect a recollection of the Plan as I should have had, had I reviewed it at my leisure. However, perhaps I will give you as good

---

1792–1812', read at the Institution of Civil Engineers (Newcomen Society), Dec. 12, 1956. I am indebted to them for much generous assistance, particularly concerning the Derby and Milford Mills and the dating of the Belper South Mill. The reader wishing to have an excellent technical survey of Strutt's work should consult their paper.

[1] Op. cit., iii, 364.

[2] Although serving the common purpose of lightening the floor the pot and tile were used in entirely different ways. The hollow tile has no structural value; it is used merely to 'block out' sections of a floor and to form a framework for the actual structural floor. Strutt's hollow pots, on the other hand, were used structurally. They formed *part* of the arch structure and seem to have served the twofold purpose of lightening the deadweight on timber beams and of reducing the thrust in end arches where these were partly supported by the walls. The 'small pottery hollow Cylinders or Cones' used at Derby, Belper and Milford were made at Smalley Common pottery (Farey, op. cit., ii, 17).

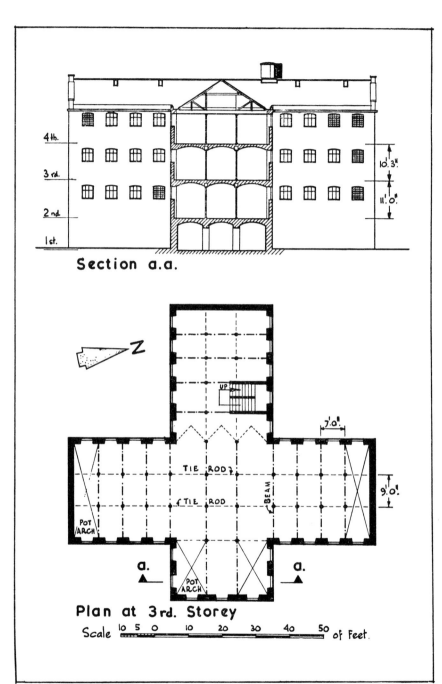

Section a.a.

Plan at 3rd. Storey

Scale — of Feet.

Fig. 3.—Milford Warehouse, 1792–93

a description as I can, least perchance I should not be able to obtain drawings at all.

The Building of the Palais Royale seems to me to be about 24 feet wide, the iron bars supporting the Arches are about four feet from each other. . . .

My friend, ye Architect, has brought into London a quantity of Paris Plaister, and has got a Parisian to shew the method of using it. Here the plaister is burnt with wood, but there is a method of burning it with coals; I scarcely recollect the contrivance, tho' I think it is not a very difficult one. . . .

The roof of the Palais Royale is of framed Iron, with a larger sort of hollow bricks to fill up the panes.[1]

It is, perhaps, improbable that Strutt got his plans, but he pushed ahead and in May, 1793, Matthew Boulton was writing to him on the use of the hollow pots:

Sirs,

I understand that you have some thoughts of adopting the invention of forming Arches by means of the hollow potts & thereby saveing the use of Timber in makeing Floors, & guarding against Fire. Allow me to say that I have seen at Paris floors so constructed, and likewise at Mr. George Saunders's in Oxford St. London, who is an eminent Architect, & who had practised that art with success. I have therefore no doubt but it might be applyd also with great success & security to a Cotton Mill.

I am with respect

Sir, your most obed. humble Servt.

Mattw. Boulton[2]

Soho May 8—93

It is clear from a plan made by Boulton and Watt in 1806 for the installation of gas lighting in 'Messrs. Strutts' Mill in Derby' that the beams used were about twelve inches wide.[3] Although no details were given we know that they were of

[1] This may have been from John Walker (1760–1804), a former partner in the Masborough firm, who had been bought out in 1783 (John, *The Walker Family, Iron Founders and Lead Manufacturers, 1741–1893* (1951), 20). The letter is in *A Memoir of William Strutt*, 28.

[2] Boulton and Watt MSS. (Assay Office, Birmingham).

[3] W. D. Shepherd, *Early Industrial Buildings, 1700–1850*. Thesis submitted in 1950 for final examination R.I.B.A.

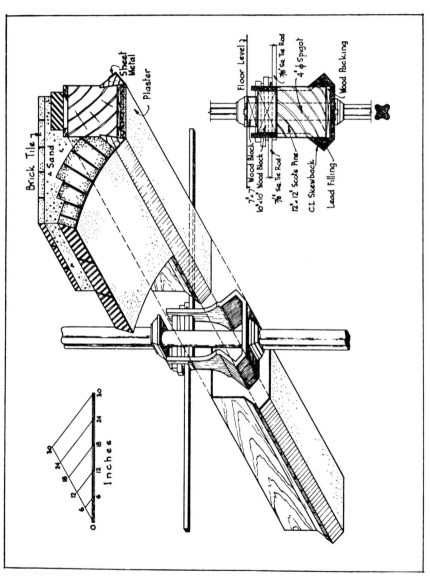

Fig. 4.—Milford Warehouse, 1792–93

timber for, reporting a fire which started in the loft of the Mill the *Derby Mercury* of July 20, 1853, stated that it

differs in the construction of its floors from modern fire-proof buildings, the arches being formed by pot cylinders, about 7 inches long and 3 inches in diameter . . . [and] the girders instead of cast iron are of Baltic fir, cased in iron.

The Derby Mill thus constituted a real break with traditional construction and was one of the major turning points in the history of structure. It is much to be regretted that it no longer survives.[1]

In 1792 also Strutt began to build the four-storey Milford Warehouse, the structural details of which are in all probability identical with those at Derby. Completed in 1793 and now known as the Cruciform Building this, the oldest surviving example of his work and the earliest existing fire-resistant mill, is a monument of unique interest in the evolution of modern design. It has arch floors, iron columns and beams of Baltic fir twelve inches square, plastered on their underside; the wooden skewbacks supporting the arches are cased in thin sheet iron and the beams span nine feet.

About the same time there was big development at Belper. His old schoolmaster there was writing to Samuel Slater in New England on January 11, 1793: 'Messrs. Strutts go on swimmingly—they are erecting a very large mill at Belper; and Mr. George is beginning to build himself a noble house on the bridge hill, just above the watering troughs.'[2] The mill was the West Mill and the accounts for its building survive. It was slow in completion, perhaps because of the setback to the trade through the crisis of 1793. It was not completed until 1795 and started working in 1796. Together with the Derby Mill and the Milford Warehouse it is the only known example of

[1] Johnson and Skempton, op. cit. Since timber beams were used the Mill cannot, however, be accepted as an iron-framed building as has been suggested by an American scholar, Professor Turpin Bannister, whose remarkable study 'The First Iron-Framed Buildings' in *Architectural Review*, cvii (1950), was the first modern historical survey in this field.
[2] White, op. cit., 105. Letter from T. Jackson; the date is given as 1792 but must be 1793 since Arkwright's death is also reported. Bridge Hill House, built at a cost of some £6,000, commanded extensive views of Belper and of the Derwent valley. It was demolished in 1938–9 (Strutt MSS.; Glover, op. cit., ii, 105).

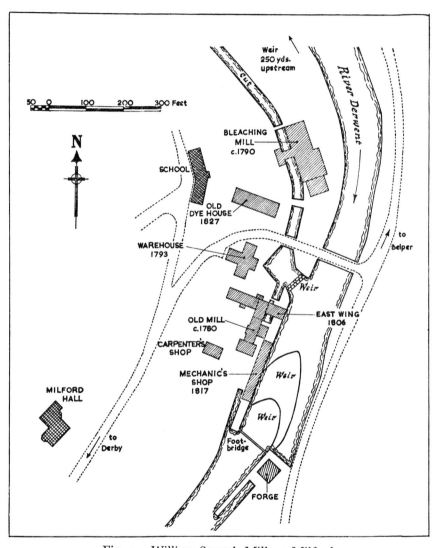

Fig. 5.—William Strutt's Mills at Milford

(The Forge, Footbridge, Carpenter's Shop, the East Wing of the Old Mill and the
Mechanic's Shop were demolished during 1952–7)

206

a building midway, both structurally and chronologically, between the timber-framed and the iron-framed mills. Britton and Brayley describe it as follows:[1]

The principal of these mills is 200 feet long, 30 feet wide, and six stories high, and like that we have described at Derby, is considered as fire-proof, the floors being constructed with brick arches and paved with brick. The two water-wheels, which work the machinery in this building, are remarkable as well for their magnitude, as for their singularity of construction; one of them being upwards of forty feet long, and eighteen feet in diameter: and the other forty-eight feet long and twelve feet in diameter. As it was impossible to procure timber sufficiently large to form the axles, or shafts, of these wheels in the usual mode of structure, they are made circular and hollow, of a great number of pieces, and hooped like a cask; one of the shafts is between five and six feet in diameter, and the other between eight and nine.

As with most of the Strutts' building the work was done by labour employed under the factory master's eye. Some of the more important items in the 'New Mill' building accounts are as follows:

	£	s.	d.
3 Labourers altering scaffold poles	2	8	0
Woods—Iron & Workmanship for 2 standards & a wallow for drawing Materials up to the Floors	1	10	0
Masons & Labourers making scaffolds	6	7	0
Brags & Nails used for braces & scaffolding		5	10

[1] Op. cit., iii, 530. One of the wheels is referred to below, pp. 210–211; the other must have been built some time before 1802. Nine years later the West Mill was powered by three wheels, the smaller of the original ones having been replaced by two wheels each 15 ft. long and 21½ ft. in diameter, built mainly from wrought and cast-iron and designed by T. C. Hewes, a Manchester engineer and mechanic. His account is in Strutts' Cash Book (Davies, op. cit., 346–7). *Rees's Cyclopædia* (article 'Water', 1811–13) states that the Belper mills had six large wheels, all of them breast-wheels. A 40-ft. wheel and one 21½ ft. in diameter and 15 ft. broad are described at length. See also article 'Mill-Work' for the governors or flying balls used to regulate the water-wheels at Belper. Glover (op. cit., ii, 101) states that in 1833 the Belper mills were powered by 11 wheels, 6 of which were used at high water and the others when the Derwent was at normal height. In 1834 Strutts estimated that the wheels at Belper and Milford gave the equivalent of 200–300 Horse Power (*Factories Inquiry. R. Com. Supp. Rep.* Part II, Section D1, p. 96; 1834 (167) xx, 578). Ure's assertion (*Philosophy of Manufactures* (1835), 344) that these mills were driven by 'eighteen magnificent water wheels, possessing the power of 600 horses', would appear to be inaccurate unless Strutts' calculation referred only to those wheels used when the Derwent was at normal height.

		£	s.	d.
36 Beams for 3 floors 30 feet long				
& 12¾ inch square 1224 feet Cube				
31½ do for 3 floors 38 do do				
& 13 inch square 1404 „ do				
6 short Beams next gable end 30 „ do				

		£	s.	d.
2658 „ @ 21d		232	11	6
Laying 72 beams upon 3 floors allowing 7 men 2 days to each floor exclusive of the other men which worked regularly at the building		4	4	0
1822 feet inch deal boards for gutters, & lineings about trap doors & sky lights	@ 1½d	11	7	9
Geting roof beams & other timber upon the building		3	10	0
52 sheets of Lead for gutters 138C 3qr 0lb	@ 19/-	131	16	3
42 Load of Crich Lime with sand & making up	@ 24/-	50	8	0
26544 inferior bricks for a stove & necessaries	@ 19/-	25	4	4
171 window sills, geting, carriage & dressing	@ 2/2	19	19	0
345200 bricks	@ 21/- pr thousand	362	9	2½
Cuting & removeing earth for foundations & laying do		8	8	6
Sundry sorts of iron work &c 1535 lbs 8 oz	@ 4d	25	11	10
Laying gutters, leading skylights, ridges, launders & making pipes &c		3	10	0

C qr lb

					£	s.	d.
4 Cast pillars	14	3	8	@ 12/3	9	1	6¾
4 do do	17	1	3	@ 12/-	10	7	3¾
3 do do	7	3	7	@ 12/-	4	13	9
3 do do	7	3	11	@ 2/-	4	14	2
4 do do	17	1	3	@ 12/3	10	11	6¾

		£	s.	d.
13 Pillars, 13 skew backs & wedges &c. from Chesterfield 64 0 19	@ 11/6	36	17	11¼
Digging 3 holes for foundation of Pillars in Counting House			7	6
5 Stones for an arch over the passage workmanship included			5	7½
Bricks for 8 Arches Counting House end 15744	@ 21/-	16	10	7½
Paving Bricks for 3				
floors do do do 9460				
do do Landings & half spaces 1792				

		£	s.	d.
11252	@ 26/-	14	12	6½
Bricks for the first Floor 26682	@ 19/- pr thousand	25	6	11½
Bricks for the Floor in the roof 7160	@ 19/- pr thousand	6	13	0½
6 Ton 11½ Cwt of plaster for the Roof room Floor	@ 14/-	4	12	0
Pots for the Top Story Counting House included				
35609	@ 52/6	93	9	5½
Carriage of Pots from the Pot House			6	0
Of Edward Mee Pots for arching 3900		10	4	9
From Milford 1050 square bricks for arching			6	3

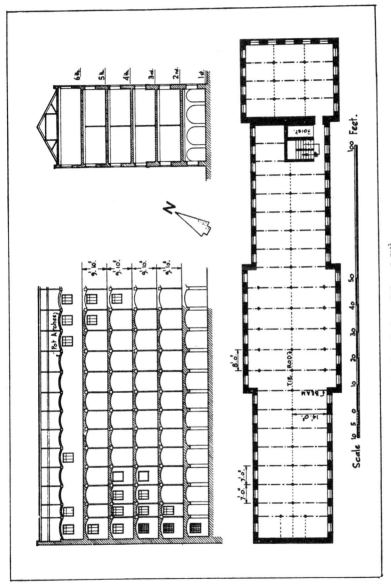

Fig. 6.—Belper West Mill, 1793-5

Doubtless much of the stone, timber and other building materials were obtained from the Strutts' estate which had several quarries as well as plantations of larch and of Scots pine.[1]

Since not all the accounts have survived it is impossible to estimate the total cost of the labour employed in building the West Mill. A single entry taken from the books reads:

'Workmens wages for building the Mill £220 13 4½.' There are, however, in addition, numerous entries such as the following for September 3, 1795:

1795:			£	s.	d.
Wm Moore	42 days @ 2/6		5	5	0
Saml Moore	43¼	2/6	5	8	1¼
John Wheateley	47½	16d	3	3	4
Josh Henry	47½	14d	2	15	5
Andrew Whittaker	41½	22d	3	16	1
Charles Cotterile	45¼	18d	3	7	10¼
Edward Cooper	44¾	22d	4	1	1½
John Rowbottom	44¼	22d	4	0	2½
George Clark	24	16d	1	12	0

Between March, 1793, and September, 1797 (by which time the Mill had started working), £4688 19s. 1¾d. had been spent on its construction. If this was the total sum then, with its floor area of 33,500 square feet, the cost came to just under 3s. per foot super, or roughly 25 per cent. more than that of a five-storey timber-framed mill erected in 1794–5 at Leeds for John Marshall.[2]

The above sum is exclusive of the outlay on a water-wheel, wheel-house and the 'West Mill Cut, Walls, Bridges &c.' Between March, 1795, and March, 1797, £629 19s. 4¾d. was spent on a wheel, built almost entirely from oak. The main

---

[1] Farey, op. cit., ii, 263. The Strutts had nurseries at Belper and Milford and George Strutt, whom Farey held 'to rank among distinguished agricultural Improvers', kept accurate and systematic accounts relating to every aspect of estate management (loc. cit.). Strutts were, however, unable to produce all the timber they needed and their records contain many entries such as the purchase on March 26, 1794, of 71 elders containing in all 506¾ feet of timber at 8d. a foot from William Slater, who was, perhaps, a relative of Samuel. They also bought large quantities of oak and ash. Farey (op. cit., iii, 245) states that they 'give 12d. to 16d. per foot, for Alder Poles, up to four inches in diameter, for turning Bobbins, spindles, &c.'

[2] Johnson and Skempton, op. cit.

Structural details, Milford Warehouse

Lower right: Hollow Pot (*Scale in inches*)

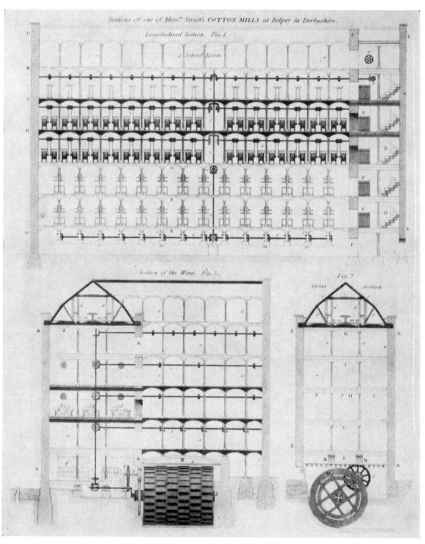

Belper North Mill, 1803–4, Section

timbers cost £117 5s. 11d.; £48 12s. 1½d. went on 'Iron for hooping the Shaft 44c 0qr 21lb @ 22/–' and £1 3s. 4d. on 'about ⅔' of a 'Barrel of Tarr'.

Construction of the wheel-house started early in 1794 and by May, 1797, had taken £323 10s. 7¾d. By January, 1796, 'Shuttles, Pillars, Arches & Bridges for [the] West Mill Cut' had cost £213 19s. 5¼d. and by May, 1797, £1142 2s. 1½d. had been spent on the 'Cut, Walls, Bridges &c.'

Liberal quantities of ale were supplied to builders working in difficult or unpleasant places. Thus on June 29, 1796, 18s. worth was given 'to Workmen while they were puting in a foundation for a Wall' and on March 1, 1797, £2 18s. 4d. worth to labourers 'for working in Water'.[1]

The years following the completion of the West Mill in 1795 saw important developments in the design and use of iron beams in framed structures for which Charles Bage (1752–1822), a friend and correspondent of Strutt, was directly responsible.[2]

During 1796–7 Bage built at Shrewsbury a five-storey flax mill modelled closely on the lines of the Derby Mill. An important difference, however, was that it had beams of cast iron in place of timber. It was thus the first iron-framed building.

The Shrewsbury mill was the starting point for the seven-storey cotton mill erected 1799–1801 for Philips and Lee at Salford. It was probably designed by Boulton and Watt whose iron beams, principally in the shape of section, were in fact a development of those of Bage.[3]

Although the Salford beams were of more advanced construction than those at Shrewsbury they were not altogether satisfactory and Bage made further improvements in their design in a flax mill completed by Benyons and Bage at Leeds in 1803. He also developed a theory for the strength of flanged iron beams which he outlined to Strutt in a letter of August 29, 1803.[4]

Strutt was soon to be rewarded for the assistance that he had

[1] Another entry records, 'To ale for the workmen £1. 5. 0.'
[2] The Strutt-Bage correspondence is in the Shrewsbury Public Library. For information about Bage's work see Johnson and Skempton, op. cit.
[3] Johnson and Skempton, op. cit.
[4] Skempton, 'The Origin of Iron Beams', *Proc. VIII Int. Cong. History of Science* (Florence, 1956), gives a full account of Bage's theory and its comparison with test results.

given to Bage, for early in 1803 Jedediah's second timber-framed mill of 1784–6 was destroyed by fire:

> About three o'clock this morning [said the *Derby Mercury* of January 13] a most tremendous fire broke out in one of the large Cotton Mills belonging to Messrs. Strutt, at Belper . . . which raged with incredible fury, and in a few hours destroyed it, and all the valuable machinery, water-wheel &c. The loss will be immense as no part of the property is insured.

The North Mill was quickly rebuilt and started working towards the end of 1804. In it Strutt adopted and improved Bage's beams and once more revealed himself a designer of the highest calibre. The new mill, iron-framed throughout, has five storeys and an attic. It is 127 feet long, 31 feet wide and 63 feet high. A wing is 41½ feet by 34 feet.

A description of it written in 1812–13 appears in *Rees's Cyclopædia*.[1] The writer spent some time at Belper and was given facilities for drawing and describing the works, which 'contain almost every improvement in the cotton trade'. His account may be summarized; the text is a lettered key to the drawings reproduced facing page 211.

The Mill.—The side and end walls are built up as usual with the usual doors and windows in them. The several floors are composed of brick arches, with a very small rise and a nine-foot span. The arches spring from iron columns, erected one upon another through the whole height of the mill. They are connected by cast-iron beams or girders, one of which extends from the top of every column to the next. In an opposite direction to these girders, each pair of columns is tied together, across the arch, by a wrought-iron bar, which has an eye at each end, to be hooked over the tops of the columns. This resists the lateral thrust of the arch. Thus, though every floor is formed of a system of arches, like a bridge, yet the lateral strain of each is supported by iron ties, so that each arch stands by its own supports, independent of its neighbours. The arches are of only one brick thickness, and are covered over at the top by a

---

[1] Article, 'Manufacture of Cotton'. The plates are drawn by J. Farey, Jr., a son of the author of the *General View of the Agriculture of Derbyshire*. The father contributed the article on 'Canal Making' and this may well be his work also or that of his son.

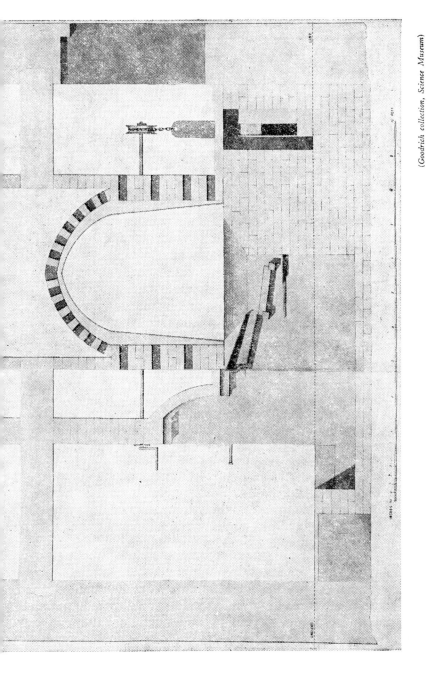

Fig. 7.—Model of William Strutt's Warming Stove, longitudinal section, 1807

P

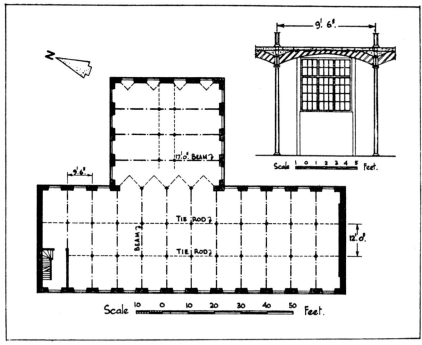

Fig. 8.—Belper South Mill, 1811–12

floor of paving bricks to make a flat surface above, the haunches
of the bricks being filled by rubbish. The iron ties across the
arches are concealed within the brickwork of the arch. The
roof is of cast-iron. The space between the two columns in the
roof forms a small room, which is used as a schoolroom for the
workpeople on Sunday.

The mill contains fifteen arches in length. The floors are
continued beyond the end wall by two additional arches, giving
a small room on each floor, which is occupied by the counting
house, staircase, and the stove which warms the mill in winter,
and also a crane for drawing up the goods to the machines on
the various floors. The wing, which consists of six arches, projects from the middle of the mill. The width, both of the mill
and the wing, is composed of three lengths of arches, having
three iron girders that they rise from, and two columns to support them. The arches in the ground floor, or cave of the mill,
are supported by very strong piers, instead of iron columns.

These piers are founded very firmly in the earth, and every precaution taken to prevent their subsiding under the great weight they have to carry. The columns of the first floor are erected immediately on the tops of these piers.

The Hoist. The writer describes enthusiastically and at length the teagle or hoist which ran by the mill's power and had been adopted in all the Strutts' mills. It was manipulated by a boy, who rode in a seat on the top of the cradle and pulled the guide ropes. The bobbins were sent up in little frames mounted on wheels and, thus wheeled along by 'little children' to the crane, are drawn up or let down without any hand labour. (The inventor—or improver—is given as 'Mr. H. Strutt'—probably a mistake for William, to whom Ure attributes it.)[1]

The Stove.—This was the apple of William Strutt's eye, and its principles were applied to hospitals and houses.[2] In the mill it was in the space below the staircase. It is very ingeniously contrived with an iron cockle, or inverted cubical vessel, beneath which a fire is made, and the smoke escapes by a flue behind into a chimney. The air is then brought in a current to strike upon the external surface of the cockle, and being thus warmed, rises up through flues into every floor of the building, where it is admitted in any quantity at pleasure by registers, regulated to produce an agreeable warmth, but, as the warm air escapes again with a draught through a proper ventilator, there is nothing of closeness. (Jedediah Strutt, Jr., told the 1816 Committee that the average size of rooms was from one hundred to one hundred and fifty feet long, thirty feet wide and nine feet high, and the cubic feet of space for each person was 1104. Pure air, warmed when necessary, was transmitted into every room constantly at the rate of upwards of 100 gallons per minute for each person.)[3]

[1] Ure, *Philosophy of Manufactures* (1835), 46–54. It always made an appeal to visitors, such as Elizabeth Grant in 1822–3. The word hoist came later; it is here called crane or teagle (Strachey, op. cit., 381).

[2] See above, pp. 170, 176.

[3] *1816 Comm.*, 217. In 1811 William Strutt gave William Edgeworth letters of introduction to Peter Ewart and to G. A. Lee and in June that year Edgeworth wrote advising him of his visit to their mills: 'Mr Lee's gas lights seem to succeed very well & his heating his mill by steam, yet he says that your plan is the best & cheapest, but as his mill is moved by steam it is no great expense to make use of superabundant steam.' Lee told the 1816 Committee of Strutt's improved stove and of his own system of steam pipes but he could not say that one had great superiority over the other (ibid., 351, 355).

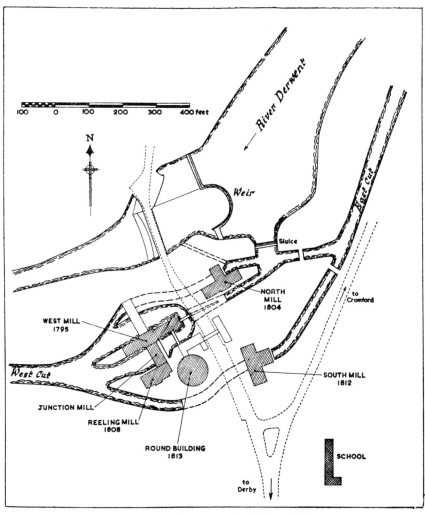

Fig. 9.—William Strutt's Mills at Belper

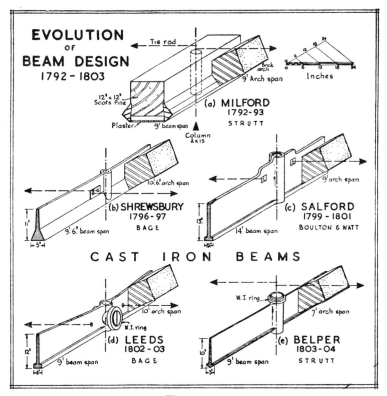

Fig. 10

Power and Drive.—The motive power came from the water-wheel which was under the wing of the mill. The wheel was eighteen feet in diameter and twenty-three feet long. Its size is so great that no cast-iron girder could be thrown across strong enough to support the arches, so a strong stone arch was put in, fortified by two strong iron bolts. The arches of the wing immediately over the water-wheel are of hollow pots. Pots were also used to build the arched floor of the roof.

The driving system comes from the water-wheel and turns a vertical shaft running up to the top of the mill. It also turns a horizontal shaft extending the length of the mill. On this, beneath every arch is a bevelled wheel turning another vertical spindle. On this the main spindles of the spinning frames are fixed.

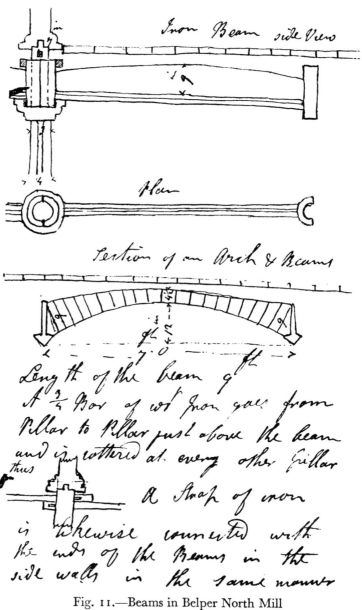

Iron Beam side View

Plan

Section of an Arch & Beams

Length of the beam 9ft
A ¾ Bar of wrot iron goes from
Pillar to Pillar just above the beam
and is cottered at every other pillar
thus

A Strap of iron
is likewise connected with
the ends of the Beams in the
side walls in the same manner

Fig. 11.—Beams in Belper North Mill

(Goodrich, *Journal*, August, 1804. Although Goodrich, does not
state that he was in Belper when he made the drawing, the accuracy
of his work has been confirmed by H. R. Johnson and A. W.
Skempton. The same sheet of the *Journal* contains a description of
the Belper Round Mill)

The two lowest floors contain the spinning frames, 28 on each floor, and 12 more in the two floors of the wing—in all 4236 spindles, 'a considerable proportion of which are, however, employed in spinning the hard twist'. The third and fourth floors contain three rows of carding engines—64 breaking cards and 72 finishers—turned by a horizontal shaft over the machines. The wing has 16 drawing frames and four stretching frames. The fifth floor has reeling, doubling, and twisting frames.

The resumption of hostilities after the short-lived Peace of Amiens did not seriously affect constructional activity in the cotton trade[1] except for occasional bad patches, as in 1805, 1810 and 1812.[2] The Strutts must have expended a good deal of capital. They rebuilt the North Mill in 1803-4, built the five-storey east wing of the Old Mill at Milford in 1805-6, and some time between 1802 and 1806 converted into fireproof construction with brick arch floors and a central row of iron columns, the two lower floors of the main block of the Old Mill. Modifications to strengthen the floors of the three upper storeys may be of the same period. The south wing appears to be structurally identical with the east wing and was built some time between 1806 and 1820. The six-storey Belper Reeling Mill was built 1807-8 and at a slightly later date this was linked to the West Mill by the Junction Mill.

In 1810 or 1811 the first Belper mill (of 1776-8) was demolished to make way for the present South Mill, 1811-12.[3] This has five storeys and an attic and is one hundred and eighteen feet long and forty feet wide. The ground storey is of stone and those above of brick. For the period there is a bold use of beams. The Mill, with its well-lit and neat interior of remarkably modern appearance fittingly represents the culmination of Strutt's work in the twenty years following his design in 1792 of the first fire-resistant mill.

Mention must also be made of that curious structure the

---

[1] Ashton, *The Industrial Revolution, 1760-1830* (1948), 150-1.

[2] Daniels, 'The Cotton Trade during the Revolutionary and Napoleonic Wars', *Trans. Manch. Stat. Soc.* (1915-16).

[3] Between March, 1812, and January, 1813, £494 8s. was spent on the South Mill Cut.

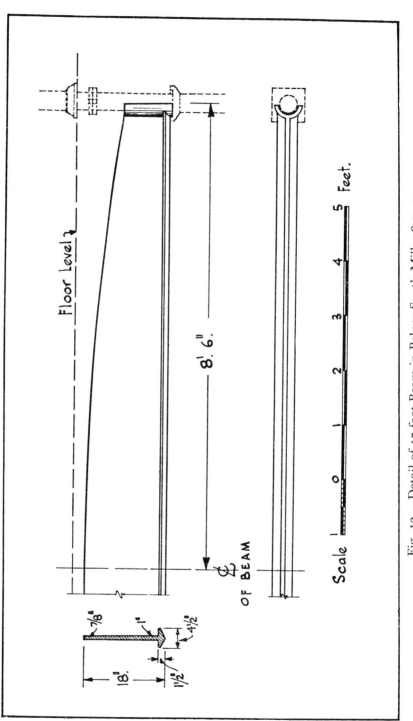

Fig. 12.— Detail of 17-foot Beam in Belper South Mill, 1811-12

Belper Round Mill which, built over the period 1803–13, commenced working in 1816. The massive stone-built Mill clearly owes much to the idea of the Panopticon of Samuel and Jeremy Bentham over which the latter wasted so much of his substance. It is divided into eight segments and the overlooker at the centre, like the spider at the heart of his web, could see everything that happened in them. Bentham held this 'simple idea in Architecture' to be of especial use in prisons. 'To be incessantly under the eyes of the inspector is to lose in effect the power to do evil and almost the thought of wanting to do it.' He even compared the position of the inspector at his place of observation to the divine omnipotence! The plan, he thought, could be extended from prisons to factories, mad-houses, hospitals, and even to schools.[1] How far William Strutt, though a friend of Bentham, was prepared to apply 'the universal inspection principle' to his workpeople one does not know, but the Round Mill had also a more utilitarian aspect. Probably it was used for scutching, a process much liable to outbreaks of fire. The overlooker at the centre could shut off any of the segments by closing the doors and letting the fire be tackled without involving the rest of the building.

The power aspects of the Belper and Milford mills were complex. The Derwent is a large but capricious stream, very subject to changes of level and to floods. It called for extensive works to overcome these handicaps. A writer in *Rees's Cyclopædia*[2] said those at Belper were 'on a large scale, and the most complete we have ever seen, in their dams and water-works'. They can still be seen and recognized as fine pieces of engineering:

The great weir is a semicircle, built of very substantial masonry, and provided with a pool of water below it, into which the water falls. On one side of the river are three sluices, each 20 feet wide, which are drawn up in floods, and allow the water to pass sideways into the same pool; and on the opposite side is another such sluice, 32 feet wide. The water is retained in the lower pool by some obstruction which it experiences by running beneath the arches of a bridge; but the principal fall of the water is broken by falling into the water of the pool, beneath the great semicircular weir.

---

[1] Halévy, *The Growth of Philosophic Radicalism* (1949), 83–4.
[2] Article, 'Water'.

The water which is drawn off from the mill-dam above the weir passes through three sluices, 20 feet wide each, and is then distributed by different channels to the mills, which are situated at the side of the river, and quite secure from all floods.[1]

The river above Belper bridge had been widened and its sides walled.

In order to prevent any ill effects from the penning of the River by their Weir (on pretence of which, several most vexatious actions were a few years ago maintained against them [the Strutts]), a capacious brick barrel-arch has been carried from below the Bridge on the W side of the River, for a quarter of a mile or more, to receive the land and soakage waters.[2]

These works developed as William Strutt's mills were built and by 1820 some 14 acres of water had been added to the Derwent in its reaches immediately above Belper bridge.[3]

The all-important water rights were zealously guarded as in 1789 when Jedediah Strutt, fearing that the proposed Cromford Canal would interfere with the level of water in the Derwent, joined with the Earl of Harrington, the mayor and burgesses of the borough of Derby and Thomas Evans in unsuccessfully petitioning the Commons against the passing of the Cromford Canal Bill:[4]

I thought it necessary to go to my father to talk with him about Belper Weir [Joseph Strutt wrote to his brother William on July 28, 1789]. He thinks if the Bill is likely to pass, such a clause should be

---

[1] Article, 'Water'.

[2] Farey, op. cit., ii, 398. The following entries of 1795 appear in the Strutt MSS.: 'Saml Bridgett assisting to make the Bank in Mr Strutts Garden to prevent high Water from injureing the Mills, £31'; '3400 Common bricks to raise Garden Wall at 20/– £3. 8. od.' 'Making a Wall to prevent Flood from Washing the bank away, £2. 14. 2½.'

[3] Strutt MSS. In order to protect their property at Belper, Makeney and Milford both Jedediah and George Strutt took an active part in the organization of the Belper Association of which the younger Strutt was treasurer. The Association offered rewards, graduated according to the type of crime for which conviction was secured; in the case of murder, burglary, highway or footpad robbery or arson, five guineas; for robbing any dwelling house, shop, warehouse or waggon, one guinea if by day, two guineas if by night; for stealing coals, or poultry (game cocks excepted), fruit, vegetables, timber, unlawfully interfering with dams or fishing therein, half a guinea, or one guinea if by night (*Derby Mercury*, Jan. 24, 1793).

[4] *C.J.*, xliv, 280, 376, 410, 422.

introduced as will impower all the owners of weirs to raise them at particular seasons, making compensation for the injury that may be done and that this compensation the proprietors of the canal should. defray.

My father is quite angry at the stupidity of Lord Stanhope about the horizontal wheels. He thinks somebody should contradict his argument and urge the failure of horizontal windmills as a reason sufficient to demonstrate the absurdity of such a scheme. Besides the works on the river are too much consequence to run the risk of untried schemes—the experiment should be made and approved before any reasoning can be made of it.[1]

Strutts' works did not detract from the beauty of the lower Derwent valley. Belper, 'with its river, overhanging woods, and distant range of hills', presented to Ure 'the picturesque air of an Italian scene'.[2] Farey painted a similar if less romantic picture of the stretch of the Derwent above Belper bridge but below this point, he observed, the river presented 'a perfect contrast . . . neglected and obstructed'.[3]

[1] *A Memoir of William Strutt*, 20–1.   [2] *Philosophy of Manufactures*, 344.
[3] Farey, op. cit., ii, 398.

CHAPTER IX

WORKERS AND WELFARE

THE number of people employed at the Arkwright and Strutt mills may be told with reasonable accuracy. In the mid-70s Cromford employed about 500 workpeople[1] and early in the 1780s the labour force was increased by the opening of the Masson Mill at Matlock Bath. Arkwright's Wirksworth mill was working by 1780[2] and by 1789 almost 200 people were employed there.[3] His mill at Bakewell then had 300 employees. It was probably built soon after that at Wirksworth and was managed by Richard Arkwright, Jr., who lived in an adjoining house until his father's death when he moved to Willersley.[4] Belper, as we have seen, started with one mill in 1778 and added another in 1786. The Milford Warehouse was completed by 1793 and the Belper West Mill two years later. All these were within a stretch of a dozen miles. In 1789 Cromford had 800 workpeople and Belper 600.[5] Arkwright did not expand much at Cromford but the Strutts went on consolidating and expanding, and reached 1200–1300 by 1802,[6]

[1] *Derby Mercury*, Sept. 19, 1776.   [2] Ibid., June 23, 1780.
[3] Pilkington, op. cit., ii, 300. About 220 workpeople were employed in 1797. Women earned 3*s.* to 5*s.* a week, children 8 to 14 years 1*s.* to 5*s.* and overseers 12*s.* a week (Eden, *The State of the Poor*, ii (1797), 130).
[4] Pilkington, op. cit., ii, 416. Richard Arkwright, Jr., owner of the manors of Cromford, Sutton, Duckmanton and Temple Normanton in Derbyshire, of Hampton Court in Herefordshire and lessee of those of Kirk Ireton and Wirksworth 'commenced life with prospects vouchsafed to few . . . [and] carried on the extensive concerns established by Sir Richard Arkwright with so much success that he was probably at the time of his death the richest commoner in England'. He left estate sworn to exceed £1m. An Anglican and a Tory, like his father, Arkwright served as High Sheriff and as Justice of the Peace for Derbyshire. A benevolent landlord, he had extensive public and private charities (*Gentleman's Magazine*, 1843, 655–7; *Derby Mercury*, April 26, May 3, 1843; Glover, *The Peak Guide* (1830), 121). In 1804 Arkwright ventured into banking when he became partner in the bank John Toplis had founded at Wirksworth in 1780. Arkwright, Toplis and Co. became Richard Arkwright and Co. in 1829. It is now merged into Lloyds Bank.
[5] Pilkington, op. cit., ii, 237, 301.
[6] Britton and Brayley, op. cit., iii, 531.

1500 by 1815[1] and 2000 by 1833.[2] Their factory villages grew apace. In 1789, Pilkington recorded, there were 433 houses at Belper and 'every year, almost every month, new houses are rising up'.[3] According to the 1801 Census the number had grown to 873 houses and 4509 persons; it was the second town of the county. By 1811 it boasted 1023 houses and 5778 persons; by 1821, 1239 houses and 7235 persons. Thereafter its growth slackened.

The increase was not wholly in the number of Strutts' employees. To them and to the nailers (200 in 1789)[4] and a few stocking makers were added workers in minor industries. It is difficult to say how far Strutts' early labour force was made up of children and adolescents and how much of adults. A cotton mill was always in part on a family basis. The adult migrant with children found work there; and the established villager— the lead miner at Cromford or the nailer at Belper—sent his children to the mill. In the first thirty or forty years of the factories there was a great preponderance of young labour in almost all processes except bleaching, weaving, machine-making, and building. This became less as the legal age of entry was raised and as machinery was improved; but in a relatively isolated community it was always to the employer's advantage to build up family earnings and local attachments by creating jobs for adults.

I. AGE AND HOURS OF LABOUR

According to their lights and in the atmosphere of their times both the Arkwrights and the Strutts were good employers. They had made money early and easily; they had an

---

[1] *1816 Comm.*, 223.

[2] *Factories Inquiry. R. Com. Supp. Rep.* Part II, Section D1, p. 96; 1834 (167) xx, 578.

[3] Op. cit., ii, 237. Unhappily there is little precise information as to Milford. In 1811 it had 150 houses and 900 persons; 600 to 700 people were then employed in its mills. In 1833 Milford gave employment to 500 workpeople (Davies, op. cit., 140, 343; Glover, *History of Derby*, ii, 215).

[4] Pilkington, op. cit., ii, 238. Their way of life is described by Farey (op. cit., iii, 508). As late as 1818 there was a considerable nail manufactory at Belper; many of the nailers had between the ages of 9 and 14 worked in the mills (*1818 Comm.*, 216).

assured position in the trade and they felt responsibility as heads of their communities.

First, as to the age and working hours of child labour. In 1774 Jedediah Strutt had told the Commons that the Cromford partners employed children of 7 years upwards but preferred to have them from 10 to 12.[1] In 1781, in advertising for labour, they repeated the 7 year figure.[2] Seven was early enough in all conscience, but domestic industry had taken children from their being able to crawl.[3] Robert Owen said that David Dale's pauper apprentices at New Lanark were 'generally from the age of five and six, to seven and eight'.[4] In 1816 many mills had a few—perhaps more than they would confess to; a Congleton silk mill had a dozen children of 6 to 7 and 23 from 7 to 8 while a Somersetshire silk mill usually took its children at 7.[5]

Night work was common in the early decades. The parish apprentices took turn and turn about in the dormitory beds, as at Peel's mills. Cromford had no apprentices but, Richard Arkwright said in 1816, it had for twenty-two years employed 164 boys at night; they 'got extravagant wages, and were extremely dissipated, and many of them had seldom more than a few hours sleep'.[6] We have no corresponding evidence from Belper; in 1834 only from 10 to 20 adults were on night shift there.[7]

The hours worked, Jedediah Strutt, Jr., said in 1816, were twelve, 'six before dinner (which is twelve to one), and six after; each of which six includes the time for breakfast and tea. This has been the invariable practice at the original silk mill in Derby . . . for more than a hundred years.'[8] The twelve-hour day had thus a venerable antiquity. The day at Cromford began at 7 in winter and 6 in summer. Except for the dinner

---

[1] *C.J.*, xxxiv, 709.

[2] *Derby Mercury*, Sept. 20, 1781.

[3] Cf. Clapham, *An Economic History of Modern Britain. The Early Railway Age, 1820–1850* (1926), 565–6.

[4] *1816 Comm.*, 20.   [5] Ibid., 74, 76.

[6] Ibid., 280.

[7] *Factories Inquiry. R. Com. Supp. Rep.* Part II, Section D1, p. 97; 1834 (167) xx, 579.

[8] *1816 Comm.*, 223. The only holidays during the period Oct., 1784–June, 1787, appear to have been those on Christmas Day, 1784 and 1786 (Reelers' Wages account).

break the water-driven machinery never stopped. Arkwright described the other meal times:[1]

As to breakfast, it is very irregular. In the summer-time the bell rings for breakfast at half past eight; those who go to breakfast, which includes the workmen, but not the spinners, go and stay half an hour. There is a room called the dinner-house, in which there is a range of hot plates or stoves, much the same as in gentlemens kitchens; the mothers, or the younger sisters of the hands employed, bring the breakfasts into this room; they bring them probably a quarter of an hour before the bell rings. As soon as the bell rings, a number of boys, perhaps eight, carry those breakfasts into the different rooms in the factory; those who come first may receive their breakfasts probably in two minutes; those who come later may not receive it for a quarter of an hour; so that possibly some of the hands may have eight-and-twenty minutes at breakfast, others cannot have more than fifteen, they cannot have less. In the afternoon, the bell rings at four, and they are served in like manner; but very few have their refreshment, probably not one in five, I should think. . . . there may be from forty to forty-five minutes allowed in the whole, in the morning and afternoon.

At some point—Arkwright thought about ten years before 1816—children under 10 were excluded. The principal reason was 'that they might learn to read before they came; I do not think their health was taken into consideration, as no injury ever appeared to me to arise from it'.[2] For all that, he himself thought boys should come in at 9 years: 'I see them often running about, and in mischief.' The girls 'have to nurse their younger brothers and sisters, or they work at home, or they do something; but boys have nothing to do unless they go to school'. But, added the practical factory owner, 'it is not so well to alter rules; it is always attended with inconvenience'.[3] It was, however, 9 that formed the compromise in the Act of 1819. Of the Strutts' 1494 employees in 1815 only 100 were under 10, and only eight of these (and eight more among the older) could not read; when the firm's Lancasterian schools, 'nearly completed', were ready no child would be taken on until able to read.[4]

If the witnesses before the Committees of 1816–19 were

[1] *1816 Comm.*, 277.
[2] Ibid., 278–9. [3] Ibid., 281. [4] Ibid., 217.

truthful, a change must have come over the practice of the cotton trade, for 10 was treated as a reasonable age of admission and few would admit having more than a handful of less than that age. The change may have come from educational motives —it was the time of Whitbread's bill and of the discovery of how factory methods might be applied to education under the Bell and Lancaster systems—which undoubtedly affected the better employers. But there was also the threat in Peel's draft bill of June, 1815, of a statutory minimum age of 10 and no night work. Certainly consciences had become a little tender. There is the point too that the number of young children had been lessened by changes in machinery. Arkwright said that there were more adults in water-spinning than there used to be. G. A. Lee (1761–1826), who, in 1790, had been at Drinkwater's water-spinning factory at Northwich, said that five times as many children under 10 had then been employed.[1]

It is less clear that there had been any improvement in hours. Lee said that hours were only half-an-hour longer than in Sir Richard Arkwright's time;[2] others said they were much longer. In Manchester the average working day was fourteen hours (including meal times).[3] Moreover night work by children (free labour) was by no means extinct. So deep did the custom of a century run that the overworking of children defied the reformers until the 1830s; it was not until then that there was much response from parents in favour of shorter hours.

It is important to remember that the twelve-hour custom was sanctioned by working-class tradition. By 1834 there had even been some retrogression at the Strutt mills. The minimum age of admission had become the 9 that had been made statutory under the Act of 1819. Even so, Jedediah Strutt, Jr., in his answers to the Factory Commissioners said: 'Many, indeed most of the females, have been previously employed, some even from five years old, at lace running or tambouring.' (He furnished a list of 150.)[4] In those unregulated jobs they had been 'shut up in small ill-ventilated rooms for twelve or

[1] *1816 Comm.*, 279, 343. For an account of Lee's career see *Gentleman's Magazine* (1826), 281–2, and *Manchester Guardian*, Aug. 12, 1826.
[2] *1816 Comm.*, 354.
[3] Ibid., 96–7 (evidence of G. Gould, twenty-two instances given).
[4] *Factories Inquiry. R. Com. Supp. Rep.* Part II, Section D1, p. 96; 1834 (167) xx, 578. On tambouring see Hutchins and Harrison, op. cit., 14.

he Weir at Belper

The Round and South Mills at Belper

The South Mill, Belper

thirteen hours a day, or even longer, at an employment more injurious to health, and particularly so to eye-sight, than any employment they would be put to in a well regulated cotton factory'. The demand for children at Belper had increased, 'having more light work than we formerly had'. So the twelve-hour day continued, the only change on the hours of the 1770s being that those under 16 worked nine hours on Saturdays.[1]

The Strutts were willing to contemplate a raising of the age of admission to 12, with a ten-hour day and two hours' schooling.[2] But the process must not go too far. Family wages must be considered since payment was by piece:

The reduction of time from twelve hours to ten, and the consequent reduction of wages, would have a most serious and lamentable effect on the working class, as well as bring a great injury to the master. Every thing should be done to enable the working class to procure sufficient food and clothing, and the comforts of life, and then there is some chance of making some moral improvement, but it is very difficult to instruct and improve the hungry and the naked, and those who are degraded (against their own will too) into pauperism.[3]

It was a dilemma that was genuinely felt by the good employer. Having grown up under a system of long hours and early work, meeting competitors who were often unscrupulous and who scamped their welfare responsibilities, he did not sense the resiliency of an industry which, when Parliament did intervene, could take the new restrictions in its stride.

There was also the thought that the cotton mills were a preventive of pauperism. They provided relatively easy work (by the standards of the day) and, even if they did not offer a progressive career to all in them, they were an aid to family earnings. Thus John Pym, the Belper constable and deputy overseer, told the 1818 Committee that the children of the town went into the mills and that besides the jobs under the Strutts of 'Blacksmiths, Labouring Men working out of Doors, making Improvements about the Works, and various other

---

[1] *Factories Inquiry. R. Com. Supp. Rep.* Part II, Section D1, p. 97; 1834 (167) xx, 579. 'Many years ago we worked $12\frac{1}{2}$ hours a day for a short time.' But there is no indication of the date.

[2] Loc. cit.

[3] *Factories Inquiry. R. Com. Supp. Rep.* Part II, Section D1, p. 98; 1834 (167) xx, 580.

Things', they went on to become nailers, weavers and stocking makers.[1] It was among these latter—domestic trades—that the problem of poverty arose; the shadow of the poor law always loured ominously.[2] For a good many the mill was bound to be a blind alley. In water-spinning, of Arkwright's labour force in 1816, 37 per cent. were under 18; of Strutts' (with their specialized yarn finishing) 48 per cent.; in mule-spinning, of McConnel and Kennedy's (1818), 47 per cent.[3]

The water-driven mills had a difficulty from which the steam-driven were largely free—broken time through flooding or shortage of water. The sense of drive made the master as much a slave of the machine as the worker. Time lost had always to be made up. And with piece wages there was reason for it. The Strutts reported in 1834 that in the previous year they had only worked an extra hour on one day owing to water trouble—a surprisingly light extension. Another instance of overtime recorded was more curious. To add a third day's holiday at the wakes of June, 1832, to celebrate the passing of the Reform Bill the operatives at Belper worked off the twelve hours at the rate of an extra hour a day for two weeks.[4]

Strutts kept a record of the reasons given by those workers who left after giving notice. A summary of 367 cases in the six and a half years between December, 1805, and July, 1812, brings out strikingly what happened to those who left the factory. It was by no means wholly a blind alley. Of the women and girls the most numerous groups were those leaving because of pregnancy, or to go into service, or to stay at home. (Even in a factory village the habit of women working was then less common than it was later to become.) Among the boys most went 'to learn a trade', with or without apprenticeship. The number who left because of positive objections to mill-work was small. The Strutts, as good paternal employers, probably took much greater interest in the future of their young workers than most.

There were, of course, others who left without notice, who ran away, or who were dismissed. To these we shall return.

---

[1] *1818 Comm.*, 216.   [2] Cf. Farey, op. cit., ii, 34; iii, 508.
[3] *1816 Comm.*, 217, 291; *1818 Comm.*, App. 16.
[4] *Factories Inquiry. R. Com. Supp. Rep.* Part II, Section D1, p. 97; 1834 (167) xx, 579.

Notices, December, 1805 to July, 1812

1. To take up other occupations:

	Males	Females
To learn a trade	28	
Nailer	17	
Apprentice (a)	15	
Shoemaker	6	
Framework knitter	2	4
To work at his own trade (weaver)	2	
Weaver	1	
Filecutter	1	
To learn the art of weaving calico	1	
Wheelwright	1	
Mason	1	
Collier	1	
To work at his trade	1	
Service	1	40
Milliner		2
To go home		6
To stay at home		30
	78	82

(a) one 'an apprentice of Messrs Strutts'.

2. To leave Belper or Milford for:

	Males	Females
London		3
Chevin (near Belper)		1
Langley (near Heanor)		1
Staffordshire ('from whence she came')		1
Yorkshire	1	
Not stated	1	8
	2	14

3. Insufficient Earnings:

	Males	Females
Cannot get sufficient wage		6
Cannot (or will not) get enough wage		1
Cannot earn her maintenance by picking cotton		1
Too little wage		2
Dissatisfied with wages	2	1
Has a large family that wastes more in her absence than she gets		1
	2	12

4. Dissatisfied with mill work:

	Males	Females
Dissatisfied with place	2	6
Says she's shifted about too much		1
Says Wm Winson uses her ill		1
Cannot give satisfaction with her work		1
Cannot give satisfaction in his place	1	
	3	9

5. *Health:*

Dust injurious to health	1	1
Pregnancy (often 'had to go before her time'—three months)		146
	1	147

Notices were handed in, but withdrawn, for the following reasons:
Going into Yorkshire in consequence of the Mill not
   suiting his wife
Cannot indure the dust in the Machine room (2)
Says the mill does not agree with her.
Standing in water so much does not agree with her
   health (a hard twist hand)

6. *Miscellaneous Reasons:*

To attend school	2	4
To live with relatives		5
To be married		2
To go to her husband		1
Lives too far off		1
To be at home with mother who is ill		1
Dissatisfied about his wife not having her own place in mill again after having been ill	1	
	3	14

Summary of Notices:

Other Occupations	78	82
Leaving Belper or Milford	2	14
Insufficient earnings	2	12
Dissatisfied with mill work	3	9
Pregnancy and health	1	147
Miscellaneous	3	14
	89	278

II. FACTORY DISCIPLINE AND LABOUR TURNOVER

For its first eighty years the factory system was on the defensive. It seemed to many a huge unnatural ogre. We see this in the tone of many of the questions put by the parliamentary inquirers, in such descriptions as those of Byng in the 1790s and of Gaskell in the 1830s, while in the factory hours agitation and the Corn Law debates in the 1840s the wickedness of the system became an article of faith of the agricultural interest. Sensitive later historians (like the Hammonds) allowed them-

selves to become a little over-influenced by the literary movement. The age was, of course, full of inconsistencies. Its conscience could be stirred by the Slave Trade and yet it hardly
felt the same urgency about the defects of the British penal
system, whose evils were just as bad. It was distressed about
the condition of children and young people in the close rigours
of the factory, yet it took for granted the sweating that went
on in the domestic trades of the cottage.

One of the aspects of the factory system that struck the
critical outsider was what might be called its private juris-
diction—the fines imposed to keep discipline among the lively-
spirited and rather wild and uncouth factory population. The
mill codes read harshly today; fining, like truck, had a very
long record in domestic industry and survived almost until our
own day. But there was an arguable case for factory discipline
imposed by the employer, especially in the earlier period, when
one thinks of the young ages of the mill hands and of the
volatility of the labour force.

By modern standards the conditions seem offensive. First
there was the length of engagement. In the factories of the 1770s
and 1780s, as we have seen, there was an engagement of a year
or more.[1] The period became shorter but in the early 1800s
the Strutts had three-month contracts and the Quarterly Gift
Money (a sixth part of earnings paid in cash at the end of
each quarter) could be forfeited for leaving without notice or
for misconduct.

We have already noted the reasons offered by those who left
the Strutts' employment after giving proper notice. There were
also those who left without doing this, who left before their
notices expired, who ran away or otherwise absented themselves
without leave. They could, if the employer so wished, be pursued and prosecuted (as in the Wirksworth case above).[2] The
newspapers had frequent advertisements of this sort. The
Strutts' list of 'forfeits' for 1805 to 1813 is worth analysing as an
instance of the millowner's difficulty in keeping his labour force
together. There is no reference to forfeits in the Reelers' Wages
account for 1784-7 and perhaps the Strutts adopted the system
some time between then and the turn of the century. A Quarterly Gift Forfeit book shows that it was in force as late as

[1] See above, p. 106.   [2] p. 106.

233

1827–8 and in 1833 Strutts told the Factories Inquiry Commission that 'small fines' were one of the methods they used to enforce discipline. Corporal punishments, they added, were forbidden in their mills.[1]

FORFEITS, 1805–13

1. ABSENCE FROM WORK WITHOUT LEAVE.

Leaving without giving notice.
Leaving before notice was expired.
Staying off without leave when wanted.
Very frequently from work without leave.
Running away.
Running away a 2nd time.
Being off drinking.
Off without leave at a wakes.
Crich fair without leave.
Going to Derby fair.
Off at Derby races without leave.
Being off at Heage Feast with a pretence of being ill.
Going without leave to a Shearring.
Being off with a pretence of being ill, when on sending up where she lives, was found washing.
Sendg word she was ill when in fact she was not.
Going home when wanted in card-room.
Off without leave with soldiers.
Going off with some Militia Men.

2. THEFT OF MILL PROPERTY.

Stealing packthread.
Having waste found on her.
Fetching a roller out of the Workmen's shop to take home.
For Stealing Candles, Oil &c.
Stealing Yarn &c., the property of Messrs Strutts.
Making good yarn into waste & pockiting it.
Stealing Nails &c.
Stealing a pair of pincers.

3. DESTRUCTION OR DAMAGE OF MILL PROPERTY.

Breaking Thermometer.
Breaking a Drawing Frame.

[1] *Supp. Rep.* Part II, Section D1, p. 98; 1834 (167) xx, 580.

Setting fire to a lamp cupboard.
Breaking a scale-beam.
Breaking a gallows iron.
Tearing roller cloths wilfully.
Stuffing a stove tunnel up.
Breaking a pair of Scales.
Putting good cotton in the Dust.

4. FAILURE TO DO WORK AS REQUIRED.

Stopping 4 Frames at once.
Lapping up without weighing.
Having 20 spindles standing without occassion for any.
Getting their doffs off without having them looked at.
Neglecting their work &c.
Making waste of good yarn.
Spoiling a parcel of cotton upon machine.
Leaving her cotton behind her.
Mixing yarn &c.
Neglecting cleaning & oiling &c.
Leaving her machine dirty.
Leaving his dust Room dirty.
Weighing sorts wrong and being saucey when told of it.
Ommitting the oiling of spinning frame rollers.
Deal of soft-twisted yarn.
Ravilled bobbins.
Making a large quantity of waste.
Counting hanks wrong.
Mixing balls wrong.
Tying bad knots.
Hiding waste (after having made a deal).
Taking laps off badly.
Spinning Double roving instead of Single.
Spoiling top-cards.
Damping her cotton.
Taking knotts out of bundles & altering the tickets of the same,
    with an intent to make them pass for good ones—when at
    the same time they were bad.
Bad work.
Bad winding.
Bad hanks.

5. FAILURE TO COMPLY WITH MILL DISCIPLINE.

Idleness & looking thro' window.
Calling thro' window to some Soldiers.

Frequently looking thro' window.

Riotous behaviour in room.

Making noises in counting house.

Riding on each other's back.

Making disturbances on Gang way.

Dancing in Room (The entire 'forfeit' of 12s. 8d. was returned to the 3 girls concerned 'by order of J. Strutt').

Going out of the room in which she works to abuse the hands in another room.

Neglecting his work to talk to people.

Making a noise when order'd not.

Quarreling.

Throwing bobbins at people.

Throwing a bobbin at F. Shipton.

Telling lies.

Telling lies to Mr Jedediah.

Striking T Ride on the nose.

Making T Ride's nose bleed on the hanks.

Throwing tea on Josh Bridworth.

Beating Wm Smith Jr.

Striking T Hall with a brush.

Playing tricks with Wm Hall

Abusing G. Haywood about her Daughters work.

Quarreling with the pickers & abusing Geo Haywood.

Quarreling in the room with Mr Hodgkinson.

Using ill language.

Fighting.

Terrifying S. Pearson with her ugly face.

Being saucy with W. Winson.

Talking &c.

Throwing Water on Ann Gregory very frequently.

Sewing in Mill time.

Throwing floor sweepings into cut.

Encouraging the hands to disobey their master.

Moving the wheel which belongs to the bell & by that means making short bell ringings.

Sending for ale into the room &c.

Indecent behaviour to a girl.

Getting into Plantation at the end of the West Mill.

Refusing to carry water.

Refusing to clean her frames.

6. MISCONDUCT OUTSIDE WORKING HOURS.

For putting Josh Haynes' dog into a bucket of Hot water.

Taking Jas Ludlum's coat.

Taking M. Coopers' packet.

Receiving potatoes of Martha Booth which she had stolen from home.

Rubbing their faces with blood and going about the town to frighten people.

Attempting to defraud Messrs Strutts by changing bad money for good.

Stealing gun-flints.

It is unfortunate that the Forfeits account gives no indication of the fraction of Quarterly Gift Money deducted from work-people's earnings. The early pages of the Quarterly Wages Book, 1801–5, however, provide just such information and it is from there that the following examples are taken:

		Forfeit		Gift Money		
		s.	d.	s.	d.	
John Sandom	Spinner	18	6	18	6	For throwing roving bobbins through window into Cut.
Sarah Varrney	Spinner	1	10½	1	10½	Left
Joseph Jepson	Carder	3	9½	3	9½	Stopd for running away [Had then been absent 5 weeks]
Mary Pym	Carder	2	4½	2	4½	Left [5 weeks before end of quarter]
Mary Hall	Picker	2	3	5	10½	Refusing to go to spin
Joseph Lievers	Workman	2	6	31	5	Off 1 day without leave
William Porter	Workman	4	9½	4	9½	To go towards paying off his Debts to Messrs Strutt
Hannah Seal	Roller Coverer	9	11½	14	3	Bad conduct
Frank Orme	Reeler	5	0	12	11	For Counting hanks wrong
Mary Buckley	Picker	2	0	7	10½	Ill behaviour
Sarah Philips	Picker	3	0	8	4½	Ill behaviour
Thomas Bunting	Spinner	1	3	14	`9	Forfeited for letting 4 Cards stand
Charles White	Carder	1	8	19	3½	Forfeited for not giving Notice when he left during Dinner hours
William Bailey	Carder	2	0	5	8½	For letting the grinding stick go between the Cylinders
Thomas Ball	Workman	2	6	30	6	Off 1 Day Drinking
Thomas Bamford	Workman	5	8	35	6½	Off 2 days Drinking
Joseph Seal	Workman	1	0	22	5	Off ½ Day Drinking
Jno Smart	Workman	2	6	24	6	Off 1 Day Drinking

That the percentage of total earnings forfeited was small indeed is shown by the following figures taken from the Quarterly Wages Book. Though individuals and families perhaps sometimes suffered hardship owing to the loss of Gift Money the Strutts can hardly be said to have made a ruthless use of their power:

FORFEITS JANUARY, 1801, TO SEPTEMBER, 1804

	Mean No. of Workers per Quarter	Total Earnings (15 Quarters)			Forfeits (15 Quarters)			Total No. of Forfeits (15 Quarters)
Spinners	219	£9650	6	8½	£70	13	9	279
Carders	234	9585	16	0	99	17	6	399
Winders	99	1956	1	2½	8	13	7	85
Reelers	164	7598	0	6	39	9	5½	163
Pickers	185	6389	13	7½	124	13	5½	703
Roller Coverers	15	457	15	5	1	10	9½	6
In and Out Workmen	107	10342	19	11	61	14	3	129
Mill Labourers	37	1625	16	3	9	8	6	51
Clerks	3	243	4	1	–	–	–	—

The three-months' notice and the imposition of forfeits were not the only methods by which Strutts sought to retain and to discipline their labour force. Together with neighbouring factory masters they agreed not to take on workpeople unable to produce a satisfactory testimonial from their old employer. The millowner's attitude is clear from the following letters of Walter Evans of Darley Abbey:[1]

Walter Evans to the Botts of Tutbury

December 14, 1787.

We are informed that some children named Bennets & Garratts who left us a little time ago are employed at Tutbury as also Jas. Allens family. We allso have had many hands (who said they came from Tutbury) offerd at Darley, and we had employed some, we believe, except Freeman whom we refused until he brought a character from you. From experience we are well satisfied it is a very impolitic measure, for different Mills (particularly neighbouring ones) to employ hands from each other without bringing a character

---

[1] I am indebted to Miss Jean Forrest for permission to quote the following letters of Walter Evans and Co.

from their last place. We do not know any Mill but yours that would employ hands from [us]. Messrs. Strutt of New Mills & Belper have empowered us to offer from them as well that no person shall be employed from them or from Tutbury without a written character provided you will do the same to them and us letting people now employed continue where they are, it appearing to us, that when your people know that they will not be employed at these three Mills it will probably damp their spirit of tramping.

Walter Evans to the Robinsons of Bulwell

June 29, 1795.

We are informed that a widow Woman named Ann Janet Holmes who took away her Children from our Cotton Mill a month or two Back has got employment for them under you and also we are told that others from us have made application at your Manufactury for employment. We desire to know if it is your intention to continue to take people from their employment under us: we do not mind the case of a family of Children but it would not be pleasant to see the Hands that we have entirely taught their Business continually drawn away from us & particularly by a Gentleman from whom we had no such expectation.

And at the same time Walter Evans wrote in similar terms to the Robinsons of Papplewick mills.

The success of Strutts' experiments in the field of labour management may be gauged from the few figures we have of time lost and of labour turnover at their mills.

The Reelers' Wages account shows the time lost (including that resulting from unavoidable stoppages) to have been as follows:

	Period	Weeks	Total possible working days	Days lost	Percentage of Time Lost
Reelers	Oct. 1784–June 1787	140	37,068	3757	10·0
Workmen, later classified as:	Oct. 1786–Jan. 1787	12	2,304	185¼	8·0
Home Workmen	Jan. 1787–June 1787	21	3,486	335	9·6
Out Workmen	Jan. 1787–June 1787	21	6,312	1215	19·2

Later records reveal that between June, 1805, and December, 1812, 1600[1] workpeople left the mills with or without giving

[1] This is not a rounded figure.

the required three-months' notice. Assuming that some 1300 persons were then employed at Belper and Milford, the labour turnover must have been in the region of 16 per cent. per annum.

III. EARNINGS AND PAYMENT IN KIND

From the scattered material at our disposal it is hard to construct a picture of the wage system. Almost all the mill workers, however low paid, were on piecework, as were some of the adult 'in' and 'out' workers. An immense amount of book-keeping and calculation was involved but only a few accounts have survived. This is a pity because there is little to show us how the Strutts surmounted the shortage of small coin which was one of the great difficulties of the millowner. The great ironmasters had been using for some time their own silver and copper token coinage (John Wilkinson began his issues in 1787), and many others, tradesmen and industrialists, followed suit. In the case of Samuel Oldknow, as Unwin has described, it led to an elaborate system of paper money and truck.

It would probably be wrong to assume that Oldknow's elaborate system at Mellor was quite typical of the factory colonies. He was in a bad way financially in 1792, before the outbreak of war and the crisis of the spring of 1793, which led to something like panic in Manchester, Liverpool and New-castle-upon-Tyne. By his shop notes of 1792–3 he almost eliminated the use of money in his wages. It was an ingenious scheme but there was a background which, as it was not familiar to Unwin, may be noted. Oldknow had just taken into partnership Peter Ewart (1767–1842), an apprentice of Rennie's and then with Boulton and Watt. Towards the end of April, 1793, Oldknow sent him to Liverpool to raise money. He called on Dr. James Currie who told the story in a letter to William Wilberforce. The firm was trying to keep its workers at Mellor together, although it had no money with which to pay them; and for three weeks they had been prevailed on to accept about a third of their wages. To raise coin the firm had entered the retail market:

They fitted up a light cart and sent a young man with it, full of goods, to supply the retailers in every part of the country, and to bring home the specie every Saturday, whatever might be the loss. The expedient succeeded for about three weeks, but had now failed, and he was come to Liverpool to try if by any possible means he could raise a few hundred guineas, to get over another week and keep his people alive. . . . They [the workers] had agreed to wait this young gentleman's return from Liverpool, and what money he was able to raise, they had consented should be laid out in oatmeal, which being boiled up with water, potatoes, and some of the coarser pieces of beef, should be shared out in fair proportions among them; and thus in the cheapest manner provide for their subsistence.

The house had many thousands owing to them in Liverpool but could not raise a single guinea. 'How he was to face the poor people he knew not, each of whom had four to six weeks' wages due.'[1] The shop notes to which Oldknow resorted were thus a crisis measure, although they continued for a year.[2]

Before he was driven to these expedients Oldknow had got his small money from Thomas Evans and Sons, the Derby bankers. In a letter to him of December, 1786, they describe how against

Bills at two months on a good House in London, either your own drawings or endorsements. . . . We believe we can supply you with £500 every fortnight, at some times probably we could spare more. . . . We apprehend you will have no cause of complaint . . . as Messrs Arkwrights have had cash from us some years & we never received a complaint nor had a guinea returned.[3]

It is not clear whether at this date Strutts also obtained cash from Evans and Sons. They drew occasional 'cash' from Abel Smith and Co. of Nottingham—£100 and £150—and occasionally from Smith, Payne and Smiths of London. Strutts' London agent sent down (in 1787 and 1788) two hogsheads of half-guineas at £100 each. But by 1794 they had an account with Thomas Evans and Sons by which they received a weekly amount of 'cash' which they covered by bills. The early rate was £150 weekly, rising in the middle of 1795 to £250, and then in March, 1796, to £400. The amounts fluctuated over

[1] Henry, *A Biographical Notice of the late Peter Ewart, Esq.* (1844), 11–14.
[2] Unwin, op. cit., 179–93.
[3] Ibid., 177–8.

the next ten years with the state of trade and the firm's mill-building activity. The half-yearly drawings in 'cash' from Evans until the account was closed in August, 1813, were:

		£			£
1794	[July–December]	1650	1805	i	9310
1795	i	3600		ii	9500
	ii	7035	1806	i	5700
1796	i	8890		ii	6800
	ii	10062	1807	i	5800
1797	i	10595		ii	7100
	ii	10400	1808	i	6650
1798	i	10300		ii	5700
	ii	10095	1809	i	5600
1799	i	9500		ii	5500
	ii	9490	1810	i	5230
1800	i	9140		ii	5430
	ii	9200	1811	i	5050
1801	i	10740		ii	5400
	ii	9450	1812	i	5000
1802	i	11780		ii	5400
	ii	11455	1813	i	5000
1803	i	10150		[To August 2]	600
	ii	10150			
1804	i	9980			
	ii	8000			

Doubt arises about the years after 1806. William Strutt (with his sister Elizabeth) was a partner in the Evans' bank until 1808.[1] In 1806 Samuel Smith of Nottingham opened a bank in Derby and in 1810 Strutts opened an account with them. It is not possible to tell from the ledgers whether some of the 'cash' drawn from them was for wages; probably it was.

But in what did the 'cash' consist? Possibly at some period the Strutts used tokens. Arkwright issued Spanish silver dollars, countermarked at the Soho Mint, 'Cromford, Derbyshire', and valued at 5s. and 4s. 9d.,[2] and Strutts' cash books show that between September, 1803, and October, 1806, Thomas Shipman, their London agent, bought and sold dollars on their

---

[1] *London Gazette,* January 9–13, 1810, 67.

[2] Davis, *The Nineteenth Century Token Coinage* (1904), 14. A Spanish silver dollar of Charles IV, dated 1801 and countermarked 'Cromford Derbyshire 4/9', is in the Public Museum, Derby. For the state of the coinage in Derbyshire at this time see Farey, op. cit., iii, 510–12; *Derby Mercury,* Oct. 30, Dec. 18, 1778; July 29, 1802.

behalf through Smith, Payne and Smiths. The cash book entries
are as follows:

1803		£	s.	d.
September 24	To cash 43 Dollars of Thomas Shipman at abt 4/7¼	9	18	6
	By cash 2 Dollars to Belper	4	15	–
1804				
June 22	By 987 Dollars to Smith Payne & Co	226	9	8
	By loss by the above 987 Dollars taken @ 4/9 each £234 8 3	7	18	7
June 28	To cash of Smith Payne & Co Dollars	100	–	–
July 12	To cash of Smith Payne & Co Dollars &c	150	–	–
1806				
January 14	By cash loss by 292 dollars on home, the price being lowered from 4/9 to 4/6 ea.	3	13	–
January 23	To cash gain'd by 329 Dollars paid at Belper	4	2	9
February 4	By cash loss by 52 dollars Jany 14 3d ea being alld for that No to those people whose silver we usually take	–	13	–
February 24	By Dollars sent Thos Shipman	300	–	–
March 14	To cash gained by Dollars recd at 4/6	2	2	6
March 25	To cash gained by 92 Dollars @ 3d	1	3	–
April 17	To cash gained by 208 Dollars @ 3d each	2	12	–
	By 208 Dollars sent T Shipman by J S @ 4/9	49	8	–
July 9	By 445 Dollars sent Thos Shipman	100	2	6
October 16	By Dollars sent Thos Shipman	58	14	6

Between March, 1802, and June, 1804, Strutts also obtained
£447 worth of seven-shilling pieces and a total of £420 worth
of seven-shilling pieces and half-guineas from Shipman and
their cash book reveals that from 1812 to 1816 James Peirce,
their London agent, was sending them silver and occasionally
copper. As late as 1825 they were still obtaining cash through
Peirce. They wrote on May 5 thanking him for 'the 200£ in
gold and silver' and on November 7 they told him, 'if you
found you could get 500£ in Silver from the Banker, it wd be
better to send it in a bale by water'.

In 1811 there appear in Evans' account to Strutts' credit
four items amounting to £370 for 'tokens', and £1 10s. 10d.
for 'expences on tokens', and in January, 1812, in Strutts'
account with the Smith bank at Derby there is £151 16s. 6d.
for 'tokens'. On August 4, 1812, £6 10s. 9d. 'expences on tokens'
was paid by Strutts to Richard Arkwright. These tokens may
have been some of the general tokens commonly used, possibly
those of the Bank of England. But it was, of course, common
for concerns of the factory colony type to issue their own tokens

at this time. New Lanark countermarked a 5*s*. Spanish dollar, a 2*s*. 6*d*. half-écu of France, a farthing on a William III Scottish bodle; Deanston used half-écus, Charles II bawbees, and George III halfpennies (countermarked 4*s*. 6*d*.); Ballindalloch and Rothesay had Spanish dollars, and so on.[1] McConnel and Kennedy bought casks of coin from Boulton and Watt in 1806, 1807 and 1808, and in 1812 their agents were scouring the country for silver. This was the time of the Strutts' tokens and it may well be, as McConnel and Kennedy suggested in their letters, that the great rise in food prices and the Luddite risings and food riots in 1812, had caused hoarding of silver and copper coin, which made payment of wages very difficult.[2]

The earliest of the Strutts' wage accounts, that of Reelers' Wages for 1784 to 1787, gives the earnings of reelers, pickers and 'in' and 'out' workmen. The latter appear to be builders and craftsmen; they would include the machine makers but not the mill foremen. Their wage rates and earnings were considerably above those of the millhands and it may be presumed that, as was the case some thirty years later, many of them had earlier worked in that capacity.[3]

Payment was mainly by time though a few seem to have been on piece. The wage rates of the Chappells and the Lidgatts, all reelers, for the six-day, 72-hour week were as follows:

John Chappell (Overseer)	Sep. 25, 1784–Aug. 20, 1785	7*s*.
	Aug. 21, 1785–Jan. 14, 1786	6*s*.
	Jan. 15, 1785–June 1, 1787	10*s*.
Christian Chappell	Dec. 4, 1785–Dec. 31, 1785	3*s*.
	Jan. 1, 1786–June 1, 1787	No rate stated- presumably on piece.
Eliza Chappell[4]	Nov. 7, 1784–Apr. 2, 1785	2*s*.
	Apr. 3, 1785–Oct. 15, 1786	2*s*. 3*d*.
	Oct. 16, 1786–June 1, 1787	No rate stated- presumably on piece.

---

[1] Davis, op. cit., 20, 23. The dates are not given, unfortunately.

[2] Daniels, 'The Cotton Trade at the Close of the Napoleonic War', *Trans. Manch. Stat. Soc.* (1917), 10.

[3] *1818 Comm.*, 216–18, 221.

[4] A sister, Martha, whose name first appears in the Reelers' Wages account in Feb. 1787, testified in 1833 that she began work at Belper when

A page from the Reelers' Wages Book

Ruth Chappell	Jan. 16, 1785–Feb. 12, 1785	1s.	
	Feb. 13, 1785–Nov. 10, 1786	1s.	3d.
James Lidgatt	Sep. 25, 1784–Nov. 20, 1784	4s.	2d.
	Nov. 21, 1784–July 30, 1785	4s.	6d.
	July 31, 1785–Nov. 3, 1786	5s.	
	Nov. 4, 1786–Nov. 24, 1786	5s.	6d.
Isaac Lidgatt	Sep. 25, 1784–Oct. 2, 1784	2s.	9d.
	Oct. 3, 1784–Jan. 1, 1785	2s.	10d.
	Jan. 2, 1785–June 11, 1785	3s.	
	June 12, 1785–Jan. 28, 1786	3s.	3d.
	Jan. 29, 1786–Sep. 1, 1786	3s.	6d.
Joseph Lidgatt	Sep. 18, 1785–Jan. 14, 1786	4s.	3d.
	Jan. 15, 1786–Sep. 8, 1786	4s.	6d.
	Sep. 9, 1786–Feb. 9, 1787	4s.	9d.
	Feb. 10, 1787–Apr. 13, 1787	5s.	

To the weekly wage rate was added payment for overtime at 1d. an hour for millhands and at 2d. an hour for overseers. Few millhands worked more than the usual 72-hour week though John Chappell and Robert Hodgkinson, the reelers' overseers, regularly put in a 13-hour day.[1]

Deductions from earnings included those for absence from work (calculated in quarter days) and—for but few of the workpeople indeed—rent and goods. Other deductions went towards the repayment of money borrowed from the Strutts. At any one time about half-a-dozen reelers were in debt. The sums involved usually came to but a few shillings and were at irregular intervals repaid to the firm. John Chappell was persistently in debt. In 1784 he borrowed various sums which he gradually repaid; then on October 6, 1786, he is recorded as owing 147s. Week by week he repaid a few shillings until on the last entry in his account (June 1, 1787) he owed 42s.

Many of the 'workmen' were perennial borrowers. Perhaps the most interesting example is that of Charles Richardson, whose weekly wage rate was 12s. His name first appears for the week beginning October 27, 1786. He did not work during that week and is then recorded as owing 64s. 4d. In the 32

five years old at 9d. a week. Hours were from 6 a.m. to 7 p.m. and included one hour for dinner during which time she went home. Breakfast was taken while standing. In 1827 she had left Belper for Old Radford, Nottinghamshire, where she was employed in a mill for 12 hours a day at 7s. a week (*Factories Inquiry. R. Com. 2nd Rep.* Section C3, p. 4; 1833 (519) xxi, 104).

[1] This would include time for breakfast and tea but not for dinner. See above, p. 226.

R

weeks ended June 8, 1787, he worked during only 15 weeks and did not repay any of the money he had borrowed. The last entry in his account reveals that he then owed Strutts £27 13s.

The workpeople named in the Reelers' Wages book were, it seems, paid weekly and in cash. By the 1800s, however (how much earlier we do not know), 'cash' represented only a fraction of the wages bill. The economy of the Strutts' mills, like those of the Gregs, must have been mainly based on truck or rents. The amount of money earned at Belper and Milford in a typical quarter, September–December, 1803, is about £3946, or £303 a week. Of this no more than a sixth was received by the workers in cash, say £50. The elaborate Quarterly Wages Book of 1801–5 lists the whole of the workpeople with either their full earnings or the sixth of their earnings that is 'allowed in money'. There are references to a Ticket Book in which, presumably, the disposal of the rest is set out, but this has not survived and we lack any details of how payment was made. It must have been on a family basis as the list of millhands in the latter part of the book also gives the name of the parent or head of the household.

Unhappily it is not possible to compile a series of earnings sufficiently long to exhibit a trend from either the Reelers' Wages or the Quarterly Wages Book but, where comparison is possible, wage rates were higher in the latter.

The greater part of the workpeople's earnings must have gone on housing, foodstuffs, coal and a variety of miscellaneous goods and services supplied to them by the Strutts. Probably this was recorded in the missing Ticket Book.

First as to housing. The 1790s, as we have seen, witnessed a remarkable expansion of Strutts' activities at Belper and Milford. The West Mill and the Milford Warehouse were under construction in 1792–5 and in order to meet the needs of their millhands, the Strutts then built the North and South Long Rows at Belper and sixty or so houses at Hopping Hill, Milford.[1] By 1801 Belper had 873 houses—double the number twelve years earlier. Its growth continued, though at a diminished rate, and by 1831 it had 1482 houses, a fifth of which were owned by the Strutts.

[1] Between February, 1793, and November, 1794, £3338 was spent on the construction of houses at Hopping Hill.

The Rent Stopped account for the years 1827 to 1837 reveals that during this period the weekly rents deducted from the earnings of the Belper millhands came to about £36.[1] Those for the week ended June 5, 1829, were made up as shown in the table overleaf.

Contemporaries were impressed by the dwellings erected by many of the country factory masters:[2]

> The cottagers throughout Derbyshire [wrote Farey in 1813] are much better provided with habitations than they commonly are in the Southern Counties of England, and they generally keep them in neat and in better order . . . the vast numbers of neat and comfortable Cottages which have been erected, by the late Sir Richard and by the present Mr. Richard Arkwright, by Messrs. Strutts, Mr. Samuel Oldknow and numerous others of the Cotton-spinners and Manufacturers, for the accomodation of their multitudes of workpeople, must have had a great influence on the general style and condition, now observable in the Cottages.

And, writing in 1836, Gaskell asserted:[3]

> An inspection of Belper, Cromford, Hyde, Duckenfield, Stayley Bridge, the villages and hamlets around Oldham, Bolton, Manchester, Stockport, Preston, Glasgow, &c. &c., will show many magnificent factories surrounded by ranges of cottages, often exhibiting signs of comfort and cleanliness highly honourable to the proprietor and the occupants. These cottages are generally the property of the mill owner and the occupants are universally his dependants.

But, he contended, 'the admirable organization of a few out-town manufactories' cited by Ure was hardly sufficient evidence upon which to support the assertion that 'there is not a better or more certain mode of benefiting a country village than by establishing a cotton-factory in it':[4]

> It would be . . . unjust [Gaskell warned] to take as the sole ground for examination, the establishment of the Messrs. Strutt, in

---

[1] Although many of the Strutts' houses had large gardens a considerable number of workpeople rented additional land known as 'Potatoe Lots' at 1d. a week. A rather exceptional garden rented by John Gratian is enthusiastically described by Farey (op. cit., ii, 209–12).

[2] Farey, op. cit., ii, 21.

[3] Op. cit., 294.

[4] Ure, op. cit., 342. The 'out-town manufactories' were those of the Strutts, Gregs, Ashtons, Ashworths and Grants (ibid., 343–52).

Rents of Strutts' Houses at Belper
(Week ending June 5, 1829)

Rents (s. d.)	St. George's Place	Smith's Court	Bridges's Lane	Scotches	Mount Pleasant	Short Rows	Field Row	Cluster Buildings	North Long Row	South Long Row	Berkins Court	William Daniels's Houses	Miscellaneous	Total
1 0–1 2½	1				1								1	3
1 3–1 5½					1	12							7	20
1 6–1 8½	5	5											4	14
1 9–1 11½					1	5		1					2	9
2 0–2 2½					3	15			13	13	19	2	5	70
2 3–2 5½				8		7		8	14	16	6	2	8	69
2 6–2 8½	6	5	3			6		8	5	3		5	16	57
2 9–2 11½	1		1	2	2	1	1	1	2	3	1	1	4	20
3 0–3 2½	1		3		3	1	3	1	2	1	1		1	17
3 3–3 5½			3		4		2	1		1			2	13
3 6–3 8½			2		1		1						1	5
3 9–3 11½					2		1						1	4
4 0–4 2½							1							1
4 3–4 5½													1	1
4 6–4 8½					2									2
Total	14	10	12	10	20	47	9	20	36	37	27	10	53	305

the valley of the Derwent, or any other country mill, conducted by men of enlarged benevolence and active philanthropy . . . The instances adduced [by Ure] are rather beautiful examples of what may be done, than illustrations of what is done.[1]

The Strutts' property, solidly built of brick or of the local gritstone, was kept in good repair. The interior walls of houses were regularly whitewashed and chimneys swept quarterly (at 2d. a time). The practice of whitewashing, Strutts supposed to be responsible for the rarity of infectious diseases at Belper and Milford[2] and, in 1835, Ure went further in claiming that a few years earlier 'not one of Messrs. Strutt's work-people was attacked with cholera, while the neighbouring handicraft people and farmers were falling victims to this pestilence'. The factory workers' immunity he erroneously believed to be 'due to the warm air which surrounded them at work, and to the comforts of their homes'.[3]

The Strutts, like Oldknow, the Gregs and the Evans, supplied their workpeople not only with housing but also with coal, milk, meat and vegetables, the cost of which they deducted from their earnings. Unfortunately we do not know the proportion of millhands that bought goods in this way though one suspects that it was high.

The Coal Stock book which runs from 1808 to 1824 shows that households regularly spent 1s., 1s. 6d. or even 2s. a week on coal and that not a few of them were often in arrears with their payments.

Similar arrangements enabled the millhands to buy adequate quantities of milk throughout the year:[4]

Messrs. Strutts of Belper [Farey tells us] in order to ensure a constant supply of Milk to the Inhabitants and make it the interest of Cow-keepers, to keep up their stock of Milking Cows through the Winter, engage for a sufficiency of Milk, at 1½d., 2d., 2½d. and even 3d. per quart, during different periods of the year according to the expense and difficulties of procuring the article, and a person serves it out to their numerous Work-people in the Cotton Works, and keeps accounts until the end of the week, when they pay for it out of their wages.

---

[1] Gaskell, op. cit., 89–90.
[3] Ure, op. cit., 378.
[2] *1816 Comm.*, 217.
[4] Farey, op. cit., iii, 30.

Strutts' Milk Account, 1806 to 1842, confirms this description of their scheme. In May, 1809, they agreed to buy milk from R. Statham, F. Needham and G. Ride at 2½d. a quart during the months of December, January and February and at 2d. a quart at other times. The milk was to be delivered to their dairy and to ensure that sufficient quantities were forthcoming during the winter months the suppliers agreed to pay Strutts 2d. for every quart by which their deliveries in December, January and February fell below one-third of those of the previous May, June and July. At any one time milk reached the Belper dairy from six or seven sources including, from 1811, the Strutts' own farms at Bridge Hill and at Green Hall.

Milk was delivered to consumers each day and we know something of the earnings of the roundswoman for a note in one of the accounts tells us that on February 5, 1813, it was 'ordered by Mr. G. B. Strutt that from May 1st to Sept 7 the allowance for the person delivering out Milk shall be 5/- per wk and from this period to May 1 4/6 per wk—and that Mary Robson the now acting person shall be pd after that rate from Jany 1st 1813'.

The Belper dairy was well supplied with milk cans, churns, pots, sieve cloths and other equipment. It was regularly painted and whitewashed and strenuous efforts were taken to ensure its cleanliness. During the period 1807–30, 524,267 gallons of milk were sold at a profit of £70.[1]

Strutts' employees bought meat and perhaps other goods also from W. Butler, a concern later known as the Belper Provision Co. The Provision Co., which is first referred to in an account beginning August, 1821, was a co-operative enterprise distributing its profits amongst its customers in proportion to the value of their purchases. Its surviving accounts may be summarized as follows:

	No. of Customers	Value of Sales	Dividend Distributed
Mar. 1818–Mar. 1821	581	£1275	£107
May 1821–Sept. 1821	265	£386	£19

The Strutts displayed an active interest in the Company's affairs and made occasional purchases from it. Thus between

[1] Sales during 1831–42 came to 172,662 gallons on which a profit of £165 was made.

1818 and 1820 Jedediah Strutt, Jr., bought meat worth £2 7s. 1d. and during the same period £14 9s. 9d. worth was supplied to Bridge Hill House, the home of G. B. Strutt. Later accounts contain references to Bridge Hill House and Farm but not to Jedediah Strutt.

It is undoubtedly the Belper Provision Co. that Ure refers to in his *Philosophy of Manufactures*, 1835:[1]

Several years ago [he recorded] a number of the operatives [at Belper and Milford] formed themselves into a society on the co-operative plan, for laying in their provisions and materials of clothing in the wholesale market, in order to benefit by the profits which usually go to the retailer. As the society wore a beneficial aspect it received the concurrence of the proprietors, and was countenanced by one of them becoming a member of the managing committee. For some years the scheme seemed to work well; the goods were bought for ready money, and ostensibly at the lowest current price, and they were distributed to the members in proper proportions, according to their wishes or their means. The money profits . . . were divided among them, and amounted frequently to as much as well nigh paid their house-rents. Eventually certain evils began to be developed, which were not at first sight foreseen. Travelling dealers, who came in quest of orders for goods, found out that a bonus might be given with advantage to an influential secretary or treasurer, and might secure a preference in the sale of indifferent article, such as tea or cloth, at a price above their ready-money value. Disputes and suspicions began to arise. The committee, though chosen freely by the whole body of the associated workpeople, were naturally selected from the more prominent among them, such as the mill-overlookers, and were therefore often continued from year to year, whereby some of them had opportunities of becoming adepts in studying their own interests more than those of the society at large. In fact, driving bargains for the society or themselves, began to occupy their thoughts too much to the exclusion of their proper mill duties. The main evil attendant on this plausible plan was its depriving the people of the habit of managing their money wages, which were in fact absorbed by the co-operative shop in consequence of their value being taken in goods, whenever they were due and in articles not of strict necessity, such as would probably have been let alone, if cash must have been paid for them. Many of the intelligent operatives having become sensible of these evils, and feeling their independence of action nullified, so to speak, signified their wish to break up the

[1] Pages 344–6.

concern. Thus after a thirteen years' fair trial, the co-operative society of Belper was voluntarily abandoned by the workpeople.

Provision books for the years 1819 to 1838 show that the Strutts sold to their workpeople large quantities of dripping, lard, vegetables and fruit supplied from Bridge Hill House and Garden and from Wyver Farm. The vegetables most commonly sold were potatoes (several varieties), onions, peas, scarlet runner beans, leeks, cabbages, cauliflowers, Brussels sprouts, cucumbers and radishes. Fruits included cherries, pears, apples, currants, gooseberries, damascenes and rhubarb. Occasionally the workpeople bought small quantities of butter, bacon, pork and ewe lamb.

By far the greatest number of entries in the accounts are for dripping which must have held a prominent place in the diet of the millhands. Lard was slightly dearer. Butter at 1s. 2d. a lb.—double the price of dripping—was rarely bought. It was doubtless a luxury beyond the means of the workpeople.

Strutts' employees not infrequently bought goods which they paid for in instalments out of their earnings. The records, unhappily, are fragmentary but the Quarterly Wages Book reveals that during the first six months of 1801, 23 workpeople bought books valued in all at 25s. 8d. and the Foreign Stoppages and Goods Stoppages accounts contain such items as the following:

			Value	Deduction per week
1829	Thomas Woolley	Wheat	15s. 0d.	3s.
	Wm. Winson	Sause pan	3s. 6d.	6d.
	Thos. Turner	Boiler & damper	28s. 9d.	2s.
	Sarah Blackham	Anvil	13s. 6d.	1s.
	Jane Walker	,,	12s. 10½d.	1s.
	Sarah Waterfall	Window Shutters	3s. 9d.	1s.
1830	Benjamin Mather	Coals, apple Trees & ashes-Grate	17s. 0½d.	1s.
	Thos. Smith	Clock	13s. 0d.	13s.
	James Hicking	Ashes Grate	2s. 0d.	6d.
	Isaac Rowland	Cloth	15s. 0d.	1s.
	Chas. Seal	,,	12s. 0d.	1s.
	Joseph Haynes	Music	10s. 0d.	1s.
	Hugh Shimmells	,,	5s. 0d.	1s.

Mention must also be made of the deductions from the earnings of the millhands in payment for the 'welfare' services they enjoyed. At Belper and Milford workpeople wishing to have a pint of tea or coffee, morning and evening, were able to do so for 1*d.* a day. A rather curious feature about this scheme was that persons participating in it 'obtain medical assistance gratis'.[1]

Medical advice for all females employed at Belper was also provided under a 'sick club' which, during the years 1821–7, had an average membership of 432. 'Abuse to which all sick clubs are liable [had, however,] . . . caused its dissolution, so far as receiving weekly pay, in the year 1828.'[2]

An account of 1828–32 shows that Strutts were then setting aside £12 a year for distribution to workpeople involved in accidents during the course of their employment. Compensation was doubtless given only in the more severe cases as on June 23, 1828, when 'William Potter hurt his Head and Legg with a fall from [the] Third Window in [the] North Mill'. His condition was described as 'Very Bad'. In 1830 an additional £2 was given to 'a boy of the name of James Bridges whose Arm was dreadfully injured at the large Wash Card'; and in 1832 '£2 [was] added for bad cases'.[3]

IV. THE FACTORY COLONIES

Religion and education continued to occupy important places in the Strutts' factory communities. Jedediah's sons built upon his work, founding, within a few years of his death,

[1] *Factories Inquiry. R. Com. 2nd Rep.* Section C3, p. 5; 1833 (519) xxi, 133; *Factories Inquiry. R. Com. Supp. Rep.* Part II, Section D1, p. 98; 1834 (167) xx, 580; Ure, op. cit., 334.
[2] *Factories Inquiry. R. Com. Supp. Rep.* Part I, Section D3, p. 313; 1834 (167) xix. The Strutt MSS. confirm the existence of a 'Female Sick Fund' in 1821. Contributions seem to have been at the rate of 1*d.* a week. There is reference to a 'Sick Fund' in the early pages of the Quarterly Wages Book, 1801–5, but no entries in the columns provided for contributions to it.
[3] Accidents, which were mainly to fingers, may be summarized as follows:

| Year ended Feb. 28 | Slight | Number of Accidents | | Total | Compensation Allowed £ |
		Bad	Very Bad		
1828	132	29	12	173	12
1829	137	28	17	182	12
1830	148	38	12	198	14
1831	167	27	7	201	12
1832	188	33	10	231	14

schools organized in accordance with the principles advocated by their acquaintance, Joseph Lancaster.[1] By 1811 they had built a Unitarian Chapel at Milford[2] and early in the 1820s they made a generous contribution towards the costs of constructing an Anglican Church at Belper.[3]

Unfortunately we do not know the date at which the Strutts founded their Lancasterian schools at Belper and Milford but it may well have been 1807, the year in which they bought 30 copies of Lancaster's *Improvements in Education* at a cost of £3. Certainly by 1811, 400 pupils were receiving instruction at Belper and a further 150 at Milford.[4] In 1817, 64 children were attending day schools and 650 the Sunday schools at Belper while 300 went to the Lancasterian Sunday school at Milford. There and at Belper the Strutts were then building schoolrooms for 400 and 500 pupils respectively.[5] The following year, 1818, 142 children under 10 attended the Strutts' day schools at Belper and Milford while 1044 pupils of all ages went to their Sunday schools. A further 660 were then also receiving instruction at Sunday schools organized by the Methodists and Calvinists.[6] By 1833, 650 children were attending the Belper Lancasterian school, 200 a charity school belonging to the Anglican Church, and 800 the Sunday schools supported by the Calvinists, Baptists and Methodists.[7]

The ages at which boys and girls were admitted to the Strutts' schools at Belper and Milford are given in the table printed opposite.

To the younger children the schools must have served as crèches. Older boys were taught the three R's as were the girls

---

[1] William and Joseph Strutt had met Lancaster during his visit to Derby in 1802. In 1809 they wrote inviting him to stay with them (Strutt MSS.; *A Memoir of William Strutt*, 54–5).

[2] Davies, op. cit., 343.

[3] *Derby Mercury*, Aug. 18, Sept. 8, 1824. The new Church, built at a cost of £12,000, was consecrated in Sept., 1824. It had accommodation for 1800 persons, six times that of the old Church (Glover, op. cit., ii, 116–17).

[4] Davies, op. cit., 343, 355.

[5] Lysons, *Magna Britannia*, v (1817), 139–40.   [6] *1818 Comm.*, 217–18.

[7] Glover, op. cit., ii, 117. In 1846, 500 pupils (including infants) attended the Lancasterian school at Belper and 400 a Sunday school held in the same premises. Scholars at the Lancasterian school paid 1*d*. a week. The Milford day and Sunday schools had 285 pupils. Children employed in the mills went to school for three hours each day. All males under 20 and females under 18 were obliged to attend Sunday school (Bagshaw, op. cit., 289–90).

STRUTTS' SCHOOLS AT BELPER AND MILFORD

NUMBER OF BOYS ADMITTED BY AGE, 1819-30

Year Admitted									Ages at which admitted											Total
	1	2	3	4	5	6	7	8	9	10	11	12	13	14	15	16	17	18	19	
1819			1	3	7	14	11	8	16	14	8	6	5	3	3					99
1820			2	4	9	7	7	12	11	4	2		1	1		1				61
1821		3	4	16	15	9	6	4	8	2	1	2	1	1	1	1	1			75
1822		2	6	9	8	16	10	11	7	7	5	3	1	1						86
1823		3	3	10	18	10	15	10	10	9	1	2	3							94
1824		1	6	11	9	11	16	7	10	7	2	2								82
1825			7	11	13	11	10	7	11	5	2		1							78
1826			4	14	13	17	16	13	2	8	3			1	1					92
1827			2	14	10	10	9	5	7	6	2	2								67
1828	1		6	10	13	11	11	7	8	5	2		4						1	79
1829		3	13	9	19	14	8	7	11	4	2	3	1	1	1					96
1830		3	7	7	9	7	13	5	5	3	1	1	2							63
Total	1	15	61	118	143	137	132	96	106	74	31	21	19	8	6	2	1		1	972

NUMBER OF GIRLS ADMITTED BY AGE, 1823-30

Year Admitted									Ages at which admitted											Total
	1	2	3	4	5	6	7	8	9	10	11	12	13	14	15	16	17	18	19	
1823		1	6	6	5	4	11	7	20	17	5	7	5	2	2	1				99
1824		1	9	7	3	8	11	5	13	18	5	5	5	2						92
1825			1	4	4	5	3	4	14	14	5	7	2	2	1	1	1			68
1826			14	20	14	10	11	12	22	14	9	4	7	3	2				1	143
1827		1	10	17	13	6	6	7	20	7	6	2		1	2					98
1828			17	12	10	7	4	7	8	4	3	2		2						76
1829			12	11	18	14	14	12	13	5	2	10	3	3	1	1				119
1830			6	13	8	5	5	9	4	5	4	2			1					62
Total		3	75	90	75	59	65	63	114	84	39	39	22	15	9	3	1		1	757

who, in addition, received instruction in sewing.[1] Classes were held each weekday but our only hint as to the number of hours' instruction provided at this time is contained in the following note written in one of the school accounts:

'James Barlow began Teaching April 13, 1818 and is employed 7 hours per Day.'

For 62 years a member of Jedediah's Chapel at Field Row, James Barlow was 'upwards of fifty years . . . the efficient and respected master of the Lancastrian School' at Belper.[2]

Most of the pupils attended school for but a few weeks or months, though a small number stayed on for several years. They left for a variety of reasons. Many of the girls are listed as having 'Gone to the Mill', as having been 'Kept at Home' or, more vaguely, as having 'Gone to Work'. A few were expelled, went to another school or 'Left Town'. Most of the boys are recorded as having 'Gone to Work', 'Gone to Work at the Mill' or as 'Wanted'. A small number were expelled owing to bad conduct or poor attendance. One boy gave as his reason for leaving the fact that he had no shoes. Many pupils who left school were subsequently re-admitted.

Children old enough to work paid 1d. a week towards their education. Those too young to enter the mills attended school free of charge.[3] Most of the pupils lived in Belper or Milford though a few were from more distant places like Heage and Shottle. Some came from workhouses. Their parents followed a variety of occupations, predominant amongst which were those of nailer, stockinger, collier and mason.

Strutts' millhands were obliged to attend Sunday school, and an entry in the Forfeits book reveals that on May 8, 1807, one, Thos. Cooper, had his Quarterly Gift Money stopped because of his failure to do so. And in 1833 Strutts told the Factories Inquiry Commission that 'all the young persons under twenty are expected to attend Sunday schools', that they required all children to have attended their elementary school before starting to work in their mills and that

all the boys that leave work on Saturday at four o'clock we compel to attend school for about a couple of hours, not only for their own

---

[1] Strutt MSS.; Lysons, op. cit., v, 139.
[2] Memorial tablet in the Chapel where he is buried.
[3] *1818 Comm.*, 218.

improvement, but to prevent the mischief which we found before the adoption of this regulation they were apt to get into from wantonness, and of which the neighbourhood began to complain. The girls are allowed to go home, to assist their mothers in sewing and household work.[1]

The Act of 1833 made the employment of children in the textile mills conditional upon attendance at school for two hours a day on six days a week and, to comply with these provisions, the Strutts established schools at Belper and Milford.[2]

Hours at the school held at the Belper mills were from 6.30 a.m. to 6.30 p.m. during which time 'changes in hands ... amounted to 14'. 'Every overlooker', reported the Inspector of Factories, 'has on a slate the hours at which the classes work, and, on the other hand, there are the names of the children who are in each separate class.'[3] The school was 'in charge of a mistress who has the assistance of two young persons during the periods when the largest classes attend'.[4] Returns for children under 13 show that in 1838, 84 boys and 119 girls were in attendance 'in seven sets'. All the pupils were instructed in reading and writing and the girls were taught sewing and knitting 'about half their time'. 'In this mill', Strutts stated, 'the education of the factory children has not been conducted until the last few months upon any very good system. Some improvement has now been effected . . . [and] it is contemplated to obtain the assistance of a schoolmistress from the British and Foreign School Society.'[5]

The Milford school had, in 1838, 'lately been removed from a cottage in the neighbourhood to a room prepared on purpose on the premises. It is under the charge of a mistress, assisted by a boy as a monitor'.[6] As at Belper no charge was made for the

---

[1] *Factories Inquiry. R. Com. 1st Rep.* Section E, p. 24; 1833 (450) xx.
[2] Before this time Strutts 'seldom took any children to work except such as were educated at our day-school . . . and it gave us the opportunity of taking those best qualified'. Owing to the 1833 Act 'the demand [for child labour] was greater than the supply, and we were obliged to take such as offered' (*Factories Act, Educational Provisions. Com. Rep.*, pp. 38–9; 1839 (42) xlii, 390–1).
[3] *Mills and Factories Regulations. Sel. Cttee. 2nd. Rep.*, p. 56; 1840 (227) x, 220.
[4] *Factories Act, Educational Provisions. Com. Rep.*, p. 38; 1839 (42) xlii, 390.
[5] Loc. cit.   [6] Ibid., p. 39; 1839 (42) xlii, 391.

instruction provided for the 36 boys and 37 girls who attended 'in three sets of relays'. The schoolmistress was able to report a marked improvement in the conduct and manners of her pupils but the mill superintendent was less enthusiastic about the attitude of their parents who, he maintained, displayed little interest in the education of their children.[1]

Like their contemporaries in many parts of the country Strutts' workpeople took an enthusiastic part in the celebrations organized to mark events of national significance.

The first of these under Jedediah's sons seems to have been that held in October, 1801, to commemorate the signing of the Preliminary Treaty of Amiens. Twelve-hundred men, women and children employed at Belper and Milford, 'attended by three excellent bands of music', marched in procession after which 'they were treated with an excellent dinner (of which two fine oxen made a part) and plenty of ale'. In the afternoon 'another ox was roasted whole, and with a proper quantity of bread, and 14 barrels of ale distributed to the populace, attended by a band of music. . . . In the evening there was a general illumination, which was brilliant notwithstanding the extreme wetness of the evening.'[2]

Great rejoicings in June, 1814, marked the break in the Napoleonic conflict preceding the Hundred Days. At Derby, where 'Messrs. Strutt entertained their workpeople with Old English fare of Roast Beef and Plumb Pudding', £10,000 is said to have been spent on festivities.

Belper and Milford were the scene of great rejoicings:

Friday se' n-night at 9 o'clock in the forenoon [the *Derby Mercury* reported] a discharge of cannon summoned the numerous people employed at Messrs. Strutt's manufactory at Belper to meet at the mills . . . [where] after parading the town . . . 750 sat down to a plentiful dinner of Roast Beef and Plumb Pudding, and the remainder, amounting at least to 450 more, were abundantly supplied with the same excellent fare, and an ample quantity of ale at their own houses. The dining room was decorated with great taste and

---

[1] Loc. cit. Jedediah Strutt, Jr., testified that owing to the necessity to employ children 'that we should formerly have rejected . . . I do not see any change at present for the better in their habits and manners'.
[2] *Derby Mercury*, Oct. 22, 1801.

elegance. On the one end over the head of the table were G.R. Peace, P.R. in large letters composed of gilt and plain laurel leaves and ribbons; the other end over a long range of barrels of ale, the word 'Plenty' was very appositely placed, and on the end of one wing along which four tables extended, appeared the immortal name of 'Wellington'.

The evening was concluded with dancing and a display of fireworks.[1]

The following day:

Messrs. Strutt's regaled their work people at Milford with the same liberality as at Belper; the decorations of the dining and dancing rooms, in which four hundred and fifty were entertained, were equally beautiful, and from the center of the dining room a 5 stone loaf was suspended by three hanks of cotton labelled 'Peace, Liberty, Industry'. 150 children dined in the mill yard, and 300 more at Mr. George Henry Strutt's house, where they sang 'God save the King' in full chorus. And the same day 200 poor inhabitants of Belper were plentifully regaled by Messrs. Strutt's at the Mills.[2]

In July, 1821, Strutts' employees at Belper and Milford celebrated the coronation of George IV. 'The whole of the work people amounting to 2,500, accompanied by bands of music walked in procession and were regaled with upwards of 300 Gallons of ale which they drank to "the King's good health, and may he never forget those principles which placed his Family on the Throne of these Realms" '.[3]

The passing of the First Reform Act, a measure to which the Strutts had given their wholehearted support, was an occasion of great rejoicing:[4]

The festivities in honor of the Reform Bill . . . have been conducted at Belper on a scale, that we doubt not will equal if not surpass any other in the country [reported the *Derby Mercury*].[5] The whole has been arranged by a Committee of Management, aided by the invincible energy of their justly popular townsmen, Messrs. Strutt. . . .

On Monday, the female hands in their employ, to the number of nearly 1000, were entertained by Jedediah Strutt, Esq. on the lawn in front of his beautiful residence, by a sumptuous *déjeuner*, the

---

[1] *Derby Mercury*, June 23, 1814. [2] Ibid., June 30, 1814.
[3] Ibid., July 25, 1821. [4] See above, pp. 188–9, 230.
[5] July 4, 1832.

excellent band of John Strutt, Esq.[1] playing the most approved airs. In the evening they adjourned in procession . . . to the large area of the mills, when the day was delightfully concluded by a merry trip on the 'light fantastic toe', in one of the large and appropriate Rooms of those immense edifices.[2]

During these gratifying festivities . . . 4,800 lbs. of beef, 3,184 lbs. of plumb pudding, 7000 penny loaves, and 2,550 quarts of ale were distributed, in the following proportions:—$\frac{3}{4}$ lb. of beef and $\frac{1}{4}$ lb. of plumb pudding, with one penny loaf, and a quart of ale, to every male; and the like quantity of beef, pudding and bread, with $\frac{1}{2}$ pint of ale, to every female and child; independently of the public dinners which were supplied to 2000 of the principal inhabitants, at the different Inns on Tuesday.

Tuesday saw a continuation of the festivities at Belper and the following day the workpeople at Milford took part in celebrations arranged by Anthony Radford Strutt.

[1] This forty-strong orchestra and choir was composed of workpeople employed at the mills. They received regular instruction which was counted as working time, and in return agreed to remain in their employment for at least seven years. The orchestra gave performances in and about Derby and to encourage its members to give of their best Strutt occasionally took small groups to the opera and to concerts in London (Gardiner, *Music and Friends*, ii (1838), 512–13).

[2] The Strutts 'have provided a dancing-room in their mill, where festoons of flowers are suspended, and a band of music is heard on holydays, as a substitute for the public-house to their female youth' (*Factories Inquiry, R. Com. 2nd. Rep.* Section D3, p. 5; 1833 (519) xxi, 133).

CHAPTER X

THE RAW MATERIAL

STRUTTS became one of the largest consumers of raw cotton in the country. We know, however, little of their early sources of supply except that they came from London importers. In the 1770s and 1780s Strutts' London agent occasionally noted the carriage paid to Derby or Belper, but not the origin or weight of the cotton. If the analogy with other firms holds it was probably West Indian and Levant. But Belper and Milford, specializing in hosiery yarns, came to be very selective in their demands. The Belper 'pickers' of 1784–5 were divided in the wage book into those of 'coarse', 'fine', and 'Surinam' (later called 'superfine'). The various kinds of long staple South American cotton had come to form the main consumption of Belper, if not of Derby.

I. THE KINDS OF COTTON

South American cotton, before the coming of Sea Island in the late 1790s, and the little from Bourbon (imported through Ostend), comprised the dearest kinds of cotton. It reached London mainly through Portugal and Holland. Thus in 1774 a Manchester merchant noted:

From Berbecia all the cotton is sent to Holland, and the quantity rarely exceeds 150,000 lbs. annually, and some years when crops fail the quantity imported is not above 5,000 lbs. weight. Surinam at most 100,000 lbs in one year. Essiquibo and Demerary not more than 50,000 lbs. in one year. These cottons are mostly consumed in Switzerland and at Brabant.

At Amsterdam in November, 1774, Surinam fetched $23\frac{1}{2}d.$ a lb. and Berbice $25\frac{1}{4}d.$, against $12\frac{3}{4}d.$ for Smyrna; the Bristol prices of West India ranged from $15d.$ to $20d.$[1] The imports

[1] *Proc. Manch. Lit. and Phil. Soc.*, X (1870–71), 142–4. From the Memorandum books of George Walker, an original member of the Society, which were destroyed with the Society's library in the blitz of 1940.

from 1768–77 show the variations in the foreign growths and the higher, though fluctuating volume of those from the West Indies; [1] the small imports from North America, especially from the Southern colonies, may have been grown there or may have been West Indian, as were probably the New England exports. Even in 1787 the total import was almost equally divided between the French, Spanish, Dutch and Portuguese colonies and the East Indies on the one hand, and the British West Indies and the Levant on the other: [2]

	Mill. lbs.		Mill. lbs.
British West Indies	6·6	French & Spanish Colonies	6·0
Levant	5·7	Portuguese Colonies	2·5
		Dutch Colonies	1·7
		East Indies	0·1
	12·3		10·3

The price range at Manchester between 1786 and 1802 illustrates the relative positions of the growths:

PRICES OF COTTON AT MANCHESTER

	1786	1794	1795	1796	1797	1798	1799	1800	1801	1802
Smyrna	14¼	10½	14½	17¼		23				
Surat		11½			19	20	18			
French	22	17	22½	24					30	
Barbados	23	17	22½	24		29	26–45	32	31	
Domingo	23½	17	23	23½				33	30	
Demerara	26	18½	27½	24½	26		50		32	
Cayenne	27			28						
Maranham	30		28	26	27	32	34–52	32½	34	27
Pernambuco	39	22	28		29			37	36	34
Georgia						21	30½	20	22½	21

Prices as of June, except 1802 Georgia (Jan.). Where two prices are given, and with 1800 Pernambuco, the lower price is apparently of October. [3]

The rising demand for cotton in the 1780s both put up the price and called forth new supplies. The first books on the Liverpool cotton market (such as Slack of 1816 and Smithers of 1825) [4] describe the appearance of more South American

[1] See Appendix D, pp. 347–348.
[2] *An Important Crisis in the Calico and Muslin Manufactory in Great Britain* (1788), 8.
[3] *Proc. Manch. Lit. and Phil. Soc.*, op. cit., 161.
[4] Slack, *Remarks on Cotton* (1816); Smithers, *Liverpool, its Commerce, Statistics and Institutions; with a History of the Cotton Trade* (1825).

cotton, though their dates are hardly to be relied on. By 1792 a list of prices in the London market gives 26 different growths, all but five from the West Indies, Brazil and the Guianas;[1] none were from North America. The Strutts took virtually no cotton from North America until 1800. McConnel and Kennedy, in the first months of their partnership of 1795 as mule spinners, used some South American and some Bourbon (the latter ranged between 37*d.* and 48*d.* for odd bags), but soon turned mainly to Georgia (at 28*d.*).[2] Birley and Hornby of Blackburn, a firm that began in 1767, used West Indian and a little Smyrna cotton, adding from 1791 some Surat; they did not use Georgia until 1798.[3] The regular exports of North American cotton began in small quantities after the peace of 1783 and by 1791 were only 189,316 lb., rising to 1,601,700 in 1794; the rise then became very rapid—9,360,005 in 1798, 17,789,803 in 1800, 40,383,491 in 1805.[4]

The Strutts' preference for South American cotton and the way in which they supplemented it by other growths during the intermittent supplies of the Napoleonic Wars, can be seen from the accompanying analysis of their cotton records, 1794

---

[1] *Manchester Herald*, May 12, 1792.
[2] McConnel and Kennedy MSS.
[3] Birley and Hornby MSS.
[4] Baines, op. cit., 302. The main growths were Bowed Georgia, Georgia and Upland; the precise differences are hard to specify. The 'bowed' referred to the primitive cleaning process before Whitney's saw gin (invented 1793) (ibid., 67, 301). The Strutts, though they did not then use American cotton, figure in the legendary history of its introduction to England. They are said to have bought in 1784 the eight bags that an unbelieving Customs official challenged because he did not know that the Americans grew cotton (Brooke, *Liverpool as it was during the last Quarter of the 18th Century* (1853), 244). The consignees were William Rathbone and Sons and Nicholas Waterhouse, the broker (Ellison, *The Cotton Trade of Great Britain* (1886), 195). The eight bags are not recorded in the Liverpool imports given in the *Manchester Mercury* for 1784 where, however, mention is made of eight bags imported together with a quantity of timber by William Rathbone in the *Britannia* from New England in 1769 (*Manchester Mercury*, Sept. 26, 1769). This was not the first American consignment; some imports are mentioned in 1770 (Enfield, *Hist. of Leverpool* (1773), 73). Another claimant was William Teasdale who, in 1839, sought reward from the trade because his uncle Isaac Teasdale had sent 'the first bag of cotton wool' grown in America, which arrived at Liverpool in the *Diana* from Charleston on Jan. 20, 1785 (*Manchester Guardian*, Oct. 23, 1839). This is confirmed by the *Manchester Mercury* of Jan. 25, 1785, but the importation was, like many others recorded in the paper, probably a re-export of West Indian produce.

to 1817 (pp. 264-7). It can be divided into two parts: (i) the period up to and including the Peace of Amiens and the short period of peace, and (ii) the years of renewed war, including the Napoleonic blockade, the American War, and the first two years of peace. The measurement is in bags of varying bulk.[1]

RAW COTTON PURCHASES, 1794–1803

Type of Cotton	1794	1795	1796	1797	1798	1799	1800	1801	1802	1803
S. American:										
Bahia		10	21		20					50
Berbice	15	39			15		38	314	114	30
Brazil			101				87		32	16
Cayenne	10	22			10	10	10	95		56
Cumana						12				
Demerara	270	134	215	10	70	294	541	678	583	567
Dutch	40		31							
Giron							215	330		
Guiana		80			23					
Maranham	293	532	304	80	167	190	85	98	117	108
Para						35				
Pernambuco	758	446	660	1393	1633	1051	285	374	489	691
Surinam	20	30			157	279	573	779	783	431
Total	1406	1293	1332	1483	2095	1871	1834	2668	2118	1949
W. Indian:										
Bahama		60	35		30		56		58	
Barbados	223	38	144	97	45	334		197	162	125
Carriacou	368	302	477	581	130	243	396	94	320	160
Dominica	26		15		90		15		44	
Grenada	78	55	50				33	73		
Guadaloupe							5			
Jamaica	35									
Martinique						33	15	153	122	
St. Lucia	24	26								
St. Vincent		21								35
Tobago	70	34	20	35						
West India						10	20	25	31	
Total	824	536	741	713	338	612	683	486	615	320

[1] See Appendix D, pp. 339–341.

Type of Cotton	1794	1795	1796	1797	1798	1799	1800	1801	1802	1803
N. American:										
Bowed										
Georgia										88
Georgia					5		49	246	168	150
New Orleans									5	157
Orleans										28
Total					5		49	246	173	423
Eastern:										
Bourbon	4				1					
Total	4				1					
Unclassified:										
Fine						12				
Total						12				

The earliest account of the use and quality of the various growths was given in *Rees's Cyclopædia* about the year 1808 in an article entitled 'Cotton' which is worth quoting:

North American:

Sea Island Georgia—is the produce of the coast of Georgia, and the small islands contiguous and belonging to it. It has a long and fine staple, but more or less silky, stained or dirty, on which account no other cotton varies so much in price. The best is preferred now to every other kind, and is often sold at very high prices to the manufacturers of lace.

Upland, or *Bowed Georgia*—is the produce of the inland districts, and either from the nature of the soil, or defective cultivation, is much inferior to the preceding. It is a light flimsy cotton, of weak and very unequal staple, having long and short fibres intermixed. It is used chiefly for inferior goods. It derives its name of Bowed Georgia from an instrument like a bow, which the planters use in cleaning it.

Tennessee—much like Bowed Gerogia, but in general cleaner, and sometimes better staple.

New Orleans—this also resembles Bowed Georgia, but it is generally preferred both to that and to Tennessee. The fibre of these

Raw Cotton Purchases, 1804–17

Type of Cotton	1804	1805	1806	1807	1808	1809	1810	1811	1812	1813	1814	1815	1816	1817
S. American														
Bahia	10				39	1169	907	707						
Berbice						119	50						5	
Cali													11	
Cayenne		53		97							60			
Ceara						40	47	51						
Cumana		16												20
Demerara	917	725	637	430	144	17	739	312			246	208	356	
Laguira				5		63	175	923	1159					
Maranham			105							3811	3164	2817	1204	1093
Orinoko			423		60									
Pernambuco		40	190	545	486	1038	253	821	967	1163	1408	1252	129	516
Surinam	443	377	322	173	276		194	134						
Total	1370	1211	1677	1250	1005	2446	2365	2948	2126	4974	4878	4277	1705	1629
W. Indian														
Bahama	215					54						20		
Barbados	51	473	538	971	764	1111	474	417	477	386	547	808	1082	171
Carriacou	15		389	214		42		37					15	
Dominica														
Grenada				35	30	39								
St. Peter's														
St. Vincent											15		61	
Trinidad													12	
West India														
Total	281	473	927	1220	794	1246	474	454	477	386	562	828	1170	171

N. American														
Bowed	114	554	476	273	86	50	421	736	40	20		146	170	97
Bowed Georgia	130	48										20	220	
Georgia	151	288											50	
New Orleans		90	123	145				30					809	12
Orleans													54	10
St. Simon								20						
Sea Island			137	103	72	242	160	145	84			2	106	26
,, Georgia	40					16								
,, Tennessee	5			90			60							
Upland							285	75				160	256	
Upland Georgia													50	
Total	440	980	736	611	158	308	926	1006	124	20		328	1715	145
Mediterranean														
Macedonia		9												
Smyrna		85	55	63	95			20	14	95	50			
Total		94	55	63	95			20	14	95	50			
Eastern														
Bourbon			160	20					10		90	229	1216	
Bengal	6	122	43	202	94	51	46						10	258
Surat				560	67	246	127							52
Total	6	122	203	782	161	297	173		10		90	229	1226	310

three kinds is weak, compared with that of West India, or Sea Island, and goods manufactured from it are unable to endure the same hardship.

South American:

Pernambuca—fine, long staple; clean and pretty uniform in quality; much esteemed; principally used by the hosiers.

Maranham—rather inferior to Pernambuca; not so even in quality, not so clean; much like good Demerara, and used for the same purposes.

Bahia—much like Maranham, sometimes it has the advantage.

Rio—a very inferior cotton; very brown; used generally for the same purposes as low West India.

Surinam—has a long staple; clean; yellow; it is a fine cotton, and much used for making stockings.

Cayenne—a fine good clean staple, preferable to Surinam.

Demerara—the quality of this cotton has fallen off since the colony has been in possession of the English. The best has a fine silky strong staple, much esteemed. The inferior sorts are rather brown, dirty, coarse, and much mixed.

Berbice—the quality of this has of late years fallen off. The best has a good staple, fine, silky, and clean; but latterly it is brown, dirty and mixed.

Carthagena—has a very long staple, but weak; it is very stringy, and rather dirty.

Giron—a brown coloured cotton, fair staple, and generally pretty clean.

Cumana—superior to Giron, and not so clean.

Carracca—inferior to Giron; still more dirty.

Laguira—inferior to Cumana, but preferable to Carracca; not so dirty.

West India:

Bahama—Cotton from the Bahama islands is of various qualities. The best is grown from Bourbon seed, but is much inferior to that kind. The staple is pretty good, fine and silky, but it is often dirty. The staple rather short but strong.

Barbadoes—is of fair middle quality, the staple not very long, but generally silky, and pretty strong; often a good deal of shell of the seed in it, which is a great objection.

Jamaica—very little cotton grown here, and that of very inferior quality; there is the long staple, which is very weak, and often very dirty, and the short, which is also very poor and dirty.

St. Kitt's—very little grown; it is in general very brown, dirty, but of fair staple.

St. Lucia—the same.

St. Thomas—the same.

St. Domingo—sometimes very clean good cotton, and likewise very inferior; not much comes here.

Carriacou—rather a coarse grain, but in general clean, fair, strong staple, used by the hosiers to mix with fine cotton, such as Pernambuca.

Grenada—a good deal like Carriacou, but not always so clean.

St. Vincent's—rather high-coloured; clean, good staple, but not very fine; a good deal cultivated for the size of the island.

Antigua—very little grown, much like St. Kitt's.

Tortola, Montserrat, Dominica—the same.

Martinique—very little comes here. It is a fair middle quality.

Guadaloupe—much the same, sometimes very good cotton.

Tobago—little grown, sometimes very fair good cotton.

Trinidad—rather short staple, and in general very dirty.

East India:

Bourbon—the most even and uniform in quality of any other. It is a fine silky staple, and very clean. It is the most valuable cotton brought hither, except the best Sea Island.

Surat—has a fine, but exceedingly short fibre, in general dirty, containing leaf and sand. It is the lowest price cotton in the market, and used in the manufacture of low coarse goods.

Bengal—much like Surat, but still shorter staple, in general cleaner, and much about the same value.

Madras—not much brought hither. It is mostly from Bourbon seed, and sometimes not unlike it in staple, but in general dirty, and contains much shell, which renders it less valuable; worth little more than Surat; some very good will fetch the price of West India.

Turkey:

Smyrna, &c.—a short mossy kind, and rather dirty, used for making candlewicks; has more substance than Bowed Georgia.

Although of good staple, South American cotton was often dirty and called for especial trouble in 'picking' or cleaning, the first of the preparatory processes. The saw gin had not yet spread to South America and more had to be done at the mills. The 'picking' was done by women, sometimes outside, sometimes inside the factory. The cotton from the bales was beaten with sticks on a square frame, across which were stretched cords between which the seeds could drop; the cotton was then picked by hand for dirt. Picking or 'batting' by hand came to be superseded by the 'devil', in which two large spiked cylinders tore open the bales and separated much of the dirt, and by batting machines, which beat the cotton with sticks on a corded frame.[1] The careless packing led to frequent demands by Strutts, through their brokers, for compensation. Thus, to take a few examples:

	Broker	Entry	Compensation Obtained £ s. d.		
Oct. 3, 1793	Charles Allingham	To Cash of Ewart & Rutson for a stone wt 12½ lb in a bag of Pernamo N 18 Lot 7 bot 13 Mar 93 at 2/–	1	5	0
Jan. 1, 1794	George Greaves	To Cash of Mr. Haussoullier for 20 lb Seeds in Lot 30 Pernamo	2	11	6
Feb. 1, 1796	Nicholas Waterhouse	To Cash of Jas Kenyon for 33½ lb at 2/1 of Iron &c in Demerara Lot 61	3	9	9
Feb. 12, 1796	Nicholas Waterhouse	To Cash of Jas Kenyon for 14 lb at 2/1 Brickends in Demerara Lot 61	1	9	2
Dec. 27, 1797	George Greaves	To Cash for 6 lb 10 oz Clay in N 1293 & 1295		16	5
Feb. 9, 1799	Nicholas Waterhouse	To Cash for 125 lb seeds in N 1245 56 lb 1248 69 lb at 2/4½ £14 16 10 Kept the Seeds at 6d £3 2 6	11	14	4
Apr. 20, 1801	Nicholas Waterhouse	To a Pair of Steel yds in a bag of Demerara bought of J. Bolton in Jan 10 5½ oz		13	6

The machines brought troubles of their own and customers found in them the explanation of bad yarn. The Strutts' agent in Nottingham was complaining in 1801:

I hope this week to get a large supply & of a better Quality. All your Customers say its nothing like so good as it used to be, they have got some report among them that you have a D——l or a machine for picking that spoils all the yarn, I tell them I know nothing of the matter, how the report has got [out] I do not know; whatever is the cause the yarn is not liked so well as it was when I first began.

---

[1] *Rees's Cyclopædia*, articles 'Cotton' and 'Machine'.

II. LONDON AND LIVERPOOL

By 1794, when the Strutts' cotton records begin, the broker-age system was apparently in full swing. They bought from many importers who were paid in bills direct by the firm, but they used a broker as their agent on the traditional commission, at Liverpool, of ½ per cent. Liverpool terms were then 10 days' credit and payment by a three months' bill.[1] London commissions were somewhat higher, ranging between ½ and 1 per cent.[2] Strutts' London brokers were Samuel Wagstaff of Bush Lane, Cannon Street (until his death in 1796),[3] George Greaves (until 1800) and, from 1798 to 1827 (when the records break off), Roger Hunt. In Liverpool the principal broker in the 1790s was Nicholas Waterhouse, a Quaker who, after a training in manufacturing, set up as a broker in the early 1780s.[4] He remained Strutts' broker until 1806 when they transferred the whole of their Liverpool business to Samuel Hope, who, formerly an apprentice of Waterhouse, set up on his own account about this time. He was noted for the excellence of his cotton circulars; his successors, George Holt and Co., remained the Strutts' brokers until modern times.[5] In 1816 Strutts began

[1] Baines, op. cit., 319; Smithers, op. cit., 140.

[2] Strutt MSS.; *The City* (1845), 176. For the commissions earned by the Liverpool and London brokers see Appendix D, p. 343.

[3] He left 'sub £5000' to his wife Eleanor who carried on his business. (Will at Somerset House.)

[4] Ellison, op. cit., 195–6. Amongst Waterhouse's clientele were John and Samuel Horrocks, Robert Peel and Co., Peel, Yates and Co., and Richard Arkwright who, in 1799, paid brokerage on 1300 bags valued at £36,000 (Dumbell, 'The Cotton Market in 1799', *Economic History* (1926), i, 142–3). Waterhouse, resident at Everton, near Liverpool, died in 1823 leaving personal and real estate worth well over £100,000. Shortly before his death he had bought land in Chapel Street, Liverpool, upon which he was building a warehouse, and estates in Bedfordshire. (Will at Lancashire Record Office.)

[5] Ellison, op. cit., 200, 202–3; *Report on Merchants*, 1823 (452) iv, 153. Samuel (1780–1837), the son of William Hope, a mercer and draper of Liverpool, took George Holt (1790–1861) as apprentice in 1807 and as partner five years later. They became bankers and, in 1823, when their partnership came to an end, Hope continued as banker and Holt as cotton broker. In 1836, Samuel Hope and Co. became the Liverpool Borough Bank, a joint stock concern with a capital of £500,000. It failed in the crisis of 1857, the loss being estimated at £94,000.
A Nonconformist, Hope was 'a man of considerable strength of character, and had pronounced Liberal views. In philanthropic endeavours he was

to buy through Kearsley and Bower and continued with them in the 1820s when they were known as John Kearsley and Sons and William Bower and Sons respectively.[1] Occasionally they used other brokers—Thomas Allingham in 1793 and Ewart and Rutson in 1801.

In the years 1794–1803 (except for 1799) the Strutts bought more of their cotton through London than through Liverpool.[2] Thereafter the proportions varied, the effect largely of the vagaries in supply during the war. The quantities (in bags) bought through their London and Liverpool brokers may be summarized as follows:[3]

COTTON PURCHASED BY STRUTTS, 1794–1817
(Bags)

	London	Liverpool		London	Liverpool
1794	2039	195	1806	1243	2355
1795	1599	230	1807	2143	1783
1796	1673	400	1808	1115	1098
1797	1679	517	1809	2981	1316
1798	1237	1202	1810	1886	2052
1799	1001	1494	1811	2854	1574
1800	2241	325	1812	2009	742
1801	2732	668	1813	3635	1840
1802	2311	595	1814	2960	2620
1803	1660	1032	1815	2920	2742
1804	622	1475	1816	1922	3894
1805	912	1968	1817	271	1984

There was not much to choose between London and Liverpool in the early years. The former was, of course, the older market and seems rather to have specialized in South American and Levant cotton. It was also the market for East Indian,

ever to the fore, and he was earnest in his promotion of educational improvement.' He worked to abolish the Slave Trade, to establish a Mechanics' Institution at Liverpool, and to achieve Free Trade. Hope owned considerable properties in Liverpool and built his 'spacious and elegant mansion' in Everton Terrace. He married, in 1816, Rebekah (1794–1838), daughter of Thomas Bateman of Manchester (Hughes, *Liverpool Banks and Bankers, 1760–1837* (1906), 205–12; Syers, *The History of Everton* (1830), 304).

[1] Ellison, op. cit., 192–3.

[2] Little is known of the early cotton markets, especially that of London. Liverpool imported more cotton than London in 1790–2 and after 1795 resumed a lead that was never lost (Ellison, op. cit., 170).

[3] See also Appendix D, p. 342.

STRUTTS' PURCHASES OF COTTON, 1794–1817

(Bags)

	1794	1795	1796	1797	1798	1799	1800	1801	1802	1803	1804	1805
London												
South American	1321	1155	1151	996	1118	821	1581	2151	1573	1191	536	678
West Indian	714	444	522	683	118	168	611	379	615	320	80	30
North American							49	202	123	149		
Mediterranean					1							94
Eastern	4										6	110
Unclassified						12						
Total	2039	1599	1673	1679	1237	1001	2241	2732	2311	1660	622	912
Liverpool												
South American	85	138	181	487	977	1050	253	517	545	758	834	533
West Indian	110	92	219	30	220	444	72	107			201	443
North American					5			44	50	274	440	980
Eastern												12
Total	195	230	400	517	1202	1494	325	668	595	1032	1475	1968

	1806	1807	1808	1809	1810	1811	1812	1813	1814	1815	1816	1817
London												
South American	598	870	859	2240	1522	2734	1749	3540	2703	2499	341	
West Indian	355	430		367	31		236		117	192	182	36
North American	32	30		77	160	100					323	50
Mediterranean	55	63	95			20	14	95	50			
Eastern	203	750	161	297	173		10		90	229	1076	185
Total	1243	2143	1115	2981	1886	2854	2009	3635	2960	2920	1922	271
Liverpool												
South American	1079	380	146	206	843	214	377	1434	2175	1778	1364	1629
West Indian	572	790	794	879	443	454	241	386	445	636	988	135
North American	704	581	158	231	766	906	124	20		328	1392	95
Eastern		32									150	125
Total	2355	1783	1098	1316	2052	1574	742	1840	2620	2742	3894	1984

which the East India Company was pressing in the early 1790s.[1] The origins of the Liverpool cotton market have still to be worked out in detail and some historical revisions of the received texts must clearly be made. The Waterhouse records, which Professor Hyde and his colleagues are investigating,[2] show that by 1800 the broker had assumed his modern functions. He was then usually a man brought up in spinning and manufacturing who used his expert knowledge to become a middleman between the non-specialist importer,[3] to whom cotton was only one side of his trade, and the spinner. He performed essential services to the latter, handling freight and insurance, compensation for defective cotton or incorrect weight, and so on. He also made things easier for the ship-owner and importer by assuring him that his commitments would be met and also by giving him credit facilities and financial assistance. Some of the outlines of the picture can be pushed still further back. In 1793, William Walton, who was broker for Peels, Ainsworth and Co. and other firms, was describing the sample system and its disadvantages. He was giving evidence in a case brought by a buyer of 820 bags of Pernambuco (for £11,196) who had evidently been caught by the slump, had fixed his selling price too high, and whose broker unsuccessfully hawked the cotton round the trade, including the Strutts and Richard Arkwright.[4]

Professor Hyde has shown that in spite of his small commission, the broker's services to his spinning client were a profitable source of revenue. They were certainly miscellaneous. As being the first such accounts we have it may be interesting to set out Strutts' record of their dealings with Waterhouse in

---

[1] Ellison, op. cit., 83. A letter from Oldknow to William Strutt of March 27, 1787, said: 'Several persons have applied to me to purchase East India Cotton yarn, and I never would, on account of its coming in so very awkward a state for our purpose and as it is a material we cannot depend on for a lasting supply I have never thought it worth while teaching children how to wind it or making things for that purpose, and even now, (however cheap) I am not inclined to buy any of it.' Trade opinion was strongly against the East India Company's monopoly and the Strutts supported the agitations (as in 1815) against it.
[2] Hyde, Parkinson and Marriner, 'The Cotton Broker and the Rise of the Liverpool Cotton Market' (*Econ. Hist. Rev.*, 2d Ser. viii, 75–83 (1955)).
[3] For the leading Liverpool importers, 1768–79, see Appendix D, p. 346.
[4] Exch. Dep., 36 Geo. 3, Mich. Lanc., 18.

1799 (from the Belper Ledger) and Waterhouse's[1] account in his ledger. The episode of the *Minerva* concerns a salvaged cargo: (p. 275–8, 280–1):

WILLIAM, GEORGE & JOS STRUTT'S ACCOUNT WITH NICHOLAS WATERHOUSE FROM 1ST JAN., 1799, TO THE 31ST DEC 1799.

1799			£	s.	d.	£	s.	d.
1 mo	1	To Balance from Old Ledger	3701	4	11			
,,	9	By Sundries for 10 Bills & Int.				3361	16	10
,,	12	To Sales a/c J Chorley for 12 Cumanas £189—& Charges £1 2 5	190	2	5			
,,	18	To Sundries for Charges on 110 Bags Cotton p Eliza	159	9	9			
,,	,,	To Thomas Mather for Remr of Insurance & c	39	19	6			
,,	,,	By John Wilson for return for Convoy &c				50		
,,	24	By Sundries for Bills & abatement				413	12	10
,,	17	By Jno Chorley for 2 Bills & Int				189	–	–
,,	,,	By Thomas Mather for Error in Insurance				75	4	6
,,	18	To John Wilson for Premm. of Insurance p Devonshire	153	15	3			
,,	22	To Sales a/c Battier & Co. for 60 Pernams £1531 16 & Charges £8 12 2	1540	8	2			
,,	26	To D a/c Thwaites & Co. & T Tarleton for 18 Bags Cotton £571 19 5 & £3 3 5	575	2	10			
2	1	By Sundries for 17 Bills & Int				2103	15	5
,,	2	To Sales a/c Jno Bolton for 25 Bags Surinam Cotton £971 11 & £5 5 5	976	16	5			
,,	4	By John Bolton for 7 Bills & Int				971	11	–
,,	9	By Jno Chorley for Damagd Seedy Cotton				11	14	4
3	26	To Sundries for Charges on 167 Bags Cotton p Devonshire & Pcess Royal	254	1	8			
,,	,,	By Sales S 15 Bags New Orleans Cotton for Nt Proceeds				201	16	8
,,	,,	By John Wilson for return for Convoy p Devonshire £1443 @ £5				72	3	

---

[1] I am indebted to Professor Hyde for access to the Waterhouse MSS.

1799			£	s.	d.	£	s.	d.
4	17	By Sundries for 2 Bills & Abatet				133	17	3
„	19	To Sales a/c J Kenyon for 30 Bags Cotton £1406 5 & Charges £7 10 4	1413	15	4			
„	24	By (Wm) say James Kenyon for 3 Bills & Int				1406	5	–
5	17	To Sales a/c T & W Earls for 50 Bags Cotton £1144 0 4 & Charges £6 9 11	1150	10	3			
„	21	To Do a/c Do & J Bolton for 106 Do £4057 0 11 & Do £21 19 1	4079					
„	22	By T & W Earle for 4 Bills & Int				1144		4
„	28	To Sales a/c J Kenyon for 50 Bags Cotton	1235	7	1			
„	29	To Sundries for Charges on Do	6	19	7			
„	30	By Sundries for 21 Bills & Int				4057		11
„	3	By Do for 6 Do & Do				1235	7	1
„	30	To Sundries for Charges on 6 Barrels Ashes		8	3			
7	12	To Do for Do on 25 Bags Cotton from T Rodie	8	14	9			
„	18	To Sales for 48 Bags Cotton a/c T Tarleton £2544 16 & Charges £13 9 11	2558	5	11			
„	25	By T Tarleton for 8 Bills & Int				2544	16	
„	31	To Sundries for Charges on 25 Bags Cotton from T Rodie	8	12	6			
„	27	By Cash for value in 1 Bill recd from R Jackson for so much Cotton sav'd from the Fortuna Campbell				21	11	–
9	2	To Cash paid for translating acct curt p Minerva	1	1	–			
„	7	To Sales a/c T Tarleton for 50 Bags Cotton £2215 6 6 & Charges £11 17 7	2227	4	1			
„	9	By Thos. Tarleton for 6 Bills & Int				2215	6	6
„	21	To Charges on Merch for Charges on adjustg a/cs concerning Minerva	17	1	5			
10	17	To Sundries for Charges on 100 Pernams from Harrison & Co	10	15	6			
„	18	To Do for Do on 50 Demeraras from T Rodie	10	14	4			
„	21	To Sales a/c T Tarleton for 27 Bags Cotton £857 15 & Charges £4 14 7	862	9	7			

1799			£	s.	d.	£	s.	d.
10	22	To Do a/c Sundries for 53 Do £1431 8 6 & Charges £8 0 6	1439	9				
,,	23	By (W G J) Thos Rodie for 2 Bills & Int				1977	12	6
,,	,,	To Thos Rodie for 50 Bags Cotton	1977	12	6			
,,	25	By T Tarleton for 3 Bills & Int				857	15	
,,	26	By Sundries for 5 Bills & Int				1431	8	6
,,	29	To John Wilson for Insce on Butt Wine p Amiable Clarissa	2	15	6			
,,	,,	To John Littledale for Do on Cotton p Do	191	9	6			
,,	30	To Sundries for Charges 64 Bags Cotton from D Whittaker	7	15	8			
11	1	To Do for Do on 15 Do from Humble & Co	2	9	11			
,,	2	By D Whittaker for value recd out of Bills & Int paid him					9	5
,,	6	To Cash for cash paid by J & S Matthews ballance of payment for 15 Bags Cotton		17	3			
,,	22	To Sales a/c Rathbone & Co for 50 Bags Cotton £1344 17 & Charges £7 10 6	1352	7	6			
,,	21	To John Littledale for Insurance on 26 Do p Ant	76	3	6			
,,	29	By Sundries for 5 Bills £1337 5 & Int £7 12				1344	17	
12	4	To Sales a/c Robinson & Co for 50 Bags Cotton £859 1 4 & Charges £5 2 1	864	3	5			
,,	5	To Do Thwaites & Co for 45 Do £853 18 2 & Do £4 19 11	858	18	1			
,,	9	By Robinson & Co for 3 Bills & Int				859	1	4
,,	11	By Thwaites & Co for 2 Do & Do				853	18	2
,,	,,	To Sales a/c Sundries for 130 Bags Cotton £3310 4 10 & Charges £18 13 11	3328	18	9			
,,	13	To Sundries for Charges on 160 Maranhams from T Ryan	20	16	8			
,,	16	By Sundries for 7 Bills & Int				3310	4	10
,,	20	To Sundries for 63 Bags Cotton £1082 17 2 & Charges £6 8 7	1089	5	9			
,,	26	By Sundries for 8 Bills & Int				1082	17	2
,,	,,	By Sales for an error of 10 lb in Bag of Surinam at 2/2				1	1	8
,,	31	To Sundries for 2 Hhds Sugar & Charges	72	6	3			

T

			£	s.	d.	£	s.	d.
12	„	To Charges on Merch for Error in Charge of Translating the Minervas Papers being included in the charge 21/9 mo				1		1
„	„	By Balance Carried down as p a/c renderd				538	4	6
			32,467	9	9	32,467	9	9

The extracts given from Waterhouse's accounts show some of his minor services. Besides the hogsheads of sugar, there was wine from Lisbon. A pipe of 143 gallons was consigned by Evans, Offley & Sealy to Waterhouse, which came to Liverpool via Ireland and for which he paid £44 7s. 9d. expenses (1800). In 1803 four pipes of wine were sent to Liverpool by the *Hawke* and the *General Prescott*, the expenses being £172. The Liverpool broker, in one instance at least, sold stockings (£21 13s. 6d.) for Strutts (1802). He bought timber for them—from Dempsey £93 9s. 2d., and from Rathbone £76 7s. 1d. (1809). He paid the firm's subscription to trade lists and to the *Liverpool Mercury* and *Gore's Liverpool Directory* (1815). In 1817 he began a custom that was to be of long-standing, the purchase of biscuits for William Strutt. And, at least once, he acted as Strutts' debt collector.

III. THE WAR YEARS

During the Napoleonic Wars and perhaps earlier some of the principal spinners imported direct from Lisbon and Oporto. The Evans were solicited for orders in 1792, as their reply to the London firm of Bolders, Adey, Lustington and Bolders shows:[1]

22 August 1792

Gentlemen,

We consume a considerable quantity of Brazil Cotton Wool which we have hitherto bought in London. We have received applications from Messrs. Bearsley & Webb of Oporto and also from Messrs. Evans Offley & Sealy of Lisbon to purchase it for us in Portugal. We are told that Evans keeps his cash at your house,

---

[1] I am indebted to Miss Jean Forrest for permission to quote the following letters of Walter Evans and Co.

and that Mr Sealy the man who has the care of purchasing the Cotton at Lisbon was brought up under Mr. Evans and is known to you: it is proper for us to endeavour to find men of fidelity and attention being unable to have any check upon them except that of putting a stop to the connection. If it is not attended with much trouble to you to make the enquiry we shall be obliged to you to learn & inform us who are the most likely Houses for the purpose of purchasing Cotton in Portugal, and any other circumstances that may occur respecting the probability of it answering a good purpose to us.

Thos. Evans

Whether the Evans placed orders with these firms is not known but later, as the following letters reveal, they imported through George Sandeman and Co., the great wine concern, who, shortly after their foundation in 1790, had acquired stores at Vila Nova de Gaia, near Oporto:[1]

9th April 1799

Sir

We thank you for your very clear statement of the insurance &c. and for your trouble in obtaining the drawback. A part of the cotton is arrived and it gives us pleasure to inform you of its proving to our satisfaction, though it comes rather higher than we expected. We do not at present wish to import to any considerable amount but if you think it advisable you may order your house to send us fifty bags of the best Pernambuco they can procure out of the new imporation. We conclude we are at no risque untill the cotton is actually on board at Lisbon and we should wish to have the bill of lading upon acceptance of the bill as below. We shall rely upon your insuring a proper amount in due time.

Wm Evans & Co.

16th Oct. 1799.

Sir

We have been expecting to hear from you with the Bill of Ladings of the cottons and we should also be glad of any information you can furnish us with of the present prices at Lisbon the Exchange &c. If these should be favourable we wish to know when the arrival of any cottons now purchased might be depended upon.

Walt. Evans & Co.

---

[1] I wish to thank Geo. G. Sandeman, Sons and Co. for allowing me to consult their early records.

Nicholas Waterhouse's Account with W. G. and J. Strutt

Dr.

1799		£ s. d.
Feb. 9	To Cash for 125 lb Seeds in N 1245 (56 lb) 1248 (69 lb) @ 2s 4½ £14.16.10 kept 1 bag seeds @ 6d £3.2.4	11 14 4
Jany 28	To 15 bags Cott Wool	201 16 8
Augt 29	To Cash for Cott. saved out of the Fortuna	21 11 0
Nov 1	To Cash Recd of D Whittaker	9 5
Dec 24	To Cash for 10 lb short in SD 850	1 1 8
	To balce	2 –
1800 Jany 21	Bills	267 14

Cr.

1799	Of Whom Bought		Sort	Whole Amt. £ s. d.	Commission £ s. d.	Expences £ s. d.
Jany 12	Jno Chorley	12	Cumana	189 – –		3 6
Octr 6	Thos Herbert Lisbon	110	Pernam	paid		
Jany 5	Josh Lyne & Co do	77	do			
17	Battier & Co	60	do	1531 16 –	7 13 2	19 8
26	Thwaites & Co	10	Barbados	309 0 9	1 10 11	3 5
Feby 1	T. Tarleton	8	Carru	262 18 8	1 6 3	2 10
April 5	Jno Bolton	25	Surinam	971 11 –	4 17 2	8 3
	By Bill for 15 bags Cotton Wool					201 16 8
Nov 4	By Cash					–
Apr 17	Jas Kenyon	30	Dema.	1406 5 –	7 – 7	9 9
May 15	T. & W. Earle	50	Pernam.	1144 – 4	5 14 4	15 7
20	do	39	Do	871 10 –	4 7 1	12 4
??	Jno Bolton	67	Dema.	3185 10 11	15 18 7	1 1 1
27	Jas Kenyon	50	Barbados	1235 7 1	6 3 6	16 1
July 5	T Tarleton	48	Carru.	2544 16 –	12 14 5	15 6
12	Thos Rodie	25	Dema	1665 7 9	8 6 6	8 3
10	do	25	do	1641 9 2	8 4 2	8 4
Sept 6	Thos Tarleton	50	Carru.	2215 6 6	11 1 6	1 16 1
Oct 15	Harrison & Co	100	Pernam.	1843 10 2	9 4 4	1 11 2
16	Thos Rodie	50	Demerara	1977 12 6	9 17 9	16 7

Date	Particulars	No.	Place	lb	s	d	£	s	d	£	s	d
	Rumble & Co	13	Surinam	440	3	1	2	4	–		3	4
Nov 11	Rathbone & Co	50	do	1344	17	–	6	14	5		16	1
Dec 2	Robinson & Co	50	Pernam.	859	1	4	4	6	–		16	1
4	Thwaites & Co	45	Barbados	853	18	2	4	5	4		14	7
2	Titherington & Co	31	Demerara	991	9	2	4	19	1		11	–
3	Jno Bolton	44	do	1440	10	2	7	4	2		14	10
3	do	55	Barbados	878	5	6	4	7	9		17	1
16	Thos Ryan	160	Maran.	3639	17	6	18	4	–	2	12	8
13	Thos Naylor	25	Barbados	426	17	10	2	2	8		8	3
13	Jno Bolton	38	Barbados	655	19	4	3	5	7		12	1
Sept 21	By expce of adjusting the Minerva's accts									17	1	5
Jan 20	By Commission on Ashes										8	3
Nov 3	By 2 hhds Sugar									72	6	3
										[190	16	4]
		1494		38169	1	11	190	16	4	504	9	1

504 9 1

1st Jany 1801.

Sir

We are favored with yours of the 29th past. As we have neither knowledge nor leisure to conduct the business of importing our Cottons, we should certainly wish to decline it, unless it can be done upon a very secure footing; but provided you can insure it from the time of the purchase till it is landed in England, we shall have no objection to purchasing 150 Bags, say about equal quantities of Pernambuco and Maranham, which we should wish to have forwarded by two Vessels to Lpool addressed to the care of our Broker Mr. Marsden. We should wish to have Cottons of the first quality & cleanness, and if a good quality of Pernamo cannot be procured, you may send the whole of Maranhams.

We should be glad to have a part of this as soon as it can be got, as we expect our stock will be exhausted by the time it arrives and we should wish to know in a few posts whether we may depend upon this being executed; as if not, we should purchase in London or Lpool—at the same time pray say how soon you think we may expect it.

Walt. Evans & Co

Messrs Sandeman Robinson & Co.
  Tom's Coffee House,
    Cornhill.

Strutts, whose dealings followed the Evans' pattern, bought from three Lisbon firms—Joseph Lyne and Co. (1796–1809), Evans, Offley & Sealy (1800–02) and George Sandeman and Co. (1798–1804). Sandeman's Order Book for the years 1794 to 1806 survives and shows that they imported South American cotton, predominantly Maranham and Pernambuco, mainly into Liverpool but also into London, Hull and the Clyde, on behalf of some eighty-odd spinners including Horrocks of Preston,[1] David Dale (a single order), Claytons and Walshman

---

[1] The great concern founded by John Horrocks (1768–1804), one of eighteen children of a small quarry owner of Edgeworth, near Bolton. Horrocks, after working for his father at 18s. a week, set up with a few spinning-frames erected on his father's premises and in January, 1791, launched out in Preston. Within a year, assisted by Richard Newsham, he built the 'Yellow Factory', the nucleus of the extensive buildings of today. By 1800 he had opened seven factories, two of them on the site of the present Yard Works. Horrocks, a Tory, represented Preston in Parliament during the last two years of his life. He is said to have been worth £150,000. (Information supplied by Horrockses, Crewdson and Company).

of Keighley, J. Simpson and Co. of Manchester, Hollins, Oldknow, Pearsce and Co. of Pleasley and Philips, Wood and Lee of Salford.

Sandeman's total importations, neglecting the numerous orders subsequently 'annulled' and also certain small miscellaneous quantities, may be summarized as follows:

	Bags	Miscellaneous Quantities	Strutts' Orders (Bags)
1798	1752	—	100
1799	1330	£1,000	100
1800	2870	—	100
1801	2280	—	—
1802	8760	£40,000	200
1803	3895	£3,500	150
1804	5290	£40,000	300
1805	2590	—	—
1806 (to October)	2200	—	—

Strutts' Lisbon cotton was consigned to Nicholas Waterhouse or to Samuel Hope at Liverpool. Between 1796 and 1802 Waterhouse paid expenses incurred on the consignments from Joseph Lyne and Co. but received no commission; between 1806 and 1809 Hope was paid commission at ½ per cent. for the same service. Sandeman's cotton was sent to Waterhouse (who again received no commission) and their Order Book contains such items as the following:

August 3, 1799: 100 Perns p conv[oy] consd to N Waterhouse L'pool whom adv for Insurance markd numbd as before & weighed 5 bags at a time—Bills not to be sent for accepce to Smith Payne & Smith's till 4 days after recd.

January 22, 1802: 50 Perns (best terms) p month consd to N. Waterhouse L'pool. Draw as before. Insure.

July 29, 1802: 50 Perns per month to be bot regularly unless there seems reason to defer the purchase: this is a confirmation of their order of 22 Jan. Sept 22—100 instead of 50.

December 20, 1802: 50 Perns (best terms) per month. Consd to N. Waterhouse. Draw on Smith Payne & Smith. Numbers to be continued to end of 1803. Square bags to be preferred. Suspended 27 June.

In addition to buying cotton Sandeman's also insured that bought by spinners from other Portuguese houses. The following examples are taken from Sandeman's account in the Belper Ledger:

		£	s.	d.
August, 1800:	By Insure of 96 bags Pernamo by the Hope, Nicholl from Evans & Co Lisbon vald at £1600 at 7 : 7 : 0 p Ct—policy £2	119	12	0
October 27, 1800:	By Insure of £3500 for 203 bags Perno by the John Andrews from Josh Lyne & Co Lisbon vald at £3500 at 7 : 7 : 0 p Ct to return £3 : 10 : 0 p ct. Policy 4 : 7 : 6	261	12	6
March 27, 1802:	By 800£ insured on 51 bags by Genl Wolfe from Evans & Co	14	12	0
July 5, 1802:	By £2200 insured on 119 bags by Gainsbro'	28	12	0

The Lisbon arrangement probably reached its full development when the 'Lisbon fleet' or convoy was in being.[1] In these years the margin of supply was often narrow. On December 18, 1800, William Strutt was writing from Derby to his brother Joseph in London:

We have nearly been without cotton wool which was very disagreeable but hope we shall have enough now. We are in daily expectation of hearing that the Lisbon fleet has safe arrived at Liverpool.

Five days later he added:

We have received but 75 Bags since you went and are now without Cotton or nearly so for the third time tho' no inconvenience (but in the mind) has been sustained yet, of 150 bags most of which should have been delivered here long ago the last bag left London 17 days ago. We expect a Boat Load today or tomorrow so that there is not much to fear but it is very unpleasant. Since you went Waterhouse has bought 30 Demerara and has orders for 70 more which he says he cannot do with till the fleet arrives. Hunt has bought 10 Demerara [and] 40 West India & has orders for 50 Demerara & George [the third brother] says some Berbice should be ordered. I meant to send Waterhouse more orders but it is useless till he can execute what he has.

Two years later (October 8, 1802), during the peace, Joseph was writing from Derby to William, then at Dr. Crompton's, near Liverpool:[2]

Josh. Lyne & Co advise of 100 Perno.—so that there are 250 bags we have advice of from Lisbon in all, & they say it has risen to 320

---

[1] For the convoy system see Redford, *Manchester Merchants and Foreign Trade, 1794–1858* (1934), 26–7, 43–4.

[2] See above, p. 174n.

and Maranm. to 260, about 20 reas. You will see Waterhouse no doubt—I have written to him this morning.

There was some pressure four years later when Samuel Hope wrote to Strutts (September 22, 1806):

We are in daily expectation of the Leeward Island fleet by which we may look for a fair supply & ere long the arrival of the fleet from Lisbon may be expected as they were to sail on the 21st. The holders in general are looking for an advance in the prices of Cotton in consequence of the opening of the trade to S. America & the smallness of our Stock tends to encourage this but I consider the present prices too high to admit of any material advance under any circumstances & I think a renewal of hostilities on the Continent would throw a damp on the trade & more than counterbalance the increased demand arising from our foreign Conquest.

In addition to the cotton which they bought thrôugh their brokers, the Strutts obtained some during 1805–8 from Thomas Ogier of Charleston, South Carolina, in part payment for hosiery which he had sold on their behalf.[1] The War of 1812, however, greatly reduced their purchases of cotton from America: they took 1006 bags in 1811, 124 in 1812, 20 in 1813, none in 1814 and 328 in 1815.

After the peace they continued to buy cotton in the United States and between February, 1817, and April, 1819, they took 925 bales, worth £16,077 from A. and C. L. Ogden of New York. It was consign^{ed} to Strutts' agent at Liverpool, William Forde and Co., who sold 174 bales for them and sent the rest to Derby. Strutts' profit was £1179. On September 28, 1824, they wrote to Forde:

It is well we purchased no Cotton in America last year, & we do not feel to buy any Alabama this year unless *good fair* can be laid delivd in Liverpool at 6¾ or 7d. If that is the case we shd like 200 bags of Alabama but not else.

On the same day they wrote to J. W. Lysdin 'at Kearsley Bowers', Liverpool':

We have done well to buy no Cotton in America last year, & we do not feel inclined to purchase any this at above 7 or 7½ for *good*

---

[1] See below, pp. 312–314.

fair Bowed laid delivd at Liverpool including all exps. If this shd occur shd like 150 Bowed but not else. Have the goodness to acknowledge. This is wishing you a good voyage.

In January, 1819, they bought 109 bales of Upland from Anthony Molyneux of Savannah, consigned to Samuel Hope, on which they lost £180. In 1826–7 they were taking cotton from J. S. Hobson of Philadelphia, and G. Hobson, New Orleans, consigned through S. J. Hobson and Son of Liverpool. They wrote to the last-named on June 22, 1826:

Enclosed are 3 Bills value £573 with which 6–7–6 Intst are in full for your acct as under. You seem extraordinarily urgent for a remittance forgetting that we never exceed 2 posts after we get the Invoice. We still think, with the accts they must have had from Liverpool, and having 'no doubt' of doing better that they were too precipitate in buying the first part even if the want had not proved it. Our other friends in America are doing better and move cautiously. We have advised Smith Payne & Co to accept your drafts. Your value of these Cottons at 7d we believe you cannot realize.

On September 26, 1827, Strutts further advised them:

Enclosed is a bill £101–15–6 which with £1–2–10 Intst to 25 Decr is in full for the charges on the 49 bales—please to send a rect. You charge 3½ p bag Porterage & 3d Carte. Why are both raised ½ p bag & why is 10/- charged for Canvas & twine? All these are *extra* charges to us on Cotton imported. You have not sent us the loadg wt of each bag please to send them in your reply. We have not determined to order any Cotton from America yet.

And the next day they wrote to G. Holt and Co., brokers:

What must be done abt Cotton not being in a proper state for carriage? It cannot be so if it will take 100 yards of canvas to repair them & we will not subject ourselves to the loss & damage we have had by their not being in a fit state.

American cotton consigned to Strutts in this way was insured by Boddington, Philips, Sharpe and Co. of London, the concern responsible for the insurance of the goods they sent to Königsberg and to Petersburg.

IV. THE 1820s

By the 1820s the Strutts were obtaining their cotton through four brokers, three of them in Liverpool and one (Roger Hunt) in London. The supremacy of Liverpool as the leading cotton market was by this time unchallenged but the Strutts who had always done a good deal of business in London and whose mills lay between the two markets had much to gain and nothing to lose through buying some of their cotton there.

Strutts kept in constant touch with their brokers, directing them to obtain from the importers cottons of varying types and qualities. Their abundant capital enabled them to lay in large stocks when prices were low and when the market moved against them they tried to avoid placing orders.

Many examples of this policy are to be found in the instructions which they sent to their brokers. Thus, on January 27, 1826, they informed J. Kearsley and Sons:

From the state of the credit at Liverpool & of the Cotton market, we think the time is approaching when we may be induced to buy freely, & we are now ready to receive offers of parcels of Demerara, Maranham & Macaio if such occur worth informing us about, & if short dated bills will induce lower offers we are ready to pay in that way. The quality of the 2 first you know—the Macaio must also be good.

The same day they wrote identically to G. Holt and Co. and on March 10, 1826, they further advised them:

We cannot help thinking Cotton Wool is at the bottom & shall wish you to purchase about 100 bags more Pernambuco. We wrote you yesterday to get 200 more Para & 1 to 200 Bowed before it may perhaps be well to get. But we leave all these to your judgement both in time & price & have no doubt it will be exerted to our Interest.

Four days later Strutts sent similar instructions to W. Bower and Sons:

Part of the Egyptian are come & we have no Invoice. Prey send it. We wrote to you on the 10th about more Egyptian &c. We see

The Belper Mills from the Air

a large arrival [and] probably you may do well in them & for a *good* offer; do not stick at 2 or 300 but make it 4 or 500 when you think it best to strike. The Barbadoes too keep in view when you can do well.

On March 22, 1826, they told R. Hunt:

We think there will be a great dulness in Wool just now and that prices may be lower than ever—if so we shall go on buying. Please to keep sending them off, but not too many in a ship, to encounter the nocturnal gales.

And on April 10, 1826, at a time of 'very wretched' trade they wrote to G. Holt and Co.:

The 65 Pernambuco bought Feb. 28 varies very much—*some* bags *very* dirty & do not work well—the rest are good fair Cottons. In Surat or *Bengal* we feel inclined to take about 300 more if you can get them as good as in the sale terms. Will you inform us what is *likely* for we are in no hurry, & if things continue we quite expect several Mills to stop. We shall go on however at these prices buying more if it still drops. Any offers at lower prices we are open for quantity.

When Strutts considered the price of a variety of cotton to be excessive they sought to buy other kinds instead. Thus, in September, 1826, they told J. Kearsley and Sons: 'Brazils are so high that Demerara does not come at our price, we are trying to substitute something else lower.'

Carthagena seems to have been even more unfavourably priced, and on June 23, 1825, Strutts advised W. Bower and Sons:

Your directions were so positive from us about the Carthagena that we cannot blame you but we could not conceive the possibility of their dropping in proportion to other sorts. Do not buy another bag of that sort for us on any account at present. It is at least 3d too high for our use & we shall probably change the sorts.

The next day they again wrote to them expressing regret that they had bought more Carthagena and advising that in future some other cotton be bought instead. A substitute must have been found for on October 20, 1825, they told J. Garnett, a Liverpool importer:

You have heard truly that we had given up the use of Carthagena.

288

You raised it to such an unwarrantable height that it was impossible for us to go on with it. It is besides a very difficult Cotton to use— loses very much in working and requires an expensive management so that unless we can get it low it will not answer to us to begin again. If you think it worth while to let us have 1000 bags at 7d we will take them.

There is no record of the firm buying Carthagena after this date.

Although Strutts' brokers served them well, one or other of them occasionally came in for sharp criticism:

'Should not you have done better *in a falling market* by waiting a few days before you had bought our order? It prevents us giving you any discretion which others have used to our interest,' they complained to W. Bower and Sons on November 11, 1825; and on March 24, 1827, R. Hunt was reproved:

We are very much surprized to see you have bought 169 bales of No. 2 sample cotton, you will find we desired not to have any of those! The object of sending samples was *for us to judge what would suit us,* & having distinctly said 'No 2 we do not wish any of' we request to know on what principle you acted differently to our directions.

Eight months later, on November 10, 1827, Strutts expressed dissatisfaction with the way in which J. Kearsley and Sons had looked after their affairs:

Of the sorts of Cotton you have latterly bought for us we are using very little & have about a years stock of all. We should not, however, be ingenerous with you if we did not tell you that you have *not* done so well for us by far as our other brokers, either in quality or price. For when we have given you an order and told you we did not *want* it it has seldom happened, even in a *falling* market, that you did not buy when by waiting a while you would have got the same thing at $\frac{1}{8}$ or $\frac{1}{4}$ lower. This has been a matter of great importance to us for we not only lose the Interest of the money but as much or more in price. We do not however mean to say we shall not when we want send you more orders.

Cotton bought at Liverpool was carried to Derby by canal. That from London also reached Strutts by canal or was sent by sea to Gainsborough and there transferred to canal barges for Derby.

Jas. Holt and Co. and Pickfords and Co. both of London, were Strutts' carriers. Pickfords ran two services, a quick light trade by fly-boat and a slower, heavy trade by barge. Fly-boats moved at 3 to 3½ m.p.h., carried a load of not more than 10 tons and, since they travelled both day and night, had a crew of four, two steerers and two drivers. A trip was usually split up into four or five stages, thus allowing relays of horses to do about 40 miles a day. Pickfords' barges carried heavy goods; their average load was 20 tons and they travelled at about 2 m.p.h. Each boat was drawn by one horse, went an average distance of 25 miles a day and was in the charge of two men. Carriage by fly-boat cost about twice as much as by barge. As traffic on the canals rapidly expanded Pickfords began building their own wharves and warehouses and set up their own stations along the various canal routes. In 1808 they took over a wharf at Derby.[1]

The canal carrying trade was highly competitive and on May 2, 1825, Jas. Holt and Co. wrote to Strutts as follows:

It is with reluctance but necessity obliges me to inform you the present rates of your Freight by Canal to and from Derby [and London] are so low that they will not cover the expences. Have lately been oblig'd to advance my servants pay who work the Boats and owing to the high price of Provisions for both Men and Horses they want a further advance which shall be oblig'd to give them. I trust the small extra charge to you will be consider'd reasonable. Namely all Goods to or from Derby to be 3s/od pr. Cwt. for Freight with 3d pr. Cwt. for Cartage on all goods to commence at the end of the ensuing general stoppage about the 21st Inst.[2]

Also on May 2, Pickfords and Co. wrote to Strutts in identical terms and on June 30, 1825, Strutts advised R. Hunt as follows:

Both Holt & Pickfords prices are 3/- but as Pickford will carry Surat at 2/9 send those by him till you know further & *some* of the Para or any other you may buy.

---

[1] *Transport Saga, 1646–1947* (1947), 15. During the summer of 1818 it took from four to six days to carry cotton from Runcorn to Derby. The boatmen from Runcorn or London often received 'Drink Money' varying in amount between 9d. and 2s. 6d.

[2] At the time of the 'general stoppage' of 1825 Strutts made arrangements for cotton to be brought from Liverpool to Belper by road.

Negative evidence as to the efficiency of the shipping, canal and road carriers is to be found in the fact that between September, 1824, and December, 1827,[1] Strutts lodged but two complaints with them. Both related to the carriage of cotton between London and Derby. The first was on February 11, 1826, when R. Hunt was told:

The following Nos. of Sea Island Cotton by F. & S. are come in so shameful a condition that we must charge somebody with the damage. The ropes are broken, the bags burst, & the Cotton strewed about in a way we never saw before. The boatmen from Gainsbro' say they received them in that state—it will be well if they can prove it because then if you prove the delivery in a good state, the damage is fixed on the Carrier between London and Gainsbro'. Please to examine into it & inform us as soon as may be.

At the same time they wrote to Sevesley and Co. of Gainsborough:

We have received 16 bags of Cotton in a most shameful state from Gainsbro'. It will be necessary for you to prove that you so received them there & we have written to our broker in London to prove the delivery in good condition there. We wait your reply before we can fix the damage.

Strutts were clearly determined to get to the bottom of the matter but we have no record as to the outcome of their enquiries.

In the midsummer of 1827 they experienced difficulties in having cotton shipped from London to Gainsborough and sent a strong protest to the shipper:

Mr. Hunt informs us that he has very great trouble & inconvenience & loss of time in getting off our Cotton by your Vessels from London & that they will not take any bags of Cotton in till they know *what other loading they shall have.* This seems very strange conduct indeed. We pay your charge—discharge the account whenever you send it—& to be thus treated is neither what we desire or will submit to. The great weight of our Cotton from London is East India bales—there has indeed been lately some of Egyptian & some very large bales of American, but if these are not to be brought with the others say so & we shall know what to trust to. We do not want the Cotton but it does not answer to pay warehouse

---

[1] The period covered by the Letter Book.

rent in London & above all it is intolerable to give Mr. Hunt so much trouble.

The condition in which the broker delivered cotton to the carrier sometimes gave Strutts cause for concern, as when on December 9, 1824, they wrote to R. Hunt:

The 50 bags by Holt are in a shameful state. He says they were received so by him & that you would not send any person to mend them. Now as we pay so very much for *mending* & loading, how is it possible that if they are properly done, they should be in this state when delivered to him? We fear this charge is often made & the work not done & it is very injurious to the Cotton & we hope will not happen again—if it does we shall object to pay that expence.

Sometimes bags of cotton reached Derby unmarked. R. Hunt was most frequently responsible for this neglect and on March 22, 1826, Strutts wrote to him as follows:

We have received 31 bags of the 37 bought of Ward on February 24 & with extreme difficulty we can make out something like 221, 222, 230. The rest we can neither find *the* Ⓢ *nor any progressive No, or anything like one in any part of the bags!* How this has happened is very odd & very neglectful in the person you entrusted to do it— who we will do the ample justice to say has generally marked them well and boldly as they ought to be. When it is otherwise we are put to great inconvenience & we hope it will not again occur.

Exactly a month later they again found it necessary to draw Hunt's attention to his failure to have bags marked correctly:

We are sorry to send you a long list of wrong marked bags below & wrong accounts too. It gives us infinite trouble when these occurrences happen for every bag has to be laid aside till the whole Lot comes & they take up the most valuable room we have. These things did not use to occur with you & we hope you will prevent them doing so again—most of the Nos are now clearly marked but not all. Many of the bags come in a sad state, and we charge the carrier with repairing them.

When seeds, stones and other waste matter were found in bags of cotton it was, as we have seen, the task of the broker to claim compensation from the importer and on September 2, 1826, Strutts wrote to W. Bower and Sons:

Annexed is Certificate of 3 bags bought of Ewart & Co. March

21 which contained 88 lb damaged Cotton which lies here at your disposal. You have not noticed the 12 lb wrote about July 21 nor the 5 lb July 25 nor the 39 lb May 5 nor the 20 lb April 22. These trifling things are better settled at once, they only cause extra trouble.

Such matters were usually dealt with to the mutual satisfaction of all parties but in October, 1827, a dispute arose concerning Strutts' claim on Rathbone and Co., importers, and on October 26, 1827, they wrote to G. Holt and Co. as follows:

We are come to the determination to compel Rathbone & Co. to pay us for the 18 lb seeds returned to you September 10. It may become a serious grievance if submitted to & we will therefore try it. For this purpose we must request you to imploy either your own Lawyer or somebody of perfect respectability to give them due notice & to furnish him with all the information necessary & to inform us what documents & evidence are necessary & when they will be wanted. You mention claiming the amount of their value at the time of their return. The difference will not be 1/6. The value is nothing, it is the *Principle* we contend for and must maintain. We have not often had occasion to contend for our right in a court of Justice & would never do it without just concern & doing so we have never yet been foiled.

Under this pressure Rathbone and Co. acceded to the demand for compensation.

From time to time Strutts' cotton reached Derby in damp condition. They believed that if too much water was used in packing injury to the staple would result[1] and, on March 31, 1826, they wrote advising W. Bower and Sons:

The Barbadoes we have had lately is generally much higher coloured than it used to be, & the Cotton in those bags which are the most stained is *caked* together, & have the appearance of having been put up wet. We think you would do well to inform the Importers of this, that they may write to the growers to prevent what, if continued, will be a serious evil.

It would be wrong, however, to leave the impression that the Strutts and other spinners were, in general, ill-served by their

---

[1] For the method of packing cotton see *Encyclopædia Britannica* (1810 ed.), vi, 693–4.

brokers. Writing of the Liverpool market in 1835, Baines asserted that:[1]

The cotton is principally bought and sold by sample, the purchasers very rarely considering it necessary to examine the bulk. By strict probity and honour invariably observed by the brokers in their dealings with each other, this immense business is conducted with a facility and despatch which have probably no parallel in any other market of the world, and which could not exist to the same extent in the sale of any description of merchandise.

The Strutts' records would appear to confirm the accuracy of this description of the Liverpool market.

[1] Op. cit., 318–19.

CHAPTER XI

PRODUCTS AND MARKETS

I. MACHINE MAKING; THE MILLS' PRODUCTION

THE records of the Strutts, unlike those of Oldknow and McConnel and Kennedy, are very weak on the side of production, giving little detail about what they produced or the machines they employed. They threw and spun silk at Derby and wove it and dyed it; and although they had dropped the spinning of yarn and the weaving of calicoes by 1815, they seem to have continued the dyeing there.[1] At Belper they spun and prepared yarn for the market and did a little weaving. At Milford they also spun, had their bleachworks[2] and did their machine-making. In very general terms this seems to have been the picture.

---

[1] Information about the Derby mills is rather sparse. The Strutts continued to weave there until the early months of 1815 but in the later years on a very diminished scale. At the beginning of 1802 'weavers' wages' averaged £52 a week; by the end of 1814 they ranged from £5 to £10 a week. The firm stopped cotton-spinning at Derby in January, 1815, and 'spinners' wages' in the 'Cotton Mill' which had ranged from £40 to £47 a week in 1802 and had dropped a little by 1814, disappeared from the books; the 'Cotton Mill's' poor rates were reduced, '1/14th part only being occupied'. The Silk Mill, however, went on; new machinery had been installed and more workpeople were employed; wages had risen from £15 a week in 1802 to about £87 in 1815. The letting of a 'fireproof Silk Mill' to a Mr. Taylor in November, 1824, perhaps marked the reduction or end of the Strutts' activities in that field.

[2] A letter of William Strutt, Jr., to Samuel Oldknow (Sept. 1, 1788) deals with Jedediah's intention to take up bleaching and thanks Oldknow for his offer to show father and son over some bleachworks (Unwin, op. cit., 240). In Jan., 1790, Oldknow was advising William Strutt about 'the New bleaching Liquor' his brother had prepared: 'Sir Richd Arkwright (only) has had several Bottles & I am sure he would make Messrs Strutts some with great pleasure—his method of making it is his own & he asserts that he is not beholden to any man for what he knows of the process. Mr W & he do not communicate nor visit in the Character of Chymists—so matters stand' (Strutt MSS.). A letter of June 28, 1801, from William Strutt to his brother Joseph advises that the capacity of the Milford bleachworks was then somewhat below 500–600 bundles of cotton a week (Strutt MSS.). The bleaching process at Milford is described by Davies (op. cit., 341–2).

Of the machinery used in the early period we have only the description in *Rees's Cyclopædia* already quoted,[1] the knowledge of William Strutt's inventions[2] and the description given to the 1816 Committee by G. B. Strutt of an improvement in scutching.[3] John Kennedy in his classical paper on the early cotton industry has a passage on the earliest process, that of cleaning the cotton:[4]

In the year 1797 [he records] a new machine for cleaning cotton was constructed by Mr. Snodgrass, and first used at Johnston near Paisley by Messrs. Houston and Co. This is called a scutching or blowing machine. Its merits were but little known till 1808 or 1809, when it was introduced into Manchester. It is now generally adopted for cleaning cotton. The labor of that operation, formerly performed by women, in a most fatiguing manner, and always considered as degrading; has been reduced by this machine to about one twentieth of what it used to be.

In a footnote he adds: 'Mr. Arkwright and Messrs. Strutts have added most useful improvements to this machine.'

It was this improvement that G. B. Strutt described in 1816. He was arguing that dust could be removed from the scutching rooms and gave a description supplied by Richard Arkwright, Jr., of a machine he himself employed at Cromford:[5]

The scutching machine most in use, is a machine for cleaning cotton from the seeds and other impurities, and is in principle similar to the thrashing machine. The cotton passes through a pair of rollers, and is struck by bars of iron or steel called beaters, which revolve with great velocity, striking the cotton with considerable force over a number of parallel bars, so placed as to allow the seeds to fall through; the current of air passing over the bars, and carrying the cotton, fly and dart forward into an apartment called the cotton chamber. It is necessary this air should be got rid of, and it is effected by a large opening, in which is placed a fine wire-grating; the air either returns into the room or is suffered to escape externally. But even by this latter mode considerable inconveniency arises to the persons employed, from the dust and fly, as it is impossible to close up every aperture and crevice so as to prevent some portion

---

[1] See above, p. 219.
[2] See above, pp. 170, 198, 215.
[3] Page 306.
[4] 'Observations on the Rise and Progress of the Cotton Trade in Great Britain' in *Mem. Manch. Lit. and Phil. Soc.*, Second Series, iii (1819), 130.
[5] *1816 Comm.*, 306.

of it from coming into the working-room. This inconveniency is now completely remedied, by the adoption of a very simple plan: a fan is placed on the outside of the wire-grating before-mentioned, which by a quick rotary motion rarefies or exhausts in some degree the cotton-chamber; consequently the air in the working-room presses in at every opening to restore the equilibrium, carrying with it all the fly and dust created by working the scutcher.

Although the water-frame survived at Cromford and Belper until Ure's visit in the mid-1830s,[1] there was always experiment and improvement in the air. Unhappily, however, it would need the eye of an expert to keep track of this in the Machinery ledgers.

II. HOME MARKETS

Our earliest source of information about the home markets is the Belper Ledger for 1792 to 1803 containing accounts of more than 800 merchants and manufacturers in all parts of the British Isles. Amongst them are to be found those of Samuel Oldknow, James McGuffog, Birley and Hornby, and Peels, Ainsworth and Co.

The greater part of Strutts' yarns went to half-a-dozen areas —Derbyshire, Tewkesbury, Leicestershire, Nottinghamshire, London and Manchester—in all but the first two of which they had their agent who sold goods upon a commission of $1\frac{1}{2}$ or, occasionally, $1\frac{1}{4}$ per cent.[2] The agents were responsible to Strutts for 10 per cent. of the bad debts resulting from their sales and, although these seldom came to more than a small fraction of their commissions, the need to recover outstanding debts and to keep a wary eye on doubtful customers must have

---

[1] Ure, *The Cotton Manufacture of Great Britain*, i, 239.
[2] Records of agents' sales for the following years have survived: Leicester, Elizabeth Copson, 1801-7; David Harris, 1808-18; Elizabeth Harris, 1819; George Bellairs, 1820-8. London, Thomas Shipman, 1804-6; James Peirce 1814-18; Thomas Marshall, 1817-26. Manchester, James Pollit, 1794-1800; James Shuttleworth, 1817-30. Nottingham, Alexander Strahan, 1800-4; Wright Coldham, 1807-16; Richard Hopper, 1816-21; George Gill, 1821-4. All except T. Marshall and J. Shuttleworth received commission at $1\frac{1}{2}$ per cent. The Nottingham agents all played leading parts in the public life of the borough (*Records of the Borough of Nottingham*, vii, 417-18; viii, 463-72).

taken its toll of their time and patience.[1] Strutts insured the goods held by their agents and allowed them one half of the cost of the Christmas boxes which they gave to their customers. The pattern was to continue for many decades.

Besides the goods which they sold through their agents, Strutts sold large quantities of yarns direct to customers who, in the early days at least, were asked to send cash with their orders or to supply the names of persons ready to vouch for their integrity.

Occasionally, however, concerns already known to Strutts agreed to stand surety for goods which they sold to a third party. Thus, on February 2, 1804, Baynes D'Antrobus of Liverpool wrote to them:

> Some time ago we gave our Guarantee to you with Wm Richards for £100 which we request you will be pleased to Extend for One Hundred & Fifty Pounds for either Silk or Cotton and you'll oblige.

And in March, 1815, W. Haines of Melbourne, Derbyshire, advised:

> I have a neighbour who is in want of a little Cotton for Stockings for which I will be responsible to you for . . . the persons name is Wm. Hemsley & shd he order more [than a small specified amount] please to send it. I am myself going a journey & it is probable he will want more before I return. I will however be responsible to the amt of £50 worth.

The years after the end of the Napoleonic Wars saw no significant change in the conditions under which Strutts sold goods in home markets. 'If you favor us with orders have the goodness to send references for inquiry, unless Cash Notes come

---

[1] The following are typical of the hundreds of agents' notes inserted in the Strutts' ledgers: 'Apl 29, 1813   Maria Watney [of Leicester] is again married. The man seems to have neither inclination nor means to pay. I [David Harris, the Leicester agent,] have tried all means but law & her situation for some time has been such as any expence in law wd have increased the debt.' [Loss, £15 3s. 6d. Strutts had last sold yarn to her in 1810.] 'Jan. 15, 1814. J. Peirce [the London agent informs that] Catherine Baguley is dead and her daughter very troublesome, owes J.P. money for which he has applied 50 times in vain.' [Loss, £9 14s. 5d.] '20 June, 1826. Geo. Bellairs [the Leicester agent advises that] In consequence of the failure of Jervis & Co Mr R Wileman has requested a little indulgence in the payment of his a/c now past due. I expect it will be paid this week. I have no doubt but that he is perfectly safe.'

AGENTS' SALES, 1794–1830*
(£)

Year Ended February 28	Leicester	London	London	Manchester	Nottingham
1794				6,360	
5				8,456	
6				14,929	
7				18,814	
8				22,985	
9				24,184	
1800				30,023	13,050
1	26,682				3,800
2	32,908				19,518
3	37,633				22,590
4	31,799	2,875			14,638
5	43,437	8,970			
6	27,648	11,753			
7	38,900				23,817
8	34,988				
9	33,520				23,220
10	24,225				23,872
1	25,861				26,189
2	24,996				21,548
3	26,388				25,805
4	30,076		32,396		32,822
5	24,903		26,274		14,827
6	43,799		45,692		29,081
7	24,352	15,015	52,918	22,874	17,197
8	25,461	9,594	60,305	16,274	33,381
9	8,834	8,194		20,835	33,466
20	17,224	3,417		14,960	21,240
1	20,889	1,962		17,319	6,633
2	26,050	1,263		13,948	16,408
3	28,364	981		14,343	19,786
4	26,437	1,345		14,847	17,600
5	29,606	1,305		13,597	
6	22,396	1,352		9,006	
7	28,013			10,813	
8	23,478			12,510	
9				8,104	
30				10,372	

* See p. 297, n. 2.

with the order,' they told New and Loxley of Evesham on February 4, 1826; and on August 16, 1827, D. and G. Holy and Co. of Sheffield were advised:

We have duly recd your favour directed to Belper (where our

Works are) instead of Derby and we now annex a list of the Prices of our Knittgs & which was reduced 1/- pr bdle on the 6th Inst. We allow 10 p ct for Cash or Bill due in 14 days or 7½ p Ct for bill at 3 Mos from date of Invoice.[1] Our Yarn is very generally approved. If you favour us with orders we shall be obliged by References.

At this time Strutts manufactured counts up to 150 but had, they told a prospective buyer, long since ceased to make candlewick.

During the first half of 1825, which year marked the culmination of the long expansion of the British economy in the early twenties, Strutts were alarmed at an almost continuous increase in the price of raw cotton. The earliest hint of what was in store came on January 17 when they advised their London agents that the prices of all yarns were to be raised by 1*s.* a bundle. A week later they wrote to J. Peirce, G. Bellairs and G. Gill:

So great an advance has taken place in fine Wool & yarn at Manchester that as a *temporary measure* we must advance all fine Sewg N 40 to 70 1/- p bundle 2/- p bundle N 70 to 100 & 3/- 100 & above to take place on rect of this letter.

This was followed on February 5 by a new list to buyers of hosiery yarns who were advised that 'from the extraordinary advance on fine Wool the highest Nos are very considerably raised'.

A fortnight later Strutts wrote to J. Shuttleworth:

Any orders you *accept* we shall hold ourselves bound to execute, but in a rising market you cannot know when we may advance, it may not be wise to do it unconditionally as we may neither have the goods by us or make them soon & by attendg to this we can advise while you wait for our answer.

An increased list of February 7, 1825, was followed by another on February 26 when Strutts advised their agents that:

From the daily advance in Cotton wool we are compelled, as a temporary measure to raise the price of *every sort & quality of our yarn* 1/- p bundle above the list of the 7th Inst. This of course includes twist. Cord must be 1d p Gross higher.

---

[1] These terms were in force, a list reveals, as late as Sept., 1862.

A fortnight later there was another increase. 'When this continual advance is to stop we know not,' Strutts told their agents and on April 2, 1825, they further advised them:

The price of Cotton wool becomes quite alarming. We shall on Monday make a *temporary* advance, & also raise bleaching it *might* be 4/- p bundle but we shall wait another week to see how the market stands before we do any more.

The same day they wrote to J. Shuttleworth:

We have very little twist by us—please to avoid acceptg many orders witht informg us. Where is this speculation to end— do have the goodness to give us your opinion of the probability of this price being maintaind or exceeded, for our list may have to be much higher but we are afraid of doing too much.

Despite Strutts' fears of the possible consequences of further increases a list issued the following week advanced the price of all yarns and twists by 2s. a bundle. Even so, this was barely sufficient to cover higher costs and on April 19 they wrote to G. Bellairs:

We are quite alarmed at the price of Cotton Wool—if our list was to be raised 5/- p bundle to day it wd not pay us. We must send you a new one this week, but are willing to do all we can for our friends before it takes place. You may sell all you have, & we will send what we can that you send orders for by *Saturdays post* for the under sorts [here followed a list of many types of yarns]. . . . You may also offer 100 bunds wte yellow tie Tambr N 8 at price of 7 March & 150 bunds yellow tie Tambr *all colrs* N 14 at 24/6 p bundle net.

Towards the end of April Strutts heard 'a vague rumour' that 'Mr Arkwright is sellg now at his old price' and asked their Nottingham agent to find out whether this was in fact the case. We have, unfortunately, no record of the outcome of his enquiries.

By June 23, 1825, the price of raw cotton had reached and passed its maximum and Strutts sent out a new circular which advised:

Tho' our last list was by no means proportioned to the enormous advance in Cotton Wool, & tho' the drop in this article will barely justify our present reduction of 3/- p bundle, yet we have made that with the hopes of the list being more permanent.

Trading conditions seem to have given Strutts no further cause for anxiety until December, 1825, when the country was shaken by the panic in the money market. Encouraged partly by the reconversion of a large proportion of the Government Debt and partly by the recovery of commodity prices following easier credit, the public had begun to speculate to such effect that in 1824–5 over 600 new companies with a total capital exceeding £372 million were floated, besides which over £17½ million was invested abroad, mainly in South America. Many projects were unsound and the position was made more dangerous owing to the boom being financed largely with small notes. Since 1821 the entire over-enlarged country circulation had been payable in gold and, for the first time, it included a large volume of small notes payable in gold on demand. There was little gold in the provinces and the stock of the Bank of England was practically the only source of supply.

Towards the end of 1825 the money market suffered a series of reverses, the most striking of which was the collapse of the South American mining ventures. The Bank, alarmed at the progress of the speculative movement, ceased to discount paper money, thereby hoping to maintain its reserves. The country banks, finding their notes coming back to them for repayment, had no place to which to turn for help. Some dramatic bank failures drained gold from the Bank of England and only by the reluctant consent of the Government that it might exceed the legal limit of its note issue by lending, if necessary, even upon goods, was the situation saved. Gradually confidence was restored, failures grew less and less, the drain on the reserve dwindled and finally came to an end.[1]

Although Strutts had been taken completely by surprise at the sudden outbreak of the crisis, they were quick to react to danger. On December 15, they wrote to J. Peirce:

Your acct of the money market is dreadful & defies all calculation. Any money you have to spare you may as well let Roger Hunt clear some Cotton with from the India house—he will want in all 896 : 10 : 4.

---

[1] For a more detailed description of the 1825 crisis see Feavearyear, *The Pound Sterling* (1931), 218–20.

The same day they told A. J. Oppenheim of Frankfurt:

The ferment in the money market is beyond all description—a great many of our first Bankers have stopped payment & what it will all lead to no human sagacity can foresee.

That Strutts had no illusions about the likely consequences of the crisis is clear from the following letter of December 16 sent to their Leicester agent:

In these most strange times it behoves you to be *peculiarly cautious* who you trust—it will be much better when you can [to] get good bills rather than let the acct run to Cash for it makes double risk. We hope there is no doubt of the remaining banks, but this convulsion must shake many of the hosiers—again we say be very cautious.

After the crisis had passed Strutts were for long ultra-cautious in their dealings with doubtful customers. Thus, on March 23, 1826, they wrote to G. Bellairs:

These people are always behind in payment & we will not trust those who do so. If you dist bills for them or any body else we think you do very wrong. Surely what has occurred lately to the ruin of thousands shd keep your eyes open. You had better have nothing to do with such shabby people as Fields witht money at the time.

The same month, after their agents' annual accounts had been received, Strutts told a customer that they had emerged 'wonderfully well' from the 'sad crisis'.

During the next two years, however, they were to complain of a severe depression in the trade and on February 6, 1826, they sent new lists to their agents. These, they advised, were necessary owing to the 'temporary depression of the Cotton market' and would, they trusted, not be in force for long. At the same time, apparently determined to increase their London sales, they wrote to J. Peirce:

Our Sewg is now so good & so low that we ought to sell more, much more, thro' you but there seems to be something yet to prevent it which we do not understand. . . . We trust all our sorts of Tambour will find a ready sale now, & having lowered the coloured we hope you will do all possible to get *coloured orders of all sorts*—for there is every reason to believe nobody can do it *better now nor lower*. We much wonder you do not sell more tie bonnet & Cord in bundles—surely the price of these 11/- & 12/- must force it now. We shd expect the large discts on nankin twist will bring you orders.

On June 21, 1826, evidently still anxious to expand their sales, they told G. Gill:

There must be a deal of runng spottg &c used & we sell little. Is it owing to the price? If so we wish you to lower all runng so as to charge it only 1/- p bundle above the same N & sort of 2ds even if made up in 1 oz or ½ oz sks. With respect to spottg Cotton we know not if much is used but we shd like to do it, do let us know abt these soon.

The list of February 6, 1826, was revised on July 31 when Strutts informed their agents that:

In consequence of other houses underselling us we have this day determined to lower each sort of Hosiery yarn 1/- p bundle from the list of 1 Feby last. No other alteration will take place in our lists & from the state of the markets we do not expect any at present [as] this seems to us very unnecessary.

This list remained in force until January 22, 1827, when it was revised owing to price-cutting by competitors and to the increased price of indigo, a material used in the dyeing of yarn. In a letter accompanying the new list, Strutts told their agents:

We now forward you new lists by which you will see that we make neither Angola nor Virginia but only Summer & Winter Merino & that this article is considerably advanced. You will also observe we have 2 articles of Sewg & 2 of Tambour & that all these as well as knittg are lower than before! Hosy yarn remains as it was except that Grey is raised 6d p bundle from the very high price of Indigo. Tho' these prices are inconceivably low, we are determined to compete in the different qualities with any house whatever & we have no hesitation in saying that our yarn in every sort is better & evener & more regular than we ever made it & that it will continue to be so.

On August 6, 1827, Strutts reduced the prices of 'all sorts & qualities except Merino & Cord' by 1s. a bundle. 'Cotton spinning is at present a most destructive trade,' they told Solgar and Co. of Manchester on September 26, 1827.

The severity of the 'sad depression' was emphasized in a letter which Strutts sent to J. Peirce on August 2, 1827. 'Mr A,' they wrote, 'has an *enormous* stock & is determined to sell it. Many spinners must break or stop. All who can buy his yarn wd do well to buy all they can from him.'

Strutts kept a close watch upon Arkwright's activities and their reactions in the face of price-cutting are to be seen in the following letter which they wrote to J. Terrett of Tewkesbury on November 1, 1827:

With respect to our prices we found Mr A was determined to sell at all events. When any article gets below prime cost & the party can hold out for a while it may be their interest to do so. This is our case & tho' our marble tie will compete with most we believe there is a turn against us. When Mr A has sold his stock we shall better know what to do but at present we 'lie on our Oars' hoping at some future time to recover your favours.

The issue of revised lists often led to dissatisfaction amongst those of Strutts' customers who considered that they should be charged according to the terms of the old or the new list, whichever was the lower. Strutts, however, never budged from their principle to sell only at the price prevailing when the order in question was received.

This they made clear in a letter of August 11, 1825, to Watson and Fry of Loughborough:

If the fine Nos you have on hand of ours had not been purchased by you they might have been by others, & probably with a view to an increase in price, and which afterwards took place to an extraordinary degree. To the advantages & disadvantages resulting from these fluctuations we are all alike liable except that the Spinners generally sell all we have on the eve of an advance & consequently our sales are lessened to that amount after the advance takes place so that by every change we are the losers. If then we were to re-purchase afterwards that Yarn at a high price which we had before sold at a much lower, in what situation are we placed for what is done to one must be done to all who require it. The same request has been made by some of our best customers besides yourselves; but forseeing to what it would lead we have been under the necessity of declining the proposal & when you consider how we are circumstanced we hope you will concur with us in the propriety of our conduct in this instance.

When, in October, 1826, William King and Co. of Newcastle-upon-Tyne asked them for special privileges they were told:

If you consider one moment how unjust it wd be to allow you the reduction for goods had 38 days before it took place, & not allow it to everyone else of our customers for all that time you can no longer think we do wrong—there is no limit to an advance or a reduction but the day it takes place—any other conduct on our part wd lead to endless dissatisfaction. We act on one general straight forward rule, & we find it meets most general approbation —if in your case you think otherwise, we trust no other person will think so, & we can only regret you shd. If it causes a diminution of your orders we shall be sorry for it—but nothing will induce us to act unjustly.

Another cause of dissatisfaction among a section of Strutts' customers arose from their refusal to allow special rates of discount to large buyers:

Your apprehension of our not running much risk for reductions similar to yours is correct [they told William King and Co. on November 24, 1826], we have none such because every one knows that it wd be absurd & impossible to comply with them, & that it is our invariable rule never to do it but to treat all alike . . . We can only repeat that no prospect of any future advante wd induce us to depart from our regular system—it is from *Principle* we act & mean to do so & we apprehend those who deal with us will not in the long run find they do worse than with others.

On April 19, 1827, G. B. Brown of Liverpool was advised: 'If your orders were for 10,000 bundles we cannot make any other price of dist *as we serve all invariably alike.*'

And on November 4, 1826, Strutts wrote to J. F. Norrington:

You are in a strange error respectg these goods being charged 20 p Ct higher than our list—they are not charged one farthing more than by our list of 6th Feby which is the last published & by which we charge those who take 1000 times your quantity! Besides yours being a difficult twist has to be made on purpose, & is worth a shillg p bundle more.

Strutts disliked making small quantities of yarns not in regular demand and often declined to execute orders for less than 50–100 bundles:[1]

---

[1] Strutts' yarn was reeled into 840-yard hanks which were packed into bundles each of 10 lb. (Davies, op. cit., 354).

We can do nothing with the Cord [they told their Leicester agent on December 1, 1824], it is very troublesome & nothing but the expectation of a quantity wd have induced us to make it. Do not take such small orders—they plague us sadly.

Strutts took great pains to ensure the high quality of their yarns and during the period October, 1798, to May, 1807, they carefully recorded some 113 letters of complaint in a book kept for that purpose.

Eleven of these letters came from A. Strahan, their Nottingham agent, who, on October 27, 1801, wrote to them:

I have had a terrible scold from Hewett & Co about the quality of the Cotton, they had Stockings came Inn on Saturday which realy appears very bad, & they say the hands would take no more of it, but would sooner give up their Frames, there was both from No 16 & 24 which appeared very bad indeed, very rough & uneven. Pray give your People at the Mills a lecture or it will hurt the Sales very much.

And on February 4, 1803, he protested:

Inclosed is a pair of Stockings from James Dufty & Co: they make very great complaints of the Marble Grey Cotton, they say the yarn is very uneven & lumpy; the coloured different shades, not only in the Bundle but in some of the hanks. I told them it might be owing to the workmen washing or soaping it, but they say if it is so with one hand or two, it might be so, but they give it out to some of their best hands & give them an additional price to keep it clean &c they therefore think it must be owing to your people not taking the pains they used to do in preparing & finishing the article. They say Mr A's common Grey @ 8/- additional makes a better stocking than yours @ 13/- there certainly appear different shades in many of the Hose they showed me. Please to return this pair & if you can make any alteration for the better I shall be glad.

The market for yarn was a highly competitive one as can be seen from the following letter of April 16, 1806, sent to Strutts by W. Coldham, who was now their Nottingham agent:

I am sorry to say your Cotton has not reachd yet to that degree of improvement as to admit of my selling it to those Houses who now buy of Hollins. Hoard & Lonsdale to whom I shew the sample would not take a Bundle nor Morley & Wilson. Mr. T. Carpenter Smith so fully convinced me (by shewing me many Dozens of Hose promiscously taken from different hands) that Arkwrights is much more even than either your 34 marked R or 40 marked L that I suppressd my sample untill I should receive some that may prove acceptable. Mr. Smith will try 3 slips of 50 with one of his best hands & if you wish it I can send over the Stockings for you to look at. Every one to whom I shew my samples said it was very far short of either Thackey or Hollins, in looking over Mr. Smiths Hose I own I was surpriz'd to see Mr. Arkwrights Cotton so good. Pritts would buy Super of you but are not satisfied with this Quality.

By the 1820s complaints regarding the quality of Strutts, yarns were few and far between and their attempts to ensure its continued high standard are to be seen in such letters as the following, addressed to their agents:

We have inquired minutely into the bleu Mr Mitchell complains of [they advised G. Bellairs on February 17, 1826]. It was fast bleu—great pains were taken with it to make it fast & even—it is well remembered by all who had to do with it. No fault was found with it in making up, where it is always minutely examd—it was done over & over again, & could not be a middle colr—in short we believe it to be as good a thing of the sort as can be. We know some dyers cover it over at the last with Logwood, to make it look darker & evener—but we never do, for that washes off, while ours being all Indigo will keep to the shade it appears. We cannot therefore in justice to ourselves make any allowe on this for we feel confident it was well worth the money charged. We never will send an ounce of yarn away which we do not believe to be perfect in all respects.

In March, 1826, they told G. Gill:

We return the hose & turkey red. If you can be sure of the bundle from which this was taken & can send us the ticket, it wd stagger us, otherwise we pronounce it at once not ours. It is from N 42 to 45, & it is many years since we dyed any of those Nos. We are remarkably particular abt our turkey red[1]—we *rewind it all* & this is so rotten that it would not bear that process—it is also all tried immediately on being recd for we once had some Sewg Cotten injured & have been on our guard ever since. That it is not ours we are convinced for not a single complaint has been made *for many*

---

[1] Strutts, in common with other concerns, experienced considerable difficulty in dyeing yarn Turkey red and between 1812 and 1824 they placed some orders for this with Robert Andrew (later Andrew and Tarlton) of Manchester. About the art of dyeing this colour see Baines, op. cit., 276-7.

years, & nothing will induce us to make any allowance whatever upon it.

And on April 6, 1827, they again wrote to him as follows:

Your remark of H & H Jenkins & Pearson complaing of the very infr quality of our mauve tie & bleu tie yarn, seems to the *general* bad quality, as no particr are given. Now we are *confident* our yarn never was *generally* better—this must refer therefore to some particular Nos or sorts which want particularly investigating, the particular complaints findg out, & those sent to us. We can then remedy the thing complained of (for some errors will creep in in spite of us) but witht this minute investigation by you we do not know what to remedy, knowg as we do that the yarn is good. When apparently *well founded* complaints are made, this investigation shd take place, & the most minute particulars sent to us, & then they will be remedied—but general complaints like this we know not how to go about remedying.

III. FOREIGN MARKETS

Before the Napoleonic Wars, if much of the Strutts' production, whether hosiery or yarn, found its way abroad, it was through London and Manchester merchants. There were, however, occasional direct exports. In 1784–7 £236 worth of hosiery was sold to Francis Bardell of Paris and in 1790 £272 worth to Michael Mahon there but it took four years to clear the latter account.[1] In 1796 the cotton firm was exporting a little cotton twist to Germany through Hull but did not do much foreign business until after the Peace of Amiens.

During the short-lived peace—in September, 1802, and March, 1803—the firm sent £305 worth of yarn to Leo Goldschmidt of Frankfurt. War was resumed in May, 1803. The achievement of British command of the seas, which was assured by Trafalgar, encouraged the Strutts, like so many other British firms, to test the markets and try to circumvent the Continental System. They first ventured through English merchants in the Mediterranean. Thus in 1805 they sent hosiery, worth £135, to W. W. Barker of Palermo, followed by £449 worth in 1806; on the two lots they made a profit of £15. In the next two years they sent a further £733 worth, on which

---

[1] These and other figures are rounded off to the nearest pound.

they lost £43. In May, 1807, they sent from London to Holland Ash & Co. at Messina, four trunks of hosiery, valued at £398. The venture was not happy; the purchaser of the trunks had complained of them and the rest had been sold by auction. Strutts lost £40 on the transaction.

A longer and more complicated story comes from Gibraltar. George Sandeman and Co., who had acted at Lisbon in the Strutts' cotton dealings, recommended to them E. Viale and Co. as a Gibraltar agent. On August 23, 1806, Viale acknowledged receipt of a bill of lading and an invoice for three trunks, containing 108 dozen men's cotton hose, valued at £256. He was to dispose of them to the best advantage and give Strutts his opinion on their quality and on the advisability of sending more. They were to defray his expenses and give him a commission of 5 per cent. on the total receipts. Silence then fell. Pressed by Strutts, Sandeman wrote to Viale who replied on July 22, 1808. The Strutts' property was safe; Sandeman reported that one of the trunks had been disposed of and the other two were in Viale's store; if he did not give satisfaction, Strutts could place the consignment elsewhere. More than a year passed and Sandeman pressed Viale to say how much was still unsold. On November, 1809, Viale told Strutts that 'however unpleasant it may be to render accounts disadvantageous to all parties, it must be done. I wait on you with acct Sales 3 Trunks Hoseiery & remittances at par for proceeds as follows. . . .' Total receipts came to £216, payable in bills at one month, ten days, and sight respectively. Strutts doubted whether this represented the prevailing rate of exchange and Sandemans said that neither they nor any merchants they had consulted, had knowledge of the rate of exchange to which Viale referred; the matter had been resolved by looking at the Gibraltar lists received at Lloyd's Coffee House. They were not satisfied with Viale's conduct but saw no method of getting redress. Strutts' estimate of their losses on the consignment was £40. In 1808 there was an attempted barter transaction with Madeira of hosiery for wine. The wine never came and eight years later the Strutts were told that the consignee was bankrupt.

Strutts' dealings with Northern Europe are obscure. McConnel and Kennedy had been sending yarn to Hamburg, through the branch of a Glasgow house, from 1805 and then, when Hamburg was closed, with Tönning, in Schlèswig, and then with Altona and Heligoland.[1] The ingenuity of British merchants and French inconsistencies form one of the most extraordinary chapters in the history of the Continental System.[2] Strutts had some part in the trade. Between September and November, 1806, they sold £2766 worth of yarn to J. G. Schuller & Co. of Vienna, and received prompt payment by bill; the route is not indicated. Samples of their goods were being sent to Hamburg. And in September, 1809, a letter from Hull to them said:

The 3 Bales are not come to hand. When they do we shall be oblig'd to land them as we have no Shipping at present for Ton-ningen *or* Hambro' nor do we expect we shall have while there's an alteration of affairs on the Continent, if you would have them any other way disposed of please let us know your directions.

Various letters to the Strutts reflect the difficulties of some of their British customers. On December 8, 1807, Daniel Barnard of Sheffield asked for forbearance in the 'very trying situation in which we are involved by events'.[3] Edward Hughes and Co. of Birmingham, to whom they had supplied yarn since 1801, told them in March, 1808, that they could not give security; 'the whole of our property being abroad we do not see how we can give any'. 'We have great hopes that we shall receive something as several of our friends have written to us to say they will remit after Easter Fairs if they can send without risque.'[4]

The first direct trade by Strutts with the United States seems to have been the sale of £628 worth of hosiery in 1803–4 to

[1] Daniels, 'The Cotton Trade during the Revolutionary and Napoleonic Wars', *Trans. Manch. Stat. Soc.*, 1916.

[2] Heckscher, *The Continental System* (1922), Part II, ch. ii and iii.

[3] Fourteen years later they were told that 'if you have received 1s. 6d. in the £ on Danl Barnard's debt it is final' and five years later still that only 1s. could be expected; 1s. 6d. had been hoped for but there was not enough money to pay the attorney's bill.

[4] He too failed and paid 5s. in the pound. In 1814 a trustee said considerable debts were owing to the estate in Hamburg, Königsberg, Danzig, Warsaw, etc., and next year advised them that no more than another 5s. was to be expected. 'Out of near £7000 esteem'd Goods before the War, with every exertion only about £400 has been yet recovered.'

William Harriman of New York. Harriman had emigrated from England in 1795 and his descendants have played a part in American railways and finance.[1] In August, 1805, Strutts entered on a consignment trade with the cotton-growing South. They sent hosiery worth £331 to Thomas Ogier of Charleston, South Carolina; he was to deduct his expenses and 5 per cent. commission and to return bills or raw cotton. He sent back a bill at sixty days for £121 and fourteen bales of Bowed Georgia cotton valued at £243 at the Liverpool price of August 20, 1806. Strutts paid expenses of £57 on the cotton at Liverpool, which left a loss on the whole transaction of £23. A second consignment of eight trunks of hosiery, worth £647, was sent on March 7, 1806; they received a sixty days' bill for £292 and 27 bales of bowed cotton, worth £477 at the Liverpool price of February 2, 1807. The expenses on the cotton were £109 and the profit was £14.

Strutts had complaints to make about the stones and dirt in two of the first bags of cotton. They wrote on August 22, 1806, and Ogier replied on January 21, 1807, that

that kind of cotton is brought from the Country in Waggons in small Quantities, and is put promiscuously into the stores of those who buy from the Countrymen, and they when they sell again to the Merchants do not know who each particular bag comes from; I bought last year from different people, and it would be necessary for me to prove from whom I bought the bags in question to enable me to recover the amount, and then I think I could not recover more than I paid for the Cotton; however having purchased the greater part from one house, altho' I cannot prove those bags came from him, yet he has promised to make some allowance, which when he does, whatever it is, I shall give you credit for it. Indeed, the persons we buy from are as innocent of any fraud as you or I, it is in the Country where the cotton is packed that the fraud is committed.

Strutts ultimately received £12 in compensation.

A further batch of six trunks of hosiery, worth £365, was sent out but Ogier warned (on November 14, 1807) that the

---

[1] He was great-grandfather of the railroad financier, E. H. Harriman (1848–1909), and great-great-grandfather of William Averell Harriman, Ambassador to Great Britain and Governor of New York (*Amer. Dict. of Biog.*).

outlook for its sale was not promising; there was talk of war and he hoped that 'all will end in Peace between the two Countries'. The interminable complications of non-importation, embargo, prohibitions and suspensions of prohibition, which were to baffle merchants on both sides of the Atlantic for six years, had begun.[1] Congress's blow did not fall with real severity until the Embargo Act substituted for selective prohibition a general prohibition of import and barred American ships also from the trade in British goods. But even so the American importation of 1808 was down only by a half, to say nothing of the increase in smuggling.

On February 16, 1808, Ogier wrote to Strutts that he had sold the six trunks of hosiery—five in December for a four months' bill and one at auction. Strutts thought he could have got a better price had he waited until the effect of the embargo was felt, but he (on September 17, 1808) contested this. 'It is not more than one or two articles that are enhanced in value by it, the reason is, money and credit are both very scarce, and People have grown great economists.' He had invested the hosiery proceeds in bowed cotton and would send it as soon as the embargo was lifted.

The Embargo Act broke down through its own severity. There was a flight of laden American ships to England and, by the end of March, Maury, the American consul, had counted forty embargo-breakers in Liverpool and expected many more.[2] Congress, on March 1, modified its policy. There was to be non-intercourse with the belligerents, Britain and France, free intercourse with the rest of the world. American ports were closed to British and French ships and goods (home and colonial). The Americans rushed to neutral ports—Gothenburg, Tönning, and St. Bartholomew (a Swedish island) by the old smuggling route of Amelia Island on the Florida border, Fayal in the Azores,—and even to Liverpool—keeping out of the consul's way. But Ogier was careful with the Strutts' cotton. He kept it until the temporary ending of non-intercourse by the Erskine-Smith agreement of April. He wrote on April 10:

Since the partial repeal on the 15th ult. of the Embargo laws,

---

[1] See the excellent description of the various phases in Professor Heaton's 'Non-Importation, 1806–1812' (*Jour. Econ. Hist.* (1941), 178–98).

[2] Heaton, op. cit., 191.

Cotton has been shipped from hence for England by the circuitous routes of Florida, St Bartholomew, & Gottenburg but from the great expence attending this mode I have not felt myself justified to ship without your order; the freight from hence to Amelia Island in Florida is 1½ cents p lb; from thence to England (at present) 12½ Cents p lb and 10 per cent primage, exclusive of which there is an import duty of 17½ p cent and an export duty of 6½ p cent, valuing all cottons at 12 Cents p lb paid there, besides commission and charges for re-shipping.

In June the cotton was dispatched. The invoice sent to Samuel Hope, Strutts' Liverpool broker, for the 39 bales was for $1422.47, with Ogier's charges:

	$
Drayage &c.	12.87
Certificate of American Produce	1.20
Commission at 5 p.c. on 9581 lb at 14 cents p lb	67.06
Storage from August 3, 1808 to June 7, 1809	71.76

On September 23 Samuel Hope sent to Strutts a note of the Liverpool charges:

	£		
Town dues &c 7s 6d duty on 9213 lb.	117	16	10
Freight &c 1¾ £67. 3. 6 primage £3. 7. 2.	70	10	8
Interest on duty from 3rd Aug to 9th Dec.	2	1	0
Bank Commission & Stamp 16. 4; Porterage, Cartage &c 19. 6	1	15	10
Postages 2. 6; Brokerage (on 9213 at 17d p. lb £652 11. 9) £3 5. 3.	3	7	11
	195	12	3

Strutts' profit on the whole Charleston venture was £88. Non-intercourse was resumed after Canning's repudiation of the Erskine agreement. For further direct purchases from the United States the Strutts waited until after the peace.

Strutts next turned to the indirect approach to the American market. On the invitation of John Jones, a Montreal merchant who had visited London, they consigned to him £83 worth of yarn. Sent in May, 1810, it reached him in September. On January 18, 1811, he wrote from New York:

the earlier vessels which had previously arrived at Quebec and Montreal, upwards of 350 Ships & Brigs, threw into the Market such a super abundance of every Description of Goods, that for my own part I thought it most prudent to keep the Majority of the Goods I had Shipped, to take the Chance of a better Market this ensuing

Spring, rather than make those Sort of Sacrifices which Several Houses were doing by making a forced Sale, a principle I conceive neither just or honourable, and from the present position of American Affairs the prospects in Canada will be very favourable to the Shipments of this year, and I trust you will give me an Opportunity of sending You a favorable Account of the Proceeds. I wrote You and Messrs Pagets & Byng in October last, and pointed out to You what I have now proposed, that the Object of a small Parcel of Goods would be of little Consquence, when times are good, but as the Circumstances stood, to hold You and myself harmless, I proposed to take them on Commission & do every thing in my Power for Your Advantage, however, I have no doubt but this Spring will enable me to make a more profitable Sale of the Goods I have on hand, and afford me an opportunity of making You an early Remittance.

Everybody was in expectation that neither the Orders in Council nor non-intercourse could last and there was a great piling of stocks at convenient ports outside America. Napoleon tricked Madison by his pretence that the French had given way and Congress decided to penalize the recalcitrant British— if the Orders in Council were not repealed.[1] By Madison's new policy of February, 1811, 'Britain could buy, but not sell. She could import American produce in American ships, but not in British bottoms. She could not send her goods to America, even in American vessels, and no neutrals could bring them in as their own property.'[2] Jones went on in his letter to comment on the effects:

twelve of the first Houses in this City are expected to stop Payment. Those already made Public are Coup Ellis & Shaw, Furguson & Day, John Patrie & Co.—That in a few Days the Non-Importation Bill will be put in force. The United States Bank have stopt all accommodation to the Merchants, and the Consequence is expected to be serious.—That the Charter of that Bank soon expires, and that the Democratic Party are using all their influence to prevent their obtaining a new One. From the general View of American Affairs our Merchants in England should not be too forward in making Shipments this Year to the States.—However it will be the means of making Canada flourish and . . . we may expect a Brisk Trade there.

On May 27 Jones comes in again to say that trade is still very

---

[1] Heckscher, op. cit., 140-3.   [2] Heaton, op. cit., 194.

bad. He then disappears from the scene. 'All lost, finished' is written in red ink across his entry in the Strutts' ledger. Things moved on to the tragedy of the repeal of the Orders in Council just before the American declaration of war. But the Strutts, for the moment, had had enough of North America.

While trade with the United States was capricious or dwindling, that with South America went through a boom and collapse. In 1808–9, the revolt of the Spanish colonies threw the cotton trade into a frenzy of exporting. 'More Manchester goods', McCulloch later reported, 'were sent out in the course of a few weeks than had been consumed in the twenty years preceding.'[1] The Strutts joined in belatedly. They had sent three trunks of hosiery, each of 33 dozen, to Benjamin and Samuel Winter of Rio de Janeiro, a firm with London and Leeds connections. On April 9, 1809, Winter wrote 'how unfortunate it was for the Sale of your Consignment, its being almost entirely rib'd Hose which are scarce at all worn here'. They had sold a trunk for which the Leeds house had remitted a bill at 30 days. They added a list of hosiery suitable 'for this Place and for the River Plate, which in several respects differ essentially'. In August, they advised of the sale of another trunk, and on August 31, 1810, of that of the third. The Strutts had been inquiring after their money and the Leeds house paid with bills on Joseph Denison and Co.,[2] London. They explained

[1] McCulloch, *Principles of Political Economy*, 2nd edn. (1830), 330.

[2] The private bank founded by Joseph Denison (?1726–1806), the son of a Leeds woollen and cloth merchant. He went up to London early in life and became clerk with Dillon and Co. before starting business on his own account. He established a connection with Heywoods, the Liverpool bankers, and with other considerable merchants in the north of England and 'by unabated industry and the most rigid frugality, worked himself into very high credit and an increasing fortune'. Joseph Denison and Co. became Denison, Heywood, Kennard and Co. in 1837, a concern now merged into the Westminster Bank. A Dissenter, he bought of Lord King the estate of Denbies in Surrey and from the Duke of Leeds the estate of Seamere, near Scarborough, for £100,000. By his second wife, Elizabeth (1739–71), daughter of a Southwark hat maker, Denison had one son, William Joseph (1770–1849) and two daughters. The son, a 'staunch old Whig, who considered that his patronymic was more in its place at the head of his own ledger, than in the pages of the peerage' though 'less penurious than his father, pursued the like policy of accumulation'. He became senior partner in the banking concern and sat in Parliament for half a century. Dying unmarried he left his £2,300,000 fortune to his nephew Lord Conyngham on condition that he took the name of Denison. (*Gentleman's Magazine*, 1806, 1181; 1849 (July–Dec.), 422–3).

that they could not have sold had the Rio house not given long credit—three months and six months. But they wished to have further goods on consignment (their commission had been 7½ per cent.) at Rio and at Buenos Aires, where the firm was styled Winter, Brittain & Co. But 'You or Your friends ought first to be informed of the Assortment best Calculated for both Markets, which We can furnish You with'. Strutts had lost £39 on the three trunks sent to Rio. The boom was over and they sent no more.

These speculative ventures on consignment were small and hardly well managed. They bring out the smallness and slowness of the returns. It is little wonder, when it took years of persistent attention to get their money back, that the cautious Strutts should not have dabbled more vigorously in foreign trade.

With the collapse of the Continental System and the repeal of the Orders in Council in 1812, it became no longer necessary for merchants to resort to extraordinary devices in order to send goods to the Continent and Strutts immediately began to sell large quantities of yarn direct to customers in every corner of Europe.

It was usual for prospective buyers to write to them asking to be advised of the conditions under which they were prepared to execute their orders:

As you request we send you a list of our prices [they told A. Kluyrer of Amsterdam on March 7, 1827]. The quality of each article can only be judged of by using it. At the same price we hope we can compete with any house whatever. You may rely on your orders being punctually & expeditiously executed. It will be necessary to send a good bill on London with your order or power to draw on a good house there.

Strutts never sent goods abroad without first having received a bill on London or the right to draw on a good house there. This and other conditions of trade is clear from their letter of September 17, 1824, to H. Degen of Königsberg:

We have received your favour of the 2nd instant & have now the pleasure to annex a List of the Prices of our different sorts of Cotton Yarn the quality of which is very generally approved. We allow 7½ per cent discount for a Bill at 3 months or 10 per cent for Cash or Bill due in 14 days from date of Invoice and we never send any Goods abroad without first having Bills or power to draw on a good House in London. We deliver any Bales well packed for exportation free in London or Hull in 4 or 5 days from date of Invoice. The present rate of insurance is about 25/- per cent, what it may be in the middle of October we do not know. From the very large Stock which we always hold[1] we shall always be enabled promptly to execute any order with what you may please to favour us & you may rely with confidence on the good quality of our Articles. We are not acquainted with a manufacturer of Scotch Thread. We cannot correspond in German as no one here understands it.

These conditions were unchanged eighteen months later when, on March 8, 1826, Strutts wrote to J. Moeller, also of Königsberg:

We are favoured with yours of 17 February which being in German we were obliged to send to London for translation & it has lost a Post.[2] If you write to us again & can do it in English or in French it will oblige us. As you desire we send a list of our prices of all sorts. Our terms are 10 per cent for *Cash in 14 days*, not exceeding a single day, *from date of Invoice*, & 7½ per cent if it does exceed that time, & Interest for the time the bill is due before the expiration of 3 months. The way therefore is to send a *good bill on London with the order* or power to draw on a good house in London. We do no foreign business on any other terms & this is the extent of our terms to everybody. We pay carriage to Hull and all orders are executed with punctuality and with articles whose quality in each sort may be relied upon with implicit confidence. We of course require no references but to learn of the respectability of the houses the bills are drawn upon. It will give us pleasure to hear from you on these terms & your orders for any bales not less than 50 bundles will oblige.

As for the home market, Strutts often declined to execute orders for less than 50–100 bundles of yarn. This is made clear in their letter to J. Moeller and on June 16, 1827, they wrote to C. F. Gleisburg of Dresden:

As this small order is only for sample it makes the expences very

---

[1] On March 1, 1812, Strutts estimated their stock to be worth £36,652.
[2] Letters were often sent to the London agents for translation, the charge for which varied between 4s. and 10s. a time.

high to us & to you too. We hope you will never order less than 50 to 100 bundles & send the bills with the order at once.

Upon hearing of a London house upon which to draw, Strutts lost no time despatching customers' goods. Occasionally, however, there was slight delay as with an order placed by David Schiess of Magdeburg to whom they wrote on September 30, 1824:

We are favoured with yours of the 11th Instant with an order for 100 bundles which has gone to Gee Loft & Co Hull to ship to F. Coqui Hambro' to whom a bill of lading will be sent & another to B. A. Goldschmidt & Co London for Insurance.[1] We have drawn on these Gentlemen at 11 days for the amount of £110 as when we allow 10 per cent we never exceed cash in 14 days. These goods would have been sent sooner but Goldschmidt & Co wrote to us they had no orders to pay & that you was unknown to them. Two days after, however, they wrote they would accept.

Under Strutts' terms it was necessary for them to draw on Goldsmid and Co. at eleven (not fourteen) days in order that D. Schiess and Co. receive a discount of 10 per cent. The British custom of allowing days of grace was unfamiliar to many Continental merchants and the firm were frequently obliged to explain a practice which often gave rise to misunderstanding.

Sometimes Strutts had difficulty in ascertaining the exact requirements of their customers. This was the case, upon one occasion, with J. C. Schlaffer of St. Gall, Switzerland, to whom they wrote on January 17, 1825:

We are not aware what you mean by *claws*, if you wish each pound to be divided into *128 hanks of 2 drams* each, we can do it, & the price will be 1/3 or 2/6 or 3/6 extra per bundle according to the N on our list but if you mean *balls* of 2 drams each, or 128 to the lb we do not make them, but we can procure them for you, of our cotton, from our Agent in London who sends a deal abroad & will charge you his regular price. We sent you a new list yesterday advancing the prices 1/- per bundle—we expect a further advance

At irregular intervals Strutts sent price lists printed in English

---

[1] The great house founded in 1777 by Abraham and Benjamin Goldschmid. *The Times* of Sept. 29, 1810, spoke of Abraham Goldschmid and Francis Baring together as 'the Pillars of the City'.

and in French to their overseas customers. They did not engage in price discrimination or in dumping and their foreign lists were identical with those supplied to customers in Great Britain. Lists were sometimes revised to meet price-cutting by competitors and in one sent to overseas customers on January 22, 1827, they said:

We are very sorry to send you a new list but we are determined not to be undersold. Notwithstanding these low prices however you will find both our Sewing & Knitting & Coloured yarn better and evener than ever & more regular in all respects. You will observe two qualities of Sewings and two of Tambour in our list. Each will compete with any other of equal price as will our other sorts. Every possible attention will be paid to your orders in every way & they will oblige very much.

An additional note included for buyers of Merino stated:

You will observe that our mixed Wool & Cotton is all Merino & called Summer & Winter. This article we are now making very nice & the price tho' raised is very low.

In August, 1827, Strutts cancelled their January list and lowered the prices of all items, Merino and Cord excepted, by 1s. a bundle. Customers at home and overseas were advised that this had been done in order to meet prices charged by competitors. The reduction was unexpected. They were 'astonished', they told a client, that their lists had had to be altered so soon.

Price changes were frequently the cause of friction between Strutts and their customers. Such was the case with M. Steinthal of Hamburg to whose London house they wrote on March 2, 1825:

You will see from the state of the Cotton Wool market at Manchester the certainty of further advances. We have very little by us but if we receive your order *by return* we will engage you shall have 500 bundles at the present price.

Their advice went unheeded and on March 9, 1825, they told Steinthal's Hamburg house:

Having in our letter of the 2nd Instant made you an offer, which we did not to any other person whatever, & from the personal knowledge you gained at Liverpool of the Cotton market, you thought it right to decline that offer. We cannot now an advance has actually taken place & the Cotton market has recovered from the depression so as to make another advance necessary engage to send it in other terms than the present list. If that is agreeable to you please to say & we will accept the order but we cannot send it just yet.

Strutts' customers sometimes accused them of delaying the consignment of goods in order that they might charge the higher prices quoted in new lists. This the firm always denied as when, on November 4, 1824, they wrote to J. Lewis and Co. of Hamburg:

The 5 bales ℞ you order can only go when you chuse them to be sent, *at the price of our list then* for we cannot, for many days ever say what the price may be. If sent now & it drops you will think yourselves ill used, & not thank us if it rises, & it will not do to accept orders now to go in Feby but at the price our yarn may be then. Under these circumstances therefore we wait more specific directions.

And on November 7, 1827, they told J. A. Lucius of Erfurt:

The Merino has to be made on purpose & takes time. All transactions in business must be subject to its vicissitudes. It is an invariable rule with us to execute all orders we may have on hand when an *advance* takes place, at the *old* price—& to put such orders at the *new* price when a drop takes place, so that in both cases we are so much losers—but it is out of all question to alter the price of goods sent off *before* such alteration takes place. We knew nothing of it 2 days before it happened. You may be assured every attention shall be pd to your orders, & every facility we can with justice grant, be allowed to you.

When the despatch of goods was unavoidably delayed, customers were always given the benefit of any changes in their price.

It is very disagreeable to us to have any alteration about prices [Strutts advised C. E. Kuhn of Königsberg in September, 1827]. Everybody in business must take the chance of a rise or fall of prices. Peculiar circumstances may arise that may render it hard upon the Parties as in the case with you of there being no ship sooner to take your goods of 21 July. We are always willing to do what we fairly & in honor can for our friends & we therefore determine to allow the 1/- on the parcel in July & it will appear in your next account & Invoice which we hope to send soon.

And on August 6, 1827, they told G. Verhoustraelin of Antwerp:

We have had so many orders for this article that we could not send it so soon as we wished. The delay, however, will serve you as we have lowered all sorts 1/- per bundle from our list of 22 July of which we give you the advantage.

From the collapse of the Continental System Strutts consigned large quantities of yarn and twist to Russia. These were shipped to 'St. Petersburg Town' from Hull or from London by Gee Loft and Co. and by Job Wright and Co. respectively. The making up of yarn into the weights required by the Russian market gave Strutts a good deal of trouble and they usually made a small extra charge for this service. In 1826, however, competition compelled them to do away with this and on July 10 they advised T. Marshall:

We have considered your letter about charging Russian weights only the weight they are in English lbs. The difficulty is the extra trouble of making all on purpose & the impossibility of doing it exactly without having too much. As the orders however are generally for a good deal of each N. we have determined to charge only the English weight sent from this day, when put in bundles, but if in $\frac{1}{4}$, $\frac{1}{2}$ or 1 lb. papers must be charged as usual.

At the same time they wrote to J. Peirce in terms more to the point than those sent to Marshall:

We find Elsten is sending Sewing & Knitting [yarns] in Russian weights charging only English weights & we have determined for the future to do so to—that is all bundles made up in Russian weights will be charged English weight only but if in $\frac{1}{4}$, $\frac{1}{2}$ or 1 lb papers those will be charged extra as at present by our list. You will pray observe this that we may not lose these orders.

As Strutts' name became increasingly well-known throughout Europe it is small wonder that they were approached by merchants wishing to sell their goods on commission. In March, 1825, in reply to one such request, they told Halldale and Co.:

Our business abroad is done by order—receiving bills with the order or power to draw on a good house in London—we have no

Established 1740.

Shipped in good order & well conditioned by *Geo Lafft & Co.* in and upon the good Ship called the ——— whereof is Master for this present Voyage *Wm Jackson* now lying at *Hull* and bound for *Elsinore & St. Petersburg.*

The Hundred Bush Cotton Twist

being marked and numbered as in the margin & to be delivered in the like good order and condition at the said Port of **St. Petersburg.** all and every the dangers and accidents of the seas & of Navigation of what nature or kind soever and fire excepted unto *Mg* ——— or *his Assigns* or *this assigns* he or they paying freight for the same

Six pence per Foot £ 10 per Cent

with primage & average accustomed. **In Witness** whereof the Master or Purser of the said Ship hath signed Bills of Lading all of this tenor and date: one of which being accomplished the other to be void **Hull** _10 April 1818_

Wm Griffith

Ship free from Lightrage

Contents Unknown to Wm Griffith

PSWT 91 @ 110

IWxr 36 @ 55
PLBt

IWNT 11 @ 75
PWT

IW S.K 1 a 35
P

IW S. 81 @ 90
P

2655/out

A Bill of Lading

PRICES OF COTTON YARN,

BY

William, George, and Joseph Strutt.

Eight Months Credit, or 7½ per Cent. discount.

BROWN.

No.	Single, Two thread and Knitting per Bundle.			Sewing, full hanks or ½ oz. hanks. per Bundle.			No.	Single, Two Threads and Knitting per Bundle.			Sewing, full hanks or ½ oz. hanks. per Bundle.		
	£.	s.	d.	£.	s.	d.		£.	s.	d.	£.	s.	d.
5	1	17	0				38	3	3	0	4	0	0
5¼	1	17	2				39	3	4	6	4	2	0
6	1	17	4				40	3	6	0	4	4	0
6¼	1	17	6				41	3	7	6	4	6	0
7	1	17	8				42	3	9	0	4	8	0
7¼	1	17	10				43	3	10	6	4	10	0
8	1	18	0	2	4	0	44	3	12	0	4	12	0
8¼	1	18	2				45	3	13	6	4	15	0
9	1	18	4	2	4	6	46	3	15	0	4	18	0
9¼	1	18	6				47	3	16	6			
10	1	18	8	2	5	0	48	3	18	0	5	1	0
11	1	19	0	2	5	6	49	3	19	6			
12	1	19	6	2	6	0	50	4	1	0	5	4	0
13	2	0	0	2	6	9	51	4	2	6			
14	2	0	6	2	7	6	52	4	4	0	5	8	0
15	2	1	0	2	8	6	53	4	5	6			
16	2	1	6	2	9	6	54	4	7	0	5	12	0
17	2	2	0	2	10	6	55	4	8	6			
18	2	2	6	2	11	6	56	4	10	0	5	17	0
19	2	3	0	2	12	6	57	4	11	6			
20	2	3	6	2	13	6	58	4	13	0	6	2	0
21	2	4	0	2	14	6	59	4	14	6			
22	2	4	6	2	15	6	60	4	16	0	6	8	0
23	2	5	0	2	16	6							
24	2	6	0	2	17	6							
25	2	7	0	2	18	6							
26	2	8	0	3	0	0							
27	2	9	0	3	1	6							
28	2	10	0	3	3	0							
29	2	11	0	3	4	6							
30	2	12	0	3	6	0							
31	2	13	0	3	7	6							
32	2	14	0	3	9	0							
33	2	15	6	3	10	6							
34	2	17	0	3	12	0							
35	2	18	6	3	14	0							
36	3	0	0	3	16	0							
37	3	1	6	3	18	0							

LESS THAN GOOD.

Inferior.

5s. per Bundle.

Waste.

9s. per Bundle.

SUNDRIES, Additional per Bundle.

	s.	d.
White Single, &c.	2	4
White Sewing,	4	2
Bleach'd Grey,	12	0
Common Grey,	6	8
Dark Marble,	8	0
One thd. White and 1 colour'd,	11	0
Randoms,	12	0
Turkey Red, per lb.	6	0
Fast Blue per lb.	2	0
Solid Colours at the usual Prices.		

agents & at present have no occasion to seek for orders. Under these circumstances the plan you propose will be of no advantage to us but we are obliged by the offer.

The same month they told F. Mieville of Milan that they did not sell goods abroad on commission and on August 24, 1827, they advised John Heyworth of Rochdale:

We are favoured with yours of the 20th respecting a Commission for Sewing Cotton in South America &c to which we beg to reply that we do not on any occasion send goods abroad without first having the money or good bills on London, or power to order on a good house there. The proposal therefore will not suit us. If you or any of your friends chuse to make a consignment of our Cotton we shall be glad to furnish excellent goods.

Yet another indication of the reputation held by Strutts' goods in Continental markets is provided by letters showing that their mark was not infrequently copied by competitors.[1] Thus a note of March 11, 1822, from J. Peirce advised them: 'D. W. Rookmaaker spins cotton & makes up with your arms &c &c in a close imitation but very inferior cotton, more hereafter.'

They asked Peirce to send them a bundle of Rookmaaker's cotton from Haarlem but, unfortunately, we do not know the outcome of their investigations into his activities.

More than three years later, Strutts heard that yarn bearing their mark was being sold in Germany and on September 15, 1825, they told J. Lewis and Co. of Hamburg:

It is very provoking to have our yarn sold as you state, but much more so to have our marks &c counterfeited, giving the idea that we sell the same thing at different prices. We have only to refer to our character & honor & to again assure you that you will never find it so. We know that 2d each has been given for our old papers, & we know not how to guard against such roguery, except by making up *the quality which they cannot mend at the same price.*

In December, 1825, they asked Lewis and Co. to send them a bundle of the yarn and this the German firm did only to find that, despite Strutts' assurance that it would be returned to

---

[1] In 1876, when Strutts applied for a trade mark for their Merino yarns, they stated that they had used the one they then submitted for sixty years (*Trade Marks Journal*, No. 80, 771–2).

Hamburg as soon as it had been examined, the Hull Customs authorities were adamant in their refusal to allow it to enter the country.

In 1827 Strutts had reason to suppose that yarn bearing a counterfeit of their mark was again being sold on the Dutch market and on September 8 they wrote to G. V. Schmidt of Amsterdam:

We thank you for informing us of the Sewing Cotton being sold at an under price but it cannot be ours for we send none away on credit & we have not sold the sorts you mention to any body in those quantities. No doubt it is some bad stuff & our mark forged.

The widespread notion that the pioneers of the Industrial Revolution were interested only in getting rich quickly will not bear scrutiny. Pride of workmanship was as highly developed in men such as Josiah Wedgwood, Matthew Boulton, Samuel Oldknow, and Peter Stubs as in any craftsman of an earlier age. It was galling for the Strutts to see cheap imitations of their wares lowering their sales and their reputation alike. But there was, for them, no question of sacrificing quality to price. Writing of the Strutts in the thirties, Andrew Ure declared that 'So high is the character of their stocking-yarns and threads for uniform excellence, that the stamp of their firm on the great bale is a passport to their ready sale without examination in every market of the world.' It is because the Arkwrights and the Strutts were not only innovators but men of firm character, able to take long views, that the businesses they created persisted throughout the nineteenth century, and, though now merged in the English Sewing Cotton Company, still preserve their identity today.

APPENDIX A

THE ARKWRIGHT FAMILY

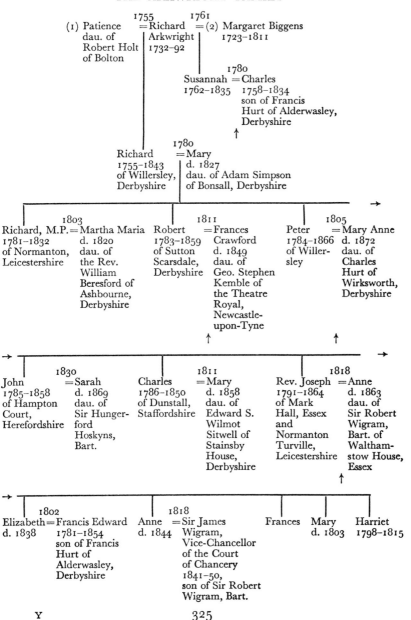

(1) Patience dau. of Robert Holt of Bolton
$\underset{\text{1755}}{=}$ Richard Arkwright 1732–92
$\underset{\text{1761}}{=}$ (2) Margaret Biggens 1723–1811

Susannah 1762–1835 $\underset{\text{1780}}{=}$ Charles 1758–1834 son of Francis Hurt of Alderwasley, Derbyshire ↑

Richard 1755–1843 of Willersley, Derbyshire $\underset{\text{1780}}{=}$ Mary d. 1827 dau. of Adam Simpson of Bonsall, Derbyshire

Richard, M.P. 1781–1832 of Normanton, Leicestershire $\underset{\text{1803}}{=}$ Martha Maria d. 1820 dau. of the Rev. William Beresford of Ashbourne, Derbyshire

Robert 1783–1859 of Sutton Scarsdale, Derbyshire $\underset{\text{1811}}{=}$ Frances Crawford d. 1849 dau. of Geo. Stephen Kemble of the Theatre Royal, Newcastle-upon-Tyne ↑

Peter 1784–1866 of Willersley $\underset{\text{1805}}{=}$ Mary Anne d. 1872 dau. of Charles Hurt of Wirksworth, Derbyshire ↑

John 1785–1858 of Hampton Court, Herefordshire $\underset{\text{1830}}{=}$ Sarah d. 1869 dau. of Sir Hungerford Hoskyns, Bart.

Charles 1786–1850 of Dunstall, Staffordshire $\underset{\text{1811}}{=}$ Mary d. 1858 dau. of Edward S. Wilmot Sitwell of Stainsby House, Derbyshire

Rev. Joseph 1791–1864 of Mark Hall, Essex and Normanton Turville, Leicestershire $\underset{\text{1818}}{=}$ Anne d. 1863 dau. of Sir Robert Wigram, Bart. of Waltham-stow House, Essex ↑

Elizabeth d. 1838 $\underset{\text{1802}}{=}$ Francis Edward 1781–1854 son of Francis Hurt of Alderwasley, Derbyshire

Anne d. 1844 $\underset{\text{1818}}{=}$ Sir James Wigram, Vice-Chancellor of the Court of Chancery 1841–50, son of Sir Robert Wigram, Bart.

Frances

Mary d. 1803

Harriet 1798–1815

Y

325

THE STRUTT FAMILY

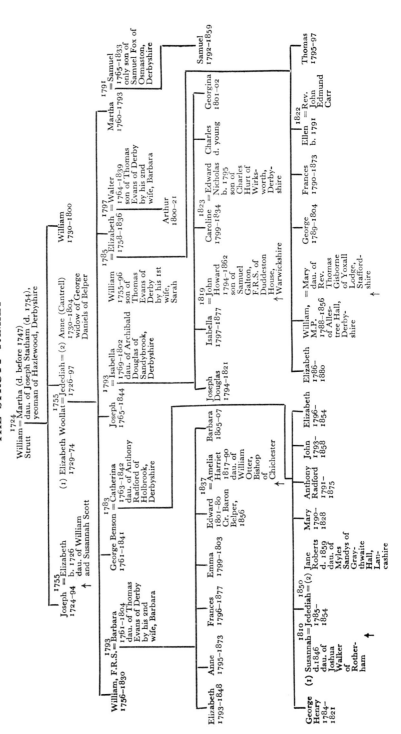

THE NEED FAMILY

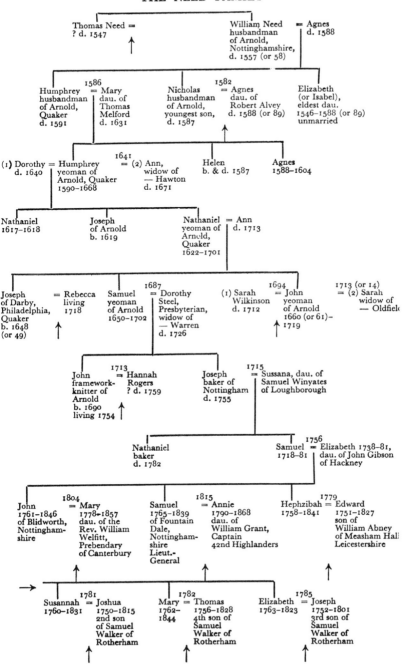

APPENDIX B

[Supplementary to Chapter II]

The following letters are printed here as further illustrating the domestic life of the period. Those of May–June, 1763, are written to Mrs. Strutt, who was staying with her friends, the Rev. Jonah Malkin and his wife, at their home at Alfreton.

Jedediah Strutt to his wife

Derby, [Monday] May 30 1763

My Dear Bett

As I coud not see you yesterday it gave me great pleasure to hear from you last Night. I am very sorry you & Mrs Malkin are so disapointed, but as the days & nights are so tedious without you if you think of no better way before this I intend to bring Jenny over on Wednesday in your Stead. I beg you will make your self very easy I was only loath to part with you. I am still in the utmost perplexity how to act in a certain affair & flatter myself you woud relieve all my douts if you was here. We are all well in health & I ought to be very busy but cannot from too much tho't. I have sent a gallon of Raisin Wine by Mrs Rowlands Bro: who will send it to his sisters. He stays while I wish my Love to Sally & Comts to Mr & Mrs Malkin. I am sorry to have so much trouble & inconvenience on our account. Fare well I am ever thine

J. Strutt

I hope nothing will prevent my coming on Wednesday Morning —but however things may be hereafter here they are very uncertain. On Saturday nigh[t] Mr Dale Brazeier at the Market head dropt down dead as he was putting on his shirt. Miss Cook was Married this morning. Billy went last night to Findern. Mr & Mrs Horwod are there & Nanny's child.

Jedediah Strutt to his wife

Wednesday Morning 5 o clock [? June 1, 1763]

My Dear

Last night I recd yours & nothing coud have given me greater pleasure except seeing you or that I might have met you today. I was at the pains to get up on Monday morning to write to you &

the post did not come. However I have sent you what I wrote that it may not be in tirely in vain. Possibly it may give you some pleasure. I shoud be glad if you woud call of Mr Cox or send to know if he have any thing to send to me. He will know. Sarahs Bro: said he must bring another Bottle of Wine or I shoud not have sent it— I will not faill for my life to meet you at the time & place. We are all well. My best service as due to All

I am thine Affect Husband

Jed Strutt

Jedediah Strutt to his wife

Derby Saturday June 4 [1763]

My Dear

This moment Mrs Rowlands Bro has called with the Empty Bottle & I shall send it again full but am inexpressibly deceivd & disapointed that I have not heard from you since Tuesday night. For that reason I have all this day particularly expected to see you every moment. If you cou'd imagine how much I want to see you & cannot you woud at least let me hear from you but I woud not chide you too much least I make you uneasy—If I coud possibly know that you woud come with me tomorrow with what pleasure woud I come—how often do I wish for that time & yet how vain my wishes. The time was surely never so slow—I am surprisd when I reflect it was but a Week yesterday since you left me & then did I not tell you you woud stay—You will wonder why I am so impatient & I cannot for my life give you a reason but so it is—I hear nothing material yet from Nottm but expect tomorrow night the post will come from Kendalls on Sunday night. Mr White expected to have heard from Mr Malkin on thursday night. If you have any possible method of letting me know I will fly to meet you —but I can now [write] no more. The Man waits & I am Boiling Silk & busy. I am glad to hear Letty is likely to do well. My Humbl service to Mr & Mrs Malkin. Adieu my dear

J Strutt

Jedediah Strutt to his wife

Derby June 6: 1763

My Dear

Last night I read both your Letters with great pleasure by which I am quite satisfied of the necessity of your staying & woud by no means have you Attribute my desire of your Coming any sooner than necessary to any thing else than that I Love you & am very sorry there shoud be occasion for your being so long away. Absence is C[lothed] like hell to real Lovers. I know not how it is nor [why] & shoud be asham'd to tell it any body else that I h[ave not] had one easy hour since you left me nor shall h[ave till] you return. But let not that make you uneasy, the de[sire] is not so great nor the time so long but we may mee[t] & I trust we shall. A little patience will Cure all. This mix'd scence of things, these hopes & fears, this [sudden] changing from pleasure to pain & from pain to pleasure, [this] variety of disapointment & success greatly tend to [ ] off ones mind & teach one not to expect too much from any [thing] here. For my own part I think if I coud have a competency I shoud be contented & leave the business of the world to those [who] better like to busy in it. But if ever I intend to arrive at that desireable point of being independent on others & makeing my family so it must be by being busy now. This is the time on Many accounts— it is with me the prime of Life. The next thing will certainly be a decline for I am already growing grey apace. Besides sickness may come—& Death. Then to have acquir'd the Habits of a Virtuous & good Mind & livd a life of honesty & usefulness to others will be the only blessing & it will be a matter of intire indifference to myself whether I am rich or poor but it will then be a fault not to have then made the best use with regard to worldy advantages, of what was justly & reasonably in my power. I never forget that I have you & 4 Children & glad I have. Give my Love to [ ]. I am very glad to hear she is likely to get so well over. I have no way of sending you any phisick. If that they give there be too strong give less of it as some may be necessary but perhaps a little treacle & Brimstone given frequently & continued longer might be abundantly sufficient. I am very sorry the wine was not good & I am afraid the last woud be the same but had no opportunity to taste of either. I wonder I shoud forget George. I was to see him last week & he continues to mend. We are all well. Don't be angry if I still beg you woud order things so that I may come on Wednesday & fix the time as well as place. I will acquint Mr White with what you say. My best service to Mr & Mrs Malkin. I am afraid Mrs Malkin shoud be uneasy & shoud be very sorry if any harm shoud come to her on our or on any other account. My service to Mrs Holms. I am much oblig'd by her kind offer as it may let you at liberty the sooner. You see I have wrote you a long Letter when less might have done but I had time & then woud not omit any I tho't woud give you pleasure. I am thy most faithful & affectionate Husband

J S

Jedediah Strutt to his wife

London Sep 8: 1763

My Dear

I did intend tomorrow morning to have set out for Derby but that being not practicable I must now stay till Monday. I am now at Mr Gibsons[1] as before & it is near 11 o Clock so that I don't know whether I have a Letter from you to day or not but wish I may— I din'd yesterday with Mr Cook who enquird kindly after you. I shall call again of him before I come away—This day there has been a sale of 78 Bales of Silk about which we have been very busy & have bo't 3 of them. Tomorrow I shall go out of town. I hope you rec'd the Letter I wrote on Monday. If it had been on Tuesday you woud not have had it as the Mail was robd—Whatever kindness or however pleasing things may be here with you only is the place of my happiness—I cannot stay to say more

my Love to Bros & the Children. If anything shoud happen that I cannot come on Monday I will let you know. I am thy most affecte Husband

Jed: Strutt

PS: desire Bro wou'd Deliver out some of the Silk to Mr Wild to throw as fast as possible & to ask Mr Stamford if he Cou'd throw us a little & also whether he has dispos'd of that white Piedmont Silk he showed me & if not to secure it at 26/ p bl which I think is the price he offerd it me at & I suppose 6 months Credit. Also if he Coud get any Marble Silk from Mr Stamford & to get forward with Mr Jardines hose & with every other sort as fast as possible as there will want a great many when I come back. There will be some Silk down on Saturday night & more next Week but he must take care to make them good & longer—At present can only get 4 guineas & half for the Buckle but shall take no such money.

Jedediah Strutt to his wife

London May 2d: 1764

My Dear Bett

You pleasd me much by Writeing in Mr Hornes Frank & again by Mr Stenson who came to me this morning. Mr Lowe has also been with me to day & tomorrow we are to go about—I have been very busy this three days & can now but just steal time to write to you. I have not been at goodmansfields since sunday morning but intend to go to night. I have sold upwards of 300£ of hose & shall sell more yet. Last night I saw Dolly. She is very well & desires her

---

[1] Thomas Gibson, brother-in-law of Samuel Need.

Love. Its uncertain whether I can see Jennys sisters or not tomorrow. There is a sale of Silk & to Day we have been looking at it. I cannot yet tell you when I shall be at home but hope it will be sometime next week—[ ] are half so uneasy in my absence as I shoud be [in] yours. I sincerely pity you & think not I shall forget you here. I often wish I coud afford & it coud be made convenient that wherever I am you might be there too, but woud my wishes stop there, no, there woud then be a thousand other things for which I shoud not fail to wish that I might still add to your pleasure & happiness as well as my own for however others may think I am far from being indifferent to the good things of this world—However after all it will be wise to remember that contentment, love & peace & a comfortable subsistence will abundantly supply the place of all the superfluous wealth & glory in the world. As it woud be the most consummate unhappiness to you to know I was unfaithful or even indifferent towards you so it must be your greatest consolation in my absence & add sweetness to my safe return to know I am your faithful & affectionate Husband J S—

I shall be very glad to hear from you soon. My love to the Children, Brother &c.

Jedediah Strutt to his wife

[London, ? May, 1764]

As Mr Stenson will be at home before me I woud not omit the opportunity of sending by him any thing I can think of to divert you for was I in your place I shoud have need of every thing—Last Sunday morning Brother & I went to see the Magdalens at Chappel & must own the appearance of more than a hundred fair penitents all innocent to look on as Vestal Virgins. The solemnity of the place, the splendid & numerous appearance of the Company together with the cause of all cou'd not but raise in my mind a thousand various reflections. The Service began with a Penitential Hymn sung Alternately to the sound of the Organ, Words so well adapted & voices so sweet coud one suppose em to be sincere woud not fail to be pleasing to the Ears of Almighty god himself—but how dreadful is the Heart of man & the Hearts of women too. How can those Eyes & affections that used to rove after every object of desire & the gratification of every Passion & Lust that intemperance & madness itself coud inspire them with be come at once & in the Bloom of youth the Calm seats of that tranquility & peace of mind the Habitually Virtuous only can enjoy—Charity prompts me to wish it may be so but my reason tells me it can hardly be—but I have not time to say more on this

Head, it is now ten o Clock & I am afraid Mr Stenson will be gone to bed & I am very Weary myself having been on foot almost all day but I am very well. I am not certain whether I shall reach you on Saturday or not but assure yourself I will come as soon as possible for I long to be with you & will omit nothing that will forward my return. I hope you have recd my Letter. I am sorry you was disapointed a day, dont be uneasy. Good night. I always wish you a good night when I go to bed. Mr N desires his Compts. My Love to the Children. Have not I wrote you a long letter. Once more good night. I must take my leave by telling you I am your most Affectionate Husd J Strutt

Jedediah Strutt to his wife

London May 10: 1764

My Dear Bett

It is now near 8 o'clock & while I expect you are pleasing yourself with reading my Letter by Mr Stenson & with the expectation of seeing me on Saturday I am writing to inform you that cannot be —Mr Need is gone to Edmonton today & I cou'd not possibly get done to get out nor wou'd it have been prudent to be both out of the Way. I shall not see him till tomorrow & then we have much to say & do so that I am not certain whether I shall get out tomorrow. At least it will be evening before [I do] but if anything shoud happen to prevent me coming th[en I] will not fail to let you know. As I cannot see you so soon as I expected my next pleasure is to write to you & to hear from you—I rec'd your Welcome Letter last night and thank you for it & I have wrote this that you may not be uneasy at not seeing me so soon as you expected. There is but few minutes pass without a tho't for you. I remember with inexpressible pleasure all your kindness constancy & truth. Your undesembled Love & goodness is for ever in my mind. Absence does not cool but kindles up anew that never dying flame that burns & will forever burn for you. Nothing coud compensate for the uneasiness I feel in your absence but the hope it will not be long. To think of seeing you no more woud be death itself but it is dark good night, may that kind providence that preserves my life & health preserve yours also & once more bring us to one anothers Arms in health & peace. Till that happy moment farewell—I am—JS

I am in perfect health blessed be god

333

Jedediah Strutt to his wife

London March 28: 1765

I have never heard from you yet which I wonder at. I also wonder how I coud forget to desire you woud write to me & to mention the Children when I wrote tho' I was very desirous of saying something more to you. I know not how it is but my tho'ts are very often as it were at some vast distance at the time they shoud be present for whatever reason I can never tell a story nor seldom say all I shoud to my present purpose. Dont forget to write to me on Saturday night about the picture frames if you have not wrote before. Did I tell you Mr Brooks was at the meeting on Sunday. He enquird after Miss & Mr Cook, desird I woud come to dine with him some day & I intend it. I was to drink tea at Mr Scots on Sunday. I think she looks as Joanish as his former Wife. She & every body about here behave with great circumspection on account of her pregnancy but it is strongly suspected it will prove a wind Egg. Have not seen Dolly yet. I hear the great cause about the frames is to come on next monday night. I have seen nobody yet that has any concern with it but Mr Moore. I have not done much to day but must Attend. I have made it some of my business to observe the taste about coats & find some with collars & some without, some with buttons at the sleeves & some with none but cannot certainly determine which there are most of. I thot it was necessary to tell you this—Since I wrote the above Bro: has brot me the Letter from you. I am very sorry to hear you are so poorly. I wanted to hear how you did. It is now near 8 & I shoud go with Mr N to Mr Hookhams. I have desird bro: to call about the letter & will see farther about myself tomorrow. I hope I shall hear from you again soon. I am in haste. I wish you much better than you are. Good night. I am your Affectionate Husband J Strutt

Jedediah Strutt to his wife

London Aprill 3d: 1765

My Dear

I have indeed recd a few lines from you but they were so few & the purport so indifferent that I have been impatient every Day since for a more agreable Letter from you but to no purpose. I was Sorry to leave you so poorly & more so to hear you was no better. I have been so busy one thing or other I have not had time to go any where. I never saw Dolly till last night & then was there but about 3 minutes. I have not been at Mr Cooks yet. I calld on Mr Bwth but did not see him. I have seen Mr Goodman once & have

334

been 4 times since to hear what they have done but cannot see him but by what I understand the opportunity is lost by their fault[1] . . . . . . But while I beguile away the time in writeing to you these transient reflections my paper gets filled, night comes on—I long to see you but cant tell when I shall. Mr Need is gone to Edmonton to day & we have many things to settle & Do that I am afraid I cannot be down this week. However I hope it will not be long now

I am only yours Jed: Strutt

I have wrote a long Letter to Bro: Woollat. There will be a Bale of Silk for us down on Saturday. [Tell him] to put it by till I come. there is nothing done yet about the frame.

[1] For missing passage, see pp. 109–110.

APPENDIX C

As so few Arkwright letters have survived, two may be given here. The first shows Arkwright's weaving specifications in 1781; the second is a letter from Richard Arkwright, Jr., on his yarn production at Bakewell in 1787. The MSS. are in the Fitzwilliam Museum, Cambridge (1781) and in the Blackburn Public Library (1787).

Mr. Robt. Dalton   Manchester, Decr. 12, 1781

Sir

Desire you will not order any Reeds but call at the Warehouse when you want as have Order'd already a Quantity of the Proper Sorts—Will forward you some Twist Tomorrow which you'll begin of Warping according to the under Directions. I am &c

Richd Arkwright

For a 60 Reed from 30 to 35 Hks Twist To Warp 54 Bears by 29 Ends should be 25 Ends 2 lb. 10 oz. of 3/s Spinning, Width of Reed 45 Inches.

For a 72 Reed—45 Inches Wide from 35 to 40 Hks Twist To Warp. 60 Bears by 27 Ends 2 lb 8 oz at 3s 6d Spinning

---

For Cravats in a 44 Reed 16 Inches wide 14 Bears⎫ Finess of Twist
by 25 Ends in the ½ Bear   ⎭ From N. 34 to 36

For Cravats in a 50 Reed 17 Inches Wide 16 Bears⎫ Finess of Twist
by 27 Ends in the ½ Bear   ⎭ From N. 38 to 42

For Cravats in a 60 Reed 18 Inches Wide   ⎫ Finenss of Twist
20 Bears by 27 Ends in the ½ Bear   ⎭ From N. 48 to 54

For Handkerchiefs in a 44 Reed 37 Inches Wide   ⎫ Finenss of Twist
30 Bears by 27 Ends in the ¼ Bear   ⎭ From N. 35 to 39

For Handkerchiefs in a 50 Reed 37 Inches Wide   ⎫ Finenss of Twist
35 Bears by 27 Ends in the ¼ Bear   ⎭ From N. 40 to 46

For Handkerchiefs in a 60 Reed 38 Inches Wide   ⎫ Finess of Twist
43 Bears by 27 Ends in the ½ Bear   ⎭ From N. 50 to 56

For Handkerchiefs in a 72 Reed 39 Inches Wide   ⎫ Finenss of Twist
52 Bears by 27 Ends in the ½ Bear   ⎭ From N. 56 to 58

For Callico's

In a 44 Reed 34 Inches Wide
24 Bears by 31 Ends in the ½ Bear to Warp

In a 50 Reed 34 Inches Wide
34 Bears by 25 Ends in the ½ Bear to Warp

In a 60 Reed 35 Inches Wide
36 Bears by 29 Ends in the ½ Bear to Warp
} Finess of Twist From N. 30 to 35

In a 72 Reed 36½ Inches Wide
42 Bears by 29 Ends in the ½ Bear to Warp
} Finess of Twist From N. 35 to 40

In a 50 Reed 45 Inches Wide
45 Bears by 25 Ends in the ½ Bear to Warp
}

In a 60 Reed 45 Inches Wide
54 Bears by 25 Ends in the ½ Bear to Warp
} Finess of Twist From N. 30 to 35

In a 72 Reed 45 Inches Wide
60 Bears by 27 Ends in the ½ Bear to Warp
} Finess of Twist From N. 35 to 40

In a 88 Reed 45 Inches Wide
79 Bears by 25 Ends in the ½ Bear to Warp
} Finess of Twist From N. 40 to 48

In a 88 Reed 57 Inches Wide
82 Bears by 25 Ends in the ½ Bear to Warp

In a 88 Reed 57 Inches Wide
109 Bears by 23 Ends in the ½ Bear to Warp

To Mr Peter Heatley, Whittle-le-Woods, Lancashire
Sir

I am favoured with your's of the 10th inst, covering your Dft. on Messrs Rawlinson & Hancock for Three hundred and fourteen pounds 8/- which balances your account.

The twist you order shall be all or a part sent the next week excepting the 20 to 22's, which we are not making at this time. The 28's I can not recommend to please the eye, however I shall send you a few bundles.

I believe some of the twist marked O was not some time since well sorted, by reason of it's being done before it was perfectly dried but with respect to its being fuller of thick threads, I can not conceive how that could be, unless the twist was in itself imperfect, and that might be the case.—They are good spinners indeed who can say their twist shall always be perfect.

I am glad to hear you approve so much of Mr Simpson's twist, and I hope it will continue to give you satisfaction. Mr Simpson informs me you have ordered of them from 56 to 70's, and that they have not, above 64's to supply you, nor could I find you any from this place, but what is marked O, of which you do not approve. We do all our fine in that way, and my weekly customers all prefer it marked O, tho some who have had of it from Mr Simpson's have disapproved, in the same manner you have done, for this I can not account, unless its laying too long in that state may injure it, but that would not make it lumpy.

If Mr Simpson can not supply you with the sorts you want, and you wish to have some done in the common method, on your noticing it, it shall be done as speedily as possible.

I am still of opinion *good* twist is better for what we do to it, and if I send you any fine I would recommend you to have some of the O.

I am

Dr. Sr.

Your very h'ble Sevt.

Richd. Arkwright

Bakewell
15 Feby. 1787.

APPENDIX D

[Supplementary to Chapter X]

STATISTICAL TABLES

I. THE WEIGHT OF BAGS OF COTTON

The size of bags of cotton varied considerably as is shown by the following examples, chosen at random from Strutts' General Clearing Book, 1793–8. Whenever possible three examples of each type of cotton have been selected for purposes of illustration. For further information about the weight of bags see Ure, *The Cotton Manufacture of Gt. Britain*, (1861), ii, 405–7; Buck, *The Development of the Organisation of Anglo-American Trade, 1800–1850* (1925), 31, n. 1, and Wadsworth and Mann, op. cit., 182, n. 2.

Type of Cotton	Number of Bags in Consignment	Mean Weight per Bag (lbs.)
Bahama	30	209
	35	228
	24	234
Bahia	10	143
	20	294
Barbados	6	138
	29	210
	37	182
Berbice	15	265
Brazil	46	143
	20	112
	38	145
Carriacou	32	276
	20	278
	37	183

Type of Cotton	Number of Bags in Consignment	Mean Weight per Bag (lbs.)
Cayenne	10	187
Demerara	2	241
	17	316
	12	247
Domingo	13	337
	3	234
	23	330
Dutch	9	306
	49	256
	2	221
Grenada	36	270
	20	294
	27	260
Guiana	50	82
Jamaica	31	261
	4	241
	9	302
Maranham	7	212
	9	187
	27	185
Martinique	1	293
Orleans	3	317
Pernambuco	9	298
	4	131
	40	136
St. Lucia	10	353
	26	316
Surinam	20	234
	10	252
	10	258

Type of Cotton	Number of Bags in Consignment	Mean Weight per Bag (lbs.)
Tobago	4	240
	25	414
	16	323
West India	11	241
	7	279
	8	204

2. COTTON PURCHASED BY STRUTTS THROUGH VARIOUS BROKERS (IN BAGS)

Broker	1794	1795	1796	1797	1798	1799	1800	1801	1802	1803	1804	1805
Hope	195	230	400	517	681	679	2220	2732	2311	240	912	1260
Hunt*	1306	606	1516	1679	1202	1494	325	457	595	1660	622	912
Waterhouse	733	993	157		556	322	41			792	563	708
Greaves*												
Wagstaff*								211				
Ewart and Rutson												
Kearsley and Bower												
Total	2234	1829	2073	2196	2439	2495	2566	3400	2906	2692	2097	2880

* London brokers. All others Liverpool.

Broker	1806	1807	1808	1809	1810	1811	1812	1813	1814	1815	1816	1817
Hope	2235	1783	1098	1316	2052	1574	742	1840	2620	2742	3764	1154
Hunt	1243	2143	1115	2981	1886	2854	2009	3635	2960	2920	1922	271
Waterhouse	120											
Greaves												
Wagstaff												
Ewart and Rutson												
Kearsley and Bower											130	830
Total	3598	3926	2213	4297	3938	4428	2751	5475	5580	5662	5816	2255

Broker	1794	1795	1796	1797	1798	1799	1800	1801	1802	1803	1804	1805
Hope	16	26	48	48	77	104	325	411	270	30	111	165
Hunt	96	63	144	167	146	191	60	64	75	179	82	140
Waterhouse	70	105	25		72	42	8			73	68	86
Greaves												
Wagstaff								30				
Ewart and Rutson												
Kearsley and Bower												

Broker	1806	1807	1808	1809	1810	1811	1812	1813	1814	1815	1816	1817
Hope	236	180	124	145	207	146	61	161	310	296	432	104
Hunt	155	296	140	331	218	190	203	313	359	291	287	37
Waterhouse	9											
Greaves												
Wagstaff												
Ewart and Rutson												
Kearsley and Bower												18	77

4. COTTON IMPORTED INTO LIVERPOOL, 1753–5 AND 1768–79 (IN BAGS)

(Figures compiled from weekly imports given in the *Manchester Mercury*)

	1753	1754	1755	1768	1769	1770	1771	1772	1773	1774	1775	1776	1777	1778	1779
WEST INDIES															
Jamaica	1060	965	2207	411	964	1636	1050	2009	924	587	717	1106	1015	668	447
Grenada				660	722	1040	736	790	867	953	753	953	194	822	694
Tortola	1008	820	1257	1336	1168	945	598	730	557	643	717	585	261	603	175
Barbados	865	845	879	581	473	294	201	647	720	469	677	550	229	671	352
Montserrat	434	153	127	220	169	158	60		48	72	64	95		81	37
Dominica				959	675	601	678	311	267	382	120	235	360	176	40
St. Kitts	470	162	268	260	125	100		51							
Antigua	661	54	214	241	24	160		34				437	11	87	29
Nevis	208	150	189												
St. Vincent				125	136	331	168	213	372	524	398	1063	493	274	181
Tobago											21			764	638
Miscellaneous	3	372	378	134	66	852	438	306	98	180	154	611	225	399	356
Total	4709	3521	5519	4927	4522	6117	3929	5165	3853	3810	3621	5635	2788	4545	2949
NORTH AMERICA															
America								4							
Boston				23		3	1								
Georgia															
Maryland					8					4					
New England				1			1		1		11				
New London				2		3	30	79	1		1				
New York							5	11	6	33	81				
North Carolina															
South Carolina	2	6													
Philadelphia	9	2	205											9	35

Rhode Island	1	8	7	20	9	4	37	67	8	6	93	131		9	35
Virginia								18							
Total	12	8	212	46	9	10	37	179	8	43	93	212		9	35
EUROPE															
Alicante & Gibraltar						3			42						
Amsterdam								339		175	288	340			
Bordeaux															
Cadiz			438	117			38			70	6		245		
Hamburg										438			42		
Ireland	44	19								30	40		597		
Leghorn	248	4			40			371		20	507				
Lisbon					132			400							
Marseilles					200										
Nantes															
Rotterdam	450									250	1354	106			
Salonica											5	585	377	326	
Smyrna											610	454	265		
Total	742	23	438	117	372	3	38	1110	42	983	2810	1485	1526	326	
MISCELLANEOUS															
Africa												143	9	158	722
Prize														100	20
Not stated															
Total												143	9	258	742
GRAND TOTALS															
West Indies	4709	3521	5519	4927	4522	6117	3929	5165	3853	3810	3621	5635	2788	4545	2949
North America	12	8	212	46	9	10	37	179	8	43	93	212		9	35
Europe	742	23	438	117	372	3	38	1110	42	983	2810	1485	1526	326	
Miscellaneous												143	9	258	742
	5463	3552	6169	5090	4903	6130	4004	6454	4903	4836	6524	7475	4323	5138	3726

5. LEADING IMPORTERS OF RAW COTTON INTO LIVERPOOL, 1768–79

(Compiled from lists in the *Manchester Mercury*. Minimum qualification for inclusion, 300 bags during the entire period. All were general importers, many of them through Lancaster in addition to Liverpool).

(BAGS)

Importer	1768	1769	1770	1771	1772	1773	1774	1775	1776	1777	1778	1779
William Allen	213	58	7	25			2		454	600	376	5
J. Brown		200	100						3		20	
Brown and Zuill		4								11	56	
Thomas Case	135	19	315	134					469		109	
T. and C. Cass					209	142	162	153	164	108	182	272
Crosbie and Greenwood	440	188	58									
Crosbies and Trafford	147	124	91	70	107	217						
Hamilton and Smythe	86	145	283	420	285	1	178	51	239	65	7	127
A. and B. Heywood	33	89	213	82	325	3	88		17			13
Hillary and Scott			369									
J. and T. Hodgson									4		389	
William James and Co.					203			100				
John Kennion	481	262	118	76	16	89	20	1605	2424	547	158	4
D. Kenyon					216		80	176	89	25	6	
Robert and Matthew Nicholson	123				28	30	242	593	47	20		
Hugh Prindle and Co.	605			1	35			32				
Rawlinson and Chorley	40	1141	1113	861	737	283	660	1026	1100	734	1536	582
Rawlinsons and Co.	53		145	59	105	435	123	48	66		111	195
Gill Slater and Co.	493		636	698	898	95	155	143	383	264		
J. Tarleton		335			228	785	931	747	290	290	511	414
Tarletons and Backhouse	95			185					152	89	20	5
Christopher Wetherherd		25				179	279	477	264	25		
Henry Wharton							116	230	80		84	271
W. Willock and Co.		3							3			6
S. Woodward		22			400	15	10			5		
Total	2944	2615	3616	2611	3792	2274	3046	5381	6248	2783	3565	1894
Total Liverpool Imports	5123	4903	6130	4004	6454	4903	4836	6524	7475	4323	5138	3726
Total No. of Importers	92	103	99	71	74	47	61	52	71	54	70	73

6. IMPORTS OF COTTON WOOL INTO ENGLAND AND WALES, 1768–1777

(LBS.)

	1768	1769	1770	1771	1772	1773	1774	1775	1776	1777
WEST INDIAN COLONIES										
Anguilla	104,474	23,507								
Antigua	134,756	88,833	15,858	2578	41,505	771	56,001	31,072	260,047	150,721
Barbados	240,466	109,683	121,755	74,687	127,992	161,139	174,088	225,991	197,658	459,849
Bermudas	200									2101
Dominica	680,281	828,568	672,411	692,626	597,531	325,028	540,014	269,819	383,642	137,358
Grenadines	757,901	876,093	866,696	593,078	973,661	955,402	1,027,513	729,949	505,963	1,136,811
Jamaica	500,448	580,880	551,780	514,233	813,727	394,703	386,677	567,716	760,107	882,274
Montserrat	111,710	100,111	57,606	26,311	36,774	32,381	61,210	38,143	41,887	62,696
Nevis	10,467	10,855	8027	150	8652	1918	12,534	6770	2791	19,557
St. Croix			13,440	617	7671	5654	5600		8028	3636
St. Eustatius	27,597		14,770	5912	33,152		10,000		400	33,226
St. Kitts	205,416	112,575	138,132	10,653	73,719	36,820	95,521	158,837	262,898	340,240
St. Vincent	59,332	46,302	63,214	67,595	80,827	99,370	342,228	271,472	374,229	218,429
St. Thomas								13,885	3878	4002
Tobago	406,433	402,276	277,570	161,932	26,400	2000	61,574	167,510	332,308	384,574
Tortola					241,021	151,289	295,037	204,754	170,803	163,457
Mosquito Shore		1400	200				600			200
Total	3,239,481	3,181,083	2,801,459	2,150,372	3,062,632	2,266,475	3,068,597	2,685,918	3,304,639	3,999,131

N. American Colonies	1768	1769	1770	1771	1772	1773	1774	1775	1776	1777
Carolina	1400	491	1161	909	1589	450		15,200	828	
Florida	320		5500	1126				1100		
Georgia		187	408	800				2276		
New England	12,436	7977		1017	12,698			2237		
New Providence	6800	27,200	3800	7344	7870	22,100	2500	11,900	16,812	21,778
New York	18,632	9122	14,773	14,825	17,563		13,455	2600	1621	
Newfoundland								4144	1110	20,200
Nova Scotia		400								
Pennsylvania	15,228	8192	1715			1306			923	
Virginia & Maryland				678	1080		206			
Total	54,816	53,569	27,357	26,699	40,800	23,856	16,161	39,457	21,294	41,978

Source: T64/275/142. Statistics compiled by Mr. K. Murphy.

Foreign Countries	1768	1769	1770	1771	1772	1773	1774	1775	1776	1777
Flanders	5844	3434			274,900		5	17,866	64,757	20,748
France	3200	21,000		4000	138,904		88,610	483,410	63,153	38,400
Germany					29,514		164,079	38,148		
Holland	31,355	12,451	145,497	97,039	199,821	27,500	664,781	546,797	335,553	20,009
Italy	349,362	441,414		85,374	723,335	187,943	364,445	526,654	409,844	399,954
Portugal		47,677			112,461	64,900	79,500	41,360	19,500	21,000
Spain	2500		9000		49,398	10,499	32,000	11,400	54,692	59,072
Straits					5498			35,000		
Turkey	439,970	645,427	604,103	127,045	568,325	321,016	1,143,073	2,175,132	1,943,736	2,423,618
Ireland	4273			15,724	1856		47,824	29,992		13,195
Guernsey						3600	106			
Jersey								784		
Total	836,504	1,171,403	758,600	329,182	2,104,012	615,458	2,584,423	3,906,543	2,891,235	2,995,996

Source: T64/275/143. Statistics compiled by Mr. K. Murphy.

BIBLIOGRAPHY

AIKIN, J. and ENFIELD, W., *General Biography*, Vol. I, London, 1799.
ASHTON, T. S., *The Industrial Revolution, 1760–1830*, Oxford, 1948.
—— *An Economic History of England. The Eighteenth Century*, London, 1955.
BAGSHAW, S., *History, Gazetteer and Directory of Derbyshire*, Sheffield, 1846.
BAILEY, J. E. (ed.), *The Palatine Note Book*, Vol. III, Manchester, 1883.
BAINES, E., *History of the Cotton Manufacture in Great Britain*, London, 1835.
BANNISTER, T., 'The First Iron-Framed Buildings,' *The Architectural Review*, Vol. CVII, 1950.
BESSBOROUGH, THE EARL OF (ed.), *Georgiana, Extracts from the Correspondence of Georgiana, Duchess of Devonshire*, London, 1955.
BLACKNER, J., *The History of Nottingham*, Nottingham, 1815.
BOWDEN, WITT, *Industrial Society in England towards the End of the Eighteenth Century*, New York, 1925.
BRAY, W., *Sketch of a Tour into Derbyshire and Yorkshire*, London, 1778.
BRAYSHAW, T. and ROBINSON, R. M., *A History of the Ancient Parish of Giggleswick*, London, 1932.
BRITTON, J. and BRAYLEY, E. W., *The Beauties of England and Wales*, Vol. III, London, 1802.
BROOKE, R., *Liverpool as it was during the Last Quarter of the Eighteenth Century*, Liverpool, 1853.
BUCK, N. S., *The Development of the Organisation of Anglo-American Trade, 1800–1850*, New Haven, 1925.
BURKE, SIR B., *Vicissitudes of Families*, Third Series, London, 1863.
BYNG, J. (ed. ANDREWS), *The Torrington Diaries, 1781–94*, London, 1954.
The Case of Richard Arkwright and Company, London, 1782.
A Catalogue of Paintings, Drawings, Marbles, Bronzes, &c. &c. in the Collection of Joseph Strutt, Derby, 1827 and 1835. [Privately Printed.]
CHAMBERS, J. D., *Nottinghamshire in the Eighteenth Century*, London, 1932.
The City: or, the Physiology of London Business, London, 1845.
CLAPHAM, SIR J. H., *An Economic History of Modern Britain. The Early Railway Age, 1820–1850*, Cambridge, 1926.
—— 'Some Factory Statistics of 1815–16', *The Economic Journal*, Vol. XXV, 1915.
COLE, G. D. H., *The Life of Robert Owen*, (2nd ed.), London, 1930.
COLLIER, F., 'Samuel Greg and Styal Mill', *Memoirs and Proceedings of the Manchester Literary and Philosophical Society*, Vol. LXXXV, 1941–3.
CONWAY, M. D., *The Life of Thomas Paine*, Vol. I, London, 1892.
COX, J. C., *Three Centuries of Derbyshire Annals*, Vol. I, London, 1890.
COZENS-HARDY, B. (ed.), *The Diary of Sylas Neville, 1767–1788*, Oxford, 1950.
CRUMP, W. B. (ed.), *The Leeds Woollen Industry, 1780–1820*, Leeds, 1931.
DANIELS, G. W., 'The Cotton Trade During the Revolutionary and Napoleonic Wars', *Transactions of the Manchester Statistical Society*, 1915–16.
—— 'The Cotton Trade at the Close of the Napoleonic War', *Transactions of the Manchester Statistical Society*, 1917–18.
—— *The Early English Cotton Industry*, Manchester, 1920.
DAVIES, D. P., *A New Historical and Descriptive View of Derbyshire*, Belper, 1811.

DAVIS, V. D., *A History of Manchester College from its Foundation in Manchester to its Establishment in Oxford*, London, 1932.

DAVIS, W. J., *The Nineteenth Century Token Coinage*, London, 1904.

DICKINSON, H. W., *Matthew Boulton*, Cambridge, 1937.

DODD, A. H., *The Industrial Revolution in North Wales*, Cardiff, 1933.

DOSSIE, R., *Memoirs of Agriculture, and other Œconomical Arts*, Vols. I and II, London, 1768–71.

DUMBELL, S., 'The Cotton Market in 1799,' *Economic History*, Vol. I, 1926.

EDEN, Sir F. M., *The State of the Poor*, Vol. II, London, 1797.

EDGEWORTH, R. L., *Memoirs of Richard Lovell Edgeworth, Esq., Begun by Himself, and Concluded by His Daughter, Maria Edgeworth* (3rd ed.), London, 1856.

ELLISON, T., *The Cotton Trade of Great Britain, including a History of the Liverpool Cotton Market*, London, 1886.

Encyclopædia Britannica
    1810 ed., article 'Cotton'
    1824 ed., *Supplement*, article 'Cotton Manufacture.'

ENFIELD, W., *An Essay towards the History of Leverpool*, Warrington, 1773.

ESPINASSE, F., *Lancashire Worthies*, London and Manchester, 1874.

FAREY, J., *General View of the Agriculture of Derbyshire*, 3 vols., London, 1811–1817.

FARRER, Lady K. E. (ed.), *Letters of Josiah Wedgwood*, Vol. II, London, 1903. [Privately Circulated.]

—— (ed.), *Correspondence of Josiah Wedgwood, 1781–1794*, London, 1906. [Privately Circulated.]

FAUCHER, L., *Manchester in 1844: Its Present Condition and Future Prospects*, London and Manchester, 1844.

FEAVEARYEAR, Sir A. E., *The Pond Sterling; a History of English Money*, Oxford, 1931.

FELKIN, W., *A History of the Machine-Wrought Hosiery and Lace Manufactures*, London, 1867.

GARDINER, W., *Music and Friends*, Vol. II, London, 1838.

GARVIN, J. L., *The Life of Joseph Chamberlain*, Vol. I, London, 1932.

GASKELL, P., *Artisans and Machinery*, London, 1836.

GLOAG, J. and BRIDGWATER, D., *A History of Cast Iron in Architecture*, London, 1948.

GLOVER, S., *The Peak Guide*, Derby, 1830.

—— *The History and Gazetteer of the County of Derby*, Vol. II, Derby, 1833.

GREIG, J. (ed.), *The Farington Diary*, Vol. I, London, 1922.

GRIGGS, E. L. (ed.), *Collected Letters of Samuel Taylor Coleridge*, 2 vols., Oxford, 1956.

GUEST, R., *A Compendious History of the Cotton-Manufacture: with a Disproval of the Claim of Sir Richard Arkwright to the Invention of its ingenious Machinery*, Manchester, 1823.

HALÉVY, E., *The Growth of Philosophic Radicalism*, London, 1949.

HAMILTON, H., *The Industrial Revolution in Scotland*, Oxford, 1932.

HAMMOND, J. L., 'The Social Background: 1835–1935', Chapter II of LASKI, H. J., JENNINGS, SIR W. I. and ROBSON, W. A. (eds.), *A Century of Municipal Progress, 1835–1935*, London, 1935.

HAMMOND, J. L. and B., *The Town Labourer, 1760–1832*, London, 1917.

—— *The Skilled Labourer, 1760–1832*, London, 1919.

HARE, A. J. C. (ed.), *The Life and Letters of Maria Edgeworth*, Vol. I, London, 1894.

HEATON, H., 'Non-Importation, 1806–1812', *Journal of Economic History*, Vol. I, 1941.

HECHT, J. J., *The Domestic Servant Class in Eighteenth-Century England*, London, 1956.

HECKSCHER, E. F., *The Continental System; An Economic Interpretation*, Oxford, 1922.

HENRY, W. C., *A Biographical Notice of the late Peter Ewart, Esq.*, Manchester, 1844.

HENSON, G., *The Civil, Political and Mechanical History of the Framework-Knitters in Europe and America*, Vol. I, Nottingham, 1831.

Historical Manuscripts Commission, The Manuscripts of the Duke of Rutland, Vol. III, London, 1894.

HOLMES, R., *Keighley, Past and Present*, London and Keighley, 1858.

Hosiers' and Framework Knitters' examinations before Committee of House of Commons, 1780. [Reprint in Derby Public Library.]

HUGHES, J., *Liverpool Banks and Bankers, 1760–1837*, Liverpool and London, 1906.

HUTCHINS, B. L. and HARRISON, A., *A History of Factory Legislation*, London, 1903.

HUTTON, W., *History of Derby from the remote Ages of Antiquity to the Year 1791*, London and Derby, 1791.

HYDE, F. E., PARKINSON, B. B. and MARRINER, S., 'The Cotton Broker and the Rise of the Liverpool Cotton Market', *The Economic History Review*, Second Series, Vol. VIII, 1955–6.

An Important Crisis in the Calico and Muslin Manufactory in Great Britain, Explained, London, 1788.

JAMES, J., *History of the Worsted Manufacture in England from the Earliest Times*, London, 1857.

JEWITT, L. (ed.), *The Life of William Hutton and the History of the Hutton Family*, London, 1872.

JOHN, A. H. (ed.), *The Walker Family, Iron Founders and Lead Manufacturers, 1741–1893*, London, 1951.

JOHNSON, H. R. and SKEMPTON, A. W., 'William Strutt's Fire-Proof and Iron-Framed Buildings, 1792–1812', paper read at the Institution of Civil Engineers (Newcomen Society), 1956.

JONES, N., *Life and Death; A Discourse, on Occasion of the Lamented Death of Joseph Strutt, Esq.*, London and Derby, 1844.

JONES, T. S., *The Life of . . . Willielma, Viscountess Glenorchy*, Edinburgh, 1822.

KENNEDY, J., 'Observations on the Rise and Progress of the Cotton Trade in Great Britain', *Memoirs of the Literary and Philosophical Society of Manchester*, Second Series, Vol. III, 1819.

KENRICK, J., *A Biographical Memoir of the Rev. Charles Wellbeloved*, London, 1860.

LOWE, R., *General View of the Agriculture of the County of Nottingham*, London, 1798.

LYSONS, D. and S., *Magna Britannia*, Vol. V, London, 1817.

McCULLOCH, J. R., *The Principles of Political Economy* (2nd ed.), London, 1830.

McLACHLAN, H., *The Unitarian Movement in the Religious Life of England*, London, 1934.

—— *Essays and Addresses*, Manchester, 1950.

MANTOUX, P., *The Industrial Revolution in the Eighteenth Century*, London, 1928.

351

MATHER, R., *An Impartial Representation of the Case of the Poor Cotton Spinners in Lancashire*, London, 1780.

A Memoir of William Strutt. [Typescript of unknown authorship in the Derby Public Library.]

NAMIER, SIR L. B., *The Structure of Politics at the Accession of George III*, Vol. I, London, 1929.

Nottingham City Council, *Records of the Borough of Nottingham*, Vols. VII and VIII, Nottingham, 1947–1952.

The [Old] Statistical Account of Scotland (ed. Sir John Sinclair), Vol. XV, Edinburgh, 1795.

OWEN, R., *The Life of Robert Owen, written by Himself*, London and Philadelphia, 1857.

PENNANT, T., *The History of the Parishes of Whiteford and Holywell*, London, 1796.

PEVSNER, N., *The Buildings of England, Derbyshire*, London, 1953.

PIGOTT, S., *Hollins. A Study of Industry, 1784–1949*, Nottingham, 1949. [Privately Printed.]

PILKINGTON, J., *A View of the present State of Derbyshire*, Vol. II, Derby, 1789.

PODMORE, F., *Robert Owen, A Biography*, Vol. I, London, 1906.

PRESSNELL, L. S., *Country Banking in the Industrial Revolution*, Oxford, 1956.

PRIESTLEY, J., *Memoirs. Written by himself, to year 1795. With a continuation to time of his decease. By his son, Joseph Priestley. Reprinted from edition of 1809*, London, 1904.

REDFORD, A., *Labour Migration in England, 1800–1850*, Manchester, 1926.

—— *Manchester Merchants and Foreign Trade, 1794–1858*, Manchester, 1934.

REES, A., *The Cyclopædia; or, Universal Dictionary of Arts, Sciences, and Literature*, 39 Vols., London, 1819. Articles 'Cotton', 'Machine', 'Manufacture of Cotton', 'Mill-Work', 'Water'.

ROLL, E., *An Early Experiment in Industrial Organisation*, London, 1930.

Royal Society of London, *Abstracts of the Papers Printed in the Philosophical Transactions of the Royal Society of London from 1830 to 1837 inclusive*, Vol. III, London, 1860.

RUSSELL, LORD JOHN, (ed.), *Memoirs, Journal, and Correspondence of Thomas Moore*, Vols. I, II and V, London, 1853.

SEYMOUR-JONES, A., 'The Invention of Roller Drawing in Cotton Spinning', *Transactions of the Newcomen Society*, Vol. I, 1920–1.

SHEPHERD, W. D., *Early Industrial Buildings, 1700–1850*. [Thesis, 1950, R.I.B.A., London.]

SKEMPTON, A. W., 'The Origin of Iron Beams', paper read at *Proceedings VIII International Congress History of Science*, Florence, 1956.

SLACK, J., *Remarks on Cotton*, Liverpool, 1816.

SMILES, S., *Lives of Boulton and Watt*, London, 1865.

SMITHERS, H., *Liverpool, its Commerce, Statistics and Institutions; with a History of the Cotton Trade*, Liverpool, 1825.

STEWART, G., *Curiosities of Glasgow Citizenship*, Glasgow, 1881.

STRACHEY, Lady J. M. (ed.), *Memoirs of a Highland Lady, The Autobiography of Elizabeth Grant of Rothiemurchus afterwards Mrs. Smith of Baltiboys, 1797–1830*, London, 1898.

STRUTT, Hon. F., 'Jedediah Strutt', *Memorials of Old Derbyshire* (ed. J. C. Cox), London and Derby, 1907.

SYERS, R., *The History of Everton*, Liverpool, 1830.

SYKES, Sir A. J., *Concerning the Bleaching Industry*, Manchester, 1925. [Privately Printed.]

SYLVESTER, C., *The Philosophy of Domestic Economy*, London and Nottingham, 1819.

TODD, G. EYRE-, *History of Glasgow*, Vol. III, Glasgow, 1934.

Transport Saga, 1646–1947, London, 1947. [Privately printed for Pickfords Ltd.]

The Trial of a Cause instituted by . . . his Majesty's Attorney General . . . to Repeal a Patent granted on the Sixteenth of December 1775, to Mr. Richard Arkwright, London, 1785.

UNWIN, G., *Samuel Oldknow and the Arkwrights*, Manchester, 1924.

URE, A., *The Philosophy of Manufactures*, London, 1835.

—— *The Cotton Manufacture of Great Britain*, Vol. I, London, 1836; Vol. II with Supplement by P. L. Simmonds, 1861.

The Victoria History of the Counties of England, Derbyshire, Vol. II, London, 1907.

WADSWORTH, A. P., 'The First Manchester Sunday Schools', *Bulletin of John Rylands Library Manchester*, Vol. XXXIII, 1951.

WADSWORTH, A. P. and MANN, J. DE L., *The Cotton Trade and Industrial Lancashire, 1600–1780*, Manchester, 1931.

WALKER, M. L., *A History of the Family of Need of Arnold, Nottinghamshire*. [Ltd. ed.] London, 1963.

WELLS, F. A., *The British Hosiery Trade; Its History and Organization*, London, 1935.

WHITE, G. S., *Memoir of Samuel Slater*, Philadelphia, 1836.

WILSON, D., 'Belper Nailers', *Derbyshire Countryside*, Vol. 50, April, 1943.

WOOD, SIR H. T., *A History of the Royal Society of Arts*, London, 1913.

OFFICIAL PUBLICATIONS

Commons Journals, Vols. XXXIV, XXXVI, XXXVIII, XLIV.

Children in Manufactories. Sel. Cttee. Rep.; 1816 (397) iii, 235.

Cotton Mills (Apprentices). Sel. Cttee. H. L. Rep.; 1818 (H. L. 90) xcvi.

Cotton Mills (Apprentices). Sel. Cttee. H. L. Rep.; 1819 (H. L. 24) cx.

Merchant Law. Sel. Cttee. Rep.; 1823 (452) iv, 265.

Factories Inquiry. R. Com. 1st. Rep.; 1833 (450) xx.

Factories Inquiry. R. Com. 2nd Rep.; 1833 (519) xxi.

Factories Inquiry. R. Com. Supp. Rep. Part I, 1834 (167) xix.

Factories Inquiry. R. Com. Supp. Rep. Part II, 1834 (167) xx.

Factories Act. Educational Provisions. Com. Rep., 1839 (42) xlii.

Mills and Factories Regulations. Sel. Cttee. 2nd Rep., 1840 (227) x.

NEWSPAPERS AND PERIODICALS

Annual Register.
Aris's Birmingham Gazette.
Christian Reformer.
Derby Mercury.
Derbyshire Times.
Fortune.
Gentleman's Magazine.
Harrison's Derby and Nottingham Journal.
Illustrated London News.

Leicester Journal.
London Gazette.
Manchester Guardian.
Manchester Herald.
Manchester Mercury.
Nottingham Journal.
Prescott's Manchester Journal.
Preston Guardian.
The Times.
Trade Marks Journal.

INDEX